P-38 Odyssey

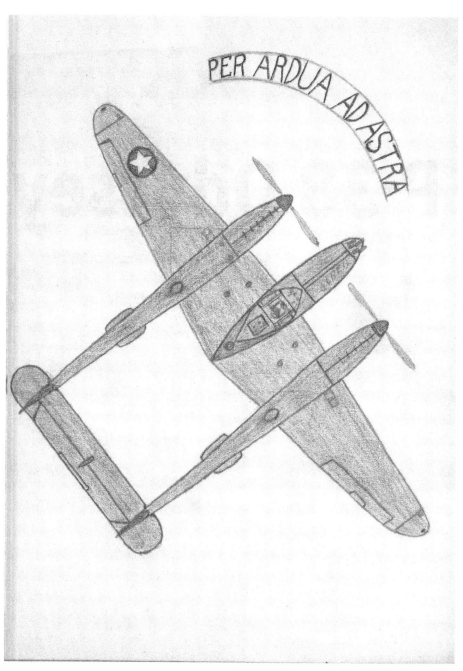

P-38 "Geneil" from the Wartime Log *(Richard M. Butler papers MSS 8849, L. Tom Perry Special Collections, Harold B. Lee Library, Brigham Young University)*

P-38 Odyssey
Farmboy, Pilot, POW

Wartime journals and letters of Richard Butler
Compiled and annotated by his son Dick Butler

Book design by Marny K. Parkin

ISBN: 978-0-578-51592-2
Revised August 2021
Printed in the United States of America

for
DAD

whose quiet selflessness
obscured this and other unsung sacrifices

CONTENTS

MAPS

. . . I wanted to look back in time to understand the world of my father, and his generation. This is partly, perhaps, because of a child's natural curiosity about the experience of a parent, a curiosity that grows stronger as the child becomes older than the parent was at that time. Such curiosity is especially acute when the father was tested by hardships that the child can only imagine.

Ian Buruma
Year Zero: A History of 1945

PREFACE

Throughout his life, my father avoided discussing his wartime experiences and in particular his time as a Prisoner-of-War. I recall only a very few occasions when he was willing to take out and look through his *Wartime Log* and talk with my siblings and me about what it represented.

Only once did I hear him discuss those experiences at length and without constraint: A few years before his premature death from cancer, when my family lived on the San Francisco Peninsula, we spent a day out with my visiting parents and two of our close friends. During an impromptu dinner after our return, something about the ambience or conversation freed Dad to speak openly and at length about those days. On that one utterly unique occasion I saw Dad talking expansively and freely, enjoying himself in recounting wartime and POW experiences.

The sole element of his wartime life he was always eager to talk about was the P-38. Few things moved him to speak with as much animation as flying, specifically flying the P-38. Nearly forty years after his last P-38 flight, he talked of that plane with the same adulation and fondness as the first time I remember hearing him speak of it. Its capabilities—and, in some sense, its capabilities as extensions of his own physical capacities—were an endless source of joyous and delighted reminiscence.

The extent of Dad's "odyssey" was considerable, given his rural origins. In addition to crisscrossing the United States, he sailed the North Atlantic on the *Queen Elizabeth*, traveled the length of Great Britain twice, sailed to Algeria and several times traversed northern Africa from Morocco to Tunisia. Fifty official missions and numerous incidental flights across and around the Mediterranean culminated in his bail-out over the Bay of Naples. As a prisoner in four different

Italian prisons, he crossed central Italy from west to east coasts, then went by rail northward to Munich and on into present-day Poland.

It was well after his early death in 1984 that I began to glimpse the real import of this period of his life. About 2010, as our mother's health declined, we were faced with sorting through a lifetime's accumulation of memorabilia. Among much else, I began sifting through several military footlockers and a number of boxes, all unopened since the late '40s or early '50s; in an unfinished basement room I began a process that has seemed like an archaeological dig.

Bit by bit, I discovered the wartime records Dad had left us. Previously, we had not known of anything more than the *Log*. It has been fascinating to find, compile, collate and transcribe the *Log* and the new discoveries; a parallel fascination has been the research necessary to interpret and contextualize what I found and to fill in the factual gaps. But far more important has been the concommitant process of discovery which has taught me that the man I knew, loved and respected as a young son was someone of greater dimensions and character than I had realized.

In 1956 we visited the remnants of Stalag VIIA at Moosburg; the photos shot that day resulted in the 3.5" × 4.5" prints common at the time. Only decades later when I saw again those small black and white prints, did I have sufficient background to imagine the stark reality of what they represented; that disjunction moved me with a powerful flow of emotion. Through the years since, and especially during research for this book, succeeding insights on specific elements of my father's combat and POW experience have struck me, each with its particular bundle of sadness and queries.

What wouldn't I give to sit with him now and ask about his odyssey! I'm staggered when I compare what I understand now about what Dad knew and felt with the blank space in our childhood comprehension of it. When we could have asked him to tell us about it and answer questions, we knew too little even to have questions. Now that I know so very much more, I seem to have more questions than answers.

A major motivation for this book has been the regret I feel at not recognizing early enough the hardships and sacrifice of his wartime years. Though I have tried to answer my own questions, to discover and to some degree even to recreate the details of his experience, nothing can truly replicate it. One thing I do know is that his odyssey was as much spiritual and emotional as it was geographical and physical.

This book on its face is one family's story. I set out to discover and elaborate details of my father's wartime experience; in the process, other people's lives became real and personal. My view of the "good" war's toll shifted quickly from historical facts and figures to individual human hardship and tragedy on a vast scale. The Greatest Generation became emphatically specific persons and families as I discovered and pondered the documents and physical artifacts, the emotions they represented and their meaning not only for my parents but for millions of people beyond our family.

I think of individuals whose lives I glimpsed: of Jo and "Doc" Holik, whose story's sadly ironic conclusion I read in one line of Jo's 1943 Christmas card to Mom. And there is the grieving mother who wrote Dad in 1946 asking for any clue to the whereabouts of her missing son. In a similar way the North Africa-period combat death of Dad's fellow Sad Sack and 82nd Fighter Group pilot Conrad Bentzlin, encountered randomly in my research, gave me a far broader perspective on Dad and Mom's three-year series of struggles.

Herb Corson, whose POW experience was so closely entwined with Dad's, had his own story. Like ours, his story had the happy ending, but even happy endings are not painless or easy. I came to see that countless happy and unhappy endings are hidden in the scores of World War II histories I'd read over the decades.

To everyone, but to the Butler grandchildren and great-children especially, keep in mind that our story in some measure tells the stories of all those others. Hold them in your heart along with Grampy and Gram as you read toward our own happy ending.

INTRODUCTION

The core of this book consists in the transcription of records left by my father, Richard Marsh Butler, of his experience of World War II. In July 1940 two farm-boys, Dad and his younger brother, Heber, enlisted together; a year and a half later they were accepted to a flight training program for enlisted men. Ultimately, they became pilots of the fabled P-38 Lightning twin-engine fighter, operating out of North Africa.[1]

On his fiftieth and theoretically final mission, after destroying a Messerschmitt 109 in a head-on dogfight over southern Italy, Dad discovered that his left engine had been badly damaged by the 109's wreckage. Forced by the burning engine to bail out, he spent the next 20 months as a prisoner of war.

After both of our parents had passed away, we siblings began to discuss how to pass on the *Wartime Log*, Dad's record of his POW years. Knowing that, if given to one sibling, it would effectively be lost to everyone else within no more than a generation, we settled on creation of a library special collection. While organizing materials for the collection, I discovered another journal, this one covering the period when Dad was overseas and in combat before the action in which he went down.

Subsequently, I discovered other journals and fragments. With all these combined, we unexpectedly had a complete first person narrative stretching from Dad's enlistment in July 1940 through his repatriation in June 1945. This unanticipated and whole personal history required background details and led to a significant research effort. What has resulted is an annotated text with Dad's narrative as structure.

---

1. Richard and Heber flew together in the same squadron until Dad went down on 20 August 1943.

The chronology falls naturally into two major parts: the time before Dad's bailout over the Bay of Naples on 20 August 1943 and the time after that event. His clear and poignant depictions are significant for us, because in them we are able both to rediscover him and occasionally to encounter otherwise unknown aspects of him.

Though his writing is occasionally punctuated with wry and sharply-observed detail, the story he tells is generally simple and straightforward. There is little digression into details of the deprivation and harrowing conditions he experienced; here, as in his later life, he has chosen not to dwell on them.

Sources

Primary

Training Journal
19 July 1940–21 August 1942

The *Training Journal*, contained in a brown 8.5" × 11" spiral notebook, appears to hold only 4 pages of algebraic equations, which I believe to be from an Aeronautical Math evening class Dad and his brother Heber took at Palo Alto High School in Fall 1940; beyond those four pages the notebook seems at first glance to be empty.

I worked for some time believing that either Dad had not recorded his enlistment and training experiences or the account had been lost. Only late in the writing process did I re-check and discover that a set of diary entries begin 8 pages from the back cover and proceed to the last page; they then pick up on the ninth page from the end and run toward the front for another 26 pages. The journal is written in typical diary style, longhand in ink.

Combat Journal
17 November 1942–18 August 1943

In a box marked "Letters," I found the account which I call the *Combat Journal*. None of us had seen it before or knew of its existence, although it was presumably Mom who had filed it away among the letters soon after the war.

Entries in the *Combat Journal* provide the content of Chapter 2, dated from 26 November[2] 1942 through 18 August 1943. They are written as though Dad were writing a long, uncensored, episodic letter to Mom. This document consists of 56 5" × 8" lined pages covered on both sides in ink and stapled at the top.

---

2. The account retrospectively begins with the brothers' departure from Tallahassee on 17 November 1942.

The content is vintage Dad; his wry commentary and witty observations and descriptions create a choice glimpse of the father we knew and loved.

Quaderno
20 August 1943–late 1943

This is an Italian student's notebook of lined pages about 5.75" × 8", complete with a blank calendar for one's class schedule. It was probably acquired in the canteen at PG 21 (Chieti). Much of its content is a portion of what I refer to as Dad's Kriegie Registry.[3]

Based on downing dates, most of what is recorded here was entered after arrival at Stalag Luft III and presumably before receipt of the *Wartime Log*. (See below.) The earliest entries were made by men with whom we know Dad was imprisoned in the first days of their captivity on the Isle of Nisida; they also give the most complete listing we have of their names. It next includes a few men whom Dad would have met in one of the Italian camps. Then it clearly picks up in Center Compound of Stalag Luft III, where the next few pages include men of Barrack 56 combines contiguous to Dad's Combine G.

On the inside of the front cover is a record of cards and letters sent home by Dad throughout his captivity. A loose unlined sheet of slightly smaller size is tucked inside the back cover and contains some multiplication and division figuring.

The Wartime Log: A Remembrance from Home through the Canadian Y.M.C.A.
15 November 1943–3 June 1945

The *Wartime Log* is a hardbound book 7.75" × 9.75" × 1.5" with an embossed Canadian red maple leaf on the cover[4]; it contained lined journal, scrapbook and blank sections as well as flap compartments for letters or, as Dad used them, for souvenir artifacts (for example, a cheese label, a package of birdseed, a train ticket). The War Prisoners' Aid of the YMCA, based in Geneva, published the *Log*.

One of the loose items inside Dad's *Log* is a letter from the War Prisoner's Aid dated 15 November 1943 introducing the *Log* to the recipient and suggesting possible uses for it. Since we know that the War Prisoners' Aid organization had its German headquarters in Sagan by that date, it's likely that Henry Soderberg,

---

3. Dad clearly began this while still in Italy, but it seems to have been the general custom in camp to have other Kriegies record their name, rank, position, home address and downing information in one's *Log*. Dad apparently continued to use the *Quaderno* for this until he received his *Log*.

4. There seem to have been different iterations of the *Wartime Log* with a variety of emblems on the cover.

who oversaw Stalag Luft III, delivered copies of the *Log* to the men there soon after that date.

Dad's entries in the *Log* include the earliest days of his captivity, but these were clearly retrospectively transcribed from an earlier draft or from memory. For example, we have one scrap from the fall of 1944 which is obviously a list of dates and events intended for later inclusion in the *Log*. Though Dad had clearly been writing and inserting mementos in his *Log* throughout 1944, it's plain that the *Kalender* entries (see below) are originals for much of the *Log's* text. On 16 June 1944 he notes in the *Kalender* that he's "Doing a little more work on my war log." Clearly, then, the *Log* was done in fits and starts and was not updated on a daily basis.

Dad's written entries are all in pencil and, until the entry of Sunday 29 April 1945, they are printed in a very careful and precise hand; with that entry, Dad reverts to longhand. Especially in the early part of that section, his pre-liberation anticipation and excitement are evident in a hurried scrawl, which was no doubt partly due to the fact that Stalag VIIA was taking fire as advancing infantry and armored forces fought their way toward, then beyond the camp.

It's important to note that, at the time of the evacuation march, many if not most copies of the *Wartime Log* were abandoned due to their weight and bulk. The Kriegies were severely limited in what they were able to take from the camp; every ounce carried and/or pulled out of the camp had to be evaluated for its survival value. Every nonessential ounce or mass of bulk meant the sacrifice of equivalent survival material. Extant copies are rare historical treasures.

Kalender
25 March 1944–29 April 1945

This is a small pocket diary about 2.75" × 4" complete with tiny pencil, again provided by the YMCA. From late March of 1944 the *Kalender* often provided a draft on which *Log* entries were based; for the period during which it was used, it seems that this was where Dad made his daily entries. That being said, there are still some things in the *Kalender* which do not appear in the *Log*, and it's likely that some *Log* entries may be original.

The 1944 *Kalender* entries are in the careful, precise printed hand that is typical of most of the *Log*. The 1945 entries are almost exclusively in cursive, often clearly hurried and sometimes illegible. This is likely because the *Kalender* was used to record events of the winter march[5] as well as others throughout that cha-

---

5. When Dad set out early on 28 January 1945 on the forced evacuation march out of Sagan, he had somehow carefully wrapped & protected the *Quaderno* and *Wartime Log*. The pocket *Kalender* was evidently kept ready to hand (though also protected from the weather). None of the three shows the least sign of damage, and it seems likely that the first two were never uncovered during the trip to Moosburg.

otic spring in Stalag VIIA (Moosburg). Every conceivable space is filled, including endpapers and expense pages.

Dad began writing in the *Kalender* 25 March 1944, returning to use the blank 1944 dates for early 1945. *Kalender* entries in this text are indicated simply as "*Kalender*" through 17 January 1945. Beyond that date Dad sometimes made more than one entry per day and wrote in a variety of blank spaces; for those reasons, entries after that date are labeled to show from what part of the *Kalender* they came (e.g., *Kalender Januar* or *Kalender Kassa*).

Flight Log
24 February 1942-November 1953

The *Flight Log* is a blue, hardcover volume 5.5" × 15" with columns on each page to record date, aircraft, hours flown and nature of flight, destination and more. I've extracted from this log essential information for each mission and inserted it into a uniform format under each date heading, I have occasionally added and adjusted punctuation for clarity and have routinely adjusted Dad's idiosyncratic capitalization.

In a few cases I have adjusted mission descriptions for clarity and have frequently footnoted additional detail and description from his brother's memoir.

Individual Flight Records
February 1942-August 1964

These are monthly reports which compile all flying done in the period: number of hours, in what aircraft, the nature of each flight. What we have from the wartime period is very nearly complete; from Dad's 1951 recall until his retirement the sequence is complete.

Dad's Correspondence

This includes letters and cards, mostly to Mom, but also to his parents and a few others. Unless otherwise noted, all card and letter excerpts in the text were addressed to Mom.

During the combat period Dad's letters took two main forms: Stationery (usually but not always onionskin) or V-Mail (billed as the fastest form of mail).[6]

During the POW period Dad was limited to pre-printed POW-labeled cards and aerograms provided by the Germans in 3's and 4's respectively per month; once a Kriegie had used up the card and letter forms issued him for a given month, he could send no more until the next month's issue.

---

6. For most of Dad's V-Mails the difference between letters' dates and post-processing US postmark dates is usually 2–3 weeks, sometimes more and occasionally less. Delivery of homebound standard-form mail seems to have been counted consistently in months.

Censorship was an important factor in all correspondence; US military home-bound mail was routinely censored for sensitive war information, and the number of censors was at least doubled once Dad was writing as a prisoner: mail was censored in both directions at both ends.

It's hard to gauge the degree to which Dad's communication was tailored to pass the censors. Dad clearly had this in mind, however, since he refers to it from time to time and portions of his letters were censored only once or twice. A wisecrack in the 17 August 1943 *Journal* entry explicitly shows Dad's awareness of the censors: "Just between the six of us. . . ."

Miscellaneous fragments and notes written by Dad

Chapter 2 uses several retrospective summaries Dad made of his final combat mission and related subsequent events.

Lost "notes and sketches"

Only after initial publication of this book did I learn that after his return home in June 1945 Dad handed Heber a bundle of "notes and sketches" which he asked his brother to keep for him and not to share. I assume that these recounted and showed aspects of Dad's life in the POW camps which he did not want Mom to know of. Among other things, they would probably have described his contribution to escape efforts and the week he spent in solitary confinement.

Late in his life Heber showed these materials briefly to his eldest daughter, but since his death they cannot be found. Heber may have considered it part of the faithful fulfillment of his brother's mandate to destroy them.

Mom's Diary and Correspondence

This is a small black leather book with clasp, roughly 4" × 6", which Mom received at Christmas 1942. The cover has "Geneil M. Butler" embossed in gold. My sister Christine, who transcribed it, says of its contents, "She recorded brief entries for 1942 through March 1944. The 1942 entries were obviously added retrospectively." Two double-sided pages from the time of Dad's overseas departure have been torn out.

Excerpts from several of Mom's letters also appear throughout the text to fill out the story or give insight into her or Dad's state of mind.

Grandma Butler's Diary, correspondence and other notes

Chris, again, took the lead in reading and transcribing portions of Grandma Butler's diary, which is quoted in several parts of this narrative, as are a number of her letters. The *Wartime Log* contains her first letter to Dad in prison camp as well as a poem and other personal material which she copied out by hand and sent him.

Heber M. Butler's Memoir I Remember When

I draw on these privately-published reminiscences of Uncle Heber for additional information or detail in Chapters 1 and 2.

Miscellaneous Military Records

These are sketchy in the early period; starting with orders issued 27 August 1942 at the end of the Luke Field training we can trace most of Dad's movements through his copies of military orders, though these become vague for security reasons once he reaches the ETO.[7]

Secondary[8]

I have drawn heavily on the official history of Stalag Luft III's Center Compound,[9] where Dad was held for fifteen and a half of the twenty-one months of his captivity. I've also used some very informative sections of the South Compound history which record the experience of Stalag Luft III internees who passed through the central Italian camps before being transported to Germany.

Steve Blake and John Stanaway's *Adorimini ("Up and at 'Em!"): A History of the 82nd Fighter Group in World War II* is frequently quoted to provide background and details of Dad's time in North Africa. Several significant photos from the book were kindly made available to me.

Another much-quoted source is Marilyn Walton and Michael Eberhardt's encyclopedic *From Interrogation to Liberation: A Photographic Journey. Stalag Luft III—The Road to Freedom.* Again, the authors were generous in sharing photographs.

Several Kriegie memoirs were very helpful in providing details of camp life. Most notable among these are Daniel McKee's *A Kriegie Recall 50 Years Later: Stalag Luft III Diary* and Albert Clark's *33 Months as a POW in Stalag Luft III: A World War II Airman Tells His Story.*

---

7. European Theater of Operations
8. For a complete listing, see Sources Consulted.
9. There are multiple copies of this history, one of them with an additional section the others lack.

NOTES TO READERS

- To avoid potential confusion in the text, Dad and Mom become Richard and Geneil. ("Dad" and "Mom" appear only where Geneil and Richard refer to their parents.)
- In a few places I have revised confusing retrospective entries so that events appear in chronological order. In all cases where I re-order events in Dad's entries, I indicate that I am doing so.
- For clarity, I have standardized spelling and punctuation except in a few cases where I felt it important to leave Dad's original as I found it. In only one case, where misspelling and poor punctuation in a secondary Kriegie source impeded comprehension, have I used a heavier editorial hand.
- Although Dad and Heber did not join the 97th Fighter Squadron, 82nd Fighter Group, until early April 1943, I have inserted through Chapter 2 relevant events in the 82nd's history. I have also inserted a few major wartime events into the narrative as points of reference.
- I refer to several works cited in the text with simplified or more descriptive names; these names are shown in brackets at the end of their bibliographic entries. For instance, "South Annexes" refers to "Annexes" (additions) to *History of the USAAF Prisoners of War of the South Compound, Stalag Luft III.*
- For help with the Kriegie patois, see *Appendix B.*
- For help reading military orders and history, see *Appendix A.*
- Production of maps which appear in the text was done on Scribblemaps.com.

- Family Names used in the text:

Heber Butler	Richard's younger brother and close friend
Martena	Heber's wife[10]
Richard (Dick), Christine, Marcia, Craig	Butler children (in birth order)
Grandma and Grandpa Butler	Richard's parents
Granny and Grampy Miller	Geneil's parents
William/Wm, Ellen, Joseph/Joe, Edwin, Willard (wife Audria), Lester, Margaret, Heber, Vida	Richard's siblings
Corson (Herb)	Fellow POW Dad met after going down

---

10. Heber met Martena Terry in Sacramento while he and Richard were stationed there. Heber proposed by mail from Tallahassee; Martena travelled across the country via troop trains, and they were married 13 November 1942.

1
TRAINING

July 1940-August 1942

Among the wartime artifacts we have is a spiral notebook ostensibly containing only notes from a math class. Lost at the back of that notebook is a record of this period. Richard began his Training Journal on the last page and from there wrote forward 35 densely-filled pages.

We also have a number of letters to Geneil and a small packet of letters and cards to other family members; these are excerpted below among the chronological listings of military assignments. With the *Training Journal,* these provide bright and tantalizing flashes of what Richard was experiencing and feeling during the two years from 19 July 1940 through 27 August 1942. His brother Heber's memoir also provides details.

We have only one official document which appears to give us a full history of Richard's enlistment and training. This consists of a copy of two columns on the back of an unknown form; Column 5 includes "Military Record, Organizations to Which Attached" and "Original Assignment and Organizations to Which Subsequently Assigned." From these two categories we can piece together Richard's first 25 months in the service, although careful cross-checking is necessary; dates are vague and sometimes contradictory.[1]

The Training Journal gives us the most precise timeline; artifacts and the correspondence help to fill out the picture of his movements and their timing. Even after Richard began flight school in early 1942, diplomas, ID cards and other personal artifacts along with the sparse but helpful Individual Flight Records are our only other sources of information before the orders received at Luke Field in late August 1942; from then on we can at least follow the track left by his copies of official orders.

Unless otherwise indicated, dates, times and events in the timeline are from the Training Journal; passages quoted in the chronological outline without attribution are from that journal. Some elements of original military abbreviations and punctuation below have been standardized.

1940

July

19   Enlisted, Federal Post Office Building, Ogden, Utah.[2]

---

1. Even his Enlisted Man's Discharge of 20 December 1942 gives a summary listing of his training which is neither complete nor in what we know to be chronological order.

2. Butler 48. Several later official documents show place of enlistment as Fort Douglas or Salt Lake City.

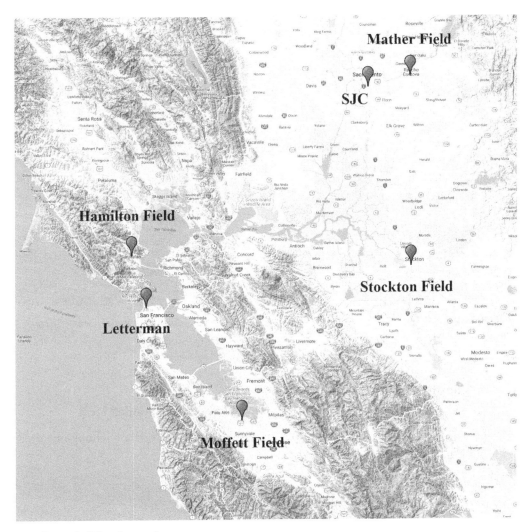

Northern California stations

22   Reported at Ft. Douglas, 6:00 a.m.

23   Departed Salt Lake City 8:00 a.m. by train.

24   Arrived Oakland, traveled by ferry to Sausalito via San Francisco, rode
the "electric car" to San Rafael, then by truck to Hamilton Field.
Base Hq[3] & 5th Air Base Sq (S), Hamilton Field, California[4]
(San Rafael, California).
Basic Training.

---

3. See *Appendix A.*
4. "Organizations to Which Attached"

Heber & Moffett Field tent (Butler family collection)

Richard soon after enlistment (Butler family collection)

September

3   Completed basic training. Traveled by convoy to Moffett Field.

25   Began evening class in Aviation Math at Palo Alto High School four nights per week.

October

1   68th A.B. Gp. (SP), Moffett Field, California.[5]
Aircraft engine/airframe mechanics and crew chief training.[6]

6   W.C.T.C. (Stockton Unit)/Moffett Field, California.

15   Caught cold, began coughing.

21   Went to sick call and was hospitalized.

23   Pneumonia diagnosed. Sent by ambulance to Letterman General Hospital, Presidio of San Francisco.[7]

---

5. "Original Assignment and Organizations to Which Subsequently Assigned"

6. Butler 51

7. Richard had contracted pneumonia due to very poor conditions living in a tent in wet weather.

*Richard, Stockton Field CA, winter 1940–41
(Courtesy of Rose Butler Hensley)*

November
29   Released from Letterman.

December
5   Richard was one of 170 men "picked to
move to Stockton."

18   68 Air Base/A.C. Advance Flying
School, Stockton, California.[8]

*Richard, possibly Stockton Field CA,
winter 1940–41 (Courtesy of Rose Butler
Hensley)*

1941

January
1   60th A.B.sq 68th A.B. Gp. (S), A.C.A.F.S., Stockton, California.[9]
Richard worked "in the instrument-training department."[10]

February
6   3-day pass for home visit.

March
21   Offered position in Link Trainer school at Chanute Field, Illinois.

---

8. Letter from brother Heber Butler (now in Letterman himself with pneumonia and
pleurisy).
9. "Original Assignment and Organizations to Which Subsequently Assigned"
10. Butler 54

27   60th A.B.A.C.A.F.S., Stockton Field, California.

April

1   Departed for Chanute Field by train.

2   Half-hour visit with family at Salt Lake City depot.
1st Sch. Sq., AC[11] (Chanute Field, Rantoul, Illinois).
Air Corps Technical School, Link Trainer Instructor Training.[12]

4   Arrived late afternoon at Chanute Field.

Postcard excerpt
to Butlers

I had a swell trip all the way. The train was late into Chicago so we had 2 hrs to look the joint over. . . . We leave pretty soon now for Rantoul 100 miles or there about.

May

1

Letter excerpts
Chanute Field (Rantoul, Ilinois)

One month out of the three has gone already and it doesn't seem like it's been very long. Maybe it's because this work is so interesting. The first three weeks were spent learning what made the trainer tick and how to keep it ticking. And for the past week and one more week will be on instruments.

We each get about a half hour flying time every day, that's what makes it interesting. I think the work is the only thing I like about this Field.

It sure seems funny. A year ago now I didn't even know you existed but now it seems as though I've known you for centuries.

Maybe it would be a good idea if I quit and got some studying done. I have a test on the three gyro-operated instruments this afternoon.

Richard, Mather Field 1941
(Butler family collection)

---

11. "Organizations to Which Attached"

12. This training "came in real handy for him after he became a pilot, because he could fly instruments like nobody ever dreamed of. Richard was the best instrument pilot that I have ever ridden with." (Butler 54)

June

28   ACTS Graduation.

July

3   End of attachment to 1st Sch. S., AC.[13]
Departure by bus for Garland.

6   Early morning arrival in Garland.

25   Departure by bus for Stockton.

26   Early afternoon arrival in Stockton. Finding
that his "outfit" had moved to Mather Field,
Richard traveled on to Sacramento.
Hq & Hq Sq 77th AB Gp. (S), Mather Fld.,
California[14] (Sacramento, California).

Richard, Sacramento (Butler family collection)

September

15   Richard and Heber registered for Fall Semester at Sacramento Junior College. Richard's
17-hour schedule included History (3), Public
Speaking (3), Orientation (1), Math 56 (10).[15]

October

10   67th AB Sq 77th AB Gp (S), Mather Field,
California.[16]

31
Letter excerpts
to Butlers
Mather Field (Sacramento, California)

Since we started school there have been seven
weeks. . . . I never thought it possible for me to
ever like math but I really do and Heber is the
same. Our math course covers Algebra, Geometry

"A sharp turn at Sac'to Junior College" (Butler family collection)

---

13. "Organizations to Which Attached"

14. "Original Assignment and Organizations to Which Subsequently Assigned"

15. Certificate of Registration. They were in class through the morning and early afternoon. "We have arranged for work at night here at the post, and are really having fun at school." After dinner on the base, Richard worked as a Link Instrument Training instructor.

16. "Original Assignment and Organizations to Which Subsequently Assigned"

& Trigonometry, and we both seem to be getting quite a lot out of the class in Public Speaking.

November

2

Letter excerpts continued

I started [this letter] last Fri night in the post library before going to work. . . . I have a pair of earphones on, instructing a cadet in the simple technique of flying a trainer. He doesn't seem to think it's so simple.

Well, I am now assis't crew chief on my trainer. . . .

We put in applications for flight training. . . .

Boy, this is sure fun trying to write a letter and figure out problems for these guys at the same time. Here's how: Climb to an altitude of 1500' at 300' per minute; at the same time make a standard one needle-width turn to the left. Stop the climb and turn together. . . . that's just what I do every night while the boys are on basic. After they get on radio beam problems is when I go nuts. Hearing those signals all the time would drive anyone crazy.

I'm figuring on getting an Xmas furlow if everything turns out the way I have it planned.

13   Entered hospital for tonsillectomy.

December

4   Successful Aviation Student exam by Flight Surgeon.[17]

18   "Had my interview with the Cadet Examining Board."

1942

January

16   Richard had a ride in a BT-13 "for about two hours & flew it for 20 min. I found out what dogfighting is."

17   He had a "hop in an AT-6-A which really turned out OK."

---

17. On 3 June 1941 Congress had authorized pilot training for enlisted men as "Aviation Students." ". . . enlisted men could apply for flight training if they passed a series of written and physical exams." (Hoover 20) By late August the first class of Aviation Students had reported for primary training. Richard and Heber were now moving through the selection process.

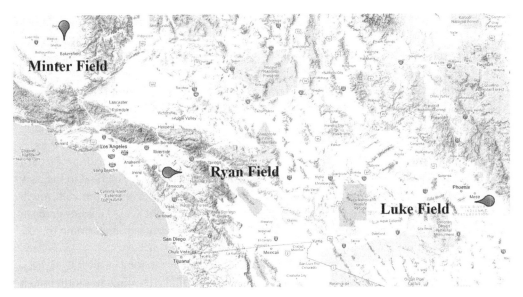

Southern California & Arizona stations

February

c. 1   Flying school applications for both brothers were approved.[18]

14   "I received orders to report at Ryan Field, Hemet Calif. by the 18th of Feb."

18   Richard arrived in Hemet at 10:30 a.m. after a stop at March Field.
Ryan Field, Hemet California; Air Force Training Detachment[19]
Elementary flight training.
Aircraft: PT-22.

24   This was the first day of ground school. "This afternoon I reported to the
Flight Line and was assigned to . . . Class 42-H,[20] Co D., Sq IV, Flight H,
Section 1. . . . I started my flight training today by logging 15 mins. of
dual time."

March

1   "Had my picture taken this morning in helmet & goggles."

16   First solo flight.[21]

---

18. Butler 60

19. *Flight Log*

20. Flight-training classes nationwide were denoted by adding consecutive letters to
the last two digits of the year.

21. "Student's Solo Log." Confirmed by *Flight Log* and by Richard's annotation on solo
diploma, Brigham City, Utah, 25 Sep 1945: "First Solo PT 22 Army."

Primary Flight Training

The basic flight schools Richard and Heber attended "had been a commercial pilot training school prior to the war and operated on a contract basis to the Army during the war. The army provided the school commandant and Army check pilots, but the instructors were all civilian. A typical day consisted of ground school for half the day, the other half being devoted to flight training." (Vrilakas 39)

"Ground training consisted of classes in navigation, weather, aerodynamics, and engine mechanics, to include hydraulics, electronics, and various aircraft systems." (Vrilakas 40)

"We learned what the system was all about, how the instruments operated, and the indications we would see under different circumstances. All the pilots then spent time in what was called in those days a Link Trainer.

"We would sit in a room that was set on an axis. It couldn't go up or down, just left or right. The same instruments we had in the cockpit were on a board before us. A controller/instructor [the position Richard trained for at Chanute Field] sat in the back of the room to observe and put us through our simulated flight. . . . [A] passing grade in the Link Trainer meant it was time to take to the air." (Hoover 24)

See Salter 77–83 for a beautifully written account of flight training at another such civilian school of the period.

Sergeant Pilot Discrimination

"I also experienced firsthand . . . the unequal treatment given noncommissioned enlisted pilots compared to officers. Our commanding officer [in fighter training] was strict and uncompromising, and he had never taken a shine to enlisted pilots. While our quarters were bare-bones, the officers stayed in much more pleasant surroundings. The enlisted men were forced to clean latrines and do KP duty, while the commissioned officers were not.

"That hierarchy seemed very unfair. Many of us made our feelings known. Fortunately for me and the other sergeant pilots, a transfer in leadership occurred. . . . The enlisted men were suddenly on equal footing with the officers and could concentrate on our fighter training tactics instead of peeling potatoes." (Hoover 24–5)

PT-22[1]

PT stood for "primary training" and "was a way of testing a candidate's [acclimatization] to a new element and at the same time taught the very basics of aviating. . . . What these instructors, aircraft and students were concerned with was the very basic concept of stick and rudder flying."

Primary Training aircraft were painted yellow and, until training was standardized in 1943, "[trainees] would be channeled off to at least four different airplanes." The other three were large and "robust" and "could keep your feet busy on the runway, yet allow you to expand your mind in the air."

"Streamlined and dainty by comparison, the PT-22 could teach its students things the [others] never heard of." It had a "swept back wing" which gave "unstable stall characteristics, such as those the students would encounter in the airplanes they would soon graduate to. . . . It was also the most heavily wing-loaded of the trainers, which meant ignoring the air speed on a botched approach could, and did, result in a disproportionate number of bent airplanes. There are many who agree that the PT-22 bears much more relationship to the AT-6 Texan than its primary trainer brethren."

Davisson describes response to controls as well as both take-off and climb-out as "leisurely." The PT-22 gave "the pilot and passenger as comfortable a ride as they'll ever find in an open cockpit airplane. The visibility is superb and the slipstream is almost non-existent. . . . The military seats [were] adjustable for height," allowing the pilot to cruise "in a low position in total calm but to also hoist [himself] up to a much better vantage point" for landing.

Ryan PT-22 Recruit (Courtesy of Julian Herzog)

---

1. Excerpted from Davisson, "Analyzing the Ryan Recruit."

"As I relax." Ryan Field (Butler family collection)

Richard studying, Ryan Field (But-ler family collection)

"Me as I look on the flightline at Ryan Sch of Aero" (Butler family collection)

"Clear!" Minter Field, May 1942 (Butler family collection)

"Flying on instruments without a hood. Taken by H. Cagle at Minter Field." (Butler family collection)

"Mixture full rich. Throttle cracked. Prime it. Energize. 'Clear!!' Engage and you're off. I was off before I started." Minter Field, May 1942 (Butler family collection)

"Those things make my ears hot. Anyway he was insulting my flying." Minter Field, May 1942 (Butler family collection)

April

22   Last flight at Ryan Field.[22]

24   Transferred to "AFBFS, Bakersfield, California."[23]
Ryan flight hours: Dual 28:08, Solo 31:52.

24   AFBFS, Minter Field, Shafter (Bakersfield) California.
Basic flight training.
Aircraft: BT-13A.

---

22. *Flight Log*
23. Individual Flight Record, 24 April 1942

Basic Flight Training
BT-13

The BT-13 "had a metal external covering except for control surfaces and was a low-wing plane with two tandem seats and a Plexiglas canopy covering the cockpits. . . . it had earned the nickname of 'Vultee Vibrator.' The radial engine, in the area of 425 horsepower, shook the entire aircraft. The metal wings also tended to flex and wrinkle under any stress." (Vrilakas 46)

Hoover notes the following item of significance to the Butler brothers: "In the 1940s, the Air Corps had a policy of sending the short pilots to fighter training and the taller ones to train in bombers and transports." (Hoover 22)

"Basic flight training finally ended and roughly half of the class was assigned to advanced training in single-engine aircraft, which pointed toward ultimately becoming a fighter pilot." (Vrilakas 47)

BT-13 Valiant (Courtesy of USAF)

25   Richard arrived Minter Field at 9:30 a.m.

29   "I went up for my first hop at the controls in the front seat [of the BT-13A]."

May
7
Letter excerpts
Air Corps Basic Flying School, Bakersfield, Califoria [Minter Field]

It was less than two weeks ago that I pulled in here, and I didn't start flying for several days after that. Even so, it only took four and a half hours until he got out and said take it up. I think the reason my instructor soloed me is because he's afraid to ride with me. If you get a chance, take a look inside a BT-13. To me it isn't so bad now, but when I first started flying here I thought I'd never get on to all the controls.

In ground school we only have three classes, but they take in everything. At primary we got mostly theory of the different subjects, but here we put it into practice. Navigation, cross country flights, meteorology, weather maps and broadcasts, and in radio communications, the headache, along with other things we are learning code. I think this will prove sort of interesting after I finish memorizing the alphabet.

When I first joined up, I was hard after some learning. Well, I got my first chance a year ago at Link Trainer School and now they're throwing it at me full force here, trying to make a good pilot out of me instead of just an airplane driver. . . . It is going to be a long hard climb even from here to the end of the course in September.

16
Letter excerpts
Air Corps Basic Flying School, Bakersfield, Califoria [Minter Field]

We're really getting into the swing of things now. I got in about sixteen hours this last week, making my total twenty-four hours of plain air work and two more hours on instruments. This is right in my line, although there is a lot of difference between flying a link trainer and flying under the hood in a plane. It's really funny when the instruments say you're flying straight and level and your senses say the wings are straight up and down.

From here on it will really get interesting. We start cross-country and night flying this next week.

Time does go quite fast when you're doing something you like. It doesn't seem like three months since I started out at Ryan Field as a lowly Dodo Bird without any wings. I was hoping each day that they would sprout and start to grow. Then one day they did. That day cost my instructor no small amount [of] anguish and possibly a gray hair or two. Anyway, today after 16 hours in the air, I am, "No better than the first day you went up." My instructor.

That's propaganda, so don't you believe it. I can't help but think he has something there, because yesterday he gave me two stars for not rolling down flaps for my gliding turns. And that ain't good. Each star costs me two bits. . . . I'm not too down-hearted—yet—because I have only two stars and the average is four or five.

24
Letter excerpts
Air Corps Basic Flying School, Bakersfield, Califoria [Minter Field]

I guess I gave you a bum stear. We started cross-country flying and formation flying instead of night—. The schedule had us starting tonight, but I think they've called it off until tomorrow night. This X-country stuff is really fun. We have sectional maps of the locality to chart our course on, and as the ground passes

Advanced Flight Training
T-6

"The advanced trainer AT-6 which we were to fly was a dream compared to the BT-13.

". . . it was fast for a trainer, had retractable landing gear, hydraulic flaps, and a dozen other features we had not experienced before. It was comparatively quiet in flight, very maneuverable and an excellent all round trainer. It also had a [*sic*] 30-caliber machine guns (mounted in the wing) for aerial and ground gunnery. Except for less engine power, it approached some of the earlier fighters of those years. . . ." (Vrilakas 48)

"A highlight of advanced training was air and ground gunnery. We were sent down in small groups to Ajo, Arizona, on the Mexico border where we learned aerial gunnery by firing at a sleeve towed behind another aircraft. We also practiced air-to-ground gunnery by diving and firing on a ground target." (Vrilakas 51)

Possibly Richard in front cockpit of this T6 (Butler family collection)

undernearth we check off the towns, railroads, etc., by their size and the time it takes to get there.

Yesterday I took my second X-C. I went from here to Fresno and back. About 100 mi each way. What really made it interesting is that the six of us flew in formation of three both ways. That's really ticklish stuff when you're flying about twenty-five feet apart. At least they think so enough to make it a five star offense if you're caught looking away from the lead ship. Even when landing. It's sort of fun to look at the lead ship and when it gets almost to the ground, level off and land your own.

This flying is a funny thing. Yesterday I went to Fresno and back while Heber was coming down here the same way. I wonder just what would happen if we ever got together in the air. Some day it's apt to happen; then you'll hear about it.

I really have a swell instructor. I thought that before I found out who he was tho'. Lt. Mathieu from Ogden. He is also a Mormon, surprising as that may seem. We are few and far between here in the Army, so it's really something at least for me to get a member of my own church for an instructor.

June

19   "My orders read Luke Field for Advanced. Near Phoenix Ariz. . . . Am going by way of home."

23   Transferred to "AFAFS."[24]
Minter flight hours: Dual 34:25, Solo 48:25, Link trainer 15:00.

24   Arrived this morning at Luke Field.

25   AFAFS/ACAFS, Luke Field, Arizona.[25]
Advanced flight training.
Aircraft: AT-6A.
"Heber and I have the same instructor, also we sleep in the same barracks side by side."

26   "I took a 40 min. back seat ride with my instructor. He showed me the area."

July

21   "The Flight Officer bill was signed. . . ."

---

24. Individual Flight Record, 23 June 1942. AF indicates Advanced Flight School.
25. Individual Flight Record, 27 August 1942

26
Letter excerpts
Luke Field/Arizona

Today marks the half-way point at this field. We beat our way to the ramp at 7:50 this morning and after a little parading, Eyes Right, etc., we stood by while some Brass Hat gave the well-known speech and presented those well-earned wings to the boys. I might add that the chest expansion of about two hundred men has increased at least six inches.

I'm not sure about the date but we are supposed to be through about Aug 27th, ceremony and all. . . .

I guess I'd better sign off and get moved downstairs. The upper class moved out so we take their place. Altho Heber and I have a separate room together, I don't think it will be as good as it has been 'cause when we fly nights and try to sleep in the mornings, the noise overhead won't be so good.

August
16
Letter excerpt
Luke Field/Arizona

Yes, this clipping very much concerns me, but I'm not sure whether they have it in running order yet or will have in time for the 27th. It won't be long afterward, tho'. Flight officers have the same pay and allowances as a 2nd Lt. without having to pay $50 to join the Officer's Club and that sort of thing.[26]

17
Letter excerpts
Luke Field/Arizona

I just mailed your official invitation. . . . I didn't put my personal seal on it, but you can take my word that I mean it.

I'll be looking for you Saturday.

P.S. It looks like tonight will finish it up. Just one more cross-country (at night) and the wings are mine. We either fly to Tucson or to Blythe, Calif. or both. It's really fun with all of those airways. Lights, city lights and so on. Right pretty.

21   ". . . I went up and flew a two-ship formation with Brentlinger out over Superstition Mountain. . . . My last scheduled flight to finish my 79 hrs.

---

26. This refers to legislation creating a new Flight Officer rank for the men known as Sergeant Pilots, whose official designation was Staff Sergeant (Pilot). It would not be effected for some months to come and would never confer the true officer status of a commission.

Heber and Richard, Luke Field (Butler family collection)

T-6s out of Luke Field (Butler family collection)

Luke Field, Richard and Heber on right (Butler family collection)

Richard and Heber, probably Luke Field (Butler family collection)

was in ship no 225. . . . To end it off I landed my last time in a typical Arizona windstorm. I guess the wings are mine."

27   ". . . completed the prescribed course of training August 27, 1942, and rated Pilot at the A.C.A.F.S., Luke Field, Phoenix, Arizona."[27]
Luke flight hours: Training (solo) 79:10, Other than pilot 7:40, Instrument Link Trainer 10:00.

30   Transferred to Dale Mabry Field, Tallahassee, Florida.[28]
58th Fighter Group (Later 338th FG, 312th Fighter Squadron).

31
Telegram

PHOENIX ARIZ
WILL ARRIVE SALT LAKE 530 PM TOMORROW SEE YOU SOON LOVE=RICHARD.

---

27. Air Corps Pilot Certification.
28. Military orders this date

September

4   Marriage of Geneil Miller and
Richard Butler, Salt Lake City.

12   338th Fighter Group,
312th Fighter Squadron.
Dale Mabry Field, Tallahassee,
Florida.[29]
Fighter training, ground gunnery.
Aircraft: P-39D1(BT-14,AT-6A).

November

18   Relieved from assignment.
Ordered to report to Fort Hamilton, New York.[30]
Dale Mabry flight hours: Pursuit
77:25, Training 14:05.[31]

*Geneil Miller and Richard Butler (Butler fam-
ily collection)*

*Richard and Heber, Tallahassee (Butler
family collection)*

*Richard, Tallahassee railway sta-
tion, November 1942 (Butler family
collection)*

---

29. Individual Flight Record, 3 October 1942.

30. Military Orders this date and Individual Flight Record, 17 November 1942.

31. The line between training and combat now becomes blurred. Flight training which ocurred after this point is sketchily reported and/or was informal; it will appear in Richard's *Journal* narrative in Chapter 2.

Fighter Training
P-39

"The P-39s, which were single-seat, low-wing fighters, had a reputation as 'widow-makers.' In fact among the fighter pilots, there was an old song that went, 'Oh, don't give me a P-39. Because the engine is mounted behind. She'll spin, crash, and burn. So don't give me a P-39.'

"The next verse went, 'Oh, give me a P-38. The props that counter-rotate. She'll not spin, crash, and burn. So give me a P-38.'

P-39 Airacobra (Butler family collection)

"The Airacobra's engine was mounted behind the pilot with a drive shaft to the propeller in a channel underneath the pilot. Most pilots felt that the midmounted engine made the P-39 susceptible to tumbling and flat spins when dogfighting. When that happened, we were told there was no recourse but to bail out." (Hoover 25–6)

Tom Watts, another sergeant pilot who kept a detailed journal, is often quoted by Bob Hoover; here is his description of his first P-39 flight:

"When I started the engine, it was like starting some powerful diesel. It frightened the daylights out of me momentarily. But the big thing was after I had aligned myself on the runway for takeoff. I was due for a surprise and didn't know it. Nothing serious: I just felt like Buck Rogers when I opened the throttle and went tearing down the runway." (Hoover 27)

Pilots and P-39s, Dale Mabry Field, Tallahassee. Richard second from front left, Heber third pilot from back left. Twenty-eight Dale Mabry trainees would become members of the "Exclusive 67" Sad Sacks; 17 of them would sign the $1 Bill. (Butler family collection)

Richard at Ryan Field (Butler family collection)

2
COMBAT

1942

November

Sunday 8

Operation Torch, the Allied invasion of North Africa began.

Tuesday 17

Geneil's Diary

"Betty Mills got a call saying that Orders had arrived. Richard and I spent our last night together."[1]

Wednesday 18

Journal

We took the train out of Tally at about 3:00 A.M. Wed morning Nov 18.[2]

Heber

Heber recalled reaching "an airbase in Georgia by 7:00 or 8:00 in the morning. We stopped and had breakfast." (Butler 70)

Postcard (Hotel De Soto, Savannah GA)

Mailed with 21 November letter from Brooklyn

I probably won't know for some time whether or not you got my telegram sent from here to Tallahassee. I didn't have time to wait for your answer. I just had to hope you weren't there to get it.

Friday 20

[In the late evening Richard and Heber arrived at Fort Hamilton, Brooklyn, New York.]

---

1. For unknown reasons, Richard and Heber had remained in Tallahassee almost a month longer than some of their friends. Along with others, "Doc" Holik, whom they later met in London, left on October 22.

2. In a blackout Geneil and Aunt Martena saw Richard and Heber off trainside; the two couples walked to the train from Tallahassee's Colonial Hotel, where they had been living. Though Richard refers in the *Journal* to "the station," in her last years Geneil recalled that the train was not in a station but was standing by itself on rails which ran through town. The nighttime departure was said by Geneil to have been for security reasons.

Geneil's Diary

[The page for 18 and 19 November has been neatly removed from Geneil's Diary. As a consequence, we don't know precisely when she and Martena left Tallahassee; the next page does tell us that she and Martena arrived New Orleans sometime early on this date and left at 2:30 p.m. in a Pullman car.]

Saturday 21

Letter excerpts (Colonial Hotel letterhead)

We're not supposed to be writing. . . .

We made the trip OK, as you can see, and I'm not very impressed with the big city. In fact, I wouldn't trade Garland for six of them. . . .

I hope I never have to take a more lonely trip than the one from Florida. I can't help but remember the way you looked at the station. I'll never get over it. If I ever hated anything in my life, it was having to leave you there to get your own way home. . . .

My address will be sent to you from the headquarters here as soon as we get there. They're really equipping us here. No one knows for what.

We got into Savannah, Ga., about 3:30 Thursday afternoon, and I tried to get in contact with you at Tallahassee. . . .

We're smuggling these letters off the post to avoid the censor. They'll get there about a month sooner this way. . . .

Geneil's Diary

[Geneil and Martena arrived Dallas 10:30 a.m. and left at 2:00 p.m., again on a Pullman.]

Sunday 22

Letter excerpts (USO letterhead)

Things are pretty dead around here this morning. There is one good change, though. The sun is shining just as tho' nothing had happened. Nothing has.

It's kind of pretty looking out over the ocean at the ships and small islands. . . .

It's fun to pretend that I am really talking to you, anyway.

It seems funny to sit here (I'm in the balcony of the Service Club.) watching the different nationalities of soldiers come and go. They don't look a bit different from any other soldier. . . . Just the uniform.

Heber and I have just been over the hill using the telephone. We walked halfway across Brooklyn to find it. We called home, but there wasn't anyone there but my nephew. . . .

I knew you wouldn't be there, but I sure was hoping. . . . We may call again before long. I hope you're home by then, so I'll at least know that you made it OK.

Geneil's Diary

[The two wives arrived Denver sometime early in the day and left immediately for Cheyenne, from where they departed at 3:00 p.m.]

Monday 23

[Martena and Geneil arrived Ogden at 4:30 a.m.]

Tuesday 24

[According to Heber, in the very early hours he and Richard transferred by river-boat from Fort Hamilton to the harbor docks, where they boarded the HMT[3] *Queen Elizabeth* along with 22,000 others; around 7:00 a.m. they left New York harbor.]

Thursday 26 [Thanksgiving]

Journal

9:00 P.M., 7:00 pm. in N. York
Mid-Atlantic Ocean
Three days out.

Since leaving Tallahassee I have been thru quite an experience. We took the train out of Tally at about 3:00 A.M. Wed morning Nov 18. I'll never forget just how you looked at the station when I left. It was about as hard a thing as I ever hope to do.

When we pulled into Savannah Ga. Wed afternoon I sent a telegram to you at the Colonial Hotel but didn't get an answer. Maybe it was because I had to leave before you could answer and maybe it was because you had already left for home. I hope that was the case.

The trip as a whole was very dull. We pulled into Washington D.C. Friday morning and could see the Lincoln, Jefferson and Washington memorials and the capital as we passed in the train but didn't get a chance to leave the station to see any of the town. From there on to New York we took a special train that took us right on through without stopping.

While our transportation was coming, we took a short look around the big city. Those big tall buildings, like the Empire State and so on, don't impress me very much. They're not as high as people would like to make out. I did get quite a kick out of the way those crazy people run back and forth. I was tempted several times to trip someone just to see whether he'd roll or skid.

Fort Hamilton loomed up just on the other side of Brooklyn, and that's where we stayed from Friday night Nov 20 until Monday night Nov 23. Heber's [21st]

_____

3. His Majesty's Troopship.

birthday was Sunday, and I saw to it that he got a warming over. He got in bed a different way that night.

After getting a bunch more clothes and equipment, we pulled out of Fort Hamilton and boarded a riverboat, or whatever they call it, and it took us on up the harbor to where the *Queen Elizabeth* was loading. The less I say about our quarters here the better. They aren't quite what we expected, but we'll pull thru. Ninety-two men in a room fifteen feet by about thirty-five feet. Four high.

This is really a big ship, about the biggest afloat, also the fastest of any near its size. Its speed is what makes it so much safer than others. I'm sure glad it is as big as it is, because that nose goes up and down too many [times] a day as it is. One time your feet will be glued to the floor like in a nine G pull-out. The next second you're six inches off the ground. That goes on all the time, and it's been worse today. At least it looks that way by the amount of sea-sick men.

To go back a little: we pulled out of New York Tuesday Nov 24 at about 7:00 A.M. and followed the coastline south for quite a way before heading out to sea.

The trip thus far has been fairly uneventful. We got hooked on an M.P. detail on the water guard (to conserve water we are only allowed to draw fresh water between 6 & 9 morning & night). Our job was to keep unauthorized personnel away the rest of the time. It turns out to be quite a job at times. They gave us the job because we had enough rank so that the men couldn't run over us. They are inclined to try that, too, every chance they get. It can be expected that with a mob of 22,000 men some of them might try to take over.

The mess deal is what kills me. We eat twice a day and I suppose that would be enough (considering the way this boat jumps around) if there was plenty to eat at those two. I guess they've found out through experience that (with every-one's stomach slightly upset and others more so) two meals a day was sufficient. The men just don't turn up for any more. (Remind me to tell you something that wouldn't look too good on paper—yes, you guessed it.)

There's something else, but you won't have to remind me about it. Every morning when I get up I look like a coarse washboard. This xo- "bunk" doesn't have a mattress, and the slats are made of good hard wood. (Probably English Walnut.) I have to roll over every ten minutes to ease the pain. I think I'll make it through. I get up every once in a while to rest. And this being the largest ship in the world, I have plenty of room to walk off the kinks.

I asked the Steward this afternoon for a mattress, but all he could say was, "Rilly, old chap, I caunt do a thing abaout it. Sorry, ol' man." I told him my sad tale about wearing out my shorts from rolling so much. He said, "Well, Guvernah you shouldn't rest so much." I was about to remind him that I hadn't rested since I boarded the sloop, but I knew I was whipped and further comment was a waste of time. (Especially when that time could be spent trying to keep this d--- boat from rocking.)

So I staggered off up the deck. I've forgotten how to walk. Anymore I just shuffle along the deck. As the nose comes up, my feet sink into wood, then as it

Aboard the *Queen Elizabeth*

The *Queen Elizabeth* had just been completed and launched and was ready for fitting-out as a passenger liner when Britain entered the war. She was then the largest and she remained for decades the fastest ship afloat. After a period of uncertainty, she was fitted out as a troop ship; only after the war was she converted for luxury passenger service.

It was here on the *Queen Elizabeth* that the "Exclusive 67" Sad Sacks met and got to know one another. (See *Appendix D*.)

"On board the *Queen Elizabeth,* the other enlisted pilots and I ran into the same discrimination that we had witnessed earlier in fighter training. We were forced to ride in what had been the gymnasium with the infantry troops while the officers occupied the luxury suites." (Hoover 33)

Hoover again quotes Tom Watts. "Our quarters were in the gymnasium. Its size was 35' × 20' × 12', and there were 92 of us in it. Bunks were four layers and made like a box. There were four strips of lumber for the bottoms, a thin mattress, no pillow. Everything was discolored with filth.

"Our life preservers were in our bunks, too, and they were shamefully grimy. Before we could even get in there, we had to remove all of our equipment and carry it because the bunks' aisles were only 25 inches apart. A soldier all decked out with his equipment could not pass through.

"We also found that we were unable to stretch out to full length, since the bunks were 5 feet in length and only 3 feet in width." (Hoover 34)

Heber says, "The bottom guy was right on the floor and the top bunk (which I picked . . .) was right up on top so I could [lie] on my bunk and write on the ceiling [where] I kept a log. . . ." (Butler 71)

"Because of the trickle-down effect, all hell broke loose when men on the top tier of bunks experienced nausea and vomiting from seasickness. The stench was awful." (Hoover 34)

Watts concurs closely with Richard on the number of men aboard: ". . . what a prize we would have been with 20,000 men and 3,500 pilots aboard." (Hoover 34)

When Cook boarded the *Queen Elizabeth* some months later, the Red Cross handed him "an OD [olive drab] drawstring bag filled with . . . things like a shaving kit, soap, playing cards, cigarettes, candy, etc." (Cook 62)

After a short cruise southward from New York with the convoy, Heber says that ". . . the captain of the *Queen Elizabeth* gave her the full throttle and we just left the escort vessels and the rest of the convoy far behind. We were moving at about 35 knots (40 mph). . . . The rest of the convoy were moving at about 15 knots. In about 15–20 minutes we were completely out of sight of the rest of the convoy." (Butler 70–71)

goes down, I float along about six inches off. (You know I don't drink.) It's kind of got me scared. I'm afraid that when (and if) we hit land, I'll try to lean over sideways and walk, like they do on this thing, and I'll fall and break something for sure.

Well, tonight again at 11:50 the clock will start running away with itself and won't stop 'til it reads 1:00 A.M. I haven't seen a 12:00 midnight since we left New York. All day today we've been in the zone three hours ahead of N.Y. Time. Tomorrow we'll be four hours away. The gun crew said that they detected two subs last night with their listening devices, but they didn't seem to hear us. From here on in they'll really be watching out. We'll get there tomorrow night sometime, and then I suppose the war will begin. We still don't know where we're going or what we'll be flying when we get there. We'll be completely blacked out, and no one will be allowed on deck or very far from quarters during the rest of the trip.

Saturday 28

Journal

We were sunk last night and all twelve thousand on board perished. That's what the German news broadcast announced. I won't have to worry any more about dying 'cause I feel pretty good. On top of that, there aren't 12,000 men on here; there are 22,000.

Every day about noon we have had an emergency drill, during which everyone presumably runs calmly to their stations. Three or four of our bunch go each day just so we'll be represented. The rest of us, if we're out of bed, just run around in circles screaming and yelling just to add to the confusion. You'd be surprised how much fun it is. Yesterday the man at the mike was wondering why boat no. six didn't have anyone in it. Someone said that's where we were supposed to be. We don't worry 'cause we know that, in case of emergency, women and flying squirrels come first.

By now I'm used to it so I can sleep thro' the ringing of that emergency bell, but this morning (about 12:30) during the drill they started shooting their big guns. I guess if we had a couple more nights on this thing I'd be tired enough to sleep through a bombing. We've had to carry our life-vests around the boat ever since we left N.Y., but now when we leave our quarters we have to take our tin helmets along. The reason for that is to keep the weight of the ship distributed more. Or to keep us from getting any taller. That's a good idea, come to think of it; this bunk is none too long.

Sunday 29

Journal

The latest rumor has it that we'll pick up our pilot (convoy) this afternoon and dock sometime tonight. I don't know where, but these sea-sick boys have been seeing land all morning. My guess is it's Ireland and we'll land in Scotland, but it could be any place. We should be starting to unload this morning, but they say we ran into a sub or two and had to change course for a round-about way.

Yes, there's land on both sides of us, and I got a glimpse of the sun for the second time since we left N.Y. We're going south between Scotland & Ireland, so it shouldn't be very long now.

Well, this thing finally came to rest. I don't know where, but we're leaving the boat at 8:50 in the morning and are taking a train for some point about 5 hrs ride from here. If they don't bomb us before morning. We're lying at anchor here in some firth (bay or what have you). Just off the coast of England.[4]

I went down about six decks to the barber shop this evening and came near being sorry of my bargain. All went well, or as near so as I could expect, until he started to use the razor. He must have been looking for the boat to rock, or something, anyway it didn't and I almost lost my left ear. (It felt like.)

Monday 30

Journal

Last night was a rough one. The boys monkeyed around packing and arguing politics until 2:00 AM and we had to get up at 5:00 to get breakfast, so I didn't get much sleeping done.

Well, we left the *Queen Elizabeth* this morning at 9:00 and took a smaller boat in to the dock. That ship is really a whopper. This morning was the first time I'd seen it from a distance.

We landed at Greenock, Scotland after spending the night in the harbor and by 11:00 were on board a train heading south. At the time we didn't know where or why. It is now 1:20 (Dec 1), and we are settled for a while at a replacement center near Stone, England about 160 miles from [north of] London. It's a pretty nice place, too. A lot better than we expected. Heber and I have a room together and are doing OK.

In Greenock we could see the results of it's having been bombed. An old boy we were talking to at the docks said, "The very first bomb hit the winery and the bloody wine was running all up and down the bloody street." It seems as though the word "Bloody" is about their worst cuss word. They sure wear it out, too. Don't say I said so, tho'.

Before we left there, the Y.M.C.A. truck came steaming up to the train with hot tea and cookies. This is all done by the women. For one (civilian) man I see about six women. I guess the rest of them are in Libya or somewhere.

They don't seem to know what milk is around here. It's either tea, coffee or water or starve to death, and it seems to hurt their feelings when you drink water so I

4. In fact, they were in Scotland's Firth of Clyde and would go ashore at Greenock, about 20 miles west-northwest of Glasgow.

guess I starve to death. (Not if I know me, I won't.)

The trip down from Scotland was quite pretty. There were the old-fashioned homes and farms with rock walls, for fences, running in every direction as far as you could see. I guess the main produce here is milk, wool, etc., because the only things inside those rock walls were cows, sheep, rolling hills and green grass as far as you can see.

We passed through a lot of towns, but some of them I remembered may trace the trip. We stopped in Carlisle, England (300 mi from London) for hot lunch (coffee). The next town of importance someone said was Blackburn. I'm not sure tho'. It was getting dark. Then Manchester Victoria [station name] and the next stop Stone. A town of about 3,000. Just a good boatload.

United Kingdom

"A row of military grips from America." London Daily Express, *7 December 1942. (Richard M. Butler papers MSS 8849, L. Tom Perry Special Collections, Harold B. Lee Library, Brigham Young University)*

Yarnfield and Duncan Hall

Richard and Heber were a couple of miles west of Stone, Staffordshire, at Duncan Hall in Yarnfield. Duncan was one of several "hostels" originally built in Yarnfield for use by women brought in to work in munitions production nearby. Stone is a market town roughly 10 miles north of Stafford; earlier in its history it had been capital of Mercia.

The brothers were stationed at Eighth Air Force's 12th Replacement Control Depot there (later Replacement Depot or "Repple Depple"); this was essentially a holding center where they underwent indoctrination and orientation and seem to have been kept busy with long walks, lectures and paperwork until a flight training unit was ready for them.

Cook arrived about 9 months after Richard and Heber. "We loaded onto Army trucks for the . . . trip [from Stone station] to Yarnfield. Yarnfield proper was a small community of a few farmhouses and one mercantile building housing a small country store and a pub. . . . This particular complex consisted of three billeting compounds with some shared and some duplicated services. . . . The headquarters offices . . . were located at Duncan Hall." (65) Beatty and Howard Halls were other similar facilities in Yarnfield; Howard contained the recreation, entertainment and food services for all three. Hoover compares the configuration of the Halls to a wagon wheel. (35)

Contemporary Yarnfield is similar to the village Richard knew; set in gently rolling country, it has a quiet and relatively short main street lined with homes in traditional architecture and a civic core comprised of the same pub and village hall he knew. The local chapel is now a hairdresser's salon.

The main difference is that today the area then covered by the Duncan Hall complex is a housing estate (as is the case with Howard and Beatty Halls), and there are other newer homes north of the center. Yarnfield is certainly less crowded and noisy today than when hundreds of US Army men flowed through it daily.

"The barracks were 'H' shaped buildings with a fat cross bar, which extended out from the legs equally on both sides. From the Commons Room, in the cross bar between the legs, hallways stretched down the center of each leg. Small 'two person' rooms, with doors, lined each side of the hallways. The extensions of the cross bar beyond the legs were mirror images. In each extension there was a utility room, with storage for cleaning equipment and supplies, toilet paper, and a very large water heater. The greater portion of the cross bar extensions contained the latrines. There was the typical row of bathroom sinks and mirrors along one wall. Unlike the usual GI latrine . . . here there were a row of commode stalls and a row of shower stalls." (Cook 66–7)

"The central structure of Howard Hall included the station theater, the [enlisted men's] lounge, administrative offices and various mess facilities. . . . two wings contain the side-by-side [enlisted men's] and Casual Officers mess hall and the Howard Hall Theater. . . . Auditorium seating consisted of very hard wooden folding chairs that were set up in one large central and two small side sections. The chairs could be folded up and stacked along the walls to create an open hall for dances or other like activities. Stage curtains concealed the retractable motion picture screen. . . .

"The theater was a primary source of entertainment, as motion pictures were screened almost every night. . . . Most of the movies were fairly recent Hollywood releases, and they were shown for several consecutive nights. . . ." (Cook 167)

There was also a small PX, where items were rationed. The men were allowed six ounces of candy per week (usually English Cadbury or Mars bars) and a choice of gum or life savers, also razor blades and soap. (Cook 81–2)

"With the morning meal, canned grapefruit or other canned fruit would frequently be served. . . .. Sometimes, for breakfast we might be served that traditional treat . . . SOS (stuff on a shingle). SOS being browned particles of ground beef in gravy dumped over toast . . . [intended] to use up stale bread."

Their meals also included powdered eggs and dehydrated potatoes, carrots and onions. "One canned meat which I thought was really appetizing was the baked ham with raisin sauce."

"The English wartime bread, which was purchased from a local bakery, was a multigrain loaf with a gray cast and a coarse texture. However, it was tasty. . . ." (Cook 106)

"The Army had encouraged V-mail as a method of sending and delivering mail quickly under adverse circumstances. Also, V-mail did not require much cargo space and could be transported by aircraft. [It was] composed on a special form, which was stamped with a serial number and then photographed. . . . The quickly-developed negative was then sent quickly to its destination where a photocopy of each letter was printed using a special V-mail processing machine. The reproduced copies were then sent via the regular local mail system to their final destinations. . . . The . . . V-mail letter was about half the size of the original and was folded to show the name and address of the recipient in the . . . window of a 3¾ by 4⅝ inch . . . envelope." (Cook 139–40)

The dancehall Richard mentions at 5 December may have been in the village of Eccleshall. Nearby communities with pubs included Eccleshall and a hamlet called Millmeece (site of the Cold Meece Royal Ordnance Factory); Stone was the closest town, and all three were within walking distance. Yarnfield's pub was the "Labor in Vain," which Cook says was off-limits to men stationed there.

Stone Railway Station (Butler family collection)

Yarnfield countryside (Butler family collection)

England is quite a place. The whole thing including Scotland & Wales isn't as big as Minnesota.

It seems a little more like home now. I have your picture up on the dresser. Take me back home. I'm homesick. I guess that's all for tonight. Goodnight.

December

Tuesday 1

Journal

Boy, it sure did seem good to sleep in a bed for a change. Even if it is a G.I. bunk (English style at that—no springs).

We had a few lectures today about safeguarding information. The colonel really told it to us straight from the shoulder. All about the ways things get out both innocently and otherwise. And about the punishment men have received who were turned in or overheard by the authorities when they talked too much. I shouldn't have much trouble trying to keep from talking. I'm too quiet even when I'm trying to talk.

*Duncan Hall aerial view
(Courtesy of Shaun Farrelly)*

Well, we get paid tomorrow for the remainder of November, and it's really going to be an occasion. I'm not too familiar with this English money yet. By the time I figure out whether I've been gyped or not it will be too late. But these are mere fortunes of war.

One good thing I can say for it here, we get our picture shows free. We saw a pretty good one tonight.

I hope the people here are not all like some the boys here were telling about. Women away from home working in the factories. . . .

I'm doing an awful lot of writing (for me), but I'm afraid I won't be able to find time, once we get settled, to do much.

The nights are really long. I mean the sun isn't out very much this time of the year. They say it's just the opposite in the summer. It doesn't get dark until 10:00 or 11 at night, and the sun comes right back up as soon as it gets down. I'm not going to like that. You know how I like my sleep.

Well, my legs are going to sleep, but I think I'll cut this short and write you a letter you can read. You may never get this.

Wednesday 2

Journal

This morning Heber drug me out of bed (I hate to get up into a cold room!) in time for breakfast. This was followed by a long walk in the country. Boy, did we tour this neck of the woods, just for exercise. There's another one coming up tomorrow and every morning we're here. Starting at 9:00 we look the country over for an hour and a half. That's better than just plain drill. It's either one or the other.

We got the payroll signed today. That should give us enough money to see London with in case we get the chance. There is a fairly good chance that we'll get our commissions pretty quick. They give ratings out right from the headquarters here instead of them having to be approved in Wash. D.C.

Thursday 3

Journal

I think they had something when they started this . . . —[V-]mail. It's even faster than air mail, they say.

There were a bunch of news correspondents on the post today, and I think that through one of them we are going to get in touch with Mother's folks here. We hope.

I sure have a pip of a cold as of yesterday. The weather is warming up a bit lately, so maybe I can get over it before we leave. I wrote my first letter to you this morning. V-mail, also one to the folks.

I was listening to a play over the radio this evening (B.B.C.), and I was certainly surprised at the amount of profanity and common slang they use. Almost every other word. The guys say it's a lot worse in their cinemas (picture show or movies where I come from). What this world isn't coming to.

V-Mail excerpts

I guess about all you will get is we're having weather and it isn't warm. This country might be OK in the summer. At least it looks like it would be by the green fields and such. It's about as damp as San Francisco but what could I expect. . . . Oh, what a cold I'm getting

We had a swell trip over and in a shorter time than we expected. [Two sentences censored.]

I always did want to see England and that's just what's happening. I'd like to have brought you and Mother along tho.'

V-Mail excerpt
to Butlers

Heber and I were talking to a newsman from London this afternoon and, by putting a piece in the paper, he thinks we can get in touch with some of our relatives there. We're going to try and get in touch with them by mail at least.

Friday 4

Journal

I went over to the hospital this morning for another throat swabbing. This sore throat has turned into just plain hoarseness.[5]

The *London Daily Express* man (Mr. Lacey) stayed overnight last night, and they took Heber's and my picture for his paper. He has quite a story about our lives and being Mormons. He wanted to know all about it. We may be able to get in touch with some of the folks here. Mr. Lacey is going to show us the town of London in case we ever get there.

We have been alerted as of today, so I guess we'll be assigned to a permanent field of operations before long.

The Western Union man finally got here, so we sent word home of our arrival. Today is our third anniversary. What a way to be spending it.

V-Mail excerpts

It sort of looks like we're going to get a permanent APO number before long. I sure hope so 'cause I can't wait much longer for a letter. I think it would be a good idea if you sent your mail by air. In most cases it will only take a week or two at the most.

Boy, they really black things out in the time sense of the word around here. On top of that the nights are so jet black that without a light you can't see three feet ahead.

Heber and I have turned publicity hunters. It looks as tho' we'll have our pictures in a London paper. Being the only Sgt Pilots over here and brothers at that, they seem to think that's something. At any rate we have a chance of getting in touch with some of our relations in London, we hope.

Well, wish me luck. I've almost mastered this money.... But this driving down the ... left side of the street has me worried. ...

Saturday 5

Journal

Saturday. What a day! To start out, it's raining. That kept up all day. We had a lecture on the gas mask, its care, etc., then went through the gas chamber again (tear gas). This is mainly to test our masks. Before leaving the shack, we always take the mask off, to test if we still have tears, I guess.

---

5. Richard probably didn't mean he went to an actual "hospital." The US military hospital at Shugborough Hall, a few miles east of Stafford, was about 17 miles away. He more likely meant the Duncan Hall Dispensary, which had a small medical staff and several ambulances. (Cook 231)

Stone

"Stone had one major street that descended through the town. There was an outlying pub just past where the road from Yarnfield connected to the main highway going into Stone. . . . Continuing on past the pub, the highway made a rounding left turn into the center of Stone and its main street. To the left, the main street ran up the grade to its end at the parking lot in front of the railroad station. To the right, High Street continued down the slope and turned right at the bottom of the grade. . . . The "Y" intersection of streets formed the town triangle, which was watched over by a bronze WWI Tommie. The right forking road continued up the hill to a residential area. Just a short way up the street, on the left side, was the location of the American Red Cross canteen." (Cook 90)

"Stafford was the county seat and was a large enough city to have a number of multiple story buildings. In the downtown area, there were several half-framed buildings with thatched roofs surviving from medieval times." There were also numerous pubs and a social club with dances. (Cook 89)

A bunch of us went over to a dance hall about two miles away (in the rain) just to see what the people were like. I guess we went to the wrong place 'cause I didn't like what I saw. Remind me to tell you something.

On the way back Johnny and I stopped at a "pub" to get him some Rum for his cold (he said). They didn't have any, so he settled for wine. I'll tell you about his cold later. He swears that's good for a cold, and I've never tried it so who am I to disagree?

This English weather kills me. One minute it will be raining, and the next the sun will really be making up time lost. Don't believe it tho' 'cause it'll be raining again in ten minutes. The sun never gets higher than a 30 degree angle from the earth any time of the day. I've only seen it three times since I landed, so I don't much care if it doesn't even come up.

Sunday 6

Journal

Sunday, one year since war began with the Japs. I was at Stake Conference when the news hit Sacramento. If I hadn't started to fly, I'd probably still be there. Who wants to be there tho'?

After quite a fight we got some bikes and took a tour of the countryside. Mostly just to Stone & Stafford, but these rolling hills all over that distance turns out to be quite a ways. Frankly, I'm ready for bed.

I haven't seen a good-looking girl for so long that it's awful. I most likely won't either for a lot longer. Anyway, who cares?

Well, the P-38 drivers that came with us left today for their station. I hope we get our commissions before we leave. Also our baggage from the hold of the *Queen Elizabeth*.

People around here sure go for their tea. War or no war, if they want some tea they close up shop and proceed to get a cup. If you don't drink tea or beer, you're balmy. I'm balmy.

V-Mail excerpts

What a day we had today . . . we drew some British bicycles and went "biking." . . . I think we pedaled up more hills than there are in Colorado.

We stopped at a tea shop (cafe) on the way back. I really went in for a drink of water, but we ordered chocolate and sandwiches . . . People think you're crazy if you drink anything but tea. She even tried to talk me out of it. . . . I don't dare ask for a drink of milk for fear they'll recommend me for a discharge (nuts, screwy, balmy).

Monday 7

Journal

This morning we had another hike, but I'm still getting over my cold.

At the lecture the major told us that we'd be commissioned within the next two or three days. That's the best news I've heard in years. I'm sure it will meet with your approval, too, what?

We're going to be here for another week or two before we're assigned and sent out. So that'll mean a lot of schooling in courts martial, some drill and that sort of thing.

The Boston Store,[6] I'm thinking, will be as glad to see us commissioned as anyone. You see we all got our uniforms on an uncertain payment deal. They took the chance. We took the clothes. I'll bet they're sweatin' us. Especially if they knew where we are.

Well, we're headin' for London tomorrow morning just to see what it's like. I'll tell you more about it when we get back. Goodnight.

---

6. This was a clothing store in Phoenix with a "military department" which apparently sold uniforms.

MORMONS PREFER SPITFIRES

Express Staff Reporter

TO a U.S. Air Corps station yesterday came two young men with a double faith—the brothers Butler, elders of the Mormon Church, fighter pilots of the American Army.

Richard Marsh Butler is 23. Heber Marsh Butler is 21. They come from their society's famous centre and home of its Temple—Salt Lake City, Utah.

And the brothers Butler, elders of the Latter Day Saints, want above all else to get cracking in a Spitfire apiece.

The Mormon fighters think there is something about a Spitfire.

They had just arrived at an Air Corps Replacement Centre with a bunch of U.S. sergeant pilots—the first to reach Britain.

They all talk about their American Thunderbolts and Lightnings. Maybe some day, they say, they will have something as good as the Spitfire. It seems, however, they want to fly Spitfires right now.

1886, AGED 6

"Say," said Elder Richard Marsh Butler, "do you know anyone around London name of Marsh?"

His mother's name is Marsh. She left England in 1886, aged six. Her sons would like to trace the family.

"Our mother married into the faith of the Church of Jesus Christ of Latter Day Saints," said Richard, "our father is a High Priest of the Mormon Church, and one brother is a bishop.

"Heber and I joined up on the same day, in July 1940. Heber started to take flying lessons before he was old enough to join."

Richard was married at Salt Lake City Temple this year and Heber at another Mormon church. Neither of the brothers smokes, drinks, or takes tea or coffee. Heber carries in his flying coat pocket his Articles of Faith.

Number 10 says, "We believe that the earth will be renewed and receive its paradisiacal glory."

Elder Heber considers that is not a bad thing to carry in a Spitfire.

London Daily Express, *7 December 1942. (Richard M. Butler papers MSS 8849, L. Tom Perry Special Collections, Harold B. Lee Library, Brigham Young University)*

Tuesday 8

Telegram

Dearest Geneil arrived safe, swell trip. Friday fourth different from three months ago,[7] wish all Merry Christmas. I miss you. Loveingly [*sic*] Richard Butler

Wednesday 9

Journal

We took the train out of Stone yesterday morning at 9:00 [with change of trains in Stafford] and arrived in London at 1:20 P.M. After registering at the service club, we got a taxi and that guy really showed us London. Just for the fun of it, I'll name some of the places we saw and visited: St. James Palace & Park, The Queen Victoria Memorial, Buckingham Palace (It's been bombed twice.), Wellington Barracks, where the Palace Guards are quartered, then Westminster Abbey. It has been bombed twice. When we got there the first time, they were having a service so we came back later. We could see where it had been bombed and part of it was rebuilt. These people don't let a little thing like a war slow them down. The next day after a raid they're out clearing the junk away so it can be rebuilt.

Some of the graves or tombs that we saw were the Unknown Soldier, David Livingstone, Sir Isaac Newton, Michael Faraday, James Herschel, O Rare Ben Jonson, Sir Charles Villiers Stanford, Wm Wilberforce, Kipling, Hardy, Dickens, George F. Handel, Samuel Johnson, Alfred Lord Tennyson, Browning, Thomas Parr (the bird that lived to be 152 yrs of age), Wm E. Gladstone, Wm Pitt the Earl of Chatham, Henry Grattan. Too many others to mention.

---

7. September 4 was their wedding day.

Also the coronation room and the room that Kings & Queens are buried in. That coronation room was really beautiful. Real gold all over in it. They keep a guard there all the time.

After we left there, we drove past Scotland Yard, the Houses of Parliament (which has the Big Ben clock 14' high), the House of Commons, which has been bombed. Drove along the River Thames past the King's University [presumably, he means King's College London], the New Waterloo Bridge, and saw Capt. Scott's ship *Discovery*, which he took to the North Pole. We saw the monument commemorating the Plague of London, drove across the London Bridge—and by the way, I don't think it will fall for a while yet. We then drove back across the Tower of London Bridge; one can be seen from the other. This bridge was built in 1700. It's a draw bridge. Then came the Tower of London, the most historical building in England, where most of the executions took place. It was built by Wm the Conqueror, took 200 yrs to build.

They [German bombers] sure did play h--- with the churches. We passed one which was built in 765 A.D. Nothing left but a shell.

This seemed funny to me. As we passed the Bank of England, the taxi driver told us that he was in it when a bomb struck, going way down in before it exploded. It killed all but seven of the people in it. He, his son, daughter & four other people were the only ones that got out alive.

We passed the home of the Lord Mayor of London town. Then came a district that was actually bombed flat. The driver told us that they were after the chemical plant. It still stood, out in the middle of the shambles. Apparently unharmed.

At St. Paul's Cathedral we saw the gate of death, through which passed all those buried there. This building cost 1,500,000 British Pounds (one pound equals $4.04).

A delayed-action bomb was dropped almost on the dome of St. Paul's. We could see the hole it made just below and to the side of the Whispering Tower. The hole was about ten feet in diameter and went down forty-five feet. A Capt. Davis had fifteen minutes to defuse it. He succeeded, by the way, or I wouldn't have been looking at the church. A bomb that size would have fairly well demolished the whole building.

From there back to where we started, we drove through Trafalgar Square, saw the statue of Nurse Cavell, on thru Piccadilly Circus, past the Burlington Art Gallery, along Park Lane to Hyde Park and back to the club.

After we'd visited the *Daily Express* and picked up some papers, we went to Piccadilly Circus to see a show. Finding the cinema turned out to be the biggest circus I've seen in a long time. London in a blackout is really fun. Ya meet more people that way. It's funny we didn't end up with a couple of black eyes. We won't talk about that now.

Yarnfield to Stone

"On the way towards Stone, the country road . . . quickly dropped down a short grade as it passed through a crowded stand of trees and terminated at Highway A34. . . . An MP was posted in the center of the road just where it ended at the highway. . . . An important part of the MP's duty was to assure the safe crossing of A34 by the GIs . . . walking to and from Stone." (Cook 133)

Stone Baggage

". . . at the railroad station, a large circus type tent had been erected on an open area between the parking lot and the railroad tracks. This tent was the location of Stone Baggage, which handled all of the gear of the Air Force personnel passing through the local Repple Depple stations. Stone Baggage was infamous throughout the Army Air Force in the ETO for pilfered luggage." (Cook 90)

STONE BAGGAGE

(Courtesy of Shaun Farrelly)

After that trip, I think I can say that I've seen everything. At any rate I've been from one end of the island to the other. Right now London is only twelve minutes flying time from the Nazis' nearest bases of operations in France. They seem to be occupied some other place right at present tho'.

Another bunch of Lt's [lieutenants] left this morning for their bases of operations. The latest rumor will have us commissioned tomorrow. Here's hoping we soon get to a permanent base, too. I'm getting tired of lying around so much. For the first week it was OK 'cause I needed to recuperate from that boat trip, but enough's enough.

They're tossing a brawl over to one of the dance halls for us tonight. These British women sure go nuts over U.S. G.I.'s. But that brings up another story. Which would be censored anyway, so I won't put it here. I'll try to forget it in the meantime. For me, that's easy.

I think I'll go to the show, I should say cinema; I've seen it already, but it's free so what the heck. It's something to do.

Thursday 10

V-Mail excerpts

What a day! I don't mean good, either. I guess I can't yell, though. We had two good days in a row while we were visiting London, and that's something.

To start out we got left and had to walk almost to [Stone]. We did catch the next train so weren't very late getting to the big city. First off we took a tour of the historical buildings and places of interest. . . .

I got something for you in London, but it'll take longer than this letter to get over there. Here's hoping it's in good shape when it gets there.

V-Mail excerpts
to Butlers

Our main trouble at first was learning the money, but that soon comes. It seems silly tho' to carry a penny which is almost as large as our dollar and only worth two of our pennies. The more money you have, the less you carry. That's a good thing in a way.

We got a pass and visited London the first of the week. That's some town. . . . that evening Heber and I took a double-decker bus to Piccadilly Circus. . . . If you want to have fun, just go to a strange town in a blackout and try to find a cinema. They really camouflage them here. I know we walked past a dozen before finding one. We went back the next morning to see.

Saturday 12

Journal

Nothing much happened today. At least not what we expected. I've spent most of the afternoon writing letters. At least I get that caught up. When we get down to business I don't suppose I'll write to anyone except you and the folks.

A bunch of R.C.A.F. boys came in today. They're transferring to the USAAF as flying Sgts. They come from the U.S. originally.

Today was really a nice day. The sun shone all day. (Both hours.)

V-Mail excerpts

It's beginning to get pretty dull around here; a good rest was just what we needed, but for me I've had about enough. I'm ready to get back on the job any day now.

There's no place to go around here to enjoy oneself, so I guess I'll take up knitting.

Monday 14

Journal

We've had a pretty nice day today but didn't do much except an interview for something or other we hope it [*sic*] something.

Among that bunch of RAF pilots that came in there was a set of twins. That makes two sets of brothers in this S/Sgt Pilot crew. We're also getting our fill of training films.

V-Mail excerpts

I guess we've been here long enough now so that I can tell you we were sunk at mid-ocean and all were lost. At least that's what came over the [Axis] radio that morning . . . we didn't get excited and start swimming. We had breakfast first. I thought I'd found the toughest chowline in the world while I was in Illinois, but no, come to find out the worst was still ahead. . . .

Tuesday 15

Journal

We had our exercises this morning, and there wasn't much time for anything else. The day doesn't begin until 9:00 A.M. This afternoon we sat thro' the film on sex hygiene again. The chaplain topped it off with a real to-the-point talk that set the boys to thinking.

Wednesday 16

V-Mail excerpts

Things are getting more boring every day, it seems. Either that or I'm getting fed up with sitting around. . . .

I guess I can start looking for a letter from you pretty soon now.

Thursday 17

Journal

Still nothing happens. All we've accomplished lately is athletics and training films. I think we're going to get final payment for Nov[ember] from this office. We took our flight certificate to the finance today.

If they don't start moving someone out of here we're going to be slightly over-loaded. Another bunch comes in every day or so. They can start on us any day now. I want to get busy on this war.

V-Mail excerpts
to Butlers

This is about as long as we've ever been without getting a letter from home, but I guess we soon will.

We've had quite a bit of time on our hands lately, so the letter writing is about caught up to date. I suppose you received our cables.

Friday 18

Journal

I really got ambitious this morning and took the hike. Just a walk out along the countryside. We accomplished something this afternoon. We finally got them to take us out on the range to shoot our 45's. That's a little progress anyway. If they don't soon send us out for duty I'll be inclined to think they don't need us in this war. If so, I know where I'm going.

V-Mail excerpt

I'll bet these letters seem awfully dry to you with all these interesting things I don't put in. At least it seems good to me. I feel, as near as possible, as though I was talking to you. I wish it wouldn't take so long for your answers.

Saturday 19

V-Mail excerpts
to Butlers

When we were in London, we saw the story they put in the paper about us. It should get some response from the folks here if they see it. As yet we haven't heard anything.

I found out that I've been sending my letters without the complete address, so if you've been using it, some of my mail may have trouble finding me. I'll get it sometime, tho'.

Flight Officers

". . . we enlisted pilots found a sympathetic officer named Colonel Grubb. As head of the reassignment group, he wondered why we had not received officer commissions.

"We had assumed that we would be promoted before leaving New York since we had learned that pilots preceding us, who were staff sergeants, had been. . . .

"Colonel Grubb was first-class and he really did go to bat for us. On December 20, 1942, a brief ceremony was held. We were designated flight officers. That rank was equivalent to warrant officer in the Army. It didn't mean we were commissioned, but we got pay and privileges similar to those of commissioned officers." (Hoover 36–7)

82nd Fighter Group

"The first contingent of 51 82nd FG Lightnings began taking off from St Eval [RAF St Eval, near the northern coast of Cornwall] around 0400 hrs on 23 December 1942. It would be an eight-hour-plus flight requiring the utilisation of two 165-gallon auxiliary fuel tanks. The destination was Tafaroui, a French airfield near Oran, in Algeria. To avoid enemy radar and possible interception, pilots were instructed to fly no more than 200 ft above the surface of the Atlantic. A twin-engine B-26 Marauder led each of the four individual formations and handled most of the navigation. . . .

"Few of the group's pilots actually made it to Tafaroui that day due to poor weather, although most of them had done so by the 26th, after landing and laying over at Gibraltar or airfields in Morocco." (Blake 11–12)

Tuesday 22

Journal

Well, what do you know? It happened. We were discharged from the Army at midnight Dec. 20, 1942, and enjoyed about fourteen hours as a civilian before being sworn in as a Flight Officer. Yesterday Dec. 21 we took the Oath and started living and acting as near like officers as is possible at such a short notice. In three months we will be eligible for 2nd Lt. which, by the way, will mean a fifteen dollar drop in pay. As Fl/Off's we get 20% increase for overseas duty; a 2nd Lt only gets 10%.

From here on we have to pay for our meals and clothes. We were lucky. They issued us a complete issue for enlisted men and a lot of it is the same as officers use, so we'll turn in about what we want to.

Today we get paid up to date as enlisted men and tomorrow we go to London for clothing allowance and to fix up all the other necessary papers. We may get to stay over Christmas.

V-Mail excerpts

We're going to have the chance of spending Christmas in London. At least we'll get to see a picture show and maybe even get a chicken dinner, who knows? They're having a Xmas party here on the post for a bunch of the kids around here. The American soldiers are doing it all over England.

I don't know whether you've been writing but, if you have, it may be sometime before I get it, so don't write any more until you hear from me again.

Wednesday 23

P-38 Lightnings of the 82nd Fighter Group began leaving the UK for North Africa.

Thursday 24

HQ 82nd Fighter Group with P-38s (95th, 96th and 97th Fighter Squadrons), was established at Tafaraoui (Oran), Algeria upon arrival from the UK.[8] The squadrons entered combat the next day.

Friday 25

Letter excerpt dated 7 May 1943

We went to London to the Hq-Air Force Christmas Eve and got our uniform allowance, then got a room at the Mostyn Chef, where we spent the next day. They had a swell Xmas dinner, too. . . .[9]

Saturday 26

Journal

Well, there went another Xmas. I can't exactly say it was wasted, but I didn't enjoy it. I can say that I've spent a Christmas in London. It's just about like any other large town, though, so what. Remind me to tell you something else about Piccadilly.

When we got into Euston Station, we were picked up with trucks and driven out to the 8th Army Headquarters. There we got our (Definite Proof) papers on the commission, also the $150.00 clothing allowance. It was already spent, tho, so that was a mere transaction with me as a go-between. I did get it sent off, thru

---

8. Tafaraoui Airfield was about 12 miles south of the Harbor of Oran at the eastern edge of the Sebkha d'Oran, a salt lake which is dry during part of the year.

9. We have the bill and two elegantly-illustrated versions of the menu (on heavy cream paper) from Oddenino's in Regent Street, housed in a high-society hotel well-known in London from the 1880s until after the war. The brothers had a choice between the restaurant and the brasserie; they chose the brasserie (no charge for orchestra/dancing and lower house charge), sat at Table 21 and had a Christmas dinner consisting of 10 courses and costing a total of 13 shillings.

the Chase Nat. Bank, so that's that bill off my mind. Before long now I'll have them all cleared up.

We ran into Holik[10] and about five more of the boys including that Lt. we met at church in Tally [Tallahassee]. . . . He was really glad to see us. They've really had an experience. On the way across they were torpedoed, and Holik spent nine days in a life boat, some of the others longer, but they all made it OK. They've been in the hospital for about a month since landing. They show it, too.

They were sunk about 600 miles out and, after a spectacular rescue hunt, the Royal Navy picked them up about 150 mi from land. Another day & a half and they'd have made it alone.

When we got back in town, it was a way after dark, so about all we did was get a room at the club and turn in. I've come so damn near freezing to death since I landed that it isn't funny. It's naturally about ten degrees too cold for comfort in the rooms (no heat). And the air is .9 water, which makes it worse. Coats don't do any good. That should be enough of my troubles for now.

We can't get Flt Off bars at present, so we're wearing 2nd Lt bars until—. Why not? The only difference between us is we make $15.00 more money. Sometime in the near future, I guess, they'll bust us down to 2nd Lt.

It looks like we're going to ship out of here [Yarnfield] tomorrow. That's good, too, cause I'm getting about fed up with this sitting around. Give me an airplane.

Monday 28

Journal

We really got together and moved out in a hurry yesterday. We left Stone at 10:40 and came here [Atcham] in trucks. This is a devil of a place to live or exist, but we'll make it.

We checked out bikes this morning and, take my word for it, they're handy. This place is scattered all over England. I don't know yet just where we're located, but my guess is we're somewhere in Wales. It looks like we're going to keep on flying the P-39.[11] Most likely for ground strafing. I'm going to like that. It's just how close to the ground you can fly without scraping it with the prop.

---

10. "Doc" Holik was someone Richard and Heber had trained with at Luke and Tallahassee. His wife's 1943 Christmas card to Geneil indicates he'd been killed in combat, a sad irony after he survived the sinking of a ship at sea.

11. That turned out to be the case, as we learn from an unheaded salmon-colored 5×8 card, which seems to be as close as we can get to an official record of Richard's flying at Atcham Field. We know that during this period at Atcham there were P-39s and P-47s as well as a few P-38s and Spitfires, but from that sole record of Richard's flight time at Atcham we learn that he flew only the P-39 while there.

I'm sure glad I got my uniform in the States, because it's like pulling teeth to get a good one here. Some of these other guys are having a pretty tough time.

V-Mail excerpts

Things have been moving a little faster than usual. We spent Christmas in London and in general just fooled around there for a few days. We had Xmas dinner at the club where we stayed. It was pretty good—considering. On top of that we had a pleasant surprise. Ott Romney[12] was there and spoke. He is the director of the Red Cross there. It sure did seem good to talk with someone from home.

We took in about every theater in London while there. Some of them are pretty nice, too. I'd sure like to see that town about a year after the war ends. I don't know what I'd do, tho', if they turned the lights on. Probably get lost. . . .

Well, we finally got moved to an outfit. How it will turn out is yet to be seen, but we're ready and willing to (take) come what may.

Tuesday 29

V-Mail excerpt
to Butlers

Heber and I just recently made it over that great barrier between enlisted men and officers. I don't think the sailing is going to be any rougher in the future than it has been, because for quite some time now we've been doing the work of an officer. There's still a plenty to work for, and we're going to be doing just that. Just what is going to be required of us to win this war we don't know yet, but we've got it and will give it all if necessary.

Wednesday 30

V-Mail excerpt

Tomorrow is New Year's Eve, but about all I can say is it starts another year and brings us that much nearer to the end of this. Here's hoping this year will write the final chapter. It think it will, but it's going to be tough.

We took off for town this afternoon on bikes. The main idea to start with was to get some things we needed. The exercise wasn't figured in to start with, but we got it anyway. This English countryside is all hills.

The other day we went down to the shop to draw a bike and found the poor guy rather swamped with work. Flat tires, broken pedals and such. I don't think he appreciated us very much because we scattered parts from one end to the other. Anyway, we came out with a ped-cycle each.

_____

12. Romney was an LDS American football player and college sports coach.

Atcham Village and Atcham Field

On Sunday 27 December Richard and Heber were transferred to the Eighth Fighter Command and moved with their group about 25 miles southwest to Atcham Field, located on the English-Welsh border five miles southeast of Shrewsbury and about a mile east of Atcham village. This small village is set on the south shore of the River Severn with an elegant one-lane bridge and picturesque riverside church along with a traditional red callbox still in place.

The village is adjacent to the Attingham Hall estate, parts of which were used for the war effort. It is today a National Trust property among whose walking paths is a World War II Walk on its eastern boundary which includes a number of remnants of Atcham Field.

Atcham Field, or Station 342, was passed to the Eighth Air Force from the RAF in mid-June 1942. ". . . in November a [USAAF] Combat Crew Replacement Center had been established there. . . .

"The duty of the unit was . . . to train pilots for operations over Europe. From the time of arrival in November 1942 and whenever the weather permitted, [pilots] flew from dawn to dusk. It was dangerous flying in an area scattered with hills and even the odd mountain. One of the closest hazards to Atcham was the large hill known as the Wrekin. . . . it rises 1,335 ft above sea level and is a danger even in the best of weather. On a good day it was plainly visible from the airfield but in bad visibility, it disappeared completely. (Brooks 36–7)

One American pilot "recalled how the Wrekin was a good weather chart: if you could see it you could fly, if not you stayed on the ground." (Brooks 38)

"We never did much flying in England because of the rain and fog. . . .

"Problems with visibility made landing pure guesswork and luck. When a pilot was vectored in over an airfield, ground control would shoot a flare to let him know he was over the airfield. Pilots would then circle until they broke out of the overcast. That alone was scary enough, but there was a hill near the base, and if the pilots' circles were too wide, they crashed into the hillside." (Hoover 36)

". . . the Americans were issued with 50 Hercules cycles because the cookhouse and mess were half a mile off the aerodrome. Not used to the British habit of driving on the left, the roadside was soon strewn with bent cycles."

"The cookhouse and mess rooms were just inside the fence that surrounded Attingham Park." (Neal 12)

Heber says that their initial quarters at Atcham consisted of "a steel Quonset building with one pot-bellied stove in the middle of the building. It took the chill off the air, but it sure didn't make it warm." (Butler 72)

"We were quartered in Nissen huts, which were round half-cylinders, capable of accommodating eight to ten pilots. In the middle of each hut was a potbellied stove.

"The English countryside, which was often blanketed in snow, was enchanting." (Hoover 35)

Training at Atcham Field

Atcham Field "served as a training centre for American fighter pilots trained in the clear blue skies of America, getting them used to British weather conditions and working them up to operational status." (Brew 9)

"Their intensive programme at Atcham included all phases of combat, with simulated dogfights, and dive bombing and ground attacks using ranges at Llanbedr, Wales." (Brew 4)

"The training schedule at Atcham was dangerous, with 167 incidents and 35 fatalities. Teaching instrument flying, formation flying and low-level flying all took their toll. There were also take-off and landing accidents together with pilots becoming lost when the weather closed in." (Brooks 38)

"The aircraft identification training was intense. The instructors had small models of German and Italian airplanes hanging like mobiles. Split-second images of aircraft were flashed on a projector screen, and we had to identify them. This was repeated over and over until we could recognize the planes and ships in an eye-blink.

"We were taught not only to identify the aircraft and ships, but to determine how many were in view.

"Fliers at Shrewsbury were instructed on how to behave if they fell into enemy hands. . . . Training personnel explained how the underground worked in different countries. . . ." (Hoover 35)

"Information for briefing lectures on evasion, especially for aircrew on operations, was also provided by Room 900 [a department of M.I.9 tasked with providing means for evaders and escapers to get out of occupied Europe]. Reports from our agents in occupied territory contained much useful advice on what to do when shot down." (Neave 64)

"From 1942 the American forces formed a fully integrated staff . . . which carried out the same functions. . . ." (Neave 65)

"Escape packs" and survival packs including silk maps, compass, a day's worth of water and food were provided to fliers across Europe, North Africa and the Middle East. (Neave 67)

Telegram
(postmarked Tremonton Jan 4 1943)

Darling doing ok address APO 637 C UT O Postmaster New York Love Richard

Thursday 31

Journal

What a set-up! This morning was the first time we've got up for breakfast since we got here. It isn't our fault if we don't wake up in time. So far all we have to do is eat

Atcham Field aerial view. Two P-38s can be recognized in the upper right near the revetments to the right off the northeast end of the main runway. (Courtesy of Sir Michael Leighton)

and sleep, and that is more voluntary than compulsory. I guess we'll be assigned to an outfit in a few days, then the schoolin' will start. Mainly identification of aircraft but some armaments & mechanics, I guess.

Heber, Johnny & I rode our bikes to Shrewsbury yesterday and took in the town. It almost took us. These crazy people drive on the wrong side of the street. If you pass them on the right side, they yell, "Get over on the right side of the street." Well, I was on the right side. It's just a case of left is right and right is wrong; and if someone doesn't run over you, someone else will unless the gods are on your side. If that's the case, why worry about the war?

Atcham bridge. Shrewsbury is to the left over the bridge; Atcham Field is about one mile to the right. (Butler family collection)

Atcham Field lay 3 miles beyond the house on left. The Wrekin can be seen in the distance on the right, 2.5 miles east of the Field. Shrewsbury is behind the viewer a couple of miles. (Butler family collection)

1943

January

Friday 1

HQ 82nd Fighter Group was established at Telerghma, Algeria upon arrival from Northern Ireland. The subordinate squadrons, the 95th, 96th and 97th Fighter Squadrons with P-38s, moved from Tafaraoui (Oran) to Telerghma.[13]

Saturday 2

Letter excerpts

We live about ten miles from nowhere in a little hut with a coal stove for company. If we succeed in finding the coal, we're lucky. Haven't frozen to death yet, though. I sure wish I'd of had a coal stove or a brown jug to carry with me while we were in London for Christmas. I had just succeeded in getting over a cold, which I got upon arrival . . . and when I got back here I had succeeded in getting another even bigger and better.

On Christmas[14] morning I drug myself out at about the same time you were getting up there, I guess. . . . I found a fireplace in the club and proceeded to see what I could imagine. . . . for a while I almost thought I was there with you having a big time. . . . I did almost succeed in getting my feet warm for the first time since landing.

This Flight Officer rank is alright. Once a guy gets over the hump, it doesn't matter what rank he holds; he's entitled to the same things. On top of that, we get $15.00 more per month than a 2nd Lt.

If I could only get a letter from you, it would certainly make things in general seem a lot brighter. I haven't yet stopped worrying about your trip home. If I could only hear from you and know that you are alright.

Undated telegram (US postmark this date)

Love and best wishes for Christmas and the New Year to all at Home. All well.

---

13. Telerghma is about 420 miles due east of Tafaraoui and about 110 miles west of the Tunisian border. Its small prewar airfield was taken over by American troops after the Torch landings, and the field was initially expanded for use by B-26 medium bombers. 82nd FG was one of a number of 12th Air Force units to use the field during the war.

14. Richard evidently meant to say New Year rather than Christmas.

Monday 4

Journal

Well, today we've been married just four months. Two and half of them were the best I've ever known. Here's to a million more of them.

I finally got my allotments made out or changed over from Enlisted to Officer. The same ones will continue until Feb 28. Then will change. The only difference will be an increase in the one to the bank. From 50.00 to $100.00.

We get paid today, final for 1942, excepting flying pay for Dec if we get 8 hrs time in this month or 12 hrs in Feb.

Our pay is as follows:

        $150.00 Base pay
          30.00 overseas pay
         180.00 + ½ for flying pay
          90.00
          21.00 subsistence
         291.00 total
          81.00 Geneil ($.70 per day subsistence & 2.00 quarters)
        $372.00
Minus
        $ 4.66 ins
           6.60 "
          35.00 Dad
         100.00 Gen. [Geneil]
        $146.26 deductions

V-Mail excerpt
to Butlers

As you know, we finally got sent to a permanent outfit. I say "permanent" 'cause it's about as permanent as anything in the Army. We may stay here for the duration, and we may pull out tomorrow or any time. At any rate, we're to a place where we can do some work. We're satisfied for now.

Thursday 7

V-Mail excerpts

We're really flush with recreation around here. No fooling, I've seen more shows (or cinema, as it's better known here) for the second and third time since coming here than I ever thought was possible. . . .

I have lost and found my bicycle about six times in the past week. Someone will need it worse than I do and whoosh there it ain't. If they only realized the chance they were taking, I don't think they'd take it. Riding a bike is faster, but it's much safe to walk. Like this morning going down the hill to mess. It was still dark. . . . I have a poem that very much describes the machine and its tricks. I'll send it to you one of these days.

I guess I can start looking for a letter from you. Start hoping anyway, as if I haven't been.

Sunday 10

Journal

The past week has been pretty slow as usual. About all we do is eat, sleep and wish we were flying.

V-Mail excerpts

What a day! This is one that reminds me of home, if that's possible. Really, this is one for the records. The first of its kind, I think, since I've been here.

I don't know whether I mentioned it but, when we were in London for Christmas, we ran into a bunch of the boys that left the States ahead of us. "Doc" and some of the others you didn't know. They had been recuperating from the last half of their voyage in a lifeboat. . . . Doc looked sort of pale in the face, but we'll probably all be that way before long from lack of sunshine.

V-Mail excerpt
to Butlers

Here goes another Sunday with no place to go to church. I wonder if we'll ever get caught up. It's doubtful.

The war can take us away from it, but it can't keep us from living our religion. It becomes a little more difficult at times than before, but that's to be expected.

Monday 11

Journal

If some -+ox doesn't quit swiping my bicycle, I'm going to ambush him, and that won't be good.

Tuesday 12

V-Mail excerpts

We're setting up housekeeping in a different place this morning. The old shack wasn't in a very good place. We only have to pedal about a mile to chow now. The bad part of it is we can't get the [censored] fire to burn very good.

If I don't get a letter from you before long, I'm going to come after it.

P-38 on Atcham Field (Courtesy of Sir Michael Leighton)

Wednesday 13

Journal

Heber went to Cheltenham[15] this morning with a bunch going for uniforms. He's sending some money home.

Friday 15

Journal

Heber didn't get that money sent off They're going to give us another $100.00 clothing allowance, so we might as well wait for that. It's getting so that if they don't pay us every weekend, and sometimes once in between, it doesn't seem right.

We're beginning to get our flying time in, so we may get back flying pay. We have it coming for 10 days in Dec. It's almost been 2 mo. since I took off the last time.

Some damn "John" Lt. ran off with my bike again today. It's beginning to get sort of old. I'm going to meet the next one with my machete. If you've seen one, you know what I mean.

---

15. West of London and about 85 miles south of Atcham.

V-Mail excerpts

Well, slowly but surely we're getting back on the beam. We've started school again, and it really seems good. . . . I guess my schooling will never cease.

You know? I'm beginning to think that it isn't all the bicycle's fault. We were flying a close formation (on bikes) and tried to take a muddy corner too fast. First someone's bike went under Heber's. He turned a half somersault over the handlebars and slid up the road backward with a silly look on his face. There was quite a mix-up of bikes and bodies. Only two out of the bunch came out OK. The two outside men and I was one of them. My luck will never cease—I hope. All in all this country is a bit hard on clothes. The hide grows back.

Say, I don't mean to crowd the wires but a telegram would really seem good once in a while. . . . I'd like to hear from you every day, but that would never do. There's a war on—it says here.

Monday 18

Journal

They turned the eagle loose again today; almost all officers here received another $100.00 clothing allowance. Tomorrow I send it off, and I don't owe anyone anything. A red-letter day, wot?

V-Mail excerpts

The schooling is in full swing. It seems like almost everything we did at home has to be changed. Whether it's a little different or a lot, it still has to be learned another way. That can become rather discouraging at times. But there's a war on, it says here, so who am I to complain.

Come to find out, I have a different address. Same difference, though. It's still, Somewhere Else in England. I guess I'll get my mail sometime, even if it is six months after duration.

About the only satisfaction we get out of life is seeing how many knees we can skin up. We have rat races up the taxi strip with half the guys going in the opposite direction. These bikes hold up pretty well, considering. If I don't stop raving about this manually-operated murder cycle it'll be turning on me one of these times.

V-Mail excerpt
to Butlers

The war's still going. Or had you heard? Life is beginning to pick up a little here, too. We've started school, anyway, even if that is about all. I guess there's going to be no end to our schooling. If they decide we've had enough of one thing, they start something new. There's just no end to the things a guy has to learn to be a flyer. The actual flying part is just the beginning.

Wednesday 20

Journal

Today noon we had a meeting, and they told us to get things together for a move to start at 8:00 tomorrow morning. We figure it is to a field a little way off for O.T.U.

Thursday 21

[With 66 of their compatriots Richard and Heber were released from duty with Hq 6th Figter Wing and Transferred to Twelfth Air Force, WPR at a secret destination.]

Friday 22

Journal

We left Atcham in trucks last night for Shrewsbury, branded our bags, boarded the train and rode all night.

This morning we arrived in Glasgow, Scotland and from there to Greenock. Here we are in the harbor in about the same place we left the *QE* Nov 30.

It looks like goodbye to England. Quite a visit we had with these limeys.

We're really in class on this ship. Our first meal was good veg. soup, fish, meat pie & potatoes with fresh young onions topped off with fruit pie all served by Indian or Hindu waiters. OK wot?

I wish they'd head west with this thing, but it looks like it's going to be Africa.

Sunday 24

Journal

Sunday again. We left Greenock this morning at 1:00.[16] The steward says we're due in Algiers a week from tomorrow. That is unless we run into some difficulty along the way.

Here's one for the books. Yesterday morning at seven the steward started pounding on my shoulder. I rolled over and he said, "'Ave some tay, Sir?" That's only half of it. We have tea at seven, breakfast at eight, tea at ten, luncheon at twelve, tea at four, and dinner at seven. All of this if you want it. Personally, I'm giving my stomach a break. We had fried eggs for breakfast this morning for the first time since I left home. If I don't watch 'em, they'll spoil me.

---

16. They were aboard the *RMS Strathnaver*, which Hoover calls "a small but luxurious passenger ship." (37)

P&O Line's *RMS Strathnaver*

Hoover again quotes Tom Watts' journal:

"When we were shown to our port rooms, we nearly dropped with surprise. Here were lovely beds with sheets and washbasins with running water. A valet was assigned to each one.

"The individual rooms were nearly as large as the entire gymnasium on the *Queen Elizabeth*. In these rooms there were twelve only instead of the ninety-two on the *Q.E.* Mmmm. Extreme comfort!

"The dining room was something out of a dream book. There were lovely large tables with fine cloths on them and . . . silverware. . . . Each meal was served in seven courses with Portuguese waiters in formal dress serving. There were no meals missed on this voyage." (Hoover 37)

RMS Strathnaver *(Courtesy of* Grace's Guide to British Industrial History*)*

This boat (Strathnaver) usually makes a trip way down around lower Africa and up thru the Red Sea, but since the 8th Army got on the ball [presumably, Operation Torch], we're going to try the Straits of Gibraltar.

We left New York Harbor the morning of Nov 24 and arrived here the next Sunday. Now we're leaving the morning of the 24th just 7 weeks since we landed. For the amount we've accomplished I could have spent Christmas at home without affecting the war a bit. I've seen England. "Great" Britain so large that if it was dropped in Texas, it may be lost for years.

I often wonder just how deep it would sink if they cut loose the barrage balloons. All in all it's a pretty good place—for the English.

I haven't written you for quite a while. I thought maybe I'd better not, being as how we're going on board ship. You know what I mean.

Tuesday 26

Journal

Somewhere in the Atlantic?

Today is the third day since leaving Scotland. Unlike the last trip over, it was the second day that was rough. We went to lunch yesterday and, as luck would have it, I was on the uphill side of the table. Oh, happy day! After all, two hands can't hold all of the dishes on the table. It started out by just sliding the dishes to one side, but that was just the beginning.

This ship is only 23,000 tons and the *Queen Elizabeth* was 85,000. I'm glad I was initiated in a large ship 'cause they hit the bumps easier.

This is about the largest in the convoy. It's a good sized convoy, too. I counted 20 ships on one side of us, and that isn't counting the destroyers all around us. This is my first convoy, because the *QE* was too fast for one, except having some destroyers the first day.

Some of the nurses on board are beginning to look sort of drawn and white-faced. I wonder why. Not only the nurses.

Saturday 30

Journal

For the past few days the sea has been considerably smoother. It's getting now so the air corps doesn't have exclusive right to the lounge like we did. Today has really been a nice day. We're getting down near the lower part of Portugal. For the first time I realize just what it is like to lounge on the upper deck in the sun. It's the first good warm sunshine since Florida.

We're traveling almost due east so I guess we'll pass through Gibraltar either tonight or tomorrow night. They don't seem to like the idea of going thro' there in the daytime.

What kills me on this trip is the salt water baths. You have to have a special soap and even that won't lather. It's sure good in fresh water tho'.

I've been reading *Les Miserables* (Hugo), and it's really good. I'm afraid the trip isn't going to last long enough for me to finish it, though.

It kills me—a pleasure cruise on the Atlantic for [$]10.00 a day. We're right in the war zone now, so it will be rather ticklish from here on.

Sunday 31

Journal

This morning really was beautiful. They talk about a Mediterranean cruise; now I know what they mean.

The steward says we passed The Rock at 2:00 this morning. When I got up, the moon was still bright but the sun coming up was slowly fading it out. I leaned against the rail for about an hour wishing you were here.

About eighteen of our convoy left us yesterday afternoon, rather we left them. It was quite a sight to see so many ships all together disappear over the horizon. They're going down around the Gold Coast to India and the Pacific war. It's about a six weeks trip all together.

We've been following the Spanish coast all morning. Just close enough to be able to [see] the Sierra Moreno Mts. I think that's what they are.

The coast of Morocco is nowhere in sight. We'll probably follow along this side, then cut straight over to Oran. Rumor has us arriving there tomorrow at 2:00 A.M.

I can't get over how calm the water is since we got down in this neck of the woods. There's sure a difference in the weather, too. I about froze to death the first few days of the trip.

Who knows? We may have some fun before the day's over. This calm sea is just right for submarines, and the weather is perfect for flying.

PM

What a day! Out on deck in the sun with the Indian crew members in their native garb. It really adds color to the whole thing. This would really be a trip in peacetime.

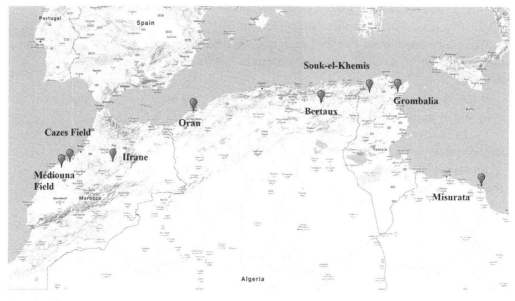

North Africa

Arrival in North Africa

Late on Sunday night 31 January Richard and Heber arrived aboard the *Strathnaver* in Oran harbor, Oran, Algeria.

According to Heber, "The ship unloaded fast, and in 30 minutes we were on the trucks and out of the harbor" where there was "great activity . . . unloading and moving equipment and troops."

"They dumped us off in an orchard . . ." with only "our parachute bags, our clothing bags, and our flying gear . . . to sleep on the ground under the trees that . . . night." (73)

Hoover says this was St. Lucian and quotes Watts on the place: "a mudhill for infantrymen." (37)

Heber reports that someone found "an old abandoned French air field nearby that had a bunch of cement buildings. Richard and I and a bunch of other guys found some remnants of steel camp cots upstairs. There were no mattresses, so we covered the springs with some of our clothes and bedded down like that." (73)

According to Hoover, this was la Senia. ". . . we were forced to sleep on the cement floor. To keep from freezing, we wore our fleece-lined winter flying clothes over our regular uniforms and then curled up in a ball. Those nights in Africa felt more like nights in the dead of winter in Alaska." (37)

February

Tuesday 2

Journal

Well, we finally came to rest in Oran harbor Sunday night. Yesterday morning they pulled us in to the dock and we debarked.

Oran is really pretty, the different colors, etc., from a distance, but these Arabs at close range aren't very appetizing. I don't mean to eat either. We got in trucks and went about 20 miles south to an infantry post. They were in quarantine for typhus and tried to keep us there, but sleeping on the ground without any bedding didn't look so good, so we got into this place. I think we should have come here in the first place. I wrote a letter to you this morning and said that we'd visited Oran. We're not supposed to say where we're located, but we can say we've been there. Actually, the city is just over the wall.

We had our money changed into francs yesterday, and today the value of the franc went up ⅓. I guess we fixed 'em.

There sure are a lot of the boys here that we graduated with. They are all flying 17's. That's quite a ship. We went out this morning and they showed us thro' their

"Thunderbird." (That's the name of their ship.) The Suzy Q and a lot of others are here, too.[17]

These cockeyed natives around here—just remind me to tell you about them. I can't do it in a letter.

Letter excerpts

I was going to pull a fast one so I wrote a few letters on the boat. [Richard later specifies that he used V-Mail forms.] That wasn't so good, because they don't use that kind of mail here. It was a good idea, though, if it had worked.

. . . the trip was a lot of fun after the weather started getting warmer.

As you've most likely already guessed we're in North Africa, where else could we be? We visited Oran, too, and it's really a pretty town. . . .

It sure does seem funny to come from a place where we are all dressed alike. Here the natives . . . all dress in their light-colored garb. I should say they drape themselves.

Heber & I are still together, by the way.

Wednesday 3

Journal

We've had a pretty good chance to look the place over and, by the looks of the buildings, it has taken quite a beating. The windows and roofs are blown out of most of the hangars and there is a pile of French planes that would cover a city block. Most of them were caught in the raids; others were set afire to destroy them. I was talking to a cook that was here when they [Allied forces] took the field. Quite a story.

We went out on the road to buy some oranges from the natives. You have to treat them like dogs or they'll gyp you blind. The oranges were really good after we got them washed.

I guess we'll leave here tomorrow or the next day for our base. I hope so. I'm getting sick of lying around.

Friday 5

Journal

It happened. Yesterday we received orders to leave at 7:00 this morning, but as usual things were a few hrs late. We left Oran in seven DC-3's and in 2½ hrs landed here at Casablanca. It looks as tho' we'll finally get put in an outfit. They have 38s here now, but there's no telling what we'll get.

We're living in a hangar here,[18] and there's everything from Lt Col on down.

---

17. This was Tafaraoui Airfield, where B-17s were based during the winter of 1942–3.
18. Cazes Field, just south of Casablanca.

Saturday 6

Flight Log: *Based in Africa [new page]*

AT-6-C; Dual with passenger: 25 mins, 2 landings.

Sunday 7

Journal

I just finished writing home. I got paid yesterday, and today I changed it to francs at rate of 75 francs per dollar. The value or price of the franc is going up. After tomorrow we will only get 50 to the dollar. Quite a little profit. We went in to Casablanca today and were disappointed.

I was checked out in the AT-6C today.

Letter excerpts

So far, so good. At least we're near enough settled so that we can get an address. Whether or not we will stay in one place long enough to get mail is a question for the quiz kids.

I did get a terrific kick out of the trip down here.

We've sure run into a lot of the boys we used to know. Even some of those in our old outfit. That was before we started to fly. It's almost like a homecoming.

I guess I've told you before that we hadn't received any mail yet. We left England in the same fix. I guess that if & when we do get it it'll be in bundles. . . .

Tuesday 9

Journal

It looks like we're going to get going. They organized us into two outfits and we've started to chisel equipment already. We left Cases Airport yesterday and are at Médiouna waiting for our new field to be completed.

I stopped off in Casablanca yesterday, and it took all afternoon to get thru the money order line, but I made it.

I got paid [$]187.00. Sent [$]186.00 home and still have [$]70.00 left. I wish I could do that every day. I finally got enough money sent home to finish everything up and get our four bonds.

They made Heber Engineering Officer of our squadron. That gives him a good job testing ships.[19]

---

19. Heber, who had studied aircraft assembly and construction before he began flying, assembled a working AT-6 from parts of three planes wrecked in offloading from ships. ". . . my commanding officer said, 'Butler, your records indicate that you have had this training. Build us an airplane!'

Cazes Field

On 5 February they arrived at what Richard later calls Cases Airport. Variously called Camp Cazes and Cazes Field, this was a French airbase just south of Casablanca; it was taken over by USAAF after Operation Torch and later became the city's Anfa Airport.

Here is a description of Cazes Field and its surroundings from a ghost-written account given by naval fighter pilots who strafed the field during Operation Torch.

"The amount of cultivation was surprising—orchards, vineyards, fields of grain. The predominating color of the countryside was a warm brown, with the white houses standing out sharply, like cubes of sugar scattered everywhere. There were belts of sagebrush, roads lined with palm and eucalyptus trees, and little red-roofed farmhouses surrounded by lush green crops. To the northeast, the great city of Casablanca shone, like a giant white palace or super-hotel.

"Cazes airport . . . has a green surface and runways, with rust-covered hangars." (Wordell, 53)

Médiouna

Médiouna, French Morocco was located about 10 miles southeast of the center of Casablanca; like Cazes, it has been engulfed by the city and is now a neighborhood or suburb of Casablanca.

"When we arrived at Mediouna, all of the pilots were disappointed to learn we had been assigned to a replacement pilots' pool. One of the men decided we should rename the group the Sad Sacks to show our displeasure with not being ordered into combat." (Hoover 38)

Around the middle of February Col. John Stevenson, the Médiouna C.O., announced delivery of a P-38 next day by a French major. "When it came time for the major to give us a demonstration of the P-38's capability, all the troops gathered, and the pilot took the plane through a few uninspiring maneuvers. No one was too impressed, since his maneuvers were performed at altitudes above three thousand feet." (Hoover 39–40)

Thursday 11

Journal

We went to town today (Casablanca) and bought a bunch of stuff.

I was writing to you when two men in P-40s tried an Immelmann in close formation. One cut the other's tail off, so he got out & I watched him float down.

"It took at least two weeks, and I finished on the 5th of February.

"When I told the commanding officer that it was ready to fly, he said, 'OK, Butler, you put her together, you are now the engineering officer. You get to test fly it and fly every morning before anyone else does.'" (Butler 73–4)

The man that did the chopping rode his ship into the ground & blew up. One of them did, I'm not sure which.

Letter excerpts

. . . we've been spending quite a bit of time in town. . . . The first time I was there I swore it was going to be the last. But things come up like getting my watch fixed, and I find myself there dodging the natives.

We just had a little excitement. Nothing that will make news but I'll remember it for quite a while. [See Journal entry above.]

I get a kick out of these natives. French is the main language here, and in the stores they speak English about as well as we speak French. It really gets interesting when they try to explain something. I'm even learning a few words of it. Necessity, of course.

*Richard, Spring/Summer 1943
(Butler family collection)*

Sunday 14

Flight Log: *AT-6-C; Dual with passenger: 1 hr, 4 landings.*

Monday 15

Letter excerpts

You know? If the war keeps going the way it looks (by the papers) we may be home pretty soon. Say, by Christmas. I was hoping it would be last Christmas, but that's a little out of the question. . . .

For want of anything to do, I got them to make me ass't tower officer. There isn't much to do, but at least I can find out a little about radio and such and in general make use of my extra time. A guy can pick up a lot of tricks just by watching other ships land. On top of that I brush up on my identification with the field glasses.

You know, it's a funny thing. People at home seem to think we're living under quite a hardship. True, it isn't what we're used to at home, but after all life is what you make it. I was out to one of the many outposts this morning where just a few men have a certain job to do. It could be pretty lonely and monotonous, but the boys have found enough wood to build some small but cozy shacks with all the comforts of home—pictures and all. I don't know where they got them, but they've picked up three or four dogs, too. Probably from the Arabs. I sort of envied the guys. At least they're settled in one place for a few days. . . . I've lived out of this flight bag and bed roll too long now.

Tuesday 16

Flight Log: *AT-6-C; Dual with passenger: 1hr 10mins, 4 landings.*

Thursday 18

HQ North African Air Force (NAAF) was set up under General Carl Spaatz, USAAF, and the Twelfth Air Force became a paper outfit. Six principal subordinate commands were specified. . . . [One of those commands, North African Strategic Air Force (NASAF), included the 82nd Fighter Group.]

Journal

I got the surprise of my life today. Last Monday I sent out my laundry and today I got it all back. We've been here a week now. I guess that makes us permanent personnel. I lost a lot of clothes when we left Tallahassee. Then we sent some to Shrewsbury while at Atcham Field. All but mine came back. It's things like that that make my unhappy.

They're effecting another change in the air force here, so we may be stuck here for months (maybe years).

We're getting our flying time in in an AT-6C. Heber being Engineering Officer is keeping it flying.

About our greatest danger here is the Arabs. They don't seem to care whether we're fighting with, for or against them. They've taken pot shots at several men in Jeeps going to or from Casablanca.

The accident rate was a little high last week. Four men killed in four days. The second one was hit by a car on the road here, and the other two a P-40 stalled out on takeoff & slid into them.

Saturday 20

Journal

We've had one AT-6C for a week now and we're all trying to get in enough flying time for this month. It's really hot.

Today we got a P-39 and later the major brought a P-38. The first of 10 that we're supposed to get. They say we'll get checked out in them we hope. This outfit has officially been made a Fighter Combat Crew Replacement Center (APO 528-1 MEDIOUNA). At any rate things look better for us and our future.

Letter excerpts

This African sunshine is making me lazier every day.

I've been having quite a bit of trouble with my watch since I broke the crystal. I just get it going what I think is good and it quit on me again. It's in the shop now under observation.

Speaking of town, I think you know which one I mean by now, don't you?

Our address changed a little today, but that does't mean much. Only that we're tracking our mail down a little closer now. From what I hear we may have mail pretty well scattered around North Africa as well as the British isles. That is, if anyone has written already. They better had or I'll be pretty mad.

Sunday 21

Flight Log: *AT-6-C; Dual with passenger: 1 hr, 4 landings.*

Wednesday 24

Flight Log: *P-39-L; Solo: 1hr 30mins, 3 landings.*

Letter excerpt

Tell me all about everything even your trip home from Tally. I know I've asked you this before and most likely you've written about it, but I still haven't received a letter. It'll be plenty OK with me even if I get a dozen letters the same. At least I know you're thinking about me. You do remember me once in a while, don't you?[20]

Friday 26

Flight Log: *P-39-L; Solo: 1hr 30mins, 3 landings*

Landing Gear Trouble–Landed on Belly.

Journal

Well, today was a red letter day. I got my second hop in a (P-39/P400) and to start out the wheel cover retracted ahead of the wheel, locking the wheels part way down. I couldn't get them to go either way by the hand crank, and the electric motor was burned out. To make a long story short, I had my first accident. A belly landing just like Heber's and just as good a job, too, they said. When I hit the ground, it broke the wheels loose and they towed it in. They'll have it flying again in a few days. It seems that every time one of us does something, the other has to do it.

We're getting some P-38s, and they say we'll start checking out in them in a couple of days.

They also made me assistant flight commander, so I have a job now.

---

20. Elsewhere in this letter Richard says, "I sent you something a while back that I think will tell you somewhere near where I am." He probably refers to the contents of an envelope postmarked 19 February; inside is a copy of *The Stars and Stripes* dated Wednesday, 27 January 1943, reporting the FDR/Churchill Casablanca Conference.

Saturday 27
Flight Log: *AT-6-C; Dual with passenger: 1hr 30mins, 5 landings.*

Sunday 28
Flight Log: *AT-6-C; Dual with passenger: 1hr 30mins, 5 landings.*

Letter excerpt

The Arabs wake up wherever the night stopped them and head their burros toward town again. I don't know how long it takes them from here or how long they've already been on the road, but they get there eventually. We find them at the different market places (or they find us most any place) with every kind of handmade article imaginable. Some real good leather goods, too. We get quite a kick out of buying things from them. It's a treat in itself. . . .

Somehow the time seems to go by fairly fast, and that is good. The reason for that may be that we came here with the idea of staying until those birds were chased back into their holes. If they told me I was going home next week, I know it would be ten years before that time arrived.

March

Monday 1
Flight Log: *AT-6-C; Dual with passenger: 1hr, 2 landings.*

Thursday 4
Flight Log: *P-39-L; Solo: 1hr 15mins, 1 landing.*

Letter excerpts

I always said that whatever happened to Heber has happened to me. At least it has so far, enough so to keep us together. Anyway what I'm getting at is this: You remember what happened to Heber in Florida the day after he was married? The very same thing happened to me a few days ago. Heber wasn't around to see it either. It was quite a bit of fun too. . . . [See Journal entry for 26 February.]

I'm still waiting for a letter. I think the Pony Express really had something there.

Letter excerpts to Butlers

It's sort of tough trying to write a letter when you can't say anything. . . . Especially when there's nothing to say anyway. I mean that nothing of importance happens that you don't hear about anyway in the next morning's news broadcast. You lucky stiffs. If we happen to be near one of the few radios, we get the news; if not, we get it (maybe) three or fours days later by teletype or some other way.

While in England, I made it a point to follow the news daily with a map of the world. It was really interesting. I got pretty well caught up on my geography, too.

Merry Old England, the island that's held up by barrage balloons. It's a good thing, too, 'cause during the Battle of Britain they really took a beating and came back fighting the harder. That spirit is about all that saved them. But now I read that they've been handing it back tenfold and will continue until it's over.

The Pony Express hasn't come through yet, but we still have hopes. Three months without a letter is quite a while.

Sunday 7

Flight Log: *P-39-M; Solo Cross-Country Cazes/Médiouna: 1hr 30mins, 1 landing.*

P-39-M; Solo: 1hr 30mins, 1 landing.

Journal

Things are beginning to move now. We're getting in a new bunch of 39-M's. I went over to Cazes yesterday to get one, and it cut out on takeoff. It's a good thing I had a long runway to get stopped on. I went back this morning and got it off the ground. It's really a nice ship, but I still want the 38.

I finally collected the last of my flying pay (three months back). For Dec. and Jan. I had $120 coming at 74F per $. I came out with $180. That's making the money.

Monday 8

Flight Log: *P-39-M; Solo: 1hr, 1 landing.*

Low Level Flying.

P-39-M; Solo: 1hr 30mins, 1 landing.

Low Level Flying.

Letter excerpts

I'm just about resigned to my fate. It looks as though I'm going to finish this war out without hearing a word from home. I suppose by now you're getting tired of hearing me say that but, no fooling, I'm getting desperate. If I can find a postal telegraph, or a reasonable replica, I think I'll try getting a message through. Then start hoping I get an answer.

My luck just ran out, or started or something. Anyway, I've been given the job of Squadron Communication Officer. That doesn't seem to help me out, tho'. I still can't yell "G" for "Genie" loud enough over that radio for you to hear. Maybe it's the radio. I'll have it checked.

Well, so far we're still quite a ways from the actual struggle, but we have hopes. After all the war can't go on forever just waiting for us to get there. We'll fix 'em when we do, tho'.

Tuesday 9

Flight Log: *P-39-M; Solo: 1hr 30mins, 1 landing.*

Low Level Flying; combat with P-38.

Friday 12: 1st P-38 flight

Flight Log: *1st P-38 pg. [new page]*

Max H.P. 1350 each

P-38-G-10-LO; Misc solo hops: 2hr 30mins, 2 landings.

1st and second hops.

Journal

Not much has been happening lately except a slow working up to what happened today. For the past week they've been working out the details of the school which ended up in the formation of three sqdrns 38-39-40. [One squadron for each aircraft type.] Heber and I finally got our long-awaited wish granted; we're in a P-38 sqdrn, and today we both checked out. I got in two hops with a total of 2:30 hrs. That's really a big airplane, 15,000 lbs., and I had my hands full, no fooling. It sure flies nice, and I'm getting in that twin eng. time, too. It has taken a year of hard work, but I'm realizing my dream. After this, any other ship I want to fly will simply be a matter of a little cockpit time—then takeoff. Next is to get good at it so I can go into combat.

Saturday 13

Flight Log: *P-38-G-10-LO; Misc solo hops: 1hr, 1 landing.*

Sunday 14

Flight Log: *P38-F-15-LO; Low Formation: 1hr 30mins, Misc Solo Hops: 1hr 30mins; 2 landings.*

P38-G-10-LO; Misc Solo Hops: 1hr 30mins, 1 landing.

Close Canopy. Set Brakes

Crack thr. ¼"

Prop low Pitch

turn on Booster.

Prime 3-4 shots ea.

turn Main & two Eng. ga.

" on Bat. switch.

Energize left.

Engage " mix to auto Rich.

turn on Gen & magneto with.

check air & hydrol Press air 50# Hyd 12 to 1500#

Energize & Eng Right.

takeoff.

Parks off & check mags at 2100 with prop switch in neutral.

Prop switches to decrease (18-1700) RPM)

Lock shoulder straps.

use Combat flaps.

line up with runway open throttle to 30" let go brakes & incr.

manifold press to 40". takeoff.

decrease man press & RPM — left wheels.

Climb at 160 M.P.H. 35# manif 2500 RPM.

Cruise (26" mercury 38" tow) 2300 RPM.) (change tanks ea 5 min.)

landing 2500 RPM. (20" merc level flight).

glide 110 lost turn 150

In dusty conditions use air filter lever (back of seat) to
utilize turbo. air filter in main wheel slots.

Richard's P-38 crib sheet (Butler family collection)

Monday 15

Flight Log: *P38-G-10-LO; Misc Solo Hops: 2hrs 15mins, 2 landings.*

Letter excerpt

Don't let anyone tell you that Africa is hot. At least not this time of the year. Maybe I'll be changing my tune a little later on, but right now as soon as the sun ducks behind a cloud, it gets chilly. I think all that's wrong with me is that I haven't completely warmed up after being in England. I think the climate here is about the same as Arizona. Only we're near enough to the ocean so that it won't get quite that hot. I hope.

I don't know whether I ever told you what ship I really wanted to fly. Whenever I was given a choice in flying school, I always asked for it. I was pretty lucky, tho', because the one I put as a second choice was the one I got. But—Surprise—time changes everything. Heber and I are still together and are flying our first choice. It happens to be the next number lower. . . . I like it even more than I thought I would. But I like to fly, so the ship I'm in couldn't matter too much, could it? Or could it? It could.

. . . I hope you soon get a letter headed this way. Or better still a telegram. That may be impossible without an emergency. The morale of the troops is one, so you can try. I know you're writing, but where they're going is what I'd like to know.

Tuesday 16

Flight Log: *P-38-F-15-LO; Gunnery: 1hr 30mins, Low Formation: 3hrs;*
                   3 landings. 150 r[oun]ds 50 Cal. Air to ground.

Wednesday 17

Flight Log: *P-38-F-15-LO; Low Formation: 3hrs, 2 landings.*

Thursday 18

Flight Log: *P-38-G-10-LO; Misc Solo Hops: 1hr, 1 landing.*
                   Oxygen-32,500'.

Friday 19

Flight Log: *P38-F-15-LO; Low Formation: 1hr 15mins, 1 landing.*

Saturday 20

Flight Log: *P-38-G-10-LO; Low Formation: 2hr 45mins, 2 landings.*

Journal

After a week of flying the 38 I can see what they mean when they say it's work. Just flying isn't bad, but when it comes to formation and combat I realize that 15,000 lbs. of airplane is a lot for one guy. I still like it, tho'. I went up to 32,500' on oxygen and everything started going wrong. The rt eng. cut out, my parachute seat blew up and I had to let the air out of it, then I ran out of oxygen. That isn't good, especially that high in the air. The eng. caught on again about 20,000' after I had about decided to feather it and make a single eng. landing. It feels pretty good to have a spare engine when one quits.

The P-39/40 men are moving to another field so that we can have this to ourselves.

Letter excerpts

According to the calendar, tomorrow is Sunday again. That day used to be what made the rest of the week worthwhile. As it is, most of the time I couldn't tell, if anyone should ask me, whether it was Monday or Saturday.

We have hopes of getting some mail now. At least some has arrived from there (about five letters). There is a rumor going around that some more is on the way from town tho'. I'll meet it half way and help them unpack it.

That P-38 is a big airplane, and the kind of flying we do is hard work in any ship. It's fun, tho—but most anything is that keeps us busy.

Sunday 21

Flight Log: *P-38-G-10-LO; Low Formation: 1hr 15mins, Misc Solo Hops: 1hr 15mins; 2 landings.*

Oxy. ALT.

Monday 22

Flight Log: *P-38-G-10-LO; Low Formation: 45mins, High Altitude Formation: 1hr 30mins; 1 landing.*

Tuesday 23

Flight Log: *P-38-G-10-LO; Low Formation: 1hr 30mins, 1 landing.*

Wednesday 24

Journal

Wow! do we have fun! We can do things in an airplane over here that wouldn't even be thought of back home. Such as going over to Bareched (where the 39

& 40's moved to) and beating up their field. There's nothing like a "dirty eight" for blowing tents over. It makes them slightly unhappy so they come over here and give us he— for a while. They haven't knocked any of our engineering tents over—yet. A P-39 did knock the weather vane off the top of operations a few days ago tho'. That's hard on wings.

One of the boys landed a 39 at 280 mph in an Arab's oat field. It sort of scattered airplane for miles, but he was at breakfast the next morning as happy as ever. Now they fine us when we come back with grass stains on the wings and prop. By the way, that native was pretty put out about the two acres of oats he harvested.

A dirty eight quit on takeoff day before yesterday and knocked off an Arab's burro. That makes the natives unhappy, too. It's getting now so that when anything like that happens you better have a gun, 'cause I don't know where they come from but they're all over you in nothing flat.

Letter excerpts

. . . The rain and mud is awful . . . this is about the muddiest mud in the world. Thank heaven it isn't as bad as it has been farther east.

. . . we need a little more training in the "Dirty Eights." Quite a bit more, considering we just started a while back. At the rate we have things going, it won't be long, though, if the weather lets up a bit.

A lot of things go unseen here that might not pass back home. Some of the boys moved to another field so we'd have room to stretch, and we have to go blow some of their tents down to show we're still alive. That starts the ball rolling, and they're soon over here trying to knock ours down with their wings. They can't blow as hard with their one-lungers as we can with two. All in all it keeps us from reading too many detective stories and straining our eyes for thrills.

Sunday 28

Flight Log: *P-38-G-10-LO; Low Formation: 1hr 15mins, 1 landing.*

HQ 82 Fighter Group and its 95 and 97 Fighter Squadrons with P-38s transfer from Telerghma, Algeria to Berteaux, Algeria.

Letter excerpts

It has been raining off and on now for quite some time. Spring in Africa, I suppose.

Someone is lucky enough to have a radio. . . . Right now there is a church program on. It sort of helps to make today seem like the day it really is, Sunday.

We have quite a place here. Open air theater, what is building up to the major league baseball every afternoon, and a library for later in the evening.

The show is held at the end of a building, so it can be used as a screen. You bring your own seats and come early to be sure of a place to put it.

Oh, yes, we had a rodeo this afternoon. . . . It was quite a kick. In fact, I did get—I wish these Arabs would cut the horns off their steers.

If I keep holding my breath, I should have a letter within the next few days, I hope. At least a few have filtered in.

Monday 29

Flight Log: *P-38-G-10-LO; Low Formation: 1hr, 1 landing.*

Tuesday 30

Journal

It finally came. We got our first letters today since coming across. Heber got one from Martena and I got one from Wm.[21] Howard Haugard wrote us each one. It really seemed good. There's still an empty place and it'll stay until I get about a bushel from you.

We were assigned to an outfit yesterday. 49th [Squadron of the] 14th [Fighter] Gp. We've been flying with their enlisted men as ground crew now for a couple of weeks. It's what we've been waiting all this time for. Now we can get down to business. Maybe to the front before many moons.

They're giving us a lot of extra high alt. work. We'll probably be escorting B-17's.

Letter excerpts
to Butlers

Surprise, we got two letters today, each. One from Wm, one each from Howard Haugard, and Heber got one from Martena. . . . You can see how we feel. It's a long way from home when the news from there is coming in regularly. It's a lot farther when it isn't.

I was glad to hear by Wm's letter that you have been getting our mail. That's a relief. Now if I knew that all was well there, I'd feel OK. Be sure and tell us all the news from the first just as tho' you hadn't written before.

Be sure and tell the Haugards how much we appreciated the letters.

We're assigned to an outfit—at last. There are several of the boys from Salt Lake. One a Cannon. It seems he knew us from an article in the *Millennial Star* (London). What do you know?

---

21. William, Richard and Heber's oldest brother.

Berteaux

Berteaux Airfield was an AAF military airfield located approximately 9km east of Telerghma. Built in late 1942 and early 1943, Berteaux was clearly not intended as a temporary field, given its asphalt runway, concrete taxiways, hardstands, parking apron and steel control tower.

"Many more new pilots arrived at Berteaux during April, of whom twenty-five went to the 97th Sq." (Blake & Stanaway 59) Heber tells us that "24 of us new P-38 pilots [were] sent forward to be members of the 82nd Fighter Group. Of those 24 pilots, I remember only 8 of us returned to the USA after combat. There were three sets of brothers who flew P-38s in the 82nd Fighter Group." (74)

Richard and Heber apparently physically joined the 97th Squadron in Berteaux, Algeria on Saturday 3 April, although the official orders are dated 4 April.

Blake mentions that, because the Allies had so successfully blocked efforts to resupply and reinforce Tunisia by sea, the Axis forces had begun trying to fly in badly-needed supplies, including gasoline in particular. He says that the 82nd was involved in operations hunting formations of such transports with considerable success (22).

"Sea sweep" was the name for patrols in search of Axis ships carrying supplies from Sicily to Tunisia. 82nd FG flew these missions both as support for bombers attacking the ships and as fighter-bombers attacking the ships; sometimes they filled both roles on the same mission. Richard doesn't appear to have been part of the missions Blake describes, though subsequent *Flight Log* entries do refer to sea sweeps.

Of one such mission, Heber says "We were four hours out over the ocean with a bomb on one side and a drop tank on the other. It was interesting flying through the mountains and over the hills and then out across the ocean." (79) Of another he reports "I was out on another mission over the ocean with drop tanks and guns. We were out there for three hours and 45 minutes, flying up and down the Mediterranean. . . . the Germans were pretty much evacuating North Africa. For seven missions in a row, I did nothing but sea sweeps, going out and patrolling the ocean, looking for enemy aircraft and transport columns hauling the army out of Africa." (79)

"April came to a close with an uneventful counter shipping mission (#151) on the early morning of the 30th. After its tremendous and exhilarating victories early in the month, things had gotten a bit rougher for the group, culminating in the loss of nine of its pilots on the 28th and 29th. Nevertheless, the unit's achievements far surpassed its losses and setbacks—and would continue to do so. There was by then no doubt that the 82nd Fighter Group had become a force to be reckoned with in the Mediterranean skies!" (Blake & Stanaway 62)

"The North African campaign was quickly drawing to a close. One of its fringe benefits, for which the P-38 units could claim at least partial credit, was that nearly a quarter of a million battle-tested Axis troops were stranded in the Cap Bon pocket. Without effective transport, the best hope the German and Italian soldiers had was a prompt and orderly surrender.

"With the situation in North Africa well in hand, the 82nd became even more involved in strategic operations over the enemy-held islands of the Mediterranean." (Blake & Stanaway 65) These included Lampedusa and Pantellaria as well as Sardinia and Sicily.

May also "finally brought an end to [the 82nd's] restriction to a height of approximately 12,000 feet. . . ." (Blake & Stanaway 66)

"After the conclusion of the Tunisian campaign the 82nd enjoyed a brief respite from operations on the 15th through the 17th. On the latter date twenty-six of its pilots received deocrations during an awards ceremony." (Blake & Stanaway 65)

"By [mid-May] life for the group at Berteaux had settled down considerably. The supply situation had improved, and an influx of new pilots and aircraft had brought the group up to strength." (Blake & Stanaway 66)

"The 82nd Fighter Group enjoyed an overall three-to-one victory/loss ratio against Axis aiarcraft during its first five months in combat. Against single-engine fighters alone, the ratio was roughly two to one." (Blake & Stanaway 73)

". . . a batch of forty-three new Lightnings . . . arrived at Berteaux in early June." (Blake & Stanaway 76)

Wednesday 31

Flight Log: *P-38-G-10-LO; Low Formation: 1hr 30mins, High Altitude Formation: 1hr 30mins; 2 landings.*

Four ship 32,000'. 12 Ship Low Formation.

First day with 49th Sq 14th Gp

Letter excerpt
Geneil to Richard

"I saw parts of the technicolor films on the invasion of North Africa. The city of Oran . . . was indeed beautiful. . . . the scenery was lovely. . . . Just think how lucky you are to get to see it."

April

Thursday 1

Letter excerpts

Heber and I received two letters. He got one from Martena but, doggone it, I didn't get one from the right person.

I thought we were assigned to an outfit but we weren't, not yet. . . . If you can, call the folks; tell them to use the Ftr. Sch. instead of the 49th like I wrote.

Note excerpt
to Butlers

Heber's here in the Post Office. He just picked up a letter from you written Mar 1. It's the first from home. Wow![22]

Letter excerpts
Geneil to Richard

"We wrote the American Red Cross . . . today, regarding your mail situation. That Field Director is supposed to cover your area and he better, too. . . ."

Sunday 4

Flight Log: **Tunis Front Combat Time**

               all Missions & "C" Time[23] **are Formation Flights**

Horse Power at 44" Hg, 1350 each (In combat 65" Hg is used.)

P-38-F-15-LO; Local and Test: 1hr, 1 landing.

Crash Landed on Dry Lake.[24]

1st Day with 97th Sq 82 Gp.

Monday 5

V-Mail[25]
Letter excerpts

As you've noticed we are assigned to a squadron, let that mean what it may. I guess one worry is over. That was whether they'd split us up or not when assigned. They didn't. . . .

---

22. I think this letter had gone directly from home to North Africa; it appears that the mail sent to Richard in England had still not caught up with him.

23. "C" Time refers to Combat Time.

24. Richard wryly refers to this crash-landing in the journal entry for Wednesday 7 April but doesn't give us the location. Chott (dry lake) Tinsilt and Sebkret (evaporative salt plain) Ez Zemoul are the nearest possibilities, lying close together 10–12 miles south of Berteaux.

25. Return address shows 97 Ftr Sq. 82nd Ftr Gp., although the letter doesn't explicitly describe that transfer.

It sure does seem good to get settled where I'll be around the same men all the time. You don't (I hope) know what it is to live out of an overnight bag, wondering you're going to move today or tomorrow.

I got a letter from Mother a few days ago, and it really did seem OK. She gave us some of the pertinent news. . . .

97th Squadron's Wildcat emblem

Tuesday 6: 1st Mission

Flight Log: **Base (Bertaux)/350 MI & return.**

P-38-G-10-LO; Local and Test: 1hr 30mins, Combat Sortie : 3hr 30mins; 2 landings.

1st Sortie; Test Hop & Formation with Heber.

Wednesday 7

Flight Log: *P-38-G-10-LO; Local and Test: 1hr, 1 landing.*

Ferrying.

Journal

We flew with the 49th just one day during which I got a high alt hop and a 12-ship sqdrn formation. [See Flight Log entry for 31 March.] That afternoon we received word that we would go back to the Sch. for some extensive flying, then go to the front. As things go in the army they changed their minds, about the training I mean. We were to fly up on the 1st but didn't get away 'til the next day.

We are now assigned to 97th Ftr Sq. 82nd Grp and are hard at it. On the 4th the new recruits took our first hop just to look the country over. Well, to start out the wrong way, I had to fly it into a dry lake. These ships are not aerodynamically designed for flying under water especially when the water is only four inches deep. Besides I didn't have a periscope so I'd have been lost even if it had been deeper. You can guess what happened to the ship—and me. An Arab and his four kids came after my clothes, but when they saw I was ok the old boy wanted to carry me to dry ground on his shoulder, but I couldn't have that. An ambulance finally came and got me. That stretcher felt good. We used it to carry my chute pack.

Heber and I went together on our first "Sortie." It was an escort mission with B-25. We had quite a lot of fun all in all. The fuel gets sort of low on a trip like that, but we got back with all ships.

V-Mail excerpts
to Butlers

Well, the long hoped-for has happened. Heber and I are assigned to an outfit and are about ready to do some good for old Uncle Sam. This getting assigned has been our chief worry, because we were afraid it would split us up, but it's over. Now our main job is to put that P-38 where it'll do the most good.

Heber's whittling on a piece of wood. Making a clamp for the hose on our gas stove so it won't burn so hot. The weather here is fairly nice in the daytime, but it gets cold as the devil at night. You don't need to worry about us now 'cause they really take care of their airplane drivers in this outfit. . . . You ought to see our little shack. Quite cozy to say the least. I didn't say it was like home. No hot and cold water (unless we heat it), but who wants running water? I do!

It sure did seem good to get that letter from you. We should have some more coming in a day or two. Both straight from home and by way of England. I was really glad to hear about Geneil in your letter. I haven't as yet heard from her.

I have reason to believe that our prayers are being answered and that the Lord is protecting us all.

Letter excerpt
Geneil to Richard

"I want you to get mail so very badly. It hurts so to think of you being without for so long. I have been writing every day now for four and a half months. If even half of it catches you, you will have plenty."

Thursday 8

Flight Log: *P-38-G-10-LO; Local and Test: 4hrs, 2 landings.*

Combat Formation.

Friday 9

Flight Log: *P-38-G-10-LO; Local and Test: 1hr 15mins, 1 landing.*

Rt Eng. caught fire during max power test.

P-38-G-15-LO; 1hr 15mins, 1 landing.

Formation.

Journal

I don't know what day of the week it is, but I think it's April ninth. I think I'll remember today, too, for quite some time to come. The ship I've been flying has had a lot of trouble with the props. Today I fixed it so they won't have any more. I was giving it a max power test and my right eng. blew something and caught afire. Well, well, crash-landing Butler is at it again. I landed wheels-up right beside an artillery camp. (The third time in less than two months.) I'm sure glad you can't find out about this stuff 'cause I know you'd worry about me a lot more than usual. Why I don't know. For that matter I don't know why you put up with me at all. I'm sure glad you do, tho'. I'm afraid Uncle Sam is going to cut off all association with me if my luck doesn't soon change. It must be luck; I can't think of anything else it could be.

Saturday 10: 2nd Mission

Flight Log: *Base/Trapani-Milo, Sicily, & return. (800 MI)*

P-38-G-15-LO; Combat Sortie: 3hrs 45mins, 1 landing.

Escorted "Foto Freddie," ran into flak.

Journal

This morning I went out to Sicily with "Foto" Freddie [a photo reconnaissance mission]. Our job was to escort him, you know, watch for enemy aircraft. There were only two of us with him and the other man was on his first sortie, so I really had my hands full watching Freddie and the other guy, too. Trapani-Milo was the place,[26] and all went well until we had almost finished; by that time they had our range and started shooting. It's funny how accurate they can be, shooting 26,500' in the air. It got rather unhealthy in that vicinity, so we headed for home but quick. It sure is fun to drop my belly tanks on most anything military in sight and watch the gas fly.

Sunday 11

Letter excerpt
Geneil to Richard

"Early in December I sent you my locket (with enclosed picture). It hurts so to think that you didn't get it before you left. I also sent you pine nuts, cartoons, jokes and several snapshots."[27]

Monday 12

Letter excerpt
Geneil to Richard

A photographer for the Ogden Standard Examiner told Geneil that "he knew a fellow who is home from Africa on a seven-day furlough. He flew here and is flying back. It is food for thought—glad, either that or dreams—both maybe."

---

26. Trapani is a town on the very northwestern tip of Sicily; Milo is a nearby village where an airfield used by the German and Italian air forces was located.

27. See 7 May *Journal* entry and Letter 1 excerpts. See also accompanying photograph.

Tuesday 13

Journal

Ah, me! Life is getting to be rather boring. I haven't flown since I was on that photo mission, and it's getting to be mighty dull. About the only kick there is in life any more is to go to Sicily or somewhere and let them shoot at us. There doesn't seem to be much going on in Tunis and vicinity. At any rate they've been closing in on the Jerries pretty fast.

We fighter boys don't get much credit for helping out around here, not that it makes a damn, but it sort of gripes us to read the big write-ups about the bombers and all of their dangerous missions with a small extra (escorted by Lightnings). All we did was to beat off several dozen fighters while they laid their eggs and ran for home.

I got a kick out of it the other day, tho'. It seems they (B-26 outfit) didn't know just what the score was and were proceeding to find out over the radio, which isn't good. Our Capt. got pretty sore and told them to return to their base. They didn't turn around, so we just headed back. You know it makes a bomber get in and go to keep up with our slow cruising, but when we looked back they were right behind us. They know who keeps 'em out of trouble and weren't about to be caught out there without us. Radio silence is the one big thing, especially on the way out because the enemy can pick us up and knows just our position and the direction we're going. That isn't good, especially when we're figuring on a surprise attack.

What the --- have I been talking about anyway? Oh, well, I guess it doesn't matter much, does it? I guess I'm just homesick. Maybe not sick, but I sure wish I was home. It's not so bad when I'm busy, but when there's a day like today with nothing to do, I about go crazy wishing I'd never heard of this place. I don't know why we didn't do anything today. Maybe they have left Tunis altogether. I wish. Not much wrong about that tho'. At the present rate, it shouldn't be long. I know what Sardinia and Sicily look like, and I'll probably see a lot more of them before that happy day.

Wednesday 14

Letter excerpt
Geneil to Richard

A pilot patient at the hospital where Geneil worked had flown P-40's, P-39's and P-38's. "He says [P-38's] are swell—better than the others. He even made it sound good (almost). I'm very suspicious still about them."

Thursday 15

Letter excerpt
Geneil to Richard

"Today I read an article in the magazine *Flying* about the use and efficiency of the P-38's in North Africa. Honestly, I fairly ate the thing up."

Friday 16: 3rd Mission

Flight Log: Base/Palermo, Sicily, & return.

P-38-G-10-LO; Combat Sortie: 5hrs 30min, 2 landings [one for refueling].

B-17 Escort. Ran into ME109's. Heber got shot up. Lost one ship: Bentzlin.)[28]

Journal

We escorted B-17s to Palermo. Heber and I in the same flight. All went well until after the bombing, then the fighters lit in on us. Heber got lost from our flight and got in on another which wasn't too good. He ended up with a cannon exploding in his left wing, which made his trip home sort of rough.[29]

I landed at Bône[30] to refuel and ran into Gimblin and a lot of the other guys, "Sad Sacks."[31] By the time we got back here, it had taken almost six hours flying time.

---

28. Escorting B-17s was an "infrequent" mission for the 82nd. (Blake/Stanaway, 58.)

Lt. Conrad Bentzlin, a Sad Sack who signed the $1 bill, "was seen to bail out over the sea" (Blake & Stanaway 58) and was lost. See *Appendix D*.

29. Heber records this mission, too, but in great detail, since his aircraft was badly damaged in that day's action. See p. 75 of his memoir.

30. I believe Richard refueled at Bône Airfield, located on the coast 9 km southeast of Annaba, Algeria. This seems likely since Bône field was located only about 40 km north of the direct line Palermo/Berteaux. The name appears to be a French version of Bona, former name of Annaba. It's unclear what the Sad Sack group was doing there, since the field was a British base.

31. The "Sad Sacks" was the name given themselves by the group of 67 sergeant pilots who also referred to themselves as the "Exclusive 67." Forty-six of them signed the $1 bill headed "'THE SAD SACKS' (EXCL. 67)" found in Richard's wallet long after his death.

See *Appendix D*.

Saturday 17

Flight Log: *P-38-G-15-LO; Local and Test: 2hrs, 2 landings.*

Test hop. Landed at Bône.

Sunday 18: 4th Mission

Flight Log: Base/north Sardinia & return. (600 MI)

P-38-G-15-LO; Combat Sortie: 4hrs, 1 landing.

B-25 escort.

Monday 19: 5th Mission

Flight Log: Base/Tunis & return. (400 MI)

P-38G-15-LO; Combat Sortie: 3hrs 45 mins, 2 landings.

Scramble.

10 Sorties: Air Medal.[32]

Tuesday 20[33]

Letter excerpts[34]

I have something coming now, and I want you to pin it on. . . . It really isn't so very wonderful. Lots of people receive them. But it's a beginning anyway and that's something. In case you're curious it's the air medal. . . . It's given for ten flights (short) across the enemy lines or for five long ones over two and a half hours. As they all know, the 38 stays up longer than the smaller ships, so naturally we

---

32. Richard notes at the top of this page of his *Flight Log* that "each mission over 2½ hrs. = two sorties," hence his total of 10 sorties. If Richard's mission on this date was the same mission as Heber recalls flying that day, it was as follows: "This was a fighter sweep; we went looking for enemy fighters out along the coast of [Bizerte], north of [Tunis]. Three hours running around, looking back and forth. We never saw anybody and returned home without any combat action."

33. Around this date Heber says "I flew my plane back to [Telerghma] to have it painted in combat camouflage color. That was a 30-minute non-combat flight." Though Heber doesn't mention anyone else doing that with him, we can presume that Richard may have had to do the same at around the same time.

34. I haven't quoted any of the relevant passages, but this letter marks a real low point for Richard. He still hadn't received any of Geneil's letters and expressed some bitter unhappiness and depression. A bit of the flavor of it can be read in the next day's letter, written after his first receipt of a letter from Geneil. Note that the letter received had been written well after Richard's arrival in North Africa; he had yet to see those still catching up with him via England. See also 7 May *Journal* entry and Letter 1 excerpts.

96th Sq. mission debriefing (Courtesy of Steve Blake)

get farther from home. Don't let anyone tell you that the seat in a chute is soft, because every time I come back I have to stand up for—.

Say, we really go in for sports in a big way here. We play volleyball just for a [pastime] but we really have a good baseball team. Plenty good, considering that the only practice they get is during the game.

Wednesday 21

Journal

On the 19th I went out on my fifth mission (over 2:30 hrs) which gave me a total of ten sorties and qualified me for the Air Medal. That's no. one for you to pin on. I hope to have a couple more by the time I get home.

Yesterday was our day off, and it rained or tried to. They got us up at four-thirty this morning for a mission, and it started raining pitchforks while we were at breakfast. Rain—no game. Maybe this afternoon.[35]

---

35. A Sgt. Abberger noted in his diary on 24 April that "For the past two days we have had such heavy rains as to ground all planes. The entire camp area and perimeter is completely swamped, making things very miserable." (Blake & Stanaway 59)

Letter excerpts

I'll take it all back. What I said in my letter yesterday. You haven't really forgotten me, have you? Your letter [written 6 March] finally got here and in just the nick of time, too. Lately, I've just had to keep on flying every day until I get too tired to move around. If I don't, I can't find anything to keep busy at. . . . Frankly, I've been about the loneliest today that I've ever been. Maybe it was just the darkness before the dawn. Anyway, I feel like a new man as of fifteen minutes ago. You probably know that it's rather hard to write one way letters, but that's all over now. I have one letter and if I never get another (which better not happen) I can read it every day. I've wondered a bit why I didn't bring some of your other letters with me, but that's over now. I've stuck it out and, believe me, it's been a long time. Just waiting for next day and hoping for at least one letter.

Friday 23[36]

Letter excerpt

I finally got my greatest wish. You know what that is, I'm sure. Take it from me, five months is a long time to wait for a letter.

. . . I'm trying to get the purple heart for being wounded in action. I just got shot in the arm. (With a needle.) I'm having trouble proving that it was in action tho'. You see, today is my day off and there isn't much action.

I'm afraid sometimes that I'm getting homesick. But I know that just can't happen to me. Oh, no? The only time I'm really, not exactly happy but can tolerate life, is when they fly me so much that I'm too tired to do anything but sleep.

Letter excerpt
Geneil to Richard

"Darling, I can't figure out why you haven't received at least one letter from me. That gripes me, too, 'cause I wanted you to get my letters first of all so you would know I have been writing. You mother has been using V-Mail almost all the time, though, so that is probably why."

Saturday 24

V-mail excerpts
to Millers

It's marvelous what one letter can do for a guy, especially after five months. I got my first letter from Geneil about four days ago, and it changed the whole war.

---

36. Heber reports a 10-day lull in the action at this point.

It's always the people that have no desires to travel that do all the chasing around. That's me. I've seen a lot of pretty country, though, and could enjoy it if I wasn't alone at it.

Sunday 25[37]

97th Squadron received a Distinguished Unit Citation for its action today during an attack on enemy airfields in Foggia, Italy. [Apparently, Richard and Heber did not participate in that mission.]

Monday 26

Letter excerpts

It seems like ages already since the day your first letter came. I'm watching for a lot more right soon, so don't disappoint me, please. I shouldn't say that tho', because I know you're writing. I often wonder just what I have done to deserve this. My being here is nothing. Thousands of people are here doing the same, but why can't my mail come?

We grabbed a jeep last night [Easter] and went to town to sort of kill the monotony mostly. That's about all that happened, too. We had supper at a R.A.F. hotel (shall we say) and then went to a picture show. Standing room was at a premium, so it was appreciated by all—I guess. If I stay over here a year or so longer, I may be able to see a show for the first time.

Tuesday 27: 6th Mission

Flight Log: Base/Sousse & return. (750 MI)

P-38-G-15-LO; Local and Test: 1hr, 1 landing.

Combat Sortie: 2hrs 45 mins, 1 landing.

Test Hop. Sea sweep, carried 500 lb bomb, anti-shipping.

---

37. Today was Easter. Richard and Heber went to Constantine for dinner and a movie. (See 29 April *Journal* entry.)

35km north of Berteaux, Constantine/Qusantinah/Kasantina was founded by the Phoenicians, then taken by the Numidians and, finally, the Romans. Built on a picturesque site atop several contiguous buttes, it's known as the "City of Bridges." For Richard's description of the city, see letter excerpts for 7 May.

Wednesday 28: 7th Mission

Flight Log: Base/Sicily & return. (700 MI)

P-38-G-15-LO; Combat Sortie: 3hrs 30mins, 1 landing.

Dive bombing, carried 500 lb bomb, anti-shipping.

Thursday 29: 8th Mission

Flight Log: Base/Sicily & return. (680 MI)

P-38-G-15-LO; Combat Sortie: 4hrs, 1 landing.

B-25 escort & carried 500 lb bomb, anti-shipping.[38]

Journal

It has been raining for about a week now and we didn't get much done, but we're back on the beam now.

They're making a dive bomber out of me. For the past three missions I've carried a 500 lb demo-bomb. That isn't good.

Last Sun. was Easter, so we hooked a Jeep and went to Constantine to a picture show. It wasn't so good, but it passed the time away. That's really a pretty town. Sort of a fortress. I guess it was quite a place in years past.

We were out on a sea sweep today, escorting B-25. I had my bomb as usual, one of the four by the way. We ran into a bunch of 109's and got 2 of them, but they got two of us so that isn't so good. We'll have to do better than that after this.

Two more missions and I will have my first cluster for my Air Medal. Each time we earn the Air Medal after the first time, we get an oak leaf cluster.

Friday 30

Letter excerpts

The end of the fifth month is here since I landed in England. I haven't been doing a whole lot of good over here, have I? At least up until about a month ago. That's when I came here, and from then on I've been finding out how much I know about flying. Or rather how much I don't know, which is a lot, but I'm catching on fast. Heber and I have been sort of promoted to leaders of the second element in a formation of four. It's quite a responsibility, too, especially when you know that if the formation isn't kept in close, I'm taking my wingman's life in my hands as well as my own. This is a place where teamwork means everything, because

---

38. Two 97th pilots were lost to enemy fighters in this action; however, Lt. Robert Congdon, a Sad Sack, $1 bill signator and novice on his first mission, was credited with a victory.

in this we don't give back the marbles, and neither do they. In a way it's fun, tho'. My adventuresome side showing up, I guess.

We have to take pills for prevention of malaria, and their aftereffects aren't good. Some of the boys are pretty sick this morning. It has me sweatin'. So far, so good, tho'.

Oh, guess what the latest rumor is. Someone said we'd be home in July. (I hope it's the 2nd.) That's too much to hope for, though, and besides I don't believe in rumors.

I've got to see the dentist, you know, social call and all that. . . .

May

Saturday 1: 9th Mission

Flight Log: Base/Sicily & return. (750 MI)

P-38-G-15-LO; Combat Sorties: 6hrs 30mins, 2 landings.

Two missions: B26 Escort, sea sweep.

Sunday 2

Letter excerpts

Things are really taking a turn for the better. When I got back from a late mission yesterday, what do you think I found? That's right, five of them. Five letters at once and all from my one and only. Boy, was I tickled? I guess they thought I was going slowly nuts by the way I ran around waving those letters. . . . I sat down and read letters for hours. Of course, it didn't take that long to finish the first time, but they were just as good the second and third times as they were the first. . . .

Three of them came by way of England. You mailed them Feb. 23, 24, 25.

. . . maybe I'm prejudiced, but there's just no place quite as swell as home. I just can't visualize what it will be like to honestly and truly be home for good. But that day is coming. It has to come. I only wish I knew when. But then if I did know, I wouldn't get anything done but wishing the time would go faster. . . . I just don't know what to do with myself when I'm not busy flying or something in that line. . . . If you do get tired of reading the same thing all the time, just throw them away as they come. But for heck sake don't stop writing. Please. I know you write almost every day, and after all I can't have everything, can I? But I could use two or three more a day, easy.

The Red Cross serves us doughnuts and stuff after each mission. The first, by the way, since I left home, and do they taste good! The poor intelligence officers have an awful time trying to get something out of us when our mouths are full.

Letter excerpts
to Butlers

I haven't been so happy in months. We came back from a late mission yesterday and what do you think met us? That's right—a whole slew of mail. We received your letter of Mar 30, and I got a whole bunch from Geneil, three from England and the last two were only written about a month ago.

We have a picture of you that Geneil took in Arizona. It's so natural I almost expect you to start talking any moment.

I guess about all we can say is we're sorry for not writing any more often and try to do better. I think we have been lately, tho', a little. Even if we don't write too much, we're certainly thinking about you and knew we ought to. It is a little bit hard to write when you're not getting any answer. It seems sort of like a one-sided conversation. . . .

After getting two or three from you and one from Wm and a couple others, I couldn't help it, but I got to wondering if Geneil was writing. I knew she was, but you know what it's like after five months. Well, everything OK now. I have enough mail to keep me reading and answering for quite a while and that is good. When I haven't anything to do, I like to write, but when I have nothing to say—well.

Letter excerpt
Geneil to Richard

"Darling, I hope you are ok. It is going on three weeks now since I heard from you. I know that really isn't long considering everything, but you know me. . . . Anyway, I'm pretty anxious."

Monday 3

Letter excerpts

We don't get many of them, but I sure get to hating these days off. There's just nothing to do. Not even a picture show within forty miles. Quite a ways to go, but we do it once in a while.

One of these days I'm going to get out the camera and take some pictures. Over on the hill, the poppies are so thick that the country is completely red in spots. Sometimes four or five acres of them just as thick as they can grow.

Don't tell anybody, but we just finished doing our laundry. The clothes look a bit gray (quite a bit), but we wear them anyway. You know? This clothes washing is something I can forget how to do in no time at all. In fact, I have to learn all over every time I do it. We sometimes have a regular place to send our clothes, but at present we're not so lucky.

It sounds like we're going to have chicken for supper. Somebody found an Arab with a few extra, so now we eat a tasty meal for a change. We officers have to pay a little extra each month for things like eggs, chickens, beef and such that don't come dehydrated in a can. You know, natural food sure does taste good. . . . Oh, for a chocolate malt with you across the table. . . .

Speaking of censors, I was just wondering if my mail had been chopped up or blacked out with the go-between's pencil. It couldn't be that I've got by without saying something.

All the time I was in England I wrote you by this speedy (?) V-. . . .-Mail. I think the first letter I sent was on Dec. 3 '42 and one about every other day after that. It seems pretty doggone bad to me that they can't fly V-Mail across the pond in two months when we came across in six days. I guess you know what's eating on me. I just got your letter of Feb 23, and you still had no mail.

Tuesday 4

Letter excerpts

. . . the weather isn't too good, so I have nothing to do but sit around and read. Oh, yes, and argue about the war. We have some pretty good strategists in the crowd, even tho' we don't help out the war effort very much along that particular line. We kill a lot of time, and that's something.

I got a letter from you today. It was mailed on Mar 11. The last one I got, a few days ago, was mailed Apr 2. . . . I suppose I'll have a bunch more coming from England. hope. Heber just got a couple from there today, so I guess they're still alive up there.

Wednesday 5: Aborted Mission

Flight Log: **Combat Cont'd** [new page]

Max speed on deck–400 MPH

Normal max H.P. 3000 RPM 44" Hg = 1350 H.P. each

Combat horsepower 3000 RPM 65" Hg develops over 1500 H.P. each

Base/Tunis & return. (400 MI)

P-38-G-15-LO; Combat Sortie: 2hrs 30mins, 1 landing.

Didn't complete mission, trouble with ship.[39]

---

39. Apparently Richard's engines were changed overnight 5–6 May. The *Flight Log* shows new engine numbers for 6 May.

Journal

Wow! Since my mail has started coming thro', I've really been writing a lot to you. At least it's a lot for me. It sure does seem good to get my mail. I know I'm not getting all that you write but, if I get one once in a while; I can't yell too much.

The war hasn't been going too fast lately because of rain, but today was really a beautiful day. We started out on a routine bomber escort sea sweep, but my wingman's ship went out so I brought him back.

A lot of the old men are just getting back from rest camp. They left about a month ago just before we got here.

Letter excerpt
Geneil to Richard

"Honey, I dashed home awhile ago and got your letter. Thanks oceans, darling, for writing. I'm terribly sorry you haven't heard from me yet. I've been writing every day and sending pictures, too. You should have received my cable, though. I sent it about two weeks ago."

Thursday 6: 10th Mission

Flight Log: Base/Sicily & return.

P-38-G-15-LO; Combat sortie: 3hrs 30mins, 1 landing.

Sea sweep, B-25 escort.

Letter excerpt
Geneil to Richard

Complaining about V-Mails. "I'll forgive everything if they will just get through to you, honey. You can't imagine how hard it is to keep writing letters knowing you never get them. Heavens, I can't imagine how hard it is on you, never getting any of them. To tell you the truth, I haven't decided which is the worst."

Friday 7

Journal

Yesterday you made me happier than I've been years, it seems like. It has really just been months, but that's beside the point.

We went out on a B-25 escort sea sweep yesterday (never saw anything tho') and, when I got back, what do you think I found? Just exactly twenty letters and Xmas cards, all from you. About ten more from others, but they weren't as important. I fooled around for half an hour trying to decide where to start. I finally sorted them into order as to date and began. I read letters all evening, then got in bed and started the second time. It's really wonderful.

Heber flew into a piece of flak the other day, and it went right into his wing. He has it for a souvenir now.

Letter 1 excerpts

It was a bit late, but it was a very happy Xmas. As much so as I could expect under the circumstances.

We came back from a mission yesterday out nearly to Sicily or somewhere and, after the doughnuts and such, my evening was really taken up. I didn't even have time to go to supper or the weekly picture show.

That was really a sweet Christmas card you sent. I'll keep it for the rest of my life. Also what I found inside. I have it around my neck and am never going to take it off.[40]

Oh, yes, I got the branch off the Christmas tree and the pine nuts, too. I'm not going to eat them all. I'm going to keep some for a souvenir or something.

It gets so darn tiresome on my days off. Nothing is interesting. I go to town once in a while, but that doesn't help any. There's nothing to do in there but look at the scenery, and it's a lot prettier from the air. . . .

You remember Constantine, the old Roman City. [See note for 25 April.] The invisible fortress and all that stuff. I've seen it from the air, and it's really beautiful. The sheer canyon walls around it with hanging bridges and stuff like that there. It was quite a temptation, that bridge. It looked so easy to fly under. . . .[41]

You know you're good for me, at least you would if you could see me each time I get a letter. Just one. So you can imagine how I felt yesterday. I've waited so darn long for those letters, and what makes me so mad is that they had plenty of time to get to me before I left England.

We went to London to the Hq-Air Force Christmas Eve and got our uniform allowance, then got a room at the Mostyn Chef, where we spent the next day. They had a swell Xmas dinner, too. . . .[42]

I may be a bit haywire but except for being able to have you with me if I were there, I would a lot rather be here flying P-38s than flying P40s. . . . I'm driving

---

40. The enclosure in the Christmas card was surely the locket Richard refers to later when he says how fortunate it was that, when he was captured, no one tried to take that or his wedding ring, a surprise gift from Geneil for his 10 August birthday. The importance of these two items for Richard while he was a POW cannot be overstated.

41. Hoover claims not only to have gleefully succumbed to that same temptation but to have twice looped around and repeated the feat of bravado. (39)

42. This account of the London Christmas trip differs a bit from Richard's earlier *Journal* entry; I believe they must have stayed at "the club" (presumably, Officers' Club) initially and then moved to the hotel for Christmas. This account is confirmed by the Mostyn Chef Christmas Day 1942 dinner menu which I found in the same box with the *Journal* and his letters.

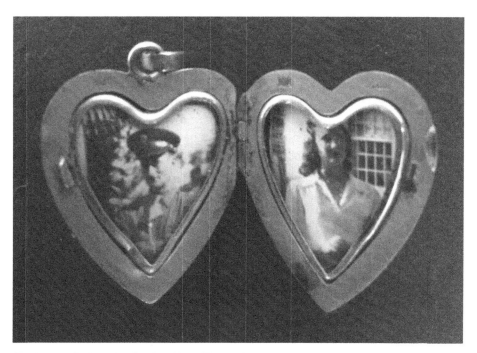

Christmas locket (Butler family collection)

Constantine, City of Bridges. No wonder Richard felt tempted. (Butler family collection)

the ship I always wanted even in flying school. I wanted twin engines, but I didn't want to drive a truck (transport or bomber). Well, here I am perfectly satisfied—with the ship I'm flying, but that's about all.

Yipe! Heber just walked in with another fist full of mail, so I'll sign off for this one. There is a package or two, too.

Letter 2 excerpts

P.M. Here I go again. I don't know what is the matter with me. Two letters in one day. . . .

We both got a pile of mail last night, and I was writing you this morning when Heber came driving in with another pile. Most of it was for me. . . .

I hope you're not worrying about the P-38. I have more time in it now than I had in the -39, and it's really a swell ship. I'd like to show it to you sometime. No matter what happens, unless it's gas, I have a spare engine. I've flown it on one eng[ine], too. Just for practice, tho', and it's really not very hard.

There really isn't much danger here. Not as much as people think. And bombing is about a thing of the past. . . . Here anyway.

. . . I've sort of been promoted to element leader if you know what I mean. You've seen our formations in Florida. Two two-ship elements. I lead the second one. I was element leader in the C.O.'s formation yesterday. . . .

I've been a F/O for nearly five months now. . . . The Gen. has had all promotions in North Africa frozen for quite some time now, so at present there's not much future.

It sure did seem good to hear you tell about the cattails and snow and ice. What would I give to have been there. . . .

Letter excerpts
to Butlers

Boy, have we been busy last night and this morning. When we came in from a mission, we found a stack of mail for each of us. I got twenty from Geneil and about ten from you. . . . I read them all through last evening . . . then this morning I started to answer them. I thought I'd answer all of Geneil's in one, so I made it a long one. Just as I was finishing, Heber came in with a bunch more. Twelve to be exact. Most of the last ones were from Geneil. Almost all that came in last night came by way of England.

This $200 I'm sending now will make it a total of $600. That should make a good down payment on the place, don't you think?

It'll take a little time before we get over the shock of having Xmas after we'd given it up for lost. We got one parcel (hankies) from Ellen & family and a lot of cards.

P.S. Someone kiss Vida for me. I got a whole letter from her.

Saturday 8: 11th Mission

Flight Log: Base/Sicily & return.

P-38-G-15-LO; Combat sortie: 4hrs, 1 landing.

Sea sweep, B-26 escort.

Journal

We escorted B-26s out on a sea sweep this morning and bombed a small ship. Adolph doesn't seem to have much left in this neck of the woods. They [Allied forces] took Tunis and Bizerte yesterday and are chasing them [Germans] out toward Cap Bon. I guess we'll just have to shove them out in the water 'til they soak up enough to come to their senses. We've been keeping the Sicilian straits pretty clear of aid. Now we'll see how many we can keep from getting back to Sicily.

One of the other sqdns dive bombed the Isle of Pantelleria just off Cap Bon and really raised havoc with the one airfield. Things are coming to a head, I hope.

Sunday 9: 12th Mission

Flight Log: Base/Palermo, Sicily & return. (909 MI)

P-38-G-15-LO; Combat sortie: 6hrs, 2 landings.

Mass bombing of Palermo, bomber escort.

Monday 10: 13th Mission

Flight Log: Base/Egadi Isl & return.[43] (730 MI)

P-38-G-15-LO; Combat sortie: 4hrs, 1 landing.

B-25 escort, sea sweep.

Journal

Well, what do you know? The radio said that the largest raid ever staged from North Africa took place yesterday over Palermo, Sicily. The docks were badly damaged and a business section was left in shambles.

Take it from me, it went off just as smoothly as one could ask. The B-17s (with escorting Lightnings) went in first and hit the docks, and it looked like an ammunition ship by the way it went up. Then we brought the B-25s & B-26s in to drop

---

43. The Egadis are a group of three islands just off the western tip of Sicily, near Trapani.

their eggs over the business section. It was fun from our end of the story. There were no enemy fighters, so we had it pretty easy. Cruel, aren't I? By the way, I flew "Genie with the light brown hair," too.

Letter excerpts

The mail is really getting in the groove now. I'm beginning to get them from you less than a month old. The latest one of the seven I got yesterday was written Apr 14. This is really OK. I have enough mail scattered around so that along with the late mail I get some old ones each time. . . . These were written between Mar 5 and Apr 14.

It came over the radio last night, so it shouldn't hurt to mention it here. Anyway there was quite a raid took place over Palermo yesterday. . . . I just wanted to tell you that Genie II took part in it. She's really a swell ship. . . . I'm going to get you a picture of it.

Your first V-Mail Mar 10 just got here. I got two others tho', Apr 6–8. They all say that V-Mail takes preference, but that doesn't seem to get it here as quick as the others.

I'm dying for a big box of popcorn. About the only thing you can do about that tho' is to buy a box and eat it for us both.

I got the blossoms, and they were still intact, too.

I still [look forward to getting mail], but it isn't as bad now 'cause I can read the old ones over again. I do that anyway every time I get a chance, which is almost every night.

Tuesday 11

Letter excerpts

. . . it really is a swell day. For what? Oh, most anything. The trouble is there's nothing to do. Our day off again, and all I can do is read your letters. Which is one thing I'm really thankful for. Every time I read them it seems like I'm just sitting there listening to you talk to me.

I finished a roll of thirty-six exposures just a little while ago, and they are developing them for me at the photo shop. . . . Anyway, I have some swell shots to show you. . . .

I just received my African Campaign ribbon . . . the one that goes beside the yellow one I wear.

I was down to Group paying a social call on the dentist a while ago and before I knew it I was in the chair. Unwillingly, of course. He put his stooge to work pedaling the mechanical drill. . . . Then he put his knee in my chest to hold me down and went to work. I thought he was going to lift the top of my head off. . . . Two little tiny fillings, but they're going to be the last.

I was going to wait for the mail before I wrote to you, but every time I wait for them to sort it I come away disappointed. That ain't good. Take it from me. It's about time I got another pile. I haven't had any at all for about three days. Just to say it, it doesn't sound like very long, but it is. I look forward to my mail now even more than I did before it started coming. . . . It is really coming in swell really. I get letters that are less than a month old with a few older ones mixed in, of course. I was just thinking now that my mail is coming in, it would be just like us to take off again.

The way it usually always works out, the guys go to rest camp after they get a little more time than I have now. So it may not be long until [I'm] pining [my] life away at some beach someplace.

Thursday 13: 14th Mission

Flight Log: Base/southern Sardinia. (550 MI)

> *P-38-G-15-LO; Combat sortie: 3hrs 30mins, 1 landing.*
>
> *Mass raid, bomber escort to Cagliari [Sardinia].*

Journal

Today turned out to be rather unlucky for the other side.[44] We went to southern Sardinia on a mass raid: 150 B-17s, 36 B-26s and 60 B-25s accompanied by about 200 P-38s and about 50 P-40s. It seemed to have done the job intended.

One more mission and I'll have my second cluster. If that means anything.

Life has promise of being rather dull here for some time to come. The colonel says we may not get more than two raids a week for maybe six weeks. He also said that there would be men going home every month from now on. That really sounded good to me.

Letter 1 excerpts

I suppose I've told you before, if you didn't already know, that the army is just a big rumor factory. You ought to hear the ones that are going around now. All about going home and that sort of stuff. It's a lot of wishful thinking but, darn, it makes a good rumor. One that I'd give the world to be able to believe. . . .

Oh, yes, Geneil II went on another tear today. I just can't seem to keep her in line anymore. What do you recommend . . . ?

. . . I'm going to get the photographer to take a picture of our ship and, if it turns out good, I'll have it framed for you. . . .

---

44. All remaining Axis forces in Tunisia surrendered 13 May 1943. Allied forces' next major goal was the invasion of Italy, necessarily preceded by removal of Sicily and Sardinia as enemy strongholds and bases.

I've read so darn many books in my spare time. That is, the ones I could find worth reading. . . . Sometimes I've been tempted to become a mystery reader. Murder and that sort of thing. But I change my mind after two or three pages. . . . You remember the Allies finished taking N. Africa sometime within the last forty-eight hours. Those crazy nuts on the other side of this pond ought to give up, so we can go home.

Letter 2 excerpts

I need a good long talk with you but this is as near to it as I can get, so it will have to do. I don't figure on sending this so it won't matter much what I say.

There isn't anything especially wrong, I guess. It's pretty bad to be away for six months and then suddenly get homesick. But the mere thought of there being a chance to go back is all it takes.

This is really a wonderful place to sit around, yes wonderful. It just isn't humanly possible to stay upstairs all of the time, but that's what I wish I could do. That's the only time that life seems to be worthwhile.

If I was in the infantry I'd most likely be doing something. As it is I just fly around and see that the wrong guy doesn't shoot somebody else up.

Saturday 15

Flight Log: *Base/Tunis/Bizerte/Bône & return (650MI)*

P-38-G-15-LO; Day off: 4hrs, 2 landings [one apparently for refueling].

Flew over Tunisia battle area. Day off.

[See Monday 17 letter excerpt below.]

Monday 17

Letter excerpts

I got the surprise of my life the other day. The Col. gave us three days off [May 15–17] and we could take our ship. The first day Heber and I flew up over the late battle area and got some swell pictures of the whole thing. Heber's up there now hunting junk to take home. I may go up and meet them somewhere this afternoon and proceed to do the same thing.

Some of the funniest tales come back from up there. They say that there are still a lot of Germans up in the some of the hills. As they run out of food, they come down and hitchhike to the nearest prison camp.

They had a couple Italian prisoners doing K.P. for them at one outfit and, when they decided to send them to Pr. Camp, they cried their hearts out. They wanted to stay where they were. I guess they had plenty to eat, at least.

As you've probably read, the Allies have taken a lot of equipment. It's the truth, too. Almost every G.I. has his private car. That's just at one place where we landed. I don't suppose it's that way all over, although there is a lot of stuff.

We got some darn good pictures of the ruins down at —- yesterday.[45] I wish you could have been there.

The stone streets were worn into ruts four inches deep at one arch where the chariots passed through. I got a shot of that and one of the archway. There was a marble monument inside of it and a place for one in the other which we had to replace. You'll see.

It really must have been quite a city in its time. The marble pillars still stood, sometimes a hundred feet high. Oh, yes, they had a big theater or colosseum?, which I have a shot of. The acoustics were really wonderful. We were over in another part of the city a half mile away while some Negro G.I.s were reenacting Romeo and Juliet. "Wherefore art thou, Romeo?" came from the balcony seats. And [from] down on the stage or where[ever] it was came back, "Heah, ah is!"

These natives must think we're souvenir happy. Well, anyway this one took the cake. The little Arabs were running around with their arms full of onions, yelling "Souvenir?"

I'm going to get that picture of my ship this afternoon. As soon as my crew gets it in shape.

When I got back last night I found your letter (V-Mail) of Apr 23. Gee, that's the quickest I've ever had a letter. It looks like mine get there pretty quick, too.

This is the first letter I've had in over a week, and I'm really glad it came. I haven't heard from Mother for about two weeks, but I should have some more today.

P.S. Here's the buttons off my flying gloves.[46] I need you to sew them on.

Tuesday 18: 15th Mission

Flight Log: **Base/Pantelleria & return.**[47] **(608 MI)**

P-38-G-15-LO; Combat sortie: 3hrs 30mins, 1 landing.

Escort B-25.

---

45. Ruins referenced here were those of Timgad. Timgad is the current name of the remains of the Roman city of Thamugas, founded c. 100 A.D. The ruins are located about 20 km east of Batna and about 60 km south of Berteaux. See Journal entry at 19 May.

46. Two red plastic "English Make" buttons are enclosed.

47. The Germans were using the island of Pantelleria as a fighter base and refueling stop for the short-range Me 109.

82nd Armorers at work (Courtesy of Steve Blake)

Letter excerpts

I guess I rate. . . . Seven yesterday. . . . There were about seven days without any mail, then I caught up again.

I keep getting old mail along with the new.

. . . I'm surely glad to hear that you feel better about the P-38. It really is a darn good ship and safe, too. I want you to feel just as safe as I do and have just as much confidence.

I'm sure I told you before that I received the locket and the other things you sent. . . . I was really took for a while when I first saw that so-familiar locket. For a minute it seemed just like you were there with me. . . . I've worn it ever since. . . .

You don't know how it is to not be able to go to Church when you feel like it.

Wednesday 19: 16th Mission

Flight Log: Base/Millis, Sardinia & return.[48] **(600 MI)**

P-38-G-15-LO; Combat sortie: 3hrs 15mins, 1 landing.

Escort B-25. Shot at 14 enemy fighters.

---

48. Heber recalls on this date a mission over Sardinia where "we picked up a lot of resistance" and he used up all his ammunition, 600 50-caliber rounds.

Journal

Things have been rather slow during the past week. We had a three-day pass Sat, Sun & Mon. [May 15–17] after the completion of this campaign. The first day Heber & I flew all over the Tunisian battle area and took pictures. [Allied forces] really took a lot of equipment and prisoners. The second day Heber & I took our crew chiefs down to see the ruins at Tim Gad near Batna. That place really has a history behind it.

Yesterday we escorted B-25s to Pantelleria without much happening. Today we went to Milis, Sardinia [escorting] B-25 and bombed an airfield. As we left there we had a little trouble with some Italian fighters. Heber & I both got out first shots at them. Scared 'em anyway.

Friday 21: 17th Mission

Flight Log: **Base/Villacidro, Sardinia & return. (550 MI)**

P-38-G-15-LO; Combat sortie: 3hrs 15mins, 1 landing.

Escort B-25. Formation leader. "Damaged" a 109. A real old mix-up dog fight with about 25 Macchi 202 & 109s.

Journal

We had a wild day today. We escorted B-25s to Villa Cidro [Villacidro][49] in Sardinia. More fun! I was leader of the formation, which was an honor, by the way, to be picked as a leader. Just as we started in over land on the bomb run, the fighters started showing up. Talk about a mad scramble. We were mixed up with Me 109s, Macchi 300 & 202s & such and when I say mixed, I mean it. We were going up and down, round and round, just like the movies. I knocked one off a 38 and followed him up with a stream of lead. Just as I got back down with the rest, one showed up underneath, rolled over on his back and opened up at me. He fell short and shot between my wingman and me. My wingman turned into him and got him. This went on for about 15 minutes, and the marvelous thing about it is everyone got home. We got about four or five victories and five probables.[50]

---

49. Villacidro was a huge Italian military airfield, the base for reconnaissance craft and for bombers attacking the Gibraltar-Malta supply line. It had also been at least partly appropriated for Luftwaffe use. See Heber's reference to an attack on Villacidro at 27 May.

50. Villacidro was a "heavily defended" target. 97th "met enemy fighters—about twenty of them—mostly ME 109s" on approach to the target. "The Axis pilots were aggressive and persistent" but the 97th "claimed three destroyed and four probables." No 97th planes were lost. (Blake & Stanaway 67)

Heber recalls a Sardinia mission on this date when "all we experienced was heavy flack coming up after the B-25s. In fact, Richard and I had swung off to the right because there were two B-25s that were way out of formation. We swung over there to give them some cover from enemy fighters and just after we passed over them and were on the outside of

I got my reward for it all when I got back. I had five letters, all from you.

You really must be having fun, dances, receptions, movies and such. Oh, if I was only home.

I received the duplicate for my second O.L.C. [Oak Leaf Cluster] recommendation yesterday. I now have 34 sorties. Getting up in the world. I have more combat time than anyone that came with me and more than some of the older men.

Saturday 22

Letter 1 excerpts

I received five V-mails last night, all from you. The latest was May 5. Pretty good, eh?

Doggone it, what's the matter? I didn't get that cable you sent. I never have received any cables from you, and that makes me pretty mad 'cause you said you'd sent quite a few.

I haven't heard from Mother for some time now.

Mother has several of us to write, so she's kept pretty busy. I know she writes once a week. She never has failed to do that since we've been away. I know they don't all get here. . . .

Well, in case you hadn't heard, the war's still going strong and we're going right with it. I have been recommended for my second cluster to an Air Medal.

I can't wait until you see the pictures of our ship. I want to tell you what's on it, tho'. You'll have to wait. I can't send them to you by mail. I can't even have them printed here. Materials, you know.

Letter 2 excerpts

. . . two letters in one day . . . I just can't help myself. It sort of comes in streaks. Every so often I get so darn lonely that I just walk in circles.

I really got some swell letters from you today. Eight of them. One came thro' England, and the rest were pretty quick coming across.

Sunday 23

Letter excerpts

I got three more letters today, two of them came by way of England. Sort of old but just as good as tho' you'd just written them. The other letter was May 4th. They're coming right along. The latest one was May 5, a V-Mail. It came day before

---

them, a big flack burst hit right between these two bombers and both of them exploded—nothing but a big ball of fire where they had been."

yesterday. . . . Heber thinks I've gone plumb nuts when he hears me laughing, then he sees that I have another letter.

I have enough letters now to almost take up my spare time reading. It seems like I have an awful lot of time off. . . . At any rate, the other guys are always yelling for a day off. When it comes, I can't find anything to do with it. I have to think of some reason to test-hop my ship. That kills monotony for quite a while.

Say, are you convinced that the 38 is a good ship? If not, I'll have to start in on you. No fooling, if I was still flying the other one, I'd probably die of inactivity. Those guys are just up there patrolling the coast, a very dull pastime.

Heber's been out jeep riding and hill climbing. Yes, we have quite a few hills here. . . . He brought some cherries back with him . . . and they were pretty good after a little washing.

Letter excerpts
to Butlers

Heber went (in a jeep) up the road a ways where we have some Arab friends. . . . Anyway, he went after some eggs . . . and brought some cherries back, too.

. . . when we want eggs and steak, we just proceed to go get some. We have to pay some extra every month for stuff like that. It's as hard for us to get as it is for you, only we're not rationed.

I got some letters from Geneil yesterday in which she enclosed a letter from a lady in Florida. Mrs. Ewing. She really treated us grand. And I'm doubly thankful to her, because she helped keep Geneil busy when I wasn't there.

I'm beginning to get some of the Red Cross letters Geneil sent, slow but sure. But I haven't yet received any of the cables she sent. Fast cable service, huh? They may catch up to me in six or seven years. If some G.I. mail orderly hasn't read them and decided I wouldn't want 'em.

That made me pretty mad. About three weeks ago, we got two letters from England. One from a woman (member of the church) inviting us to spend Xmas at her home.[51] The other was from the Church office there. The letters were both written at least six weeks before we left there.

Well, my experience seems to be doing me some good. The last time we went out I was put in as formation leader for one of the several [formations]. Heber's been an element leader for a long time, too.

---

51. The woman who had sent the Christmas invitation was Martha Gregory, a Welsh LDS church member who had read the *Daily Express* article about Richard and Heber. Our family remained in touch with Martha and later her daughter, Kathleen Gregory Downs, until Kathleen's death around 1990. The family visited us in Garland after the war.

Monday 24: 18th Mission

Flight Log: *Base/Alghero, Sardinia & return. (579 MI)*

P-38-G-10-LO; Test hop: 1hr, Combat sortie: 4hrs 15mins, 2 landings.

B-26 escort.[52]

Tuesday 25: 19th Mission

Flight Log: *Base/Licata, Sicily, & return. (850 MI)*

P-38-G-10-LO; Combat sortie: 6hrs, 2 landings.

B-25 escort.

Refueled at Kairouan.[53]

Letter excerpts

Oh, Boy! I got three more letters from you last night. Two letters and a cable. It really came thro' in a hurry, too. You sent it at 5:31 PM Feb 28 '43. Some service, eh? It went to England, too, so I guess it wasn't so bad considering that no one knew where I was.

The other two letters were V-Mail May 6 & 10. Not bad service, although not good enough. . . . There isn't generally enough difference in the two kinds to make much difference.

Heber and I have fun now. We're both in the same formation. We are always seeing which one can fly the closest. That in a way is a darn good thing, because the good formation almost never gets attacked. They had us both in the Colonel's formation yesterday. Some fun, eh?

Thursday 27: 20th Mission

Flight Log: **Base/Villacidro, Sardinia, & return.**[54] **(600 MI)**

P-38-G-15-LO; Combat sortie: 3hr 30mins, 1 landing.

---

52. According to Blake & Stanaway, this "was a combination dive-bombing mission and bomber escort. . . . Four flights of P-38s were covering the Marauders. . . . Three other flights. . . . would go in first through the flak and fighters to dive-bomb with 500-pounders from 4000 feet." (68) Pages 68-70 give a fabulous retrospective account of this mission from take-off to landing by Lt. Gerry Rounds.

53. Al-Qayrawan, Tunisia, 160 km south of Tunis.

54. Heber says ". . . we hit the aerodrome at [Villacidro, Sardinia] to wipe out the base so the German fighters couldn't come up from there. We had five missions in a row that we escorted bombers on missions over Sardinia. On two of those missions we evidently

B-25 escort.

No opposition.

Friday 28[55]: 21st Mission

Flight Log: **Base/Castel Vetrano, Sicily & return. (750 MI)**

P-38-G-15-LO; Combat sortie: 4hrs 30mins, 1 landing.

B-26 escort.

ME 109 jumped us.

Letter excerpts

We had an awfully late mission and a long one at that. Boy, was I tired. Mostly from sitting down so long. I'll bet that when I get home, I'll stand up for a week at a time. . . .

   I couldn't get the photographer to take a picture of our ship, so I took the best ones I could with this thirty-five mm. I took enough of them so one should come out. I've really showed Geneil II around this country. We went to Palermo twice and different parts of Sicily, also Cagliari and other parts of Sardinia.

   There's a dirty rumor going around that Heber & I and two or three others are leaving for rest camp in a few days. I don't know what I'll do if all of my time is "spare time."

   I have a lot more combat time than anyone else here (that hasn't already been to rest camp). Almost one hundred hours already. I don't know why, but I always did get more time than the others with me. . . . Oh, yes, as of yesterday you have a number three cluster for your Air Medal. By the way, have you seen the Air Medal? I haven't. All we get here is the ribbon to be worn under my wings. . . . The medal comes when I get back.

   I'm not eligible to go home until I have 125 hrs. combat time, and it may be quite a while now that I'm going to concentration camp.

Saturday 29

Flight Log: *P-38-G-15-LO; Test: 1hr 15mins, 1 landing.*

   Test hop.

---

had some good resistance, because when we got back I was low on fuel on one mission and had to land at Cape [Bon, Tunisia] to refuel. . . . I had used up all my 50-calibre ammunition. It had been an obviously eventful day. . . ." (Butler 80)

   55. "Although both missions flown [today] were for the most part uneventful, there was one notable aspect: The group made a maximum effort that day and eighty-eight P-38s were put into the air. This was the 82nd's biggest single-day's total to date." (Blake & Stanaway 72)

"My brother Richard taking a nap after returning from a combat mission."
(Butler family collection)

Letter excerpts[56]

I just received sixteen more letters. . . . There were some pictures with them, too. All but one of this bunch came through England. . . .

I got another Postal Cable and a letter. . . . Written Jan 29. By way of England. The telegram gave me your new address. . . .

Since I've been getting your mail, my conscience has been clear. I've been writing more and more often. . . . No kidding, tho', it was awfully hard to write when I first got here. I didn't know just what I could write, and I was so darn worried about you. Well, anyway, I did write more often than you think I did while in England. I wrote every other day and never missed it more than a couple of times. I agree with you that the V-Mail isn't what it's cracked up to be. But they said it would go across in a week, and that is what I was trying to have them do.

I have a total of 42 sorties and eight-nine hours combat. . . . The minimum to be eligible to go home is one twenty-five hours and fifty sorties, so after I get through with rest camp, it won't take long.

Doggone! News, no matter how small, sure gets around. If I'd have known it was going to get that far, I wouldn't have let him spread it so thick. Just in case you read it, I never did want to fly that airplane and told him so, but I said I would like to check out in it. It's too simple. Not much larger than a primary trainer. It

---

56. This lengthy letter seems to have been written in two sittings; the second section seems unusually disjointed, and that appears to be because Richard was then responding to things he'd read in a letter or letters from Geneil.

did a good job in the Battle of Britain, so they like to say it's the first. The Battle of North Africa sort of changed their minds, tho', wot?

You remember J.E. Bath? He flew that ship here and almost made himself an ace. When you get that far along, you sort of have a tendency to let caution go to heck just to get another victory. I hear he didn't get that one.

To me it seemed like I was an awful long way from home when I landed up there [England]. The weather was so damp and cold I almost froze to death. That day that it snowed, you remember, was about the warmest of them all. It froze up the moisture and warmed up the place. . . . Anyway, when we got on the boat to come down here, I was almost happy. At least I was going to get warm, even if I did regret it later on. This is about the same latitude as Arizona, I think, but the Mediterranean is near enough so that it stays pretty nice. Not at all like "Africa."

I was in Constantine a while back, trying to get something for your birthday, but I didn't have much luck. I'll see if I can get that far again soon.

I had a lot of fun the other day in town. I was sitting in the jeep, knocking off little Arab shoeshiners . . . but in the crowd was a little French kid and his younger brother. The older one spoke English fairly well and understood it OK. He kept telling me what the others were saying about me. I thought I'd croak. His little brother didn't like the others to be begging bonbons, chewing gum, etc., so he proceeded to chase them away. He was such a little wart, I thought he was going to have a fight on his hands a time or two but he succeeded. I gave him some gum and life savers. He sure was cute. He said, "Merci," and looked rather conscience-stricken as tho' he hadn't chased them away so I'd give him candy. It seems funny to see and hear such little kids speaking another language.

Monday 31[57]

Journal

Well, here we are at the place we hoped we wouldn't have to come. But now we're here, we're not sorry. It's quite a place. Good food, too. We had ice-cream for supper and it doesn't seem to be at a premium either.

We left Telerghma this morning at eight on a DC-3 and, after the longest and most tiresome five hours that I have ever flown, we landed at Fez, Morocco.[58] Not far from Casablanca. This place is about 40 miles from Fez, about 5600' high. Plenty cool at night.

---

57. "By this time the pilots were being given ten-day leaves after completing 25 missions. . . ." (Blake & Stanaway 73)

58. Richard's interminable five-hour Telerghma/Fes flight would have covered about 550 miles. Fes is 250km northeast of Casablanca. Richard and Heber enjoyed this R&R at the Hôtel Balima in the alpine setting at Ifrane, a French colonial mountain resort in the Middle Atlas Mountains just 40 miles south of Fes.

The only thing I lack to make this rest enjoyable is you know who. As it is, I'm afraid life will continue to be empty right when it counts most. But I'll be home soon.

V-Mail excerpt

Heber and I left the outfit this morning rest camp-bound. We flew all the way back here and if you don't think that's tiresome—well, it is. I'm almost ready to drop. I feel a lot worse than I ever did after a six-hour mission. I said I didn't know what I'd do at a rest camp, but right now it feels pretty good to sit down and relax.

It certainly doesn't take long to get a long ways away from the war. . . . This is really quite a place. Fishing, swimming, good picture shows (they say) and good food. That's the main thing. They say we get ice cream here every once in a while.

June

Tuesday 1

Letter 1 excerpts

This is really a pretty place up here. Pretty high, too. Almost six thousand feet, I think. That makes it nice and cool. In fact it's a little too cool this afternoon. This place is almost exactly like Brigham Canyon, only not quite as pretty. We got out the bikes this morning and proceeded to look over the countryside.

Since I got here I'm about convinced that I'm ready for rest camp after all. Back at the outfit we had been buying a lot of fruits and vegetables from the natives. All was well and good until that truck (transport) ride back here yesterday. . . . I slept better last night than I have in months almost. That may be because I was tired.

I came over Oran again yesterday. . . . Anyway I was going to look and see if it was really a beautiful city after all. Not bad from the air. . . . It's the color in the buildings. You should see Constantine from the air. Tunis and Kairouan are quite pretty, too. From above is the only way I've seen them, tho'. . . .

I think I'll go fishing tomorrow morning and see how wet I can get. I sit down beside the stream here and shut my eyes, and I'm home just like that.

Letter 2 excerpts

We spend most of the mornings just fooling around. They have pinball machines and junk like that and a pretty good library to take up a guy's time. I know where Heber would be ten hours out of the day if the cockeyed swimming pool wasn't contaminated. He really likes to swim.

This place here is so much like the hotel in Florida that every time I come in I half expect to see you standing there. I thought this was going to be really OK at first, but it brings up so many fond memories—I don't know.

It's going to be pretty lonely for a week at least. I won't get any mail from you. . . .

The last letters I received were V-Mails written on May 7. It's funny they both came on the same day. That doesn't happen very often. I think the latest letter I've had was May 14, and it came in about fourteen days. That really made home seem a lot nearer.

V-Mail excerpt
to Butlers

Heber and I and a few others flew back here yesterday to this rest camp. It's going to be pretty good, too. We have rooms with bath and clothes closet and two "beds." Boy, I slept like a log last night, quite a bit different from sleeping in a tent on a G.I. cot and washing and shaving in my steel helmet. . . . So far we haven't done much resting. We were out bike riding this morning. Boy am I tired. The food is sure good, too. "Ice Cream."

Wednesday 2

Letter excerpts

I took another bike ride this morning, and this time I went uphill first.

I've been trying my best to send a telegram to you, but they say it's still impossible. I'll get it done yet if I have to hire a tug and lay my own cable.

They're going on a boar hunt tomorrow (Morocco's great for that sort of thing in certain parts). We're going to try and get in on it, too.

Oh, yes, I finally found a place where I can get my negatives printed. I sent them out this morning, and it shouldn't be more than a couple days.

Tennis, horseback riding, bicycling, fishing. . . .

I almost wish I was back fighting the cockeyed war. It doesn't seem to be ending very fast.

Thursday 3

Letter excerpts

Things are sort of odd still. I just don't feel like chasing around very much yet. I feel better than I have been tho'. . . .

I'm going to send you a napkin holder from the hotel where I stayed.

When we went through Fes . . . I tried to send you a cable, but it didn't work. The French just don't seem to send them from there to the states. Too bad, too, 'cause I was figuring on getting one to you before I came back.

I have my recommendation for the third cluster to your Air Medal.

Hôtel Balima (top left) and Ifrane town (Butler family collection)

Friday 4

Letter excerpt

There are some pretty good ruins . . . near here and that's where we spent the day.[59] I got some more pictures. Some of them should be good. I'm not going to mention pictures any more, tho'. I said I was going to send you some but they didn't turn out. At least that's what he said. And he didn't print any. I'm pretty mad, too, 'cause they look to me as tho' they'd be good. I guess I'm just not so hot at photography maybe, huh?

Saturday 5

Letter excerpts

Oh, what a life. This rest camp stuff is the real thing, that is if you're tired. I wasn't until I got here, but I've told you about that, haven't I? Anyway if I get completely rested up, I'll be here for the duration. . . .

There's no telling just how long we'll be here. . . . I won't get any mail while I'm here, and I'm getting anxious for some.

---

59. See *Journal* entry below at 9 June.

. . . I am awfully lonesome or whatever it is that borders on homesickness.

I don't know why I do, but I spend too darn much time in this room, reading and such. The reason is, I guess, that it's so much like the one we used to have.

I'm sorry about those pictures. You probably think I'm holding out on you. . . . The old goat just didn't print any of the four rolls I sent. They were good, too. Most likely he just didn't have the equipment to print off from a roll like that. That's the only excuse I can think up for it. Oh, well, I got one roll of 36 shots developed for twelve Francs (24 cents). They develop in the outfit for nothing, and refill my spool.

Sunday 6

Letter excerpts

If I don't soon get to doing something I'll go crazy. This rest stuff is OK for a few days if you're tired, but it's certainly getting monotonous now.

I laid in bed most all of the morning. . . . Then I got up, shaved, and went for a bike ride. This could be really pretty country, but as it is I'm not very impressed. I did run into a lot of pretty white roses and picked a bud for you. I had to carry it back in my mouth, but I got it here.[60]

We're hoping they have some ships here for us to fly back to the outfit when we go. I'm dreading that cockeyed transport ride. . . .

I don't know which is better, being here with a lot to do if you feel like it—where everything is quiet—or being up there with a wee bit of excitement and your mail coming in. I prefer the latter. Honestly, I miss your letters more every day.

I was over to the local swimming pool this morning (just watching) and did I ever get a kick out of it all. These people are so different in customs and everything. . . . The French have a custom of shaking hands, I think to the excess. . . .

Monday 7

Letter excerpts

We've been out playing tennis all morning, and I'm about on my last lap . . . I sort of overdid it and strained my wrist.

Sounds like quite a gay and easy life, doesn't it? It could be, too, if, as I said once before, a few things were changed.

It may seem rather one-sided to you at home for some of us to be enjoying (?) life like this and others up there fighting. . . . But then think of the thousands of battleworn, brow-beaten, pencil-pushers here in headquarters. The poor cusses have to eat steak and ice cream and eggs, etc., because it's frozen and will spoil

---

60. This letter contains a dried rosebud folded into a separate sheet of paper whose edges are secured by 3 paperclips.

if sent any further. They can't have the dehydrated delicacies that come in cans. And another thing, we can drive our jeep into the open air theater twice a week and enjoy the cool evening breeze while they have to sit in a stuffy old theater.

I sent a few things to you, one at a time, in my letters, such as a napkin holder and such. . . . I hope they get through.

Remember the pictures? I might try sending the roll of negatives, but I know some of them won't get through, so there isn't much sense in that, is there.

The photo shop in the outfit will have some paper by the time I get back there, I hope. If not, I'll have to see what the Germans left in Tunisia.

Wednesday 9

Journal

The time has almost come for us to leave for the outfit again. We're undecided whether to go tomorrow or take a few days longer. We can always say the transportation was bad.

I'll never learn. I've been out playing tennis again today, and my arm is really sore now.

We went to Meknes to see the ruins[61] on about our third day here. They were nothing like the city at Timgad (Batna) but good nonetheless. If I could get my mail here, I would be content to stay a while, but as it is I'm ready to go back.

Letter excerpts

We've been having a regular game of tennis every morning for several days now. I still have a hard time holding my own with the rest of them. . . .

There's a little French girl that's out to the courts every day playing. She speaks fairly good English with a definite French accent that makes it sound funny as the dickens. We get a kick out of talking to her while she is playing. The first time someone said, "Get on the ball," she had to take time out and find out what good that would do. Now she says, "Oui, you make beeg joke."

I suppose in peacetime this place is quite a summer resort. At present there aren't too many people here. Is good! We can have the run of the place without it being crowded.

I'll be sort of glad to get back to the outfit. Even tho' it will mean going from innerspring mattresses & private rooms to a tent and G.I. cot. This gets pretty dead for me. . . . I don't go in for all of the things they have here to do.

---

61. The ruins Richard mentions near Meknes must be those of the Roman city of Volubilis, a large and spectacular site today.

Friday 11

Letter excerpts

I swore that I wouldn't eat any more of this cockeyed G.I. ration candy, but here
I go. We don't get any of it up there, so while we're here we sort of stock up on it
. . . I'm certainly not going to eat all I have alone. . . . I'll give it to my crew, I guess.
They certainly have it coming. I have to hand it to those boys. They sure did keep
my ship in tip-top shape. I think I only missed two missions while I was up there.
Take it from me, that's a record 'cause on a ship of that size so many unimportant
things can go wrong. Just enough so we can't go on.

I'm surely going to get my old crew back when I get to work again.

When I first got here I thought I'd really be glad when the time came to go
back. I'm getting used to the place, I guess. There isn't a whole lot here to hold
one's attention, but also there isn't much future up there.

You probably think we have quite a soft life. Well, right now I'm sort of inclined
to agree with you. This rest camp stuff is just what they meant it to be. I've almost
got to the point where I can sit around idle without pacing the floor. I read some
crazy book yesterday and last night. They had a dance downstairs, but the book
looked better. . . . No, I'm not a bookworm. If there's something fun to do, I'm
for it.

I played tennis all morning, and surprising as it may seem, I'm getting so I can
return the ball every once in a while.

You remember my red nose, don't you? No! It's still caused by the sun, too.
Honestly, it's taking a beatin'.

Sunday 13

*HQ 82 Fighter Group and its 95, 96 and 97 Fighter Squadrons officially transferred
with P-38s from Berteaux, Algeria to Souk-el-Arba, Tunisia.*

Journal

Here we are still [Ifrane] watching the war go by. We were supposed to have gone
back about three days ago, but the transportation is none too good so we hang
around and make callouses.

A bunch of B-26 boys left this morning, but they had one of their own ships
here. We're trying to get some 38s from the fighter school to fly up as replacement
ships. Hope it works out. I sure dread those truck rides.

One of the French waiters is a watch-maker. I almost got my ticker fixed, but
he can't get to Fes to get the spring.

I finally got rid of what's been bothering me all during the past two weeks. But
we won't talk about that. [Added later in pencil:] GIs.

Letter 1 excerpts

It's another beautiful Sunday morning. The mornings here at the town where the rest camp is are all pretty as one could ask for. It sometimes turns off a little different by night tho'.

They had a stage show downstairs last night. It was all in French, so you can guess about how it was. Some of the songs and the orchestra were pretty good.

Boy, I really slept last night. As you know I haven't been feeling too well since I got here. After yesterday there is a turn to the better. I didn't eat much of anything all day—then last night.

I guess I'll be going back to the outfit in a few days now. The transportation isn't too good, so it may take quite a while. Maybe a week.

I'm really getting anxious to get back.

Letter 2 excerpts

I was out front for quite a while this afternoon playing the radio record player. I couldn't find the one I wanted, so I just had to be satisfied with what they had. That tune we used to play way back when. It never does get old. Every time I play it, it brings back a million memories.

I still haven't been able to talk myself into taking a swim over there in the village pond. I'm not going to, either. Today cinched it.

You know that thing that I was telling you about—that play? They're putting it on again tonight for the natives and charging admission. Aren't we just the lucky things? We saw it for nothing. Tonight? No, I don't think so.

Letter excerpts
to Butlers

There's nothing I'd like better than to be there so I could go to church with you this morning. A guy sure gets to miss that one thing an awful lot here.

It has been two weeks since we left up there [their squadron base], and they don't send mail here. If they did, it would just serve to mix up an already mixed-up mail service.

Monday 14

Letter excerpts

Boy, am I mad. I went into town this morning to see about my watch, and I figured on buying a few things. To begin with, the nearest two towns must be forty miles, quite a distance anyway, quite a ride in itself, too, especially when one rides you-know-how. To make the story short, today is flag day, I found out, another native holiday for which everyone takes time out.

Anyway all of the cockeyed stores were closed. I don't think I need to tell you that I was terribly unhappy.

I did get a kick out of one thing, which helped to save the day from being a complete failure. We ate lunch at the G.M. Staff table and had a hearty little chat with some of the more expensive brass. It's amazing just how little some of these guys know about the war. (They were ground officers, so that may have a little to do with it.) Even tho' some of them do wear more ribbons than a French general. I never thought about that; maybe they trade cigarettes to the natives for ribbons here like we do for Arab rugs to go in our tents up there.

Right now I'm pretty anxious to get back to the outfit and get in the saddle. First off, tho', after I get back there, I'm going to spend the following two days reading my mail.

Tuesday 15[62]

Letter excerpts

Doggone, it's been so long since I had a letter from you that I'm beginning to get that old half-lost feeling again.

Boy, it's going to be so much fun to ride around the country and look at all of the old familiar things I used to know. I hope I still recognize people when I get back there.

Are my eyes ever sore tonight! I'm certainly a demon for punishment. We've been chasing the country over in a quarter ton truck all day. My face and clothes were almost completely covered with dust, and my eyes are as red as though I'd been staying out 'till all hours.

The prisoners over at the Sultan's Palace are just finishing their daily chant. We were talking to a Dutch girl that's been here for quite a while, and she says it's a sort of prayer. . . . The natives here aren't true Arab. A guy was telling me that they are Berber . . . a higher and cleaner class of people.

Wednesday 16

[Today Richard and Heber left Fes on the first leg of their return to their squadron. They flew from Raz el Ma (Fes) to Algiers, where they spent the next two days awaiting ongoing transportation.]

---

62. "Later that day the 97th also flew to Sicily as escorts for a formation of B-25s, which was attacked by enemy fighters." They bagged several enemy planes as destroyed, probable or damaged. (Blake 32)

Friday 18

[This date Richard and Heber caught "a hop" on a two-star general's plane from Algiers to Souk-el-Arba.]

Saturday 19

Flight Log: **Souk-el-Khemis/Cap Bon area/return. (400 MI)**

P-38-G-15-LO CQ; Undesignated: 4hrs, 2 landings.

Landed at Bou Fiche.[63]

Sunday 20

Flight Log: *P-38-G-15-LO CQ; Demonstration (Test): 2hrs 40 mins, 2 landings.*

Led a training formation.

Letter excerpts

Here we are again after a terrific battle for transportation. When I say battle, I mean just that. We fought it out, though, and finally ended up by finishing the trip back in some General's ship. He was a pretty good sort of guy. . . .

I'm pretty mad at the whole deal. First you get my mail and I don't get yours, then I start getting it by the bushels . . . and you don't get any.

They're either taking a lot of time getting there or I'm talking just too much. . . . Honestly, I was expecting a letter from you saying not to write so much 'cause you can't read them.

That rest camp is OK for a rest, but who wants a rest? . . . you see, the more I fly the shorter the time will be before (damn flies) I pass the Statue of Liberty again, going the other way. I have to go fly pretty quick now. We have another new man, and I'm showing him our style of formation.

One of my French friends—the waiter—made me a souvenir. Here's hoping they don't bend it up too much in the mail. It's just glued, so it won't take much wear & tear.[64]

---

63. This was likely Bouficha/Bou Ficha, located on the coast about 50 miles south-southeast of Tunis.

64. This is a sheet of buff paper approximately 4" × 7" and slightly thicker than normal printer paper. This collage was made with very small pieces of colored paper, most recognizable as bits of postage stamps.

Ifrane postage stamp collage (Butler family collection)

Souk-el-Khemis

"Around the 1st of June, an advance echelon of the group moved from Berteaux to its new base, called Marylebone, near Souk-el-Arba in western Tunisia. By the middle of the month the 82nd was fully installed there, despite the first bouts of malaria and other health problems which were to plague its personnel for a time. . . ." (Blake & Stanaway 73) This is the base that Richard consistently refers to as Souk-el-Khemis.

Souk-el-Arba is now part of the university town of Jendouba in western Tunisia about 90 miles west-southwest of Tunis; Souk-el-Khemis is about 14 miles northeast near Bou Salem/Boussalem.

"Although the 82nd was fulfilling its combat role in an exemplary fashion, the situation on the ground at Marylebone wasn't nearly as satisfactory. According to the group's intelligence officer (S-2)/historian, the 'intense heat and constant dust storms complicated mechanical problems and made living and eating miserable.' The terrible North African summer was upon them." (Blake & Stanaway 76)

Sgt. Tom Abberger of the 97th says the following in his diary: "Daytime temperatures here are now up to 137 degrees. Under orders we take Atabrine daily to prevent malaria. The men cover their backs with hydraulic oil as protection against the sun. Our pilots climb into their sweatbox cockpits and are wringing wet before they get off the ground." (Blake & Stanaway 79)

"When the temperature was high the pilot [after landing] would exit the P-38 very carefully to avoid touching any part of it. The midday sun in North Africa in the summer is so merciless that the metal skin of an aircraft soon becomes unbearably hot to the touch." (Blake & Stanaway 87)

Letter excerpts
to Butlers

Well, here we are back in the outfit and eager to get at it again. It has been almost three weeks now since we flew last, and it seems sort of funny (but good) to get in the clouds again.

Yes, we've had quite a rest, and it has done us a world of good. That place really did seem a lot like home. Right up in the mountains, where the streams begin.

I guess this is just the place for me this time of the year. . . . We are right out in the middle of nowhere with wheat fields all around. Just like home. If this Arab has a combine, he may find one [*sic*] each G.I. airplane driver out there helping. I'd sure like to get back on that old sacker box again. As a general rule, tho', they harvest their wheat by hand. Cut and tie it into little bundles, then haul it to stacks by burro. . . . I saw an Arab with three mules on top of a wheat stack driving them in circles.

There were quite a few letters waiting for us when we got here.

Monday 21: 22nd Mission

Flight Log: Souk-el-Khemis/Naples & return.[65] **(800 MI)**

P-38-G-15-LO CQ; Combat sortie: 5hrs 15mins, 1 landing.

B-25 escort. Led 2nd element.

Journal

We finally caught a hop out of Raz el Ma (Fez) to Algiers on June 16. Stayed there for two days and caught a hop on a ** General's ship to here. This is quite a place if you like it. We're right out in the middle of an Arab's wheat field. Just like home this time of year—only different.

I had about twenty letters waiting when I got here. Most of them came thro' England, so that just about winds up the scattered letters. It was lots of fun getting them and the date didn't change them a bit. I wish there were more. I'll hope so anyway.

We went on our first mission today since rest camp. To a field near Naples, Italy. Got a good look at the Isle of Capri, too. It isn't much to sing about. They haven't had any missions in the group here for almost a week now, and after today I've about come to the conclusion that we're just waiting for an armistice. A good dream, anyway. Honestly, there wasn't enough opposition to make us drop our tanks. No flak and only two fighters took off. I'm looking for tougher days to come, tho'.[66]

---

65. Today "was another notable day, as it saw the group's first, albeit rather uneventful, mission to Italy escorting B-25s to a rail junction near Naples. It also marked the first appearance of American fighters over the Italian mainland." (Blake 34)

66. Heber says ". . . we escorted bombers to Salerno, Italy [on the coast about 25 miles southeast of Naples]. . . . The mission was 5 hours and 15 minutes. . . . We had two

Letter excerpts

In this first two days I got thirty letters and a telegram. What do you think I did that first night here? That's right—I went to bed and read letters and fought mosquitoes, by flashlight for half the night.

I have the piggy-back tomorrow. . . . Honestly, I'd give anything if I could only be there and take you up. You still don't trust it (the P-38), do you? Some day I'm going to show you just how good a ship it is. . . .

I knew some of those boys that were interned back there you-know-when. We were at the same place.

Tuesday 22

Flight Log: **Souk-el-Khemis/Hergla/Hammon & return (325 MI)**

P-38-G-15-LO CQ; Cross-coountry: 2hrs 30mins, 3 landings.

Tunis & Cap Bon & landed twice.

Wednesday 23

Flight Log: **Souk-el-Khemis/Tunis/Bizerta & return (280 MI)**

P-38-G-15-LO CQ; Cross-country: 3hrs, 3 landings

Pick-a-back. Took Crew Chief up.[67]

Letter excerpts

Wow! Was today ever a busy day. I didn't really accomplish much, but I did a lot of flying. The pick-a-back finally got in commission, so I took my crew up for a ride, one at a time, of course. By the time I'd given them their fill, I had a line of about six more that wanted up. It's a long story, but by suppertime someone else had his fill.

The last letter I got was written May 30. A V-Mail. . . . These V letters are so small that I just get started and it ends.

The day that I complete my fiftieth mission will be the next happiest of my life, I'll bet. The real day will be that wonderful day that I see you again.

Messerschmitt 210's follow us for about 30 minutes, but they didn't dare get in too close to the bombers or to the fighters. I guess we had them pretty much buffaloed and they just hung back a couple of miles behind us. . . ."

67. ". . . late in April some [ground] crews in the 97th Sq built two 'piggy-back' Lightnings. By removing the radio from behind the pilot's seat and installing a simple bucket seat and safety belt on its shelf there was room—barely—for a passenger. The radios were reinstalled in the gun compartments. The piggy-backs were used mainly to train new pilots and to give rides to the non-flying personnel." (Blake & Stanaway 66)

There must be something to this telepathy stuff. I wake up in the middle of the night sometimes with the funniest feeling.

Thursday 24: 23rd Mission

Flight Log: **Souk-el-Khemis/Terranova, Sardegna & return (680 MI)**

P-38-G-15-LO CQ; Combat sortie: 4hrs 45mins, 1 landing.

B-25 escort. Bombed airfield. Flak & fighters.

Letter excerpts

Don't expect too much. I'm writing on my knee again. I hope I don't get used to writing like this. It may be rather hard to change and write on a desk. . . .

Hot dog—I hope I'm not yelling to loud or too quick. I saw "Pap" hand Heber some mail. Here he comes in a jeep. I'm holding my breath.

Yeah! Two letters, June 7 and 8 they're postmarked. Time out while I read.

Gee t'anks for the letters and pictures. It really seems good to get them.

Heber has latched onto that picture of the two of them already. Every one that you send, like that, disappears soon after they arrive. . . . He hasn't had any pictures besides what you've sent. . . . We probably have gobs of mail between here and Casablanca, but it takes so darn long to get it here that it doesn't help much.

Friday 25

Flight Log: **Telerghma/Souk-el-Khemis (125 MI)**

Souk-el-Khemis/Hergla/Cap Bon[68] (300 MI)

P-38-G-15-LO CQ; Cross-country: 3hrs 30mins, 3 landings.

Ferry trip from Telerghma.

Letter excerpts

Jerry, the operations officer, asked me if I'd take some of the other boys and go ferry some ships up. I had my first ride in a B-25. In the top turret at that. It's so thrilling—really you should try it some time. Honestly, I don't see how those boys can stand to drive those trucks. They say the 25 is one of the best, too. What I can't get is why they put two men in there, when one pilot could do it just as well. Maybe for the safety of the crew. That's a point. One man can sleep at a time or one can drive while the other drinks cold chocolate and dunks doughnuts. No

---

68. Hergla, also on the Tunisian coast is about 30 miles further south from Bouficha.

kidding, that's what they do on the way back from a mission. Guess they'd park and have a picnic up there if they weren't afraid we'd leave them.

I need you all the more now because I can see myself arriving home in the near future. How soon I don't know—maybe by our anniversary.

Letter excerpts
to Butlers

Heber and I still have our own ships. The same ones we had before. It really is good to have a ship that you know you can trust. It helps the confidence, especially when one is a couple hundred miles out over the Mediterranean.

I was fooling around up near Cap Bon a few days ago in Heber's ship (our day off) and some of the boys in the photo section asked me to give them a buzz job, so they could take my picture. It turned out pretty good, too. They're making me some prints of it. The only thing wrong is the left wheel wasn't completely retracted at the time.

Saturday 26

Letter excerpts

Things are smoothing up a little here now. I got another letter today (May 25). Not as late as some I already have. . . . I have a total of one hundred thirty letters counting the one I got today.

It takes about two months for me to get every letter you write, but I don't care (much). I get them, which is the main thing. Eighty-two of the letters were written before Mar 31.

You were talking about taking a week off. You must have been vacationing about the same time I was.

Sunday 27

Flight log: *P-38-G-15-LO CQ; Demonstration (Test): 1hr, 1 landing.*

Formation training: new replacements.

Monday 28: 24th Mission

Flight Log: **Souk-el-Khemis/Terranova, Sardinia & return (680 MI)**

P-38-G-15-LO CQ; Combat sortie: 4hrs 30mins, 1 landing.

B-25 escort. Hit an airfield.

Richard flying Heber's ship, northern Tunisia, about 22 June 1943. Note the partially unretracted left wheel. (Courtesy of Rose Butler Hensley)

Letter excerpts

I really look forward from one day to the next for any word at all from you, no matter how short.

Speaking of my morale. If you only knew just how much I depend upon you to keep me going. There isn't anything special to do here in our spare time and a guy can't fly all day, so you see what Africa is.

I had my annual bath the other day. About two miles from here there's a stream that we use for that purpose. . . . It wasn't exactly clean, but I didn't expect too much. . . . We just don't have the G.I. showers set up yet.

These African flies are terrible. They can't take a hint at all.

Well, I'm getting out of the Army pretty soon now. My three years will be up on the 19th (wot a laugh).

The engines are being replaced in my ship. It will be ready for showtime tomorrow. I'll have to break it in just right so it will be as good as it was before. . . . When the other engines weren't so old, I had about the fastest ship in the outfit.

Richard at left, Heber hanging laundry. (Courtesy of Rose Butler Hensley)

Urban Stahl second from left, Richard standing, Heber doing laundry. Probably Souk-el-Khemis June/July 1943. (Courtesy of Rose Butler Hensley)

You remember the cellophane bags that I used to keep my hat in? I finally found something to use them for. I put all of your pictures in them to keep the dust off. I can see them almost as well, too.

Tuesday 29

Letter excerpts

Wow! Was it ever hot today. I had heat prostration or something. At any rate I was flat on my back almost all afternoon. It's a funny thing. Little did I realize not long ago that I'd be sitting on the ground in the middle of miles of wheat fields in (of all places to be) Africa.

I want to know how much Washington has sent [to their hometown bank account]. This allotment stuff never did satisfy me, but it seems to be the only way. Or is it? The money orders seem to be just as effective.

My ship is really in nice shape now. I haven't flown it yet with the new engines, but I'm going to tomorrow. They really run out smooth on the ground. The real test is in the air when I give it full throttles. That really makes those superchargers whine. I won't have any belly tanks on tomorrow, so I can find out if I still have the fastest airplane.

Wednesday 30: 25th Mission

Flight Log: **Souk-el-Khemis/Sciacca, Sicily & return (450 MI)**

P-38-G-15-LO CQ; Demonstration (Test): 2hrs 30mins, 1 landing.

Combat sortie: 3hrs, 1 landing.

Slow time on my ship. New engines.

B-25 escort.

V-Mail excerpts

This month has certainly gone fast. I guess the reason is because we spent most of it in rest camp. At any rate, that helped a lot. Making the time go by is my biggest job. At least I work longer doing that than I do fighting the war.

Oh, yes, as of very recently I have earned another oak leaf cluster for that imaginary medal that I gave you quite a while ago. This makes the fourth one.

July

Thursday 1

Letter excerpts

I got two more letters today. Thanks a million. They were written in March, but that doesn't matter. I like them just as much. They were especially good, because they linked together a few things that weren't quite clear.

The wind is raising the devil with my paper as usual. If this isn't a heck of a place I don't want to see one. About noon it starts getting hot as hell's kitchen and remains that way until about 3 or 4:00, then the whirlwinds begin and last until evening. It was really wonderful down at the mess tent a while ago. A whirlwind hit just as I was filling my plate. It saves pepper. I sure got a kick out of watching the Col. pick straw out of his hash.

Friday 2

Journal

Time has crept its pace along until now. We're about ready for the so-called invasion of the continent. Anyone's guess is good as to when it will start, but it can't be many moons from now. We're getting final instructions as to radio procedure, escape and such. They seem to think it's going to be tough and dangerous. Maybe so, but I think we're ready for it any day now. The sooner it starts, the sooner I get my other twenty-five missions. That's my prime purpose, and my greatest victory is getting myself back in one piece. So far it has been that way, and I'm going to do my best to keep it up. There are a few victory-happy boys here, but I don't figure on being one myself.

Letter excerpts

I got three letters from you today (May 31, June 6 & 9), and they were really swell. . . . Incidentally, I get a lot of my mail in close to three weeks. The two air mails, written on 6-7, got here about ten days ago. . . . Most of my mail does take about a month, though. I think that the last two weeks of that time is spent on the continent of North Africa. . . . Honestly there is a lot of time wasted from the time it hits land 'til we get it. That can't be helped, but it may be the reason the boys fighting the war get their mail first.

   . . . Heber and I both earned our Air Medals, and possibly the first cluster, during the month of April. I now have four Oak Leaf Clusters, and Heber has slightly over three. For some reason things turn out so that I get a little more time than some.

Saturday 3: 26th Mission
Flight log: Souk-el-Khemis/Al Gherra [Alghero], Sardegna & return (620 MI)

P-38-G-15-LO CQ; Combat sortie: 4hrs 15mins, 1 landing.

B-25 escort. Bombed airdrome.

V-Mail excerpts

It's so darn hot or it has been today. It's not going to be this way every day (I keep telling myself). It's ten P.M. and is still too hot to go to bed or anything else. I just finished shaving. It's a pretty good idea to do it at night while the water's hot. It's too cold by morning.

   We've been out practicing for the award day which is to be soon. Personally, I'd almost as soon earn them as go through all of that junk to receive them.

Sunday 4: 27th Mission
Flight Log: Souk-el-Khemis/Malta/Gerbini (near Catania), Sicily & return. (850 MI)

P-38-G-15-LO CQ; Combat sortie: 4hrs 45mins, 1 landing.

B-25 escort. Bombed airdrome.

Damaged 1 RE2001 & 1 ME109.

Journal

Today has been one for the record. We bombed an airfield about 20 mi west of Catania [on the east coast of Sicily]. There was a whole bunch of fighters jumped us, and they got one of us. We got three of them, too. There were about three 38s and four 109s in a big fury, and I broke that up by damaging one Re 2001 [Italian fighter]. Then a 109 got on my tail and was raising h---. I finally shook him and got in a good burst but didn't knock him down.[69]

I was pretty worried about Heber. He didn't get home with the rest of us. Come to find out, he and four others stopped at Cap Bon for gas and took a swim in the Med. While we sweated.[70]

Letter excerpts

This, besides being Sunday (I think) and a holiday at that, has been one of the hardest days I have had to take. The Fourth of July was well-celebrated here-abouts. Fireworks and all such fun!

The African Sirocco is now in progress. . . . that is a wind that blows off the desert, sand, heat and all. The wind is really hot. I never have to heat water to shave with. They have a shower fixed up on the sides of the water truck, and, no fooling, the water was almost too hot to get under. . . . We can dress as we please and no one cares. We even go around in our shorts. Most of us tho' have swimming trunks.

Sometimes I wonder if this being together is good or not. I do more worrying about Heber, but I guess it's worth it. He stopped for gas this afternoon and couldn't get a call to us. I had a reason for being worried. . . .

I've been having troubles with Heber's Arabs. He sent his laundry with them, and they're back with it and he isn't here. More fun! I made 'em wait, but they're getting impatient. They really stick us up for what we get. Their policy is to ask more than they really expect. Well, when the Americans first came here, the prices were so low that unknowingly we paid it and maybe a little extra. Well, we really messed things up for the French. . . .

---

69. "First off . . . at 1040 hrs, was the 97th FS on a B-25 escort to the airfield complex at Gerbini. Enemy fighters were encountered and three destroyed, one probably destroyed and seven damaged, against the loss of a P-38." (Blake 34)

70. Heber likely would have refueled at Korba Airfield, on the eastern coast of the Cap Bon Peninsula 13 km north of Korba.

Monday 5: 28th Mission

Flight Log: **Souk-el-Khemis/Gerbini (near Catania), Sicily & return. (795 MI)**

P-38-G-15-LO CQ; Combat sortie: 4hrs, 1 landing.

B-25 escort. Bombed airdrome. Opposition: only flak.[71]

Tuesday 6: 29th Mission

Flight Log: **Souk-el-Khemis/Biscari, Sicily & return. (720 MI)**

P-38-G-15-LO CQ; Combat sortie: 4hrs, 1 landing.

B-25 escort. Bombed airdrome. No opposition.

V-Mail excerpts

Am I ever tired tonight! It gets so darn hot during the day that it, among other things, just saps the life right out of a guy. There has been a hot old wind blowing all day, but it has cooled down to about ninety degrees and feels really good.

Darling, I've seen two or three things since I came here that I definitely won't have happen to you. I'll even stay here for the rest of my life to prevent it if necessary. Home is a wonderful place.

Letter excerpts
to Butlers

[Richard describes the hot Sirocco blowing.] Heber's been sitting here with a wet towel over his face to keep the straw and trash out of his face. That didn't keep it from piling up all over him, tho'.

Well, we had a big parade and decoration ceremony last evening with all of the trimmings that one could expect under the circumstances. . . . Anyway, we were awarded our air medals along with a few of the oak leaf clusters that we've earned. The Col. congratulated each of us and pinned 'em on.

Heber's been sitting here tearing up his shorts. (That's what Africa does to you.) When I looked up, all he had left was the seams around his waist, etc. He says the rest is to go into his first rug. If you could only see him.

I finally got Heber on my wing. Flying I mean. It's good to have someone there that you know will stay.

---

71. On this date the 97th went out in two groups on separate missions to the same target. Richard was in the first group of 14, since he reports no fighter opposition; the second group encountered heavy and violent fighter opposition. (Blake & Stanaway 81–2)

Wednesday 7: 30th Mission

Flight Log: **Souk-el-Khemis/Gerbini, Sicily & return. (875 MI)**

P-38-G-15-LO CQ; Combat sortie: 5hrs, 2 landings

B-25 escort. From Gerbini east 75 mi, then south to lower Sicily & west—home.

Thursday 8

Flight Log: **Souk-el-Khemis/Misourata [Libya][72]**

P-38-G-15-LO CQ; Cross-country: 2hrs 45mins, 1 landing.

Detached service for two days. [See Friday 9 below.]

Friday 9: 31st Mission

Flight Log: **Misourata/346° & return. (230 MI)**

P-38-G-15-LO CQ; Combat sortie: 2hr 45 mins, 1 landing

Convoy escort. No. 1 man. Heber no 2.

Journal

We've been flying pretty hard lately, shaping things up for what I could tell you about now, but it wouldn't do any good.

Yesterday we loaded up our beds and a skeleton crew on transports and by noon were eating lunch near Misurata [added later in pencil:] Tripoli. What is to come will soon be known by all. At least parts of it will be. The rest will do just as well untold until the war is over.

[The following description from 22 July entry appears to refer retrospectively to this date.]

Heber and I went out together on convoy patrol and were relieved by Spitfires from Malta.

---

72. Richard spells the town as both Misurata and Misourata; located about 200 km east of Tripoli, it's Misrata on current maps.

Of this brief posting in Libya Heber says, "We flew from the north coast of Tripoli to Sicily, escorting everything that was going on: convoys, the bomber aircraft, the aircraft towing gliders, etc. When we got to Malta, Spitfires came up to help us. It was over Sicily that a big, hairy dogfight took place. Really, there was a lot of opposition. Richard got in on some of those fights. My assigned flight was to keep the bombers from being attacked by the enemy fighters. So it was fighter to fighter that day, and we did lose 7 pilots and aircraft that day—including Lt. Stover." (Butler 80)

Misurata

"From 8 through 11 July the air echelons of the 96th and 97th FSs operated from the RAF base at Misurata, on the coast of Libya. This placed the units closer to the Allied invasion convoys that they were to cover as the vessels sailed from Egypt to Sicily. . . ." (Blake 35)

They operated there ". . . under the direction of the RAF's 320 Wing. The pilots flew their P-38s there on July 8 and their crew chiefs were flown in by transports." (Blake & Stanaway 82)

Lt. Fred Wolfe of the 96th described conditions at Misurata: "We had little pup tents to sleep in and had to bring in all of our water and food. We didn't have any water to wash with during our stay of four days. The temperature in the daytime would get so hot we couldn't touch any of the metal on the airplanes, and it would melt the rubber in the cockpit. Scorpions were so numerous that you could always find at least one under anything that was lying on the ground. One of our pilots had one in this parachute and it stung him several times on the back before he could land the plane." (Blake & Stanaway 82–3)

V-Mail excerpts

. . . the decoration ceremony took place. Now I have one each Air Medal. They only present the ribbon over here. It seems they can't get enough of the medals to go around. . . . I hope you've seen a picture of the medal. I haven't, and someone in the family has to know something. You're elected.

I'm getting awfully anxious to be home.

Saturday 10: 32nd Mission

Flight Log: **Misourata/Souk-el-Khemis**

P-38-G-15-LO CQ; Cross-country: 3hrs, 1 landing.

(Sicily attacked.)

Souk-el-Khemis/W. Sicily & return. (750 MI)

P-38-G-15-LO CQ; Combat sortie: 4hrs 15mins, 1 landing.

Fighter sweep.

Operation Husky, the invasion of Sicily, began before dawn this date with Allied landings along the southern coast.

Journal [Retrospective entry from 22 July.]

Then the morning of the tenth we flew back here and went on a fighter sweep in the afternoon.[73]

Sunday 11

Letter excerpts

Well, how is the war going by now? I wouldn't be knowing a thing about it myself. You know we don't have radios, newspapers and such in this part of the country. I have heard rumors of a little change in headlines lately tho'. Is there anything to it?

We went up to the creek for a swim this afternoon.

I did get your birthday greeting, tho'. It was as you figured, slightly early, but who cares? I like it just as much.

This just isn't any place to live. I probably sound pretty sour on the whole situation, but I'm not. I've just spent the last twenty-four hours digging sand out of my eyes, ears, hair and skin. Just an African dust storm is all.

Monday 12: 33rd Mission

Flight Log: **Souk-el-Khemis/near Licata, Sicily & return. (650 MI)**

P-38-G-15-LO CQ; Combat sortie: 3hrs 30mins, 1 landing.

B-26 escort: Agrigento.

Letter excerpts

I have a picture of me and my ship. I should say the ship 'cause you can't see me very plainly. Anyway it's me driving it. Some of the boys in the "foto" section wanted me to buzz them for a shot. They almost missed me.

It has been rather warm for a few days past. Everything almost normal now, though, except my shaving cream. It squeezes out but doesn't lather quite like it used to. Oh, me! Do I have troubles!

Tuesday 13: 34th Mission

Flight Log: **Souk-el-Khemis/Caltanissetta, Sicily & return.[74] (705 MI)**

P-38-G-15-LO CQ; Combat sortie: 3hrs 45mins, 2 landings.

---

73. Of this mission Heber says it consisted of "4 hours and 15 minutes of chasing enemy fighters and escorting bombers" along the north side of Sicily.

74. Heber records that ". . . we escorted bombers over Mt. Etna, Sicily and there were P-40's with us flying around and they kind of got in the way, because single engine planes were what we always shot down, so we had to watch that we weren't on the tail of our own P-40's and make sure that they weren't on our tails." (Butler 80–81)

B-25 escort. Canopy came loose on one side. Held it on and landed with left hand.

V-Mail excerpts

I suppose you know more about the so-called invasion than I could tell you, so we won't go into it. It does seem good, tho', to be able to see a change taking place.

I sent a sort of postcard some time ago that one of the waiters at rest camp made for me out of stamps. I hope you got it. I just sent a picture of what I look like in the air.

Letter excerpts
to Butlers

We just received your letter of June 20th, and in it you mentioned my letters from rest camp. At least some of our mail gets there in a hurry, doesn't it? Now if it would work the same this way, it would be OK. Twenty-two days time really isn't so awful long, tho', I guess.

This country was sort of pretty for a while. During the time the wheat fields were green and the poppies and [bluebells] were in bloom. There is a slight difference in things now, tho'. The wheat is yellow, and everything is hot and dry. . . . For a while we had what they call the Sirocco, a Death Valley–hot wind that lasted for several days.

Wednesday 14: 35th Mission

Flight Log: Souk-el-Khemis/Messina, Sicily & return.[75] **(824 MI)**

P-38-G-15-LO CQ; Combat sortie: 4hrs 45mins, 1 landing.

B-25 escort. Made a complete circle of Sicily. Bombed docks.

Thursday 15

Letter excerpt

Every air mail I have received has come just as quickly as the V letters. Seeing as how my long letters don't get to you very quick. Well, I guess the answer is short V letters. I haven't written more than three V-mails since I was at rest camp. Maybe that's why you haven't been getting any mail.

I just completed for my sixth O.L. Cluster. The fifth was, as you probably know, silver. I already have the medal and three of them. They have to be presented by the Colonel. More parades and stuff.

_____

75. Heber says ". . . we escorted bombers over Messina, Sicily . . . getting ready for the late August–September invasion of the mainland of Italy." (Butler 81)

According to the teletype news, the war for Sicily is coming along according to schedule. . . . You know if one gets a little way up in the air, he can see the whole island. It seems sort of funny to look at a map, then at the original and see that the map is right.

I think someone's been misleading you about these veiled women. They don't wear veils very much.

Friday 16: 36th Mission

Flight Log: **Souk-el-Khemis/Vibo Valentia, Italy & return. (974 MI)**

P-38-G-15-LO CQ; Combat sortie: 5hrs 15mins, 1 landing.

B-25 escort. Vibo Valentia airfield. Circled Sicily.

Letter excerpts

I have received a letter a day from you for several days now. It doesn't take much for me to get into the habit of expecting it every day.

We just received some news that doesn't take too well. It's bad enough to get calluses from a parachute, but now it'll be from sitting on benches (if they can be found). Surprise! We're going to have some more schoolin'. If I could get college credits for all of this, I'd have B.S., A.B. and A.O. attached to my name already. . . .

Our little drive-in theater was on the beam again last night. It gets going about three times a week—sometimes. We can't yell too much, tho', 'cause we get in the best shows. Last week I saw *Syncopation* again. You remember we saw it in Talla-hassee 'cause we were late for the beginning of the *Pied Piper* (I think). By the way, I've seen that again, too. It was worth a second time, tho'. *Andy Hardy's Double Life* is another late show. Last night took it, tho', when *The Daltons Rode* again.

I didn't quite have time to finish [this letter] before the jeep went down to chow, then I needed a slight change in my propeller settings, so I had to get that done.

Saturday 17: 37th Mission

Flight Log: **Souk-el-Khemis/Naples, Italy & return. (900 MI)**

P-38-G-15-LO CQ; Combat sortie: 5hrs, 1 landing.

Flak and fighters.[76]

V-Mail excerpts

Am I ever tired tonight. It's all in one spot, too, almost. . . . Anyway this going so far to work isn't so good. Commuting, I think they call it. I guess I'll have to quit my job and find one closer.

---

76. Heber says they flew bomber escort missions on both 16 & 17 July. (Butler 81)

I got a letter from you dated June 17 this morning and three more this evening mailed 29 & 30 & July 1. That isn't taking so very long at all, is it!

Sunday 18

Flight Log: *C-47;[77] Unknown: 1hr 30mins, 3 landings.*

Made one landing from Co-Pilot seat and two landings as First Pilot.

P-38-G-15-LO CQ; 1hr 30mins, 1 landing.

Pick-a-back. [See letter excerpt below.]

Letter excerpts

Buchanan is here trying to get checked out in the 38, but we can't do it for him. Regulations and such, you know. Heber's taking him up in the pickaback [Piggy-back, a two-seater P-38], and they want me to take his co-pilot up.

. . . while Heber and Buch were up in the piggy, I got checked out in the DC-3. My first landing was perfect, but after that—well, the other two weren't so good.

I did get it on the ground in one piece, tho'. Just in case you don't know what a DC-3 is, it's the twin eng. transport that flies over home all the time. . . . It's a little different to land 'cause the nose is so far out in front but, as they say, if you can fly the 38, you can certainly fly this. It's the truth. Nothing much to it.

Squawkin' Hawk, 82nd Fighter Group's C-47. In all likelihood, this is the plane in which Richard did his C-47 check-out on 18 July 1943. (Courtesy of Steve Blake/Will Hattendorf)

---

77. As we grew up, we four siblings knew the DC3/C-47 only as the "Gooney Bird." Richard flew it all over Europe in 1953–6 and intermittently thereafter.

Monday 19: 38th Mission

Flight Log: **Souk-el-Khemis/Rome, Italy & return.[78] (886 MI)**

P-38-G-15-LO CQ; Combat sortie: 5hrs, 1 landing.
Demo/Test column: 1hr.

B-25 escort. Airdromes at Rome. Thick flak accurate. 4 fighters attacked.

V-Mail excerpt

It's getting lately so that I have to stand up to eat, and that ain't good. Why? Oh, for no special reason. (Ha!)

Tuesday 20: 39th Mission

Flight Log: **Souk-el-Khemis/Monte Covino airdrome [Foggia], Italy & return.[79] (941 MI)**

P-38-G-15-LO CQ; Combat sortie: 5hrs 30mins, 1 landing.

B-25 escort. Airdrome at Monte Covino. A B-25 went down in the water.

Letter excerpts

I just figured out why V letters take so long to get printed and sent on to us. They have a staff of French gals cutting and putting the letters into envelopes. Well, they all can't read English very well (I guess), so it takes time. You know someone has to censor the mail from the States. The regular censors are kept pretty busy with the other mail.

You hit the nail right on the head when you mentioned funny shops. There are a plenty around here. Just between you and me, I think you'd have your fill of shopping around here in one trip. . . . it isn't like home. . . . In the larger cities it is OK in an old-world sort of way. Very few show windows and such.

Thursday 22

Journal

Since I stopped writing, there has been a lot of history made [invasion of Sicily]. Heber and I went out together on convoy patrol [from the temporary base at

---

78. Heber says ". . . we escorted B-17 bombers and hit the railroad yards towards the mountains behind Rome." (Butler 81)

79. Heber reports that ". . . we escorted bombers again to Monte Covino, Italy, which took us 5 hours and 30 minutes." (Butler 81)

Misurata, Libya] and were relieved by Spitfires from Malta. Then the morning of the tenth we flew back here [Souk-el-Khemis, Tunisia] and went on a fighter sweep in the afternoon. That day began the campaign on Sicily which is going right well. For the first few days of the invasion we bombed several points in the island such as the airfields near Catania, Messina and a few hq towns further west. Lately, we've just left the island to the invaders and headed north first to Vibo-Valentia on the instep of the boot, then Naples, Rome and on down this way a little again. One B-25 went in. I watched it. [Added later in pencil:] I met the pilot in Germany.

At Naples we saw a few fighters and a lot of flak but didn't have any trouble. At Rome the flak was accurate and we had trouble with several fighters, but everyone got back. The last mission was to Monte Covino Airfield.[80] Nothing happened except I think two 25s collided. One went right on down and the other landed about five miles offshore in the water. Probably prisoners of war now.

We are having yesterday and today off. Right now I'm resting up from the ride to Tunis yesterday. We went up and took our physicals for 2nd or 1st Lt. We are eligible for the latter, but that depends upon the number in the sqdrn. Here's hoping they come through before we leave the place.

Friday 23: 40th Mission

Flight Log: Souk-el-Khemis/Crotone, Italy & return.[81] **(1070 MI)**

P-38-G-15-LO CQ; Combat sortie: 6hrs 30mins, 1 landing.

B-25 escort. Bombed airdrome.

V-Mail excerpt

Life is hell as usual except for a double feature show last night. "Mr. Deeds Goes to Town" and "White Cargo." I sat on the fender of the recon 'til two this morning before they finished. That's my recreation.

---

80. This was the fourth of a famous series of nine raids on Foggia, which was a consistent target during this campaign because it was the center of a concentration of airfields of strategic importance (including Monte Covino), because it was a rail center and because it was cursed with a concentration of German forces.

81. Crotone is located at the eastern end of the instep of the "boot" of Italy.

Heber records that ". . . we hit the aerodrome at [Crotone], Italy. That was a long mission, because we got into a big, hairy dogfight that took up a lot of time. That mission took 6 hours and 45 minutes there and back." (Butler 81)

Saturday 24

Letter excerpts

I broke the fasteners off two of my clusters. They aren't any good but, just so you will know what they're like, I'm going to send them. You can throw 'em away if you want after you've seen them. I can only get two on the ribbon that I wear, so it doesn't make much difference. They'll give me my other handful before long, I guess. I have four coming. The fifth (a silver one) and two more bronze. If I get ten of them earned I can wear two silver ones, but I hope to get headed for home before that time. . . .[82]

What do you know? It's the 24th of July. What I wouldn't give if I could be there. . . . At the present rate I should be off combat flying status inside of the next month. After that I won't say. All I can do is hope. . . . At any rate I won't be flying as much—in that direction.

Sunday 25

Journal

At this rate I'll never get home. We have only been on three missions this past week, and I have ten more to go. Heber has 18, and I'll probably stay 'til he's through so it'll most likely be six weeks before that happy day.

Pop, the intelligence officer, says they're putting in my recommendation for the D.F.C., so that's a consolation even if I don't get it. I'm holding my breath, tho'.[83]

Letter excerpts

If I stay over here very much longer I'll be an armchair strategist for sure. I was down to Intelligence a while ago trying to tell them how the war should be run, but they don't seem to take much stock in what I say.

The major (at Intelligence) is really a swell guy. I think he worries about Heber and I as much as anyone almost. He seems to have adopted us.

It must be pretty hard for you, because you have no idea at all the way things are. I hate to say because I don't want to disappoint you and myself, too. In short, I have ten missions to go. It may take two or even six or eight weeks. After that I hope to come home.

---

82. A studless bronze oak leaf cluster (without fastener) was taped inside the letter of 25 July.

83. On 23 August Heber wrote to the Butler parents ". . . R[ichard] has two silver [oak leaf clusters] coming & I think he will get the D.F.C. He has been recommended for it." (Letter in author's possession)

V-Mail 1 excerpt
to Butlers

A couple of the boys just came in and wanted one of us to take them to [censored] in the Piggyback. They had a pass and want to get there in a hurry.

V-Mail 2 excerpt
to Butlers

Heber and I rounded up the group photographer yesterday and had our pictures taken in front of our ships.[84] Now if they'll just turn out good, we'll have something to remember by or sompin'. We've been through quite an experience with that piece of flying metal.

Tuesday 27: 41st Mission

Flight Log: **Souk-el-Khemis/Scalea airdrome, Italy & return.**[85] **(885 MI)**

P-38-G-15-LO CQ; Combat sortie: 5hrs 15mins, 1 landing.

B-25 escort. Flight Leader with Heber as 2nd Element leader.

Letter excerpts

Here it is at the end of another day. One nearer to the last.

We have been having one of Africa's rare (every afternoon) dust storms. The dust gets so thick that if you're lucky and have a good tight tent, you can see the person next to you. . . .

Remember that napkin holder I sent from rest camp? It has the name of the hotel and the town where I stayed. It's just a little resort town in Morocco. . . . You asked me where & how I got it. Remember those souvenirs you asked for? Well, I'm trying to get them. . . .

We were up to Tunis a while back on business (personal) and looked the joint over. One of these days I'm going to visit Bizerte,[86] then I'll have been in about every big city (and a lot of small ones) in N.A.

---

84. One of these is the cover photo. In another of them, between Richard and Heber is Urban Stahl, whom they had met on the *Queen Elizabeth* and who was another Sad Sack and signator of the $1 bill. The three of them flew together in the 97th and bunked in the same tent. (Butler 86)

85. Heber says ". . . we escorted B-25's to Scalia, Italy—a five hour flight with little opposition." (Butler 81)

86. Bizerte is the northernmost city of Tunisia.

Wednesday 28

Letter excerpts

Gee whee, am I ever surprised. It has been nice and cool all day with a slight breeze. I hope I'm not talking too soon, because it's almost the time of day that the big wind starts. It's been OK so far, anyway.

I had my ship photographed (with me in front of it, but I didn't cover much up), and it came out pretty darn good. I may even have it enlarged for you when I get back. . . . I don't know whether I dare trust it to the mail or not. . . . My camera doesn't take very good pictures, so we'll have to be careful with these.[87]

There is always the chance that I may not be home for six months, but it is a slim chance and I hope to be through here by the last of August at latest.

Thursday 29

V-Mail excerpts

Boy am I getting lazy. I guess I'll have to take up ditch-digging or something. I've read so many stories that my eyes are going bad.

The mail situation . . . is pretty bad, and that ain't good. One of these days I'm going to come and get my mail firsthand.

Friday 30: 42nd Mission

Flight Log: **Souk-el-Khemis/Rome, Italy airfield & return.**[88] **(860 MI)**

P-38-G-15-LO CQ; Combat sortie: 5hrs, 1 landing.

The Varsity was out (much fighters). No losses.

Letter excerpts

It looks like it's going to be Christmas before I get home. If I don't hurry. I am hurrying, tho', so it won't be that long I keep saying.

If I don't stop talking about coming home, people will think that I'm homesick. (I am.) And on top of that maybe the censor is a spy, and it would never do to tell him that they try to send us home after fifty missions.

I guess I'm ready for rest camp again. I've read about all of the old Reader's Digests. I'll have to go back there and swipe some more.

. . . here comes the mail—I hope.

---

87. This is the iconic photo on the cover, loved and cherished in the family. After Richard went down, Geneil carefully tore her print, apparently so that she could see Richard without seeing her name on the plane behind him; we believe she didn't want to be reminded that "her" plane had potentially killed him.

88. Heber says ". . . we had bomber escort to Cracadia di Roma. That was a fairly long mission—5 hours. . . ." (Butler 81)

"I wish you could have been along to all the places it's taken me. Oscar is my substi-tute mascot." (Butler family collection)

Three friends and P-38 "Geneil" in North African desert. From left, Heber, Urban Stahl, Richard. (Butler family collection)

I did get some more. As long as I get at least one from you [written 7 July], I'm satisfied. . . . It lifted me out of a rut that I've been in for several days. I guess things aren't as black as they seem.

(The daily wind is coming on. I should say, dust storm.)

I'm going crazy waiting for that record you said was coming.

I got a couple of real nice [birthday] cards from the folks.

Saturday 31

Flight Log: P-38-G-15-LO CQ; Demo/TEST: 2hrs, 1 landing.

[1 hour of] Air to ground gunnery within 50 MI of field

1:00 of acrobatics in formation.

Letter excerpts

Boy, am I a lucky son-of-a-gun. (Yes.) I just got three letters from you today. I mean four. I sure have fun reading them.

Heber and I have fun up flying. We went up to fire our guns, at least that was the excuse. We ended up by doing aerobatics in formation. It's a ticklish but thrilling pastime. . . . It's OK as long as you know what the leader is going to do next, but I didn't. I was flying Heber's wing, and he's plumb crazy in an airplane. First he did a loop, then an immelman and a few others. After that, things were getting monotonous, so he started diving thru clouds and looping it. Thrill, thrill. Where was I? Just ask him.

I haven't yet received that record, darn it!

. . . as yet I haven't acquired the bad vice of being victory-happy. . . . In short I've led flights in places where I could have had two or more victories if I had just wanted to set my flight out on a limb. As it is, I just have several damages to my credit. My greatest victory is coming back.

August

Sunday 1

Letter excerpts

I just came past the photo lab . . . and picked up those pictures I told you about. . . . I'll bring them with me when I come . . . we'll hope that you get the pictures pretty soon.

Did you get that small shot that I sent you some time ago? I was about so far off the ground. It may look like I was just taking off, but I was having a little trouble getting the left wheel up. It did come up, tho', shortly after that. It was Heber's ship, and when he starts raving about his good aircraft, I just show him the picture.[89] We have fun even if it doesn't seem like it.

---

89. See photo page 127.

I'm going to stop talking about coming home. That's just too far-fetched to think about ever.

Tuesday 3

Letter excerpt

I got Pop (Capt C, Intelligence officer)[90] . . . to censor a couple of pictures,[91] so here they come. Hope you get them.

Letter 2 excerpts

Today is my lucky day. I got a letter that really came in a hurry. A little quicker anyway. You mailed it on the 22nd. It wasn't a V-letter either.

There's a guy here in the tent who . . . keeps talking about malts with big double dips of chocolate ice cream. And just as I'd finished convincing myself that things of that sort don't exist. I think I'll clunk him with my wash basin (steel helmet to you). He's just been over here for a month tho', so I'll try my best to tolerate him.

That would never do to have a case of assault and battering on my hands. Especially when I'm within one to six months of going home.

If Italy gives up, I may be here for years before I finish my missions. What a future! (Joke)

Wednesday 4

95, 96 and 97 Fighter Squadrons of 82 Fighter Group complete transfer from Souk-el-Arba, Tunisia to Grombalia, Tunisia.

Friday 6

Letter excerpts

I just received two more letters today. The first in quite a while. It seems longer than it really is, but every day is a week when I'm not as busy as it's possible to be.

Gee, do I ever feel dirty, and it can't be helped. We were over swimming at the beach. . . . Riding the waves and such. It's quite a lot of fun, but the water is dirty as heck. The breakers stir up a lot of junk off the bottom.

As yet I haven't run into "Dirty Gerty,"[92] but I hope to look over her old haunts pretty soon. I have been over Bizerte lots of times (who hasn't), but that's as close. One of these days I'll see that town, then I will have been in all of those that you read about.

---

90. Captain Clarence H. Corning ("Pop") was one of the squadron's two S-2 (Intelligence Officers). The other was "Uncle Wally" Reyerson.

91. See photo page 127.

92. "Dirty Gerty" is a reference to a bawdy wartime troop ditty called "Dirty Gerty from Bizerte."

Grombalia

"... on 30 July ... 82nd began moving to its new base of Grombalia, near Cap Bon in Tunisia. This move, which was completed by 4 August, would place the group closer to its targets in Sicily and Italy.

"With the success of the Sicilian campaign by now a foregone conclusion, the 82nd FG's missions alternated between supporting it and attacking strategic targets on the Italian mainland." (Blake 40)

Richard lists Tuesday 3 August as the date for 82 Fighter Group's transfer from Souk-el-Arba, Tunisia to Grombalia, Tunisia. That was probably the day Richard himself made that physical move.

Grombalia sat at the base of the Cap Bon Peninsula about 20 miles southeast of Tunis. The peninsula juts out northeastward into the Mediterranean toward Sicily, which at its nearest point is only 100 miles or so from Grombalia. It was a temporary field for light aircraft (fighters) purpose-built by Army engineers with runway, parking and dispersal surfaces of PSP (pierced steel planking).

"The airfield was located in a vineyard. Sergeant Abberger happily noted in his diary that, 'We no longer are forced to dig foxholes, now that we have aerial superiority over the Mediterranean, and have put up pyramidal tents close to an orchard.' The new field was much cooler than Souk-el-Arba and was by far the group's most comfortable base since it left Britain." (Blake & Stanaway 87)

However, things were not ideal. One of the pilots said this: "In general, the living conditions were austere. The personnel lived in four-man tents with dirt floors. We slept on canvas cots, with an air mattress and a summer wool sleeping bag under mosquito nets. Mosquitos and flies were a continual nuisance. We were often brushing flies off our food, and the DDT dispenser was essential as the nets around one's bunk were thick with masses of mosquitos. Water was scarce, and we washed, shaved and bathed in our helmets." He felt that the food, too, left something to be desired. (Blake & Stanaway, 91)

Still more significantly, he notes that "Maintenance was excellent, under extremely difficult conditions, such as shortages of parts, extreme heat, dust, and sand storms. A number of missions could not be flown because of a shortage of fuel and/or ammunition—or one squadron would fly instead of all three. . . ." (Blake & Stanaway 92) Grombalia was often short of a range of supplies due to its location at the far reach of the distribution system.

Grombalia colonial administration building (Butler family collection)

82nd Fighter Group tents (seen here in Telerghma). In foreground enlisted men's shelter halves over a dugout. Upper-crust pyramidal tents in background. (Courtesy of Steve Blake)

. . . I hope you don't worry about some of the things I put in letters. It's all in the way I feel and, as you know, I always get over my troubles shortly after I tell you.

Saturday 7: 43rd Mission

Flight Log: Grombalia/Crotone, Italy & return.[93] **(840MI)**

          P-38-G-15-LO CQ; Combat sortie: 5hrs, 1 landing.

          B-25 escort Italy.

Monday 9

Flight Log: Grombalia/Tunis/Cap Bon & return. (350 MI)

          P-38-F-15-LO; Cross-country: 2hrs, 1 landing.

          Pick-a-back. Took some of the P-40 boys for a ride.

V-Mail excerpts

Boy, am I happy. I had yesterday off, so a bunch of us went up to what-do-you-call-it. . . . There's a dozen of them up there that we knew.[94] It's not far from here except by road. Take it from me, don't go driving on a road that's been bombed. That was the father of all bumpy roads.

It was dark when I got back last night and what do you think I found. That's right. They were here. The two packages I've been waiting for and three more letters. Honestly, Darling, you couldn't have picked a more perfect present to send me.[95] Gee, I love it. The fit couldn't have been any better either. How did you do it? The record got here, too. I'm going to play it this morning. This is truly a happy birthday.

---

93. Heber recalled that ". . . we had a five hour-long bomber escort. We didn't see any enemies, but some of the other pilots on that run got into some dogfights." (81)

In a V-mail of this date he told his parents ". . . writing . . . is something to do while it is getting dark. After that the show will start. The show tonight is supposed to be *Mrs. Miniver*; it's about the start of the war in England. We are still at it & R & I are still together & having a lot of fun."

94. Possibly some of the Sad Sacks. More of this visit is described at 11 August, Letter excerpts, Paragraph 4.

95. This birthday surprise was Richard's wedding band, as he says explicitly in the V-Mail to his parents below at 11 August.

Letter excerpts

Darn! I don't know what to say. I'm so happy! Yesterday I got a bunch of mail and the record.[96] (I have found a record player, but there are too many droops around. It was just for me, wasn't it? That's what I thought.) Also that birthday present came, but I haven't opened it yet. Oh, no? I have had it on my finger ever since the minute it arrived. Honestly, Darling, it was wonderful. You can't know just what it means to me. I think this has been my best birthday ever, in spite of the circumstances.

How did you know what size my finger is? You must have known 'cause I don't think anyone could guess as perfect as that. That will probably be one of my unsolved mysteries.

When I got here last night (late) there were your letters and package. This flashlight sure takes a beatin', but it's worth it. I can't wait 'til morning to read them. Our mail doesn't come in 'til sort of late here, so you see?

I just received four more letters tonight with pictures, too.[97]

Tuesday 10 (Richard's 24th birthday)

[Richard's Flight Log lists nothing for this date. As he says below, he didn't fly on his birthday.]

Wednesday 11: 44th Mission

Flight Log: **Grombalia/Vibo Valentia, Italy & return. (780 MI)**

P-38-G-15-LO CQ; Combat sortie: 4hrs 15mins, 1 landing.

B-25. Bombed a railroad bridge.

---

96. According to Richard's V-Mail of 11 August to his parents, this was a recording of Geneil's voice; it was made through some sort of special arrangement on a Red Cross device, probably thanks to Geneil's previous employment with that organization. The record is indecipherable.

97. V-mail excerpts: Heber to Butlers (Letter in author's possession)

"Richard and I are together & will be for quite a while.

"Richard received a package from Geneil yesterday; it was his birthday present, and a very nice ring it is. . . . We have moved again, but we are still in North Africa. The place we moved from was a whole lot dustier than it is here and hotter, too, so I kind of sorta like it here. Richard and I aren't flying together now, but we aren't very far apart and we keep track of each other all the time. R. is up flying around having a little fun, and this evening we are going to go up and have a little rat race together."

P-38s on final at Grombalia (Courtesy of Steve Blake/G.T. Lewis)

Letter excerpts

Gee! What a birthday! I didn't fly or anything except typewrite. I was typing a questionnaire a mile long that has to be in triplicate, and the portable wouldn't carry to a second sheet.

It was my birthday, so I took the day off. . . . It was dark by the time I'd finished with the typing.

Sometimes I think of a lot of things that I want you to send, then I think maybe I'll be home before it could get here. If you sent a lot of stuff, then most likely I wouldn't be here when it came. As it is, we know the Army—don't we? All I can do is hope and pray that they don't need me here [or] someplace else when I finish six more missions. That doesn't sound like very many, but it usually takes a long time.

Brentlinger and the rest of them are pretty fed up with the ship they fly and even more with the job they have. (They're training pilots.) I was up there[98] with the piggy and took one of them up. It didn't help their estimation of their ship. I don't need to say—do I?—that our ship is winning the war. (With a little help here and there.)

---

98. Given where P-40s were based then, Brentlinger and company were at either El Haouaria airfield (80 km to the north-northeast at the tip of Cap Bon) or Menzel Heurr airfield (55 km northeast on the eastern coast).

Your letters have been coming in here quite regularly, too (except I didn't get any yesterday). Keep it up. . . .

V-Mail excerpt
to Butlers

A few days ago I received some pretty nice cards, then on the eighth I received Geneil's present. She sent a phonograph record of her voice. . . . That isn't the main thing, tho'. I got a little square box which held another little square box. To make the story short, I found a gold wedding band. It fits perfect, too. . . . I never did ever wear a ring for any length of time, but here's where I start.

Thursday 12: 45th Mission

Flight Log: **Grombalia/Grotone, Italy & return. (825 MI)**

P-38-G-15-LO CQ; Combat sortie: 4hrs 30mins, 1 landing.

B-25. Bombed airdrome. Flight leader.

V-Mail excerpts

Boy, am I tired tonight. I had a tough day on the farm. Being formation leader isn't all romance. A guy has too many guys to watch.

Well, Bob Hopeless and the bunch are coming to give us a laugh this evening. Guess I'd better go get a seat (on a recon fender).[99]

Friday 13: 46th Mission

Flight Log: **Grombalia/Pizzo, Italy & return. (750 MI)**

P-38-G-15-LO CQ; Combat sortie: 4hrs 15mins, 1 landing.

B-25-G. 75 MM in nose. Flight Leader. Lost 1 B-25.

Letter excerpts

Oh me, sometimes I wonder if it's worthwhile. Just as a guy gets the requirements for one thing, they change the whole cockeyed war. In short, I'm in a bad mood, but don't mind me. I'll get over it. Maybe when I get home, I'll be a colonel—or something. Mostly "or something."

I was going to say the mail is coming thru swell, but it suddenly stopped. I haven't had any at all for several days. It seems like weeks.

---

99. Hope and actress Frances Langford entertained 3,000 men at Grombalia that night. (Blake & Stanaway 89)

Heber's mail comes about as fast as mine, only his wife doesn't write nearly as often as mine.

Between the wind and these xoox— flies (one more dead) I'm just about as mad as I can get without blowing my top.

Congratulations. You now have eight clusters on your medal.

Saturday 14

Letter excerpts

We've been chasing around in a jeep finding a place to get our pictures taken. Finally found it. Now if they'll get on the beam and develop them, I'll be almost satisfied.

When I came thro' Nevada from Calif, it was so hot that even in the car it burned my nose. . . . So far Africa hasn't hit me too hard. I wear an oxygen mask when I fly. The rest of my time is spent at the mosque.

Say, where in heck did you get that clipping? This old stuff must cease. We can't have everyone knowing that I'm just a poor henpecked hasbeen. No kiddin' I really got a hoot out of it. Things are in quite a state even in the newspapers. Too bad.

By now I suppose you have the pictures I sent. I mean of the ship. I'm sort of anxious to know just how they came thru.

You know that ticket I sent? The name of the town is on it [Constantine]. It's a street car ticket.

Letter excerpt
Geneil to Richard

Geneil received the famous photo of Richard standing by his plane (referred to in letters of 25 and 28 July). "The moment I saw you standing by the plane I knew just how much more I really loved you. . . . It is so very much like I remember you. . . . It's been many a moon since I cried so joyfully about you.

"I just can't quit looking at the pictures. How did you get my name printed on it? I'm so proud I could scream. I even like the darn old P-38 now. . . . If any picture I have sent you has made you one-half as happy as these did me, then I'm starting a new picture campaign."

Sunday 15: 47th Mission

Flight Log: Grombalia/Catanzaro, Italy & return. (750 MI)

P-38-G-15-LO CQ; Combat sortie:4hrs 45mins, 1 landing.

B-25 escort. Bombed RR junction. Flight Leader.

V-Mail excerpts

All we hear is rumors, but there doesn't seem to be much future in trying to win the war in a hurry. . . . In other words, a guy might as well take it easy 'cause the war will end just about as soon anyway. I often wonder, tho', just what is happening to all of those thousands of pilots that graduate back there every month or so.

I received three more letters and a card from you today. You're all I need to keep me going. I am thankful for a few things, even tho' I don't sound much like it.

Tuesday 17[100]: 48th Mission

Flight Log: Grombalia/Borgia, Italy & return. (810 MI)

P-38-G-15-LO CQ; Combat sortie: 5hrs, 1 landing.

B-25 escort. Bombed highway. Flight Leader.

Journal

We moved from Souk-el-Arba [Tunisia] to Grombalia [Tunisia] on Aug 3. We're right here at the base of the Cap Bon Peninsula. It saves about 180 miles of seat wear on each mission. Just between the six of us, I appreciate it. My resting end feels like I'll never sit down again after today's mission. It was only five hours, just average.

There has been a lot of rumor going one way and another about our going home. I'm just afraid we won't. The latest says they have too many pilots in the states. Personally, I think they could try sending a few of them out or send them back to the farm—over.

I'm going to hold my breath for fair now. We finally got our applic's in for direct commissions. Mine is for 1st Lt. I hope it comes thru. We've certainly earned it.

It isn't pilot fatigue because I'm not tired of flying, but at times I don't give a damn if I never see another airplane. Right now is one of those times. I'll get over it tho'. But if they think they're going to make a two-bit ground officer out of me in some base section (H.Q.), they're crazy. I'm sort of worried about what I am going to be doing after my next two missions. Oh, well, who cares—if I don't go home.

---

100. "American and British ground forces entered Messina" this morning, officially ending the Sicily campaign.

In the evening "There was an air raid alert at Grombalia. . . . The actual target turned out to be Bizerte. . . ." (Blake & Stanaway 90)

Letter excerpts

Oh, me! What a day. Am I fatigue[d]—I am. Not only that—I'm getting just plain tired of everything. . . . I'm just tired, I keep telling myself. Maybe I should take a pilgrimage to Tunis or someplace. . . .

The boys seem to be cornering them up in Sicily while we sit here and watch. A ringside seat, one would say but definitely.

I've only written home once in the past two weeks. Pretty bad, aren't I? Maybe my morale is in a slump.

Yes, I still have my old ship and crew. They're good boys, too. I think the best. There's no doubt about the ship. It has the best record of any ship in the sq. and maybe the group. I'd tell you how many missions it has been on, but that would be telling, wouldn't it?

Wednesday 18: 49th Mission

Flight Log: Grombalia/Pizzo, Italy & return. (700 MI)

P-38-G-15-LO CQ; Combat sortie: 4hrs 15 mins, 1 landing.

B-25 escort. Bombed bridges. Flight Leader.

V-Mail excerpts

Different parts of N. Africa aren't so bad to live in. Those parts are hard to find, but we did succeed once. There is a cool ocean breeze blowing most of the time. Quite unlike most of this o x country. That, I think, is the only good point I've found yet.

For quite a while now yours truly has been a flight leader. A job which is supposed to be held by capt's [captains]. That doesn't mean anything except that one man does the job and the other gets the pay. That's the Army, so we won't try to change it now.

By the time, maybe before, this note leaves North Africa, I will have finished my fiftieth mission. I wish I could figure on going home—don't we?

Editor's Note: I intrude here, departing from the format in order to provide the most complete possible chronological account of the action of Richard's final mission. Here I combine several of Richard's written accounts of the day with my personal background knowledge as well as description from several other sources. Richard's words are shown in bold.

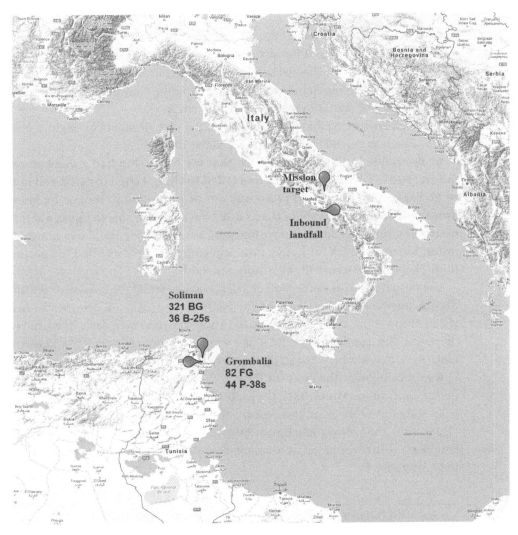

Last mission overview

Friday 20: 50th Mission (incomplete)

Flight Log   **Base/Benevento/Gulf of Naples**

P-38-G-15-LO, CQ; Combat sortie: 3hrs 15mins, 0 landing.

*ME109 confirmed & ME109 & FW190 damaged. Head-on
with 109. We shot each other down. I landed by parachute in
Gulf of Naples & was liberated from the Germans by the 3rd
Army on April 29, 1945.*[101]

---

101. Richard completed this *Flight Log* entry after his liberation.

Forty-four Lightnings of the 96th and 97th squadrons left Grombalia to escort thirty-six B-25s of the 321st Bomb Group from nearby Soliman on a mission targeting the railyards near Benevento, Italy, 30 miles northeast of Naples. Richard says the 82nd Lightnings joined the bombers "over the Gulf"; I take that to mean the Gulf of Tunis, not far to the north of both bases.

As had been the case for some time, Richard was the leader of his flight, a position normally occupied by an officer well above his rank.

At the rendezvous point I noticed that my No. 4 ship had a mechanical failure, and his nose-wheel door had failed to close. I tried to call & tell him to go back, but either [his] radio was out of commission, too, or he knew more about running my flight than I did. I haven't been able to figure out just what was wrong, because after we had gone on course for about two hundred miles, he turned back for home. (Mission completed.)[102] #3 filled in another flight, leaving me a rear flight w/only 2 aircraft.[103]

The formation crossed the Gulf of Salerno and reached the coast near Amalfi. "Shortly after the bombers crossed the coast around 1:30, ten Me 109s passed ahead of and above them. The 109s made a 360° turn and then came down out of the sun on the rear flights of 82nd P-38s, which were straggling. . . ."[104] Elsewhere, Blake says they "shot down a straggling 97th pilot."[105]

As we came over the coast of Italy, we were attacked by fighters & were under continuous attack until they left the coast outbound.[106]

"In spite of the attack on their escort, the B-25s reached the target and made a good run. The railroad junction at Benevento was well covered with hits, and buildings north of the target were seen in flames as the bombers turned and dived to pick up speed.

---

102. Richard Butler, "My Story in Short," 13 May 1945, Camp Lucky Strike (St. Valery France). This is a separate sheet found folded inside the *Wartime Log*.

I have omitted the No. 4 man's name, since I think Richard would wish it. Of him, Heber says ". . . . he refused to return until he had crossed the bomb line, so he could get credit for a combat mission. Then he turned around and came back, leaving Richard's flight group shorthanded, with only himself and his wingman. . . . The German fighters immediately honed in on the two lone fighters. . . ." (Butler 82.)

Ironically, Heber flew that day as a relief pilot and could have filled a slot in Richard's flight had he known he was needed; but the relief pilots had already turned back when Richard's No. 4 dropped out. Heber was waiting at Grombalia, watching for his brother's return.

103. After the war Richard penciled in some additions to the *Journal*; this passage is from a brief account he wrote at that time on the back of the last page.

104. Blake & Stanaway 90.

105. Blake 41.

106. Richard Butler, "My Story in Short."

"During the withdrawal another group of about fifteen enemy fighters—Me109s, Fw190s and at least one Italian type—again jumped the P-38s from the rear. . . ."[107]

One detail mentioned nowhere else emerges in Heber's letter of 5 September to Geneil and the Butler parents. For those of us who know and love the man, this point has great significance in Richard's story. The emphasis added is mine. ". . . after the bombing & [as the squadron's flights] were leaving the target, some-one called for help in the rear of the formation. So Richard took his flight[108] back & helped the man out & then proceeded on."[109]

"F/O Richard Butler . . . had already damaged an Fw190 and an Me 109 when he got into a head-on duel with another 109 west of Avellino."[110]

Two fighters from a formation of four continued the attack & I turned into them with my wingman. One of the enemy turned away, but the other kept coming in a head-on attack with me. I further backed up the fact that American planes have the best firepower in the world. His canopy flew off with other bits at about one hundred yards, then his left wing came off. To the best of my knowledge the bulk of [his] ship went under me, but the wing went over my ship. I thought I could be fairly certain of a victory from the engagement.[111]

"Second Lieutenant Al Schneider, then a novice combat pilot, was Richard Butler's wingman that day. Many years later he still remembered his fright at not being able to see the German fighters which were being called out on the radio. He stayed close to Butler and saw the smoke of his leader's guns trailing back from the nose of the P-38. Then he saw the Me 109, which came at them head-on until it was only fifty yards away. At that point a wing separated from the Messerschmitt's fuselage and Schneider watched in helpless fascination as they tumbled away in opposite directions and the two Lightnings flew between the broken pieces."[112]

When I started to feel my wounds, I found that he had been using real bul-lets, too. The only thing I noticed to my right was a hole about a foot from the cockpit in the leading edge of the wing. It was about eighteen inches long and six? wide, a strip of metal laid back over the top of the wing. The left eng. was pretty well shot up. . . .[113]

---

107. Blake & Stanaway 90.

108. A flight of two aircraft, rather than the four he should have had.

109. Heber Butler letter of 5 September 1943. Copy in author's possession. Presumably, this information came to Heber from Lt. Schneider, Richard's wingman.

110. Blake & Stanaway 90.

111. Richard Butler, "My Story in Short."

112. Blake & Stanaway 91.

113. Among "various and sundry other things," the engine lost coolant, according to Richard's letter of 12 May 1945.

At roughly this point in the action Richard and Lt. Schneider were passing along the southern flank of Vesuvius on their right.

I feathered [the left engine], but it soon started to burn anyway. The smoke entered the cockpit & I let the windows down and released the canopy, but it wasn't enough. I couldn't see & soon started to cough. My glasses weren't sufficient for open cockpit flying so, even tho I tried it, standing up was no good either.[114]

By now Richard had overflown Pompeii and crossed the coast out over the Gulf of Naples with Castellammare not far off his left wing. He was moving toward Capri parallel to the Sorrento Peninsula, which encloses the southern side of Castellammare Harbor and the Gulf of Naples. "Lt. Schneider then noticed that Butler's left engine was smoking. The latter's radio was also apparently damaged, as Schneider could not raise him. He stayed with his element leader until he bailed out. . . ."[115]

About that time the fire burst out & lay back over the turbo, so I figured I'd had it. I pulled up into about a 20 degree climb & stood up to get out. The wind hit me then & pinned me to the cockpit. In my struggle I caught my right foot between the seat & window, so when I got free & fell out it skinned my shin & twisted my right knee pretty badly but nothing permanent. It probably saved my neck anyway, because I'm sure I was going too fast at first to go under the boom like I finally did.[116] . . . I went between the booms. I wouldn't do it as a regular procedure, tho'.[117]

This is where I left old C.Q.#432326 A.C. P-38-G-15-LO. The best ship in the outfit did a wing-over to the left and buried itself just off the Isle of Capri in the Gulf of Naples not far from where I finally hit a belly-gutter in the water. That was funny, come to think of it. After I got out & the ship drove off without me, it was so quiet that I didn't realize I was falling for several seconds. All this time I'd been watching the ship half-roll & start down. When I realized what was happening, I pulled the ring, watched the silk string out, billow, felt a jerk, changed ends, then passed out when the chest snap hit me on the chin someplace. All in all it was a very enjoyable ride down after I got my senses back.[118]

The Missing Air Crew Report states that Richard went down about 1400 hours under a slight haze up to 8000 feet. "Richard's parachute opened OK and he landed in a spot where he would be picked up soon . . . he is alive & well; he could

114. Richard Butler, "My Story in Short."

115. Blake & Stanaway 91.

116. Richard Butler, "My Story in Short."

117. Richard Butler, letter of 12 May 1945, Camp Lucky Strike. Copy in author's possession.

118. Richard Butler, "My Story in Short."

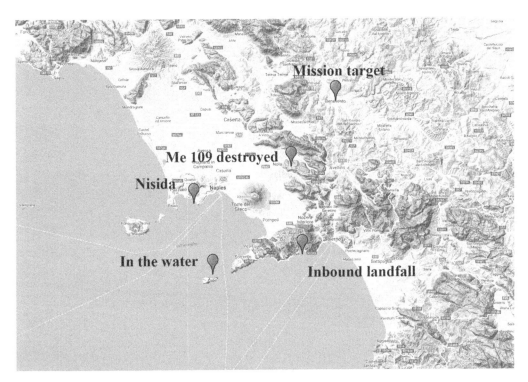

Last mission detail

not have been hurt and still flown his plane so far & when it became necessary he was able to bail out safely."[119]

I hit the gulf of Naples very easy-like after being knocked out by the parachute snap. I had quite a knot on my chin for a few days. . . .[120] That would have been off the northern coast of Capri four or five miles west of the tip of the Sorrento Peninsula.

An "Iti" patrol boat picked me up & took me to Naples where I was kept on a small island [Nisida] west of the city. . . .[121]

Decades later, Heber told his son Michael how, that evening after Richard was reported missing, Heber came upon Richard's crew chief sitting on an empty fuel barrel and weeping as if his heart would break. Heber went on to explain that ground crews, the chiefs in particular, were generally older men than the pilots and often looked on their pilots as a father would his son.[122]

---

119. Heber Butler, letter of 5 September 1943.
120. Richard Butler, letter of 12 May 1945.
121. Richard Butler, "My Story in Short."
122. Michael Butler, personal conversation, Summer 2013.

3
PRISONER
OF WAR
1943

Prisoner of the Italians

After the arrival of Richard's group at Stalag Luft III, American POW staff in the compounds wrote contemporary reports based on interviews with those men. "The Italian policy in handling air prisoners was patterned to a great extent on the German plan. . . . The sequence was on the whole: (1) capture, (2) Air Force interrogation and incarceration in nearest civil or military jail, (3) subsequent transfer to either the quarantine camp at Poggio [Mirteto], Italy, or . . . confinement at the nearest Air Force HQ., (4) final arrival at Chieti." (South Annexes 1172)

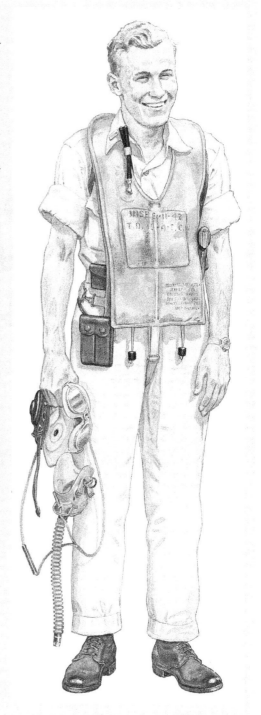

How Richard would have been dressed
when he went down.
(Courtesy of Osprey Publishing)

Introduction to
History of Center Compound

"It is paradoxical that 12,000 American flying officers have lived to tell the story of life inside Germany after a total war that struck at the defenceless and innocent and was no respecter of persons. Walking from under the shadow of death that covered Nazi Germany, these men have lived an experience unique in the history of the United States. . . . for the first time in our history thousands upon thousands of Americans have been the prisoners of a foreign power.

"How they lived and thought, how they were shaped into a military organization, how they struggled to escape physically and mentally from the atmosphere of the barbed wire, is the substance of this report. . . .

"The prisoners of war were the forgotten men, the 'missing-in-action' who returned. Although they were scratched from the rolls of their combat organizations, they continued to write letters home, and live for the end of the war with a degree of intensity unequalled in the combat zones. . . ." (Mulligan, Burbank and Brunn 5–6)

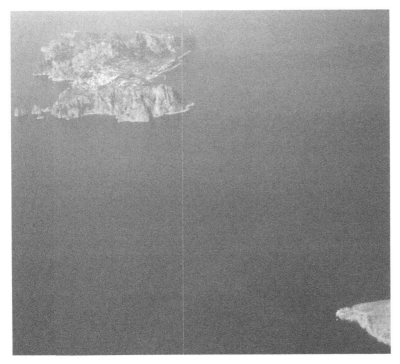

Richard's 1956 photo of Capri, shot en route to Izmir, Turkey. Richard and his P-38 would have hit the water somewhere off the north coast of Capri (to the island's right in this view). Western tip of Sorrento Peninsula can be seen bottom right. (Butler family collection)

Nisida

Nisida is a tiny circular islet on the south end of the Gulf of Pozzuoli just a few hundred yards from the seafront west of central Naples. It's a volcanic caldera, the seaward side of which drops away spectacularly to create a circular bay with a small opening to the sea. The landward side rises steeply several hundred feet from the water; from the causeway a road winds back and forth to climb to the top. On Nisida's highest point, at the northern end of the landward side, is a nineteenth-century Bourbon prison which had become an Italian state penitentiary; this is where Richard was kept.

A three-sided harbor is formed by the island, the twentieth-century causeway and the mainland. Here was the seaplane station Richard mentions; it had a large hanger with crane, several smaller buildings, a long quay and a slipway. The base housed the Italian CANT Z.501 (a single-engine, high-wing flying boat with crew of 4–5) and is also listed as a Luftwaffe airfield. Richard's description suggests that the Red Cross used it as well.

Nisida (Butler family collection)

1943

August

Friday 20

Log

Parachuted into the Gulf of Naples and was picked up & taken prisoner by an Italian patrol boat. Later searched, questioned & taken to a Red Cross seaplane base[1] where I was put under guard by the Carabinieri.

Saturday 21

Log

I was given a shave by the village barber.

Sunday 22

Log

I was taken to the air raid shelter, where I met Corson,[2] Church, Rickless, Heinberg, Vandergrift, Marks and Hammond, also some enlisted men.

---

1. This is certainly the Italian seaplane base at Nisida. It seems Richard was taken directly to Nisida after being pulled from the water near Capri and was subjected to search and preliminary questioning after reaching Nisida. In his 13 May 1945 account Richard says, "I was kept on a small island west of the city for three days" and that he spent his first night alone.

2. See first page of the *Quaderno* in *Appendix F*.

Corson says "First met Dick in an Italian Pen [penitentiary, as he later called it] located on an island connected by a causeway in the middle of the Bay of Naples. . . ." Herb was a B-26 navigator/bombardier who went down the day after Richard did. He goes on to say that "Dick presented some problem to enemy & Germans later inasmuch as he had no crew member to vouch with (common fighter pilot problem)." (Corson letter)

Herb and Richard moved together through the Italian camps and on into Germany. They lived together in Combine G during their time in Stalag Luft III, along with Curtis Church (the same Church Richard mentions here).

Herb kept in at least annual touch with Richard and, later, with Geneil all through the years until his death in 2010. (See his description of Richard as perceived by his fellow POWs at 4 February 1944.)

104

Chronological Order of Events.

Aug. 20, '43. Parachuted into the gulf of Naples and was picked up & taken prisoner by an Italian patrol boat. Later searched questioned & taken to a Red Cross Sea plane base where I was put under guard by the Carabineri.

Aug. 21, '43 I was given a shave by the village barber.

Aug. 22, '43 I was taken to the air raid shelter where I met Corson, Church, Rickless, Heinberg, Vandergruth, Hanks, and Hammond also some enlisted men.

Aug. 24, '43 After two more nights of running down the hill to the raid shelter we were awakened for our last ride in Naples at 3:00 A.M. That over we piled into a bus and started for Rome but another raid caught us about half way across town. Twenty or thirty miles from Naples the bus broke down so we had a five hour wait for another. We arrived in Roma that evening in time to see part of the town. A few comical things too. Nine-thirty P.M. found us at Poggio-Mirteto in a two by four room with nine, maybe ten, for ten at us.

Aug. 28 '43 My first Red Cross parcel (Canadian).

Sept. 8, '43 Went from Poggio to Chieti by delux bus service. Were searched again then let into the compound where I met Phillips from my group. He had talked to Hober since I had. This place was like a college campus in comparison.

Sept. 9, '43 Italian Armistice "You Are Free". One can readily imagine how we acted.

First Journal page from the Wartime Log. *(Richard M. Butler papers MSS 8849, L. Tom Perry Special Collections, Harold B. Lee Library, Brigham Young University)*

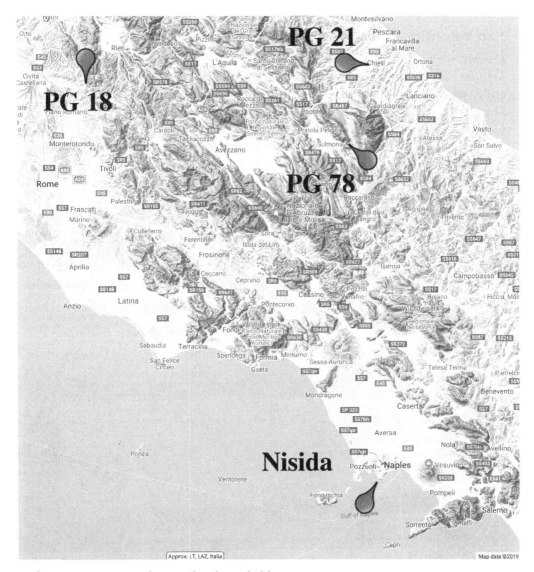

Italian prison camps where Richard was held

San Valentino/Poggio Mirteto (PG 18)

Corson says he and Richard were interned in the same cell of a monastery. (Corson letter) Actually the Convento di San Valentino near Poggio Mirteto, this was Prigione di Guerra (PG) 18, a processing center in the mold of the Germans' Dulag Luft.

The San Valentino convent was "a three-story stucco structure," where POWs slept in 5'x10' rooms (formerly nuns' quarters) "with one large, barred window," "a straw mattress on the floor" and a "small blue light . . . in the ceiling." (Caine 232) Views from the convent are expansive and beautiful, thanks to its ridgetop placement in the wooded foothills overlooking Poggio Mirteto and a wide valley to the west.

Richard's group crossed paths with Sonny Fassoulis, a navigator who arrived in the late evening of 4 September; the next morning he "looked out his window into a tree-covered, walled courtyard and saw several prisoners taking their . . . morning walk. Most, he noted, were airmen; they were still wearing their flight suits or jackets." (Caine 234)

The food issue was "very small," and no clothing was available. "Sanitation facilities were considered inadequate." "The last American officers to reach Chieti from here left Poggio September fifth, 1943." (South Annexes 1179–80)

The Convent of San Valentino today (Butler family collection)

Tuesday 24

Log

After two more nights of running down the hill to the raid shelter, we were awakened for our last one in Naples at 3:00 A.M. That over, we loaded into a bus and started for Rome, but another raid caught us about half way across town. Twenty or thirty miles from Naples the bus broke down, so we had a five-hour wait for another. We arrived in Roma that evening in time to see part of the town. A few comical things, too. Nine-thirty P.M. found us at Poggio-M[i]rteto in a two-by-four room with nine mattresses for ten of us.[3]

Saturday 28

Log

My first Red Cross parcel (Canadian).

September

Sunday 5

[This date Richard's group left the Convent of San Valentino (PG 18) near Poggio Mirteto and traveled to PG 21 near Chieti. (South Annexes 1179)]

Wednesday 8

Log

Went from Poggio to Chieti[4] by deluxe bus service. Were searched again, then let into the compound, where I met Phillips from my group.[5] He had talked to Heber since I had. This place was like a college campus in comparison.[6]

Thursday 9

Log

Italian Armistice. "You Are Free." One can readily imagine how we acted.[7]

---

3. Corson recalled "constant bombing—it was really a mess." He remembered traveling to Poggio Mirteto after the Italians "paraded us around Naples in trucks, like in the zoo, showing the people the American gangsters. . . ." (Corson /Thobaben 151–2)

4. The Poggio-Mirteto/Chieti/Sulmona/Stalag VIIA/Stalag Luft III itinerary seems to have been a common one for downed Allied fliers captured in southern Italy at this time.

5. This was likely Eugene Phillips of the 95th Squadron, who went down on 25 August.

6. This impression would not last.

7. The armistice between Italy and the Allies was announced on Italian radio and heard in the camp at 2030 that evening. (Lett 192)

Chieti (PG 21)

PG 21 was located in the river valley below and northwest of Chieti and 12 miles west of Pescaro on the Adriatic coast. It was situated among fields near the Pescaro River and had expansive mountain views to the north and of Chieti and its cathedral on a hilltop above in the other direction.

The camp consisted of a huge walled rectangle with six large, white stuccoed brick barracks built three on each side of a large open oblong; each was U-shaped around a central courtyard facing the 13' perimeter wall. The gates were at the north end of the compound; arriving Kriegies saw Chieti on its hilltop directly ahead with the large curve-roofed cookhouse at the far end of the compound and the tall squarish water tower in the far right corner. The first building on the left contained offices, hospital and a small chapel; first on the right was the barrack housing the Italian guards. The remainder of the compound was isolated behind wire fencing.

At the time of Richard's arrival ". . . we are getting practically no food from the Ities, and [Red Cross] parcels have been reduced to a half per week." (Lett 187)[1] For the entire POW population, drinking water "was provided by 2 slow-running taps. . . . It was customary to fill all available Klim cans, jugs, canteens, etc, in the A.M. and thus provide oneself with a water supply for the day and night." Red Cross clothing "was dispensed largely to incoming American officers," so

Richard may have added to his lightweight flight clothes on arrival here. He probably also bought his *Quaderno* notebook from the camp shop, where toiletry essentials were sold along with such things as cardboard suitcases. (South Annexes 1185–91)

With the armistice, senior officers in several camps in southern Italy gave their men the option of taking to the hills. At PG 21 the Senior British Officer, Lt. Col. William Marshall, forcibly kept them there, citing orders issued many months before and based on assumptions of very different conditions. Despite the increasing presence of German troops in the area, the stay-put order was enforced; in fact, the Senior American Officer told his men that "courts martial proceedings would be instituted against violators of the order," and "POW personnel [were] posted as guards and put under orders to stop any attempt at escape by other POWs." (South Annexes 1194)

". . . shortly after midnight on 20/21 September, the Germans arrived in force to take over Campo 21. They were paratroopers, dressed in full battle order, and equipped with light automatic weapons. . . . The men awoke next morning to find themselves in custody, now guarded by seasoned German paratroopers who would clearly stand no nonsense. Each sentry box atop the wall now contained two tough, steel-helmeted German paratroopers, instead of a single slovenly Italian sentry. For most it was a devastating realization." (Lett 214)

---

1. Mystery writer Michael Gilbert was a British inmate of PG 21. He gives a vivid picture of camp life in his 1952 novel *The Danger Within* (*Death in Captivity* in the UK), where PG 21 becomes Campo 127.

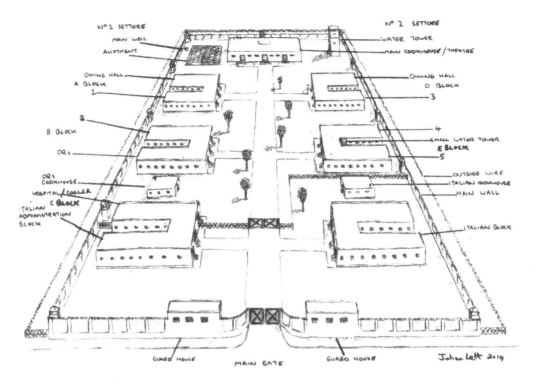

Outline plan of Campo P.G. 21 at Chieti Scalo.

PG 21 plan (Courtesy of Brian and Julian Lett)

PG 21 The wall still stands. (Butler family collection)

Fonte d'Amore/Sulmona (PG 78)

Sulmona is southwest and inland about 50 km from Chieti; PG 78 is actually located in the village of Fonte d'Amore, a few kilometers north of and above Sulmona on the skirts of bare and steeply rising Montagne del Marrone, which thrusts abruptly up from the valley.

From the camp entrance on the south, four rows of large, brick & stucco garage-like buildings stretched northward down the mountainside, each with a few small, high windows and a single door. Each was roughly 20' × 100' with 12'–15' peaked tile roofs; 45 of them, usually in groups of four, were interspersed with infirmary, latrines, guard stations, stores and "punishment" blocks.

By the account in the South Annexes, each compound of four barracks was surrounded by glass-topped walls and comprised an area of 15,000 square feet where "approximately 500 men were confined 24 hours per day." The entire camp was surrounded by "a 16-foot brick wall and outside was a series of 4 barbed-wire fences. Between the third and fourth fences were located the sentry boxes, spaced about 100 feet apart.... a tower stood in the center of the upper camp level" from which guards could see into all compounds. The camp "was dirty and well populated with rats and insects."

Conditions worsened after the arrival of the PG 21 prisoners, but food was plentiful under the German administration. Latrines were essentially holes in the ground and water was scarce. (South Annexes 1195)

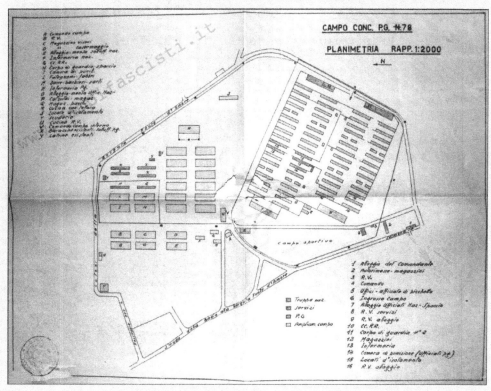

PG 78 Plan (www.campifascisti.it)

Monday 13

Telegram to Geneil

I regret to inform you that the commanding General North African area reports your husband Flight Officer Richard M Butler missing in action since twenty August. If further details or other information of his status are received you will be promptly notified.   Ulio, The Adjutant General

Tuesday 14

Log

Italians evacuate the camp (PG-21). It was comical to watch those "Ites" going over the wall. They tried to get us to come along with them, but we weren't going to be suckers. We're waiting for the Allies.

Saturday 18

Log

Germans take over P.G. 21. After doing our own guard duty for several days, the Jerry paratroops took over the posts. "Wir es Gehabt." [We have it.][8]

Tuesday 21

Telegram to WC Horsley, American Red Cross, Brigham City Utah

Regret no additional information received concerning whereabouts Flight Officer Richard M Butler when further reports received his wife will be notified immediately. Pleased to inform you casualty reports received to date do not contain name of Flight Officer Heber M Butler.   Ulio, The Adjutant General

Thursday 23

Log

Transferred to P.G. 78 at Sulmona. At 5:00 A.M. we were awakened and told to prepare to move out.[9] As we were loading on the trucks, one of the "Goons" opened up with several rounds of machine gun fire. (Harmlessly, of course.)[10]

---

8. It would seem that Richard was himself on sentry duty that night given his quotation of the paratroopers. As to the date of the takeover, he diverges from Lett and the South Annexes account, both of which put it on the night of 20–21 September.

9. All the Americans were moved in this first group to leave PG 21 for the Fonte d'Amore (Sulmona) camp, PG 78. (South Annexes 1194)

10. The Carabinieri marshall who escorted us through the former PG 21 in Chieti told us a similar story during our visit there on 31 August 2017. He showed us marks high up in the bricks of the water tower which he said were made by German machine

Remnants of PG 78 today (Butler family collection)

Then they went back into the camp and asked for ten more Englishmen. That caused quite a "flap" among them, as can well be imagined.

Thursday 30

Letter excerpt
Grandma Butler to Richard

[From Grandma Butler's typed letter to Richard of Sunday 21 November 1943. Spelling, punctuation and capitalization are original.]

Heber arrived in Salt Lake 9/30/43 at 8:30 A.M., by plane, Father, William, Vida and Myself met him, it was hard to meet one when we were expecting two. But we had rec'd a letter from Heber before, also Geniel Rec'd a telegram on the 14th of Sept stating that you were missing.

---

gun bullets fired to discourage hidden British POWs from further delaying the loading of trucks bound for PG 78.

October

Friday 1

Log

After a week of ducking appels [roll calls],[11] we were finally herded together and taken by truck to the station where boxcars were waiting to take us to der Vaterland. That, by the way, isn't the best mode of travel.

Saturday 2

Log

Twenty-eight less men this morning. The car behind us had one window without grating on it. More than that actually got away out of other cars & still more later on. We tried "3."

Monday 4

Log

My thirteenth anniversary[12] and almost my last. We pulled into Bolzano, Italy[13] about 11:30, and the siren went off at 12:00 noon. The Forts[14] lined up on us shortly after. We were right in the middle of a small RR yard. Even the hope of them hitting another part of the yard was gone. They couldn't miss us. But it so happened that they were after the RR bridge about seventy-five yards from the train. It also happened that every ship hit the target. They couldn't have been dropping more than five hundred-lb.'ers, being that close to us or we'd have suffered some concussion. We picked up several shrapnel holes in some of the cars tho'. "Bucking Box Cars."[15]

---

11. Although the German word is spelled with the double-L, Kriegies generally used the more common French spelling. With the exception of his last use of the word, Richard follows this convention.

12. The anniversary reference is to the number of months since his marriage.

13. Bolzano is in the South Tyrol province of Italy, near the Swiss, Lichtenstein and Austrian borders about 100 km south of Innsbruck.

14. "Flying Fortresses," B-17s

15. The South Annexes account says they had previously escaped any Allied "train busting," but just after arrival in Bolzano they experienced the near miss Richard describes. Corson called it "A very close call. Worse than bailing out in Aug." (Corson letter) In 1984 Richard was asked to describe one of his worst experiences as a prisoner. He responded, "Being bombed by our own forces while on a box car train in Bolzano, Italy. . . ." [See page 377.]

"The prisoners were placed in a large courtyard and slept in the open" that night. "Some civilians looted the evacuated rail cars, but the Germans upheld and protected prisoners' rights and property by shooting looters.

"The prisoners were returned to their cars on the morning of Oct. 5, 1943, and after waiting on the siding for several hours, the train pulled out at 1:15 PM. At 1:25 PM a

Sulmona to Moosburg: The Rail Journey

The South Annexes account has the Americans leaving PG 78 by truck on 2 October rather than on the first; I believe 2 October is the correct date. Richard's account and that of the South Annexes agree on 4 October as the date of the Bolzano arrival.

"On arriving at the [Sulmona] station, men were provided with 3 days rations of Italian bullybeef and hardtack, and a full [British Red Cross] food parcel per man, plus a wooden slop bucket; after which the cars were loaded with 35 men to each car and locked. These cars were German, Italian, and French in make, and varied greatly in size and construction" from wood to steel. (South Annexes 1199)

From Sulmona they traveled either east to the Adriatic coast and along it northward to Bologna or west to Rome and north from there via Florence to Bologna. From the South Annexes we learn that they spent most of the night of 3 October on a siding; that would likely have been somewhere near Bologna.

From there, only the one route was possible: through Verona and up the ever more narrow Adige River valley, passing vineyards and orchards as the Alps rose higher and more precipitously around them. Finally, they passed through Bolzano, barely escaping with their lives, and climbed up over the Brenner Pass, descending to Innsbruck and beyond.

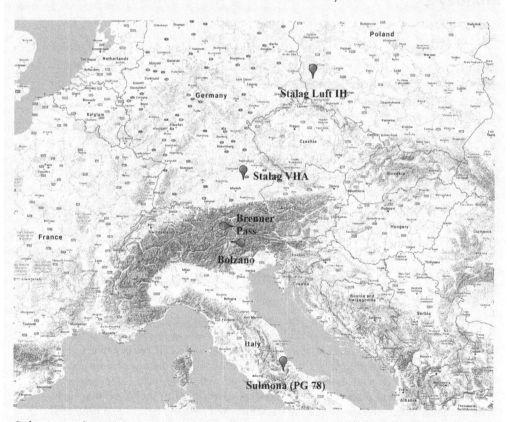

Sulmona to Sagan

The Bolzano railway bridge today (Butler family collection)

Tuesday 5

Log[16]

Through the Brenner Pass to Innsbruck. They told us this morning, after spending the night on a cement sidewalk, that we were to be marched about 35 km to a camp and would go on to Germany sometime later. After we'd discarded our excess stuff, we were marched to the train and took off for Brennero. We'd spent the night in the courtyard of an apartment. Corson and I tossed to see who got the outside of the walk. It was good to have the bed hold still for a change.

Wednesday 6

Log

Arrived at Moosburg, Bavaria (Stalag 7A).[17] A sgts' camp with every nationality in the world, including Siberians and Mongolians. Here we were kept for a

---

formation of Fortresses hit the station and demolished it." The trainload of Kriegies arrived in Innsbruck that night and were in Moosburg the next morning. (South Annexes 1200–1)

16. This entry is a bit confusing; it makes sense if one reads the first sentence as an introductory summary. They slept the night of 4–5 October on the streets of Bolzano, then reboarded the train to go on over the Brenner Pass to Innsbruck on the 5th.

17. Moosburg is about 40 km northeast of Munich.

Stalag VIIA, Fall 1943

When George Millar arrived in Moosburg on 21 September, he found the town "small and muddy" set in a "leaden, soggy landscape." The camp entrance was an "imposing oak and barbed-wire gateway." "The first thing we saw . . . was a German guard strutting along with a fierce-looking Alsatian police dog held on a long chain." (164-5) ". . . Stalag 7-A was extremely crowded. It was filthy and run inefficiently." (Daniel 44)

"There was an asphalt street running the whole length of the camp, with barracks on both sides." (Daniel 42) "Stammlager VIIA was cut up into many Lagers separated from one another by barbed wire and locked gates. This arrangement was designed to keep men of different nations or ranks separated." (Clark 159) "The compounds were separated by double fences of long-pronged barbed wire stretched on oak saplings 14 ft. high. Between each double fence was an 8-ft.-wide strip of criss-cross low wire with loose barbed wire laid on the top." (Millar 168)

"At intervals the central roadway passed through guarded gateways, and the gateway to each compound was also a sentry post. Around the perimeter, where the scrubby pine-woods had been razed for some hundreds of yards to give a field of fire, the German sentry posts were little log cabins raised high on stilts." (Millar 165)

"Each barrack was divided into two sections, each section bedding about 250 men with a sort of wash room in the middle. The wash rooms consisted of a cement floor with drains and two or three cold water faucets. There was always plenty of cold water. . . . The old-fashioned toilets were outside. They had to be emptied once or twice a week." (Daniel 42) "The beds were three-tiered erections of unseasoned deal fixed together in batches of eighteen; that is, with six people sleeping on each tier. . . . Each of us was issued with one tattered and verminous blanket." (Millar 165)

"We filled out more forms for the Germans, who told us that they were not only for their records, but also so they could notify our families of our whereabouts. We received better rations than we had eaten up to that time. We were given Red Cross parcels. . . ." (Daniel 42)

Stalag VIIA, October 1943 (Lt. Gen. Albert P. Clark Collection, SMS 329, Clark Special Collections Branch, McDermott Library, US Air Force Academy)

week in mighty dirty and crowded conditions.[18] We received our first American RC parcel (No. 9). I also sent out a card and telegram to Geneil which arrived March 1, 1944.

Thursday 7[19]

Log

Left Moosburg on a third-class train. Much better even tho' I did have to sleep on the coat rack. I really got ribbed about that, but I surely sawed the logs.

---

18. Trains carrying arriving prisoners were switched onto a branch line which took the Kriegies close to the camp. I believe they arrived at the small 2-story station photographed by Richard during our 1956 visit. (See photo page 324.)

19. The departure date is incorrect. Richard says they were kept at VIIA for a week, and Corson's account agrees. The *Log* entries at this point were retrospective and subject to approximation. If for no other reason, the timing is impossible because it would have required an overnight turnaround for all the Nazi processing. 13 October would be the likely date.

Moosburg to Sagan: The Rail Journey

Clark traveled from Dulag Luft near Frankfurt and arrived much earlier than Richard, but he, too, traveled to Sagan by third-class passenger coach. "We were very crowded in this car and were heavily guarded. Our shoes were taken from us for the duration of the journey, and we sat on wooden seats for the two or three days and nights that it took to reach Sagan. The seats were in pairs, back to back, so we sat knee to knee. Above the seats were luggage racks." (37)

Based on period rail maps, it seems most likely that Richard traveled northeast from Moosburg to Landshut, then north through Regensburg and Weiden to Eger (Cheb, Czech Republic).[1] From there a northeasterly line ran to Aussig (Ústí nad Labem, Czech Republic); a somewhat roundabout line probably took him then to Reichenberg (Liberec, Czech Republic) and from there through Zittau to Görlitz. The last stage of this presumptive journey would have wound from Görlitz through some of the same countryside Richard would later cross on foot in the opposite direction and would have arrived at Sagan from the southwest.[2]

Alternatively, Richard and friends might have gone from Eger via Plauen to Dresden, then through Görlitz to Sagan. The first possibility seems likelier given their low-priority status as prisoners traveling in third-class cars.

The length of this itinerary is about 600 km; as with Clark's journey, Richard's would probably have taken more than one day.

---

1. At that time what is now the northwestern corner of the Czech Republic, with a long history of ethnic dispute, had been given to Germany under the 1938 Munich Agreement.

2. This evidently was the line on which Lisa Knüppel was traveling when she passed the Center Compound Kriegies marching south from Stalag Luft III on 28 January 1945.

New purge arrives in Center Compound. View to south from Vorlager; Barracks 40 (left) and 39 are visible in upper right. (From Kimball & Chiesl, Clipped Wings*)*

Sunday 10

Postcard excerpts

. . . I'm OK and haven't been hurt. Please don't worry about anything. . . . Be careful what you write. No return address as yet.

Postcard excerpt
to Butlers

I suppose for quite some time now you have been in quite a worry. Here's hoping this gets to you. They say the war is over for us and as long as we're here I suppose that's the truth.

Friday 15[20]

Log

Arrived at Sagan. The old Kraut counted us and said how happy he was that we were all gentlemen and didn't try to escape. Then we took a short walk and began

---

20. The arrival date is also in some dispute. As noted above, the South Compound history puts it on 14 October, as does Hopewell: "We were receiving more and more purges, and on October 14 an unusual one came into camp. This was an American group of officers who had been held in an Italian prisoner of war camp in Southern Italy. . . . The Americans, most of whom had been shot down over the Mediterranean or while flying out of Africa, suddenly found themselves abandoned by their Italian captors and were left alone in their own compound. They were quickly recaptured by the Germans, and then transported to our Stalag." (96)

Richard says his group arrived on the 15th, as do a fragment of Mulligan's handwritten notes for the compound diary as well the fragment of another Kriegie's journal. The 15th is also the arrival date recorded on his Personalkarte. Unfortunately, there is a gap in Center Compound's typewritten official daily history between 29 September and 11 November 1943, so we can find no confirmation there.

Sagan, Lower Silesia

Sagan (Zagan) at that time was a town of about 20,000 people; it was located in the province of Lower Silesia, some 90 miles southeast of Berlin in forested farming country on the Bober (Bóbr) River, a tributary of the Oder (Odra). Sagan was important strategically because it was a rail hub and had both Wehrmacht and Luftwaffe bases as well as significant industrial works at the Ostbau Werke, which mounted anti-aircraft guns on tank chassis.

Contrary to the Geneva Convention, several POW camps were placed contiguous to the town, and Sagan thus escaped the kind of attacks and destruction visited on other German places of its significance. Nonetheless, the Kriegies experienced one or two close calls. Stalag Luft III and two other camps were located along the southeast edge of the town just beyond the rail station and yards.

Stalag Luft III

Stalag Luft III was cut out of a scrubby pine forest which surrounded it on all sides; stumps protruded everywhere within the camp. When Richard arrived, Stalag Luft III consisted of Center and North Compounds, located respectively on the east and west sides of the German Truppenlager (command and housing compound for the 2500 guards). The south and west compounds were still in planning and construction phases; East had yet to be conceived. All compounds used the facilities in the Vorlager of Center (and, later, East) for delousing and showers. Over one hundred Russian prisoners were housed in that Vorlager as well.

"This was from several points of view one of the most important POW camps in the Third Reich. Here was a concentration of intelligent and brave young me[n] with advanced knowledge and skill, youthful determination and enthusiasm. At my first

The Sagan camps. Center is second compound from right; 56 is bottom right barrack. Vorlager runs along the north end of both East and Center; Truppenlager is dark rectangle west of Center. Rail station is north of tunnel "Harry." (Courtesy of Marek Lazarz)

Center Compound from southeast. 56 is at far left. (From Kimball & Chiesl, Clipped Wings*)*

our life at the Luft by being searched again. After a vigorous half day of making up our sacks, etc., we started to getting acquainted.[21] It looks as tho' life here will be rather dull—I hope.

Saturday 16

Log

All set up for living. Having our first movie *Shall we Dance* with Fred Astaire & Ginger Rogers. Pretty good! Only about five years old. Also a three-act play coming soon. English actors are OK both at male & female parts.

Saturday 23

Letter excerpt

I was pretty disappointed but I'm getting over it. Maybe I was a little over-confident about "Thanksgiving."

Sunday 31

Letter excerpt

I said once before that I hoped I wouldn't be here long enough to get mail. I can still hope, but write anyway.

---

21. Richard arrived as Colonel Spivey was beginning his reorganization and renewal of the Compound during its transition to an all-American camp. "The new men entered a barrack without rooms.... During the first six months nearly everyone was engaged in some way in helping to organize our community or in building up a combine and making it fit for living." (Mulligan, Burbank and Brunn 14)

What Richard could not know when he moved into Block 56 was that there was a tunnel beneath his feet. A month or so before his arrival, when an earlier tunnel elsewhere in the compound had to be abandoned and an alternative tunnel was discovered, the Brits started a new one under 56. (Official History 248–9)

visit [in] early 1943 there were . . . only a few Americans in the camp. . . .

"In the beginning of the summer 1943, keeping pace with the accelerating bombing activities, the number of 'inhabitants' in Stalag Luft III increased very quickly. . . . When visiting the camp during the summer and the early fall of 43 I found it in a permanent state of growing pains—with both compounds South and West being planned for. There was a great demand . . . for equipment within my field of activities." (Soderberg 4)

Since Richard arrived at Stalag Luft III early in the massive influx of Kriegies that began with the invasion of Sicily and Italy, life in the camp was more informal and less structured than it progressively became from the summer of 1943 on and with increasing intensity throughout 1944.

"Upon entering the barbed wire enclosure, the new Kriegie found a community with its own language, customs and code of ethics. Being captive on enemy soil made a bond that held those men together and was strengthened by a common cause. Tolerance and consideration for others grew from the confinement and restricted life. . . ." (Holmstrom introduction)

Arrival

"I vividly remember this arrival and the stark scene that met my eyes; the barbed wire, the guard towers, the bare gray ground, and the weathered gray huts. I felt overwhelming sadness at the grim prospect of my uncertain future in this godforsaken place." (Clark 38)

". . . regardless of the season of the year, the sun rarely shown [sic] and our lives were played against a background of monotonous, dull, gray." (Hopewell 187) Still, when Chaplain Daniel arrived at Stalag Luft III

early in January 1944, his assessment was that "Living conditions were much better at Stalag Luft III than at Stalag 7-A. Life was cleaner and far more orderly." (Daniel 68)

Since Richard and his fellow Kriegies traveled by passenger train from Moosburg, they would have disembarked at the Sagan station, where there were two platforms above street level on the north side; on the south, the station was on a level with the camp. Richard would have descended from the platform to the street level tunnel where the ticket booths are located, but he would have turned to the left, crossed under the rail lines, passed through a bomb shelter with blastproof doors and climbed a set of enclosed stairs on the south side of the platforms and rail lines.

From there it was about ½ km to the camp's northern perimeter road; again, Richard would have made a left turn and walked about the same distance along the sandy road to the Truppenlager on the south side of the road, passing through its northeast corner to reach the gate of the Vorlager[1] giving access to Center Compound and, later, East.

Center Compound

Between compounds ran a set of "two, 12-foot fences. There was a distance of about six feet and rolls of barbed wire between the two fences, except on the north end of the compound where the Vorlager . . . was located. Here, the double 12-foot fences formed the south end of the Vorlager, and a single fence surrounded" the Vorlager. "Inside the main compound, about 30 feet

---

1. *Vorlager* means literally pre-, or before-, camp. These were transition areas between the high security parts of the camp & the outside world.

Life in a combine before triple bunks. Combine G began with 6 men. (Lt. Gen. Albert P Clark Collection SMS 329, Clark Special Collections Branch, McDermott Library, US Air Force Academy)

Letter excerpts
to Butlers
(undated pre-POW photo enclosed)

Surprise! I'm in Germany seeing the world (whether I like it or not). It really isn't half as bad as you might think. Being cooped up isn't my idea of a vacation, but the best of it can be made if one tries.

We have a pretty good library to take up some of our time, also a theater, which plays sometimes, and educational courses, mostly languages and sports. It sounds like a lot, but one's time still drags.

[Censored][22] with the German ration and the Red Cross boxes combined we have enough. . . . At present they call me the fat man, but I'm looking forward to a hard winter.

---

22. At the camp there were more than 40 young English-speaking German women who censored Kriegies' mail. "Each of the censors was assigned a letter of the alphabet and directed to censor the mail of all the men whose last names began with that letter. Over the months, they learned much about the POWs assigned to them." (Walton & Eberhardt/Lindeiner 344–5)

Richard's letters and cards show a variety of different censor numbers.

Double fences and the warning wire (Lt. Gen. Albert P Clark Collection SMS 329, Clark Special Collections Branch, McDermott Library, US Air Force Academy)

Guard tower (Lt. Gen. Albert P. Clark Collection SMS 329, Clark Special Collections Branch, McDermott Library, US Air Force Academy)

in from the fences, was a low, one-wire fence that marked the warning line. Any prisoner caught between the warning line and the high fence would be shot by guards standing in one of the 25-foot high watch towers that dominated the camp and were equipped with search lights and machine guns." (Bender 277)

In the Vorlager they were searched, fingerprinted and photographed for the German POW Personalkarten.[2] There were two

_____

2. The Personalkarten would follow the Kriegies throughout their time in the stalags; many of them, along with Richard, would salvage the cards as souvenirs after their liberation in Stalag VIIA some nineteen months later.

It's heartening to see from his photo that by this time Richard had been able to add at the least a warm coat to the summer flight outfit in which he went down. It's likely that occurred in Moosburg; the American National Red Cross *Prisoners of War Bulletin*

Richard's Kriegie ID short card (Richard M. Butler papers MSS 8849, L. Tom Perry Special Collections, Harold B. Lee Library, Brigham Young University)

of these on heavy deep pink stock; presumably, the larger one was kept in the office as a permanent record and the smaller was used by the Germans for verifying identification during photo appells.

At some point Richard would have had to don the double-oblong German POW dog tags bearing his name and prisoner number 2721. In theory, at this point any personal effects confiscated at time of capture were returned; happily, Richard had managed to keep his treasured locket and ring when processed by the Italians.

Once they had been processed and passed into Center Compound itself, Richard and his group would have attended an orientation meeting in the theater with Senior American Officer Colonel Delmar Spivey. He would have welcomed them and begun to explain about blocks (barracks), combines (rooms), the chain of command and security in the compound. At some point, each man was issued a blanket or two,

_____

for January 1944 mentions a shortage there of Red Cross-supplied clothing because so much had been used for POWs in transit through VIIA.

November

Friday 5

[Richard makes no mention of this day's excitement. The tunnel under Block 56, already reaching beyond the perimeter fence, was discovered; its entrance inside the barrack was put under guard, but 5 RCAF and RAF men got into the tunnel by crawling under the barrack (Murray, Center Compound 5); they "worked at the face in an endeavour to make an exit. After a time the air became so bad that they were forced to retreat to the entrance. The Germans had heard them moving and had thrown a cordon around the barrack." (Official History 249)]

Sunday 7

Letter excerpts

. . . it's beginning to get pretty chilly around here. . . . There's no snow yet but sometimes it feels an awful lot like it.

I would give most anything to get a letter from you, but I know I can't expect any for months to come.

I got a little infection in my finger a few days ago, and it made me feel pretty bad for a while. I guess I'll take care of my barked knuckles after this.

Saturday 13

Postcard excerpts

I just finished three days as cook.[23] Thank the Lord I'm thro' for a while. . . . It's Armistice Day today, altho' the above date doesn't show it. We have to post-date our letters for reasons.

Sunday 14

Letter excerpts

It has been so long that being home really is a dream. An unreal one. But then it can't be too much longer, can it?

. . . I hope you weren't too upset about my tough luck. . . . I have everyone's sympathy, even tho' I don't want it. When some guy thinks he has a sad story, someone tells him mine.[24] It usually shuts them up.

---

23. ". . . it was unique to see a P-38 pilot and a bomber colonel trying to bake a cake." (Corson/Thobaben 154) Corson must certainly have been referring here to Richard as the P-38 pilot, but who the colonel would have been is a mystery. In the combine the highest rank was first lieutenant.

24. This no doubt refers to Richard going down on his 50th and presumably final mission. Here are some sample reactions from Richard's Kriegie registry: "You deserved a far

a sheet and pillow case, bowl, cutlery and a mug, and a roll of toilet paper.

Center Compound ran southward from the Vorlager. From the main gate the "Avenue" led to the fire pool at the compound's center; it bisected the first two rows of four blocks (west/east 39–42 and 43–46). In the central strip, from west to east were the west wash house; the west cookhouse/ kitchen; the rectangular fire pool; the east cookhouse, containing Foodacco, the mail room, and in the south end the library and situation or "gen" room (with news reports and war maps openly posted); and the east wash house. To the south beyond the fire-pool on the west side of the compound were two two-block rows of barracks (west/east 51–52 and 55–56); in the southeast corner

was the sports and appell ground. Large pit-latrines were located on each side of the compound (two on the west, one on the east) between the barracks and the warning wire.

"The new men entered a barrack without rooms. It was a dirty place to live at best. Straw lay on the floor and the black-out shutters banged against the outside wall in the breeze. The block was a long (approximately 130 feet) narrow [about 45 feet wide], single-story structure covered with a pointed tarpaper roof. It was built of flimsy preconstructed sections of light pine and appeared rather weather-beaten on the outside. . . . In the early days, when there were more beds than men, double-decker wooden beds lay around the empty barrack

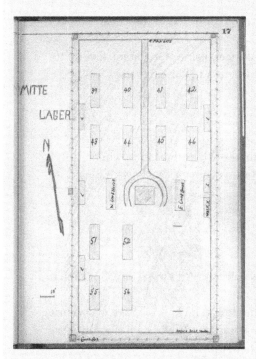

Richard's plan of Center Compound, from the Log (Richard M. Butler papers MSS 8849, L. Tom Perry Special Collections, Harold B. Lee Library, Brigham Young University)

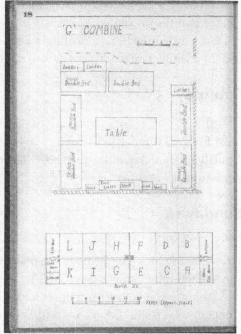

Richard's plans of Block 56 and G Combine, from the Log (Richard M. Butler papers MSS 8849, L. Tom Perry Special Collections, Harold B. Lee Library, Brigham Young University)

Monday 15

[This is the date of the letter from the International Committee of the YMCA accompanying their gift of the *Wartime Log*. Since the group's oversight of German POW camps was now headquartered in Sagan, it seems safe to assume that the Kriegies of Stalag Luft III would have been the first to receive their copies. If so, Richard could have begun working on his *Log* soon after.[25]]

Sunday 21

["A survey of Red Cross clothing showed that the American Red Cross clothing supply was far in excess of the British and the Canadian supply in Stalag Luft III. The American shipment included gloves for each and G.I. shoes to cover immediate needs." (Mulligan, Burbank and Brunn 260)]

Wednesday 24

[Camp History records Colonel Spivey's concern over "the decline in morale amongst the men. . . ." (Mulligan, Burbank and Brunn 260)]

Friday 26

Letter excerpts

Surprising as it may seem, I still have my ring and locket. It's a good thing for me that no one tried to take them 'cause, you know me, I'd've been hard to get along with about then.

   . . . tomorrow is Thanksgiving, so we're going to have a big splurge and eat up all the R.C. chocolate we've saved, if any. The cookhouse cat is in hiding for a few days. On the level tho' the food has been good & there's enough.

---

more decent break" (2nd Lt. Oliver Morton), "Happier landings next time, 'Panda'" (2nd Lt. J.V. Lilly), "But yours is a much sadder tale, Panda!" (Charles H. Midgley).

   25. Richard's first reference to the *Log* appears on 16 June 1944: "Doing a little more work on my war log." Twice during July he mentions working on it.

   Dates in the diary-style *Log* entries are not always dependable; we know that several are incorrect. They begin 20 August 1943 and were based on memory or adapted from earlier notes.

   The escutcheon listing Combine G internees could not have been compiled until after 2 July 1944, since it includes the names of 2 men who arrived on that date. This illustrated feature of the *Log* appears early in the book and was obviously carefully prepared; one sees clearly the difference between the names of the first ten occupants and the four who arrived later in 1944.

in no apparent order and these had to be arranged in a square-shaped area so that a 'combine' of eight men could live together." (Mulligan, Burbank and Brunn 16)

"In the middle half way from either end, was a wall with a door. . . . Each end of the block had an entrance door. The entire building was raised about two and a half feet off the ground by concrete piers that had wooden beams pier to pier. . . . The hallway was made by lining up wooden lockers along each side. . . . Each locker was about three feet wide by seven feet high and sixteen inches deep. It had two doors, one beside the other. . . . Breaks in the rows of lockers became the entrances into the combines." (Keefe 218–20) All but one of the Center barracks had an open bay in the middle. (39 was rebuilt in fall 1943 without one.)

"Each block has two kitchens (north-south) and each one is shared by six combines. The kitchens have one coal stove . . . and a few pots and pans for cooking. Therefore, each stove has to cook for 75 to 80 men, so our cooking schedule is very critical. . . ." (McKee 44)

Block 56, like most, was somewhat ramshackle. On 8 September 1943 Col. Spivey had formally called the attention of the Kommandant to the following list of items at Block 56 needing repair or replacement: "1. 45 windows missing or broken; 2. South kitchen sink blocked; 3. Bucket for night latrine deficient; 4. South kitchen stove deficient; 5. Leaks in roof; 6. 7 light fixtures deficient." (Mulligan, Burbank and Brunn 22)

"Each combine is independent and cooks as they choose except that we must abide by the stove schedule. The stove is only on at 8:00 to 9:00 AM for hot coffee, and 11:00 AM until 7:00 PM for preparing meals. So

being on cook duty is a harrowing experience." (McKee 44)

"In one corner of the room was an old-fashioned stove and a sink, but there were no water taps or running water. All of our water was procured from the cookhouse and brought back to our combines in our keintrinkwasser. . . .

"When we arrived . . . the furniture in the room consisted solely of a long table and two long benches. Eventually every room in the compound had a chair or two that was made from the wooden boxes containing Red Cross parcels, and a stool made from the same materials.

"The room had windows, but no screens. There were shutters that we closed during bad weather, and were ordered to close during air raids. . . ." (Hopewell 77)

"The beds within the combines were double-deckers of the crudest construction. . . . Men displayed positive genius in improving their beds to make them more comfortable. If a man was fortunate enough to accumulate enough string from various sources such as personal parcels, he devised a string hammock to replace the usual eight wooden slats in his bunk. . . .

"Keeping warm in the winter months absorbed a great deal of every prisoner's time. One of the methods which became almost universal was to create a 'flea bag.' This ingenious piece of equipment was made by taking a German ersatz blanket and folding it so that it formed three thicknesses. Each edge of the blanket was sewed to the fold so that there were two compartments. . . . One compartment was very carefully stuffed with shreds of paper, bits of cloth such as wornout underwear or socks, and anything else that would provide insulation. This compartment was then quilted. . . . The bottom of the flea bag was

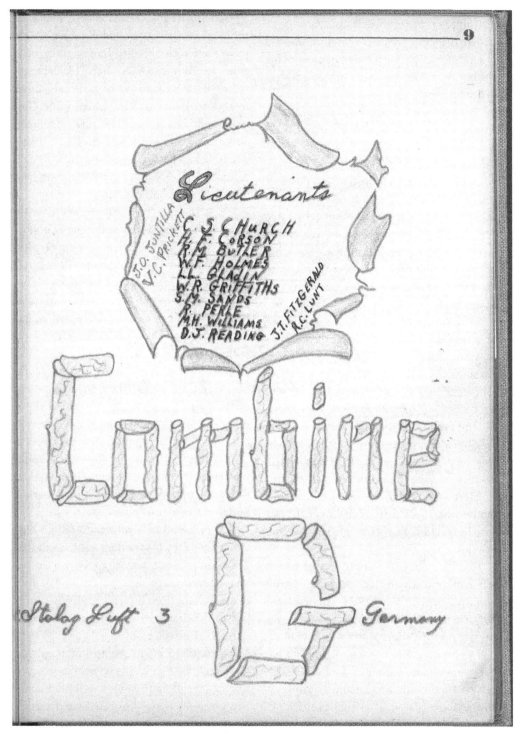

Richard's Combine G escutcheon, from the Log. *(Richard M. Butler papers MSS 8849, L. Tom Perry Special Collections, Harold B. Lee Library, Brigham Young University.)*

sewed up and the POW carefully wriggled his way into the open compartment with the quilted portion above him. . . .

"During cold weather it was common practice for everyone to sleep in most of his clothes, with the rest of them piled on top of him." (Spivey 59–60)

Richard, Herb Corson and C.S. Church, who had travelled together since Nisida, were shown to Combine G of Block 56 on the south end of the compound. The windows of Combine G looked out to the west toward Block 55. They found themselves there initially with three others. By January 1945 their combine would expand to 14 men in triple-decked bunks. (For a list of the Combine G internees see *Appendix E.*) Their Barrack Commander was a Major Hall.

"Dick & I spent 18 mo. in same combine of prisoners (8 to a combine), 20 combines to a barracks. Very close groups. Peeled potatoes, cooked, read, played cards, talked, follow[ed] news, prayed together. On the light side, we were all nosey & sometimes ill-tempered. No fights tho." (Corson letter)

"There are other things [that I have learned] such as tolerance of others, unselfishness, and an ability for companionship. . . . Here you have to learn to get along no matter what, because hard feelings can't last very long and have no place here." (McKee 45–6)

"Our 'Combine' system of living, which was communistic in that everyone shared equally, probably worked successfully because it was the only way that we could survive on such short food rations. . . .

"I did notice that the few times that we had an adequate supply of Red Cross parcels, people tended to become more possessive about personal belongings and food." (Burwell 33–4)

Food and Clothing

"I learned that the Germans provided us a minimal quantity of boiled potatoes which were semi-rotten, boiled barley grain, or a soup. . . . They also fed us hard, black bread, really bad margarine, occasional sugar beets or rutabagas, sometimes some German 'hand cheese,' and, on rare occasions, some semi-spoiled horse meat. . . . The whole boiled barley grain contained weevil grubs which were white in color and slightly larger than the barley grains.

"Each breakfast is alike, one piece of toast with jam or honey and a cup of coffee. Lunch is variable with barley, soup, or pate or cheese sandwiches and coffee or tea. . . .

"The evening meal is the big one and the one that keeps us alive. It consists of potatoes, meat, one or two vegetables (when we have them) and always a dessert with tea or coffee." (McKee 48–9)

"The young flyers were hungry from morning until night. They devoted much of their spare time trying to extend their meager rations. When 'parcel day' arrived . . . much thought went into means of combining the well-balanced Red Cross food packets with the monotonous German diet of half-rotten potatoes, black bread, barley, and occasional turnip jam." (Diggs 50)

"I later found that you could tell an old-timer in camp by the fact that he didn't bother to pick out the maggots when eating his barley. It was a slow starvation diet and it would have been difficult to survive without the British and American Red Cross parcels." (Burwell 25-6)

"Up until July and August of 1943 the English Red Cross had been able to furnish English-speaking prisoners with a change of underwear, two pairs of socks and a shirt, a pair of trousers, an overcoat, a cap, a pair

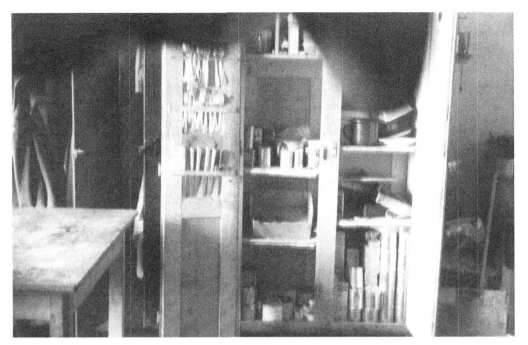

Combine storage (Lt. Gen. Albert P. Clark Collection, SMS 329, Clark Special Collections Branch, McDermott Library, US Air Force Academy)

Crowded barrack kitchen (Lt. Gen. Albert P Clark Collection SMS 329, Clark Special Collections Branch, McDermott Library, US Air Force Academy)

of shoes, and toilet articles. However, about this time, due to our stepped-up bombing raids, so many Americans began to arrive that the entire reserve of Red Cross articles was gone and none of us received the customary issue of clothes. The Germans took away most of our GI clothing and gave everyone barely enough to hide his nakedness. But there was plenty of Red Cross food. Without exception, we blessed the Red Cross and devoured the good things they sent us." (Spivey 25–6)

"The American kriegies were attired in all sorts of clothing—made-over pieces of uniforms, some old sweaters, and 'long johns' when they could get them, with as many layers of clothes as each man could scrounge and swap for. They looked vaguely like a bunch of tramps.

"Sometimes khaki scarves appeared in a Red Cross shipment, and these were quickly made into odd-looking hats to keep the ears warm. . . . Wooden clogs were worn by many, who claimed that they were surprisingly warm and dry even though not very practical for walking or playing baseball. Washing clothes was a special problem . . . as the cold water removed little of the accumulated grease and dirt. So home-made washing machines were invented. . . ." (Diggs 50–51)

Enriching Camp Life

In a letter home YMCA representative Henry Soderberg said the following about visiting the camps: "At the end of the day, we [are] sweating, very dusty, very tired, dirty and with a horrible smell. It seems that there always is a bad smell in the prisoner-of-war camps which we carry with us in our coats and clothes when we come back to the hotel." (Diggs 16) "Even the air that hung over the camp was always full of dust and smoke." (Clark 41)

". . . we live a rather simple life. Always talking about our past lives and reliving those instances of happiness many times, either in our minds or relating them to some other Kriegie who will listen. At times (not too often) we talk about the future, and what we are going to do when we get back home. What we are going to eat is the most popular subject. . . ." (McKee 50)

"To exist, the prisoner had to develop talents and latent skills to provide the necessities of life. Materials from Red Cross parcels were converted into tools such as hack saws from the steel bands around the cardboard cartons. Canadian packing crates of plywood yielded cupboards and room furniture. Another sourse of supply was the heavy wooden boxes in which the Y.M.C.A. shipped school supplies. Tin cans supplemented by barbed wire were converted into practical appliances such as cracker-grinders, stoves and even ovens." (Holmstrom introduction)

"We have a dance band that plays jam sessions, a dramatic club for the plays, a Glee Club, and other organizations. We usually have a jam session at least once a week, and a play about every six weeks. I have seen two movies since being here. . . . There are two record sessions each week, one popular and the other classical. . . .

"The most trying times here are the rainy or cold weather days, where we have to stay inside to keep dry or warm or both. These times are what we have to look forward to this winter and it causes us to have a grim outlook on life.

"Reading grows tiresome and you can't stay in bed all of the time. This on top of being hungry makes this a very unbearable place at times." (McKee 47–8) "We have a camp newspaper (*Gefangenen Gazette*) that is a piece of cardboard on the side of west cook house. There is one of these bulletins

Walking the circuit filled the time and helped keep the men fit.
(Arthur A. Durand Collection SMS 792, Clark Special Collections
Branch, McDermott Library, US Air Force Academy)

Monday 29

Postcard excerpt

Thanksgiving is over. Now for Xmas. We tried to kill ourselves overeating and almost succeeded. At any rate the day was somewhat as it should have been. I sent my address to Geneva to be called to you, so by now I suppose you have it.

Tuesday 30

Postcard excerpt

I've been out playing basketball. Before long it will be freezing up, then the hockey will start. They say we'll have some ice skates by then.

December

Saturday 4[26]

Postcard
to Butlers

It's trying its best to snow but isn't succeeding very well. I'm afraid it will, tho', before long. Another Xmas away from home. Sometimes I wonder if I'm not wasting a lot of good lifetime. Certainly, life isn't at its best. How is everything and everyone at home?

---

26. "The advent of very cold weather . . . forced the Germans to cut off all water to avoid freezing of pipes; prisoners of war made their first 'ice cream' in hand-made freezers." (Mulligan, Burbank and Brunn 265)

each week and carries only camp news."
(McKee 55)

Camp Newspapers

Two competing weeklies appeared in Center, *Gefangenen Gazette* and *Kriegie Times.* The original multi-page typed copies were submitted to Col. Spivey for censoring of sensitive material, then posted on the bulletin board on an outside wall of the west cookhouse. Both papers published features and news stories from within and outside the camp. Reporters "were not remiss in their duty to keep the administration honest" and are said to have irritated Spivey at times but "he was wise enough to appreciate the public service being performed." (Durant 232) What was perhaps most notable about them, however, were the cartoons that highlighted both; these often channeled a humorous take on Kriegie hardships and difficulties and frequently had a racy edge to them.

Gefangenen Gazette writer/editor 2nd Lt. Ronald T. Delaney published the *Gazette* roughly twice per week in a remarkable run from 27 October 1943 through 28 January 1945. 2nd Lt. Thomas E. Mulligan, creator and editor of the *Kriegie Times,* was also one of three official camp historians and a writer of "gen" (BBC radio news summaries quietly circulated through the combines after lockup). The *Times* put out 30 editions running from 1 January to 27 August 1944 and published a special Home Edition on 8 February 1944. Ultimately, Mulligan's official duties forced him to close down the *Kriegie Times.*

The official history also speaks of Pulse, Center Compound's version of the Gallup Poll; its results from queries about camp problems were also posted on the cookhouse wall. The wide-ranging bounty flowing from the YMCA included a microphone and loudspeaker which facilitated a compound radio station. WPOW operated two

Checking the compound newspapers (Thomas E. Mulligan Collection, SMS 603, Clark Special Collections Branch, McDermott Library, US Air Force Academy)

afternoons a week and "broadcast musical programs, lectures, camp sports activities and humorous forms of advertisements." (Mulligan, Burbank and Brunn 128)

Mail

"Mail meant the world to us. We lived for it, and just about the worst punishment we could receive was for our captors to withhold our mail. Mostly it brought us good news, but not always. Some men received hundreds of letters; others spent years with no word from home, and when it came it sometimes didn't matter any more." (Greening et al.)

". . . mail to the camp arrived at unpredictable times and usually by the carload from Switzerland or Sweden. . . . There was no limit on how much a *kriegie* could receive, but outgoing mail was strictly limited." (Clark 47) For Richard this meant that each month the Germans furnished him with 3 letter forms (similar to an aerogram) and four postcards for his use.

Later, on the winter march, Clark found he had to lighten his load by discarding the carefully packaged letters received from his wife. "I came to realize that I had discarded an irreplaceable treasure. Inspiring and loving, those letters reflected the great courage and devotion of my dear wife." (143)

Thursday 9

Letter excerpts

We get four cards and three letters [to send] per month. . . .

I have been in Germany for almost two months now and personally can't complain about mistreatment.

I'm not forgetting how to read tho'. We have a pretty good library here, thanks again to the R.C. Well, a letter for Xmas is the most welcome thing I can think of but slightly far-fetched.

Very likely Richard leaning against the library wall. (Lt. Gen. Albert P Clark Collection SMS 329, Clark Special Collections Branch, McDermott Library, US Air Force Academy)

Friday 10

["A warning was issued . . . to all Kriegies on the acute shortage of coal and a strict rationing program was outlined. . . ." (Mulligan, Burbank and Brunn 267)]

Wednesday 15

Letter excerpts

. . . I am in the best of health and being treated well.

We're preparing, or planning I should say, a big blow-out for the 25th. We're to receive a special Christmas parcel from the Red Cross,[27] which I'm sure will take care of the food problem. Now if we only had a good cook. That brings something

---

Sunday 5 December: "Red Cross parcels are being held up due to bombings and all rolling stock being derailed on lines leading from Berlin." (Mulligan, Burbank and Brunn 265)

27. "When the Red Cross boxes would come in you'd go down to the outer area [Vorlager], where the boxes came in from Switzerland, and the Germans would open up the box with a knife . . . and there were all the different ingredients with a manifest of what was in there. . . . They wouldn't give you the box it came in because there might be something

else up. The steak was rather tough this evening. I don't know whether I cooked it wrong, failed to pound it long enough or maybe someone just forgot to take the hide off. At any rate a lot of teeth took a terrible beating.

I get awfully homesick at times but soon get over it. Hope it isn't too much longer.

Thursday 16

Letter excerpts

I suppose there are a lot of things you'd like me to tell you about, but it's all so commonplace now. . . . The main thing is "all is well that ends well," and a whole lot has ended very well.

Here's hoping you are all as healthy as I am, but I hope you're a little more contented.

Postcard
to Butlers

We were just speaking about how far behind times we'll be when we get home.[28] I suppose the best way to avoid that is to throw rocks at the guards, but there may be other good ways not quite so sudden. All is swell and we're looking for a white Xmas.

Saturday 25

The Glee Club entertained with a very good Xmas program. The Christmas Cavalcade was put on New Years Eve. It was a sort of a musical, ending with an air raid.

---

secret in there. . . . And you had to check off on a receipt that you got it. . . ." (Corson/ Thobaben 154–5)

28. I think he refers here to the daily family and cultural sorts of things. In point of fact, they were well up-to-date on war news.

The Luftbandsters, Center Compound Christmas concert 1943 (Lt. Gen. Albert P. Clark Collection SMS 329, Clark Special Collections Branch, McDermott Library, US Air Force Academy)

Christmas 1943

According to Jack Rowan, Center Compound enjoyed "unheard-of delights" in the special Christmas Red Cross parcel distributed to each man: Canned turkey, condensed honey, Crosse & Blackwell Plum Pudding, pipe and tobacco, playing cards, checkers, salted nuts, wash cloth. He says "we bashed the gash all day. In Kriegie terms, gash is anything extra, surplus, over-and-above. To bash it is to use it up heedlessly, recklessly, with no thought of the future." His combine "prepared Kriegie Bread/Fruit Cake with Butterscotch Icing and offered tiny pieces to our visitors."

Rowan also tells of creating a makeshift manger scene with Ivory Soap from the Red Cross and wood shavings from his mattress. A highlight for him was being able to attend midnight mass and stopping in the bitter cold afterward to listen to "Silent Night" coming from one of the barracks. (Rowan)

A document among the Mulligan papers records the gift of just over 7,000 cigarettes contributed by Center Compound Kriegies to 150 Russian prisoners housed in the Vorlager under brutal treatment and more primitive conditions than those in which the Americans lived. (Thomas E. Mulligan Collection SMS 603, Clark Special Collections Branch, McDermott Library, US Air Force Academy)

4

PRISONER
OF WAR
1944

What was it like to be a Prisoner of War?

To be a Prisoner of War is to experience cold. Not the cold, blustery winter when you wished you had worn your gloves or a heavier coat. I am talking about standing for hours in soup lines or other needless lines in freezing weather, pelted by sleet and snow, your feet numbed and your fingers nearly frozen. Enduring forced marches in subzero temperatures wearing summer clothing. You are sick, your body is racked by uncontrolled shivering and your mind is a mask of pain. Dysentery knots your stomach, adding to your misery. You begin to wonder if death can be the answer. Death never comes, it only teases.

To be a Prisoner of War is to experience fear, stark terror as you lie packed in a railroad boxcar, doors locked and barred, while friendly aircraft bomb and strafe and you not knowing if you will be blown to bits the next second. The terrible fear of catching a disease that runs rampant throughout the camps and no medicine nor strength to fight back. The haunting fear that you might never be free. The fear of execution ordered by a frantic dictator.

To be a Prisoner of War is to know hunger. I am talking about the hunger from lack of solid food for days, then weeks, and then months. A hunger that gnaws at your stomach and your other vital organs, that burns the fat at first, then strips the flesh from your bones. A hunger that forces you to eat anything and everything available: black stale bread made largely from sawdust, watery soup infested with worms, made from only God knows what. Rotten potatoes and turnips, dug from a muddy field and, if you are lucky, some salt to season the half-cooked vegetables.

To be a Prisoner of War is to experience anger and deep depression. Anger knowing that your enemy counterparts imprisoned in the United States are well fed and clothed. Thoughts of your family and your home lock your mind in a bottomless depression, and this is the cruelest torture. The anger and hate you have for your captors.

To be a Prisoner of War is to suffer the agony of rehabilitation. Suddenly you are in an alien world. The frustration of trying to cope as your youth was lost in a prisoner of war camp. Trying to fit into a society that suddenly seems foreign, a society unable to relate to your experiences. Their personal problems seem pale to comparison. The recurring nightmares that plague you for the rest of your life.

I believe there was a purpose. I believe the ex-Prisoner of War has a much clearer perspective of what is real and what is genuine. Perhaps he better understands what is really important in life. I do!

Thomas P. Griffin,
West Compound, Stalag Luft III
(Wright 243–4)

1944

[Winter/Spring]

Log

[The following undated letter drafts were written in nearly illegible pencil below some German grammar and vocabulary notes and tucked inside *A Wartime Log*. For the conclusion to this letter's request, see 8 August 1944.]

Was shot down
while ops over Italy ship set afire by enemy
bailed out and life saved by your chute

Dear Sir:
While on an operation over Italy, my plane was set on fire by enemy action, forcing me to bail out. My life was saved by one of your chutes. Will you kindly enroll me in the Caterpillar Club. Please send membership card here and my pin.

January

Tuesday 4

Letter excerpts

Letters are beginning to filter thru to some of the boys who came up with me. Here's hoping mine are on their way, too. I could certainly use a bunch.

Christmas & New Year's have rolled by much as I expected them to. We spared nothing in the line of eats. With the help of a big Xmas parcel from the R.C. we did wonderfully well, considering the cooks.

We've had swell weather for a week or two. A little wet but not as cold as it was for a while.

Postcard excerpts
to Butlers

Christmas hasn't been as bad as I had expected.

Everything's OK. I'm still enjoying good health and have been all along.

Friday 14

Letter excerpts

I'm waiting very impatiently for your first letter to Germany. You know this is the second five months I have spent with no word at all from you, and it isn't funny.

Colonel Spivey's Administration

"From August 1943 until the spring of 1944 the newly-arrived Americans were absorbed in building a community. . . . later we had established our own administration, our own rules and regulations. . . ." (Mulligan, Burbank and Brunn 13–14) In early September 1943, as Center was becoming a solely American compound, Spivey began a major campaign of administrative reorganization and infrastructure refurbishment. This included moving to Center from North Compound a group of older and experienced American POWs to "set up an efficient and workable organization" to meet the influx of new Kriegies like Richard. They were to help the new men "to orientate themselves" as they confronted the daily reality of unexpected imprisonment.

One important element of this effort was to do what was necessary "to give every man one change of essentials. There was a meager stock of Red Cross clothing available. However, the major problem was shoes; the men were wearing their 'shot-down' clothes and the weather was warm." (Mulligan, Burbank and Brunn 250) As Autumn progressed, the need for warm clothes and blankets became urgent.[1] ". . . timely arrival, in early November, of coats, blankets and other winter clothing from the ARC was a great comfort." (Mulligan, Burbank and Brunn 35)

When Spivey took command, "the men were cooking, bathing and washing clothes in the same basin." The property officer made it a goal for each combine to have two basins. Eventually, he managed to obtain "two cooking pots . . . for each Block of approximately 80 kriegies." Other such necessities were created by the men from tin cans. (Mulligan, Burbank and Brunn 250–1) A complex system of classes, theater and musical productions and sports activities was created under Spivey's direction with equipment provided by the YMCA. (Mulligan, Burbank and Brunn 251)

On the occasion of a camp inspection on Saturday 12 August 1944 ". . . General Vanaman drew a sharp contrast to the camp last year when a handful of American and British officers barely 'existed' here. The camp was felt to be 'temporary' then. Optimism and wishful thinking then. No gardens . . . and little military organization. The barracks were dirty, the men were dirty and unwilling to do anything practical for themselves. There had been complete ignorance among new arrivals of the Protecting Power, RC and other agencies cooperating to help prisoners. A year later, however, the barracks and the men were spick and span, there was military order and regular exercise required, swimming in the fire pool, performances by a 'top-notch' band, the camp office was in order, camp papers were being published and educational and library facilities operated at capacity." (Mulligan, Burbank and Brunn 336–7)

---

1. Spivey's goal was for each man to have one each of the following: overcoat, blouse or jacket, pair wool trousers, 1 sweater, 1 pair high shoes, 1 scarf, 1 belt or suspenders, 1 cap, 1 blanket; he also hoped to get each one 2 shirts—wool or cotton, 2 pair winter underwear, 4 handkerchiefs. (Mulligan, Burbank and Brunn 35)

We hear quite a bit from home thro' letters and such. I understand that the location of some of these camps was published there at home. If so, maybe you know where I am. . . .

Postcard excerpt
to Butlers

When you send a box slip in a pencil or two (nothing expensive). Some of those things we don't have too much of.

Sunday 16

Had our first Sunday evening Classical Concert. It turned out very well and has promise for the future, possibly a P.A. system later on.

Friday 28

Postcard excerpts
to Butlers

Everything's fine and I'm in good health.

I'm pretty anxious to get a letter or parcel from home. Some should start coming soon tho.'

Saturday 29

Letter excerpts

It has been so long since I was there at home with you that time just doesn't count or matter any more. It's a funny thing to explain but events, instead of days, mark the passing of time.

It has been surprisingly warm for the past month, so you can see that I'm doing well.

February

Friday 4

Letter excerpts

Everything is swell here. Not quite so good as the Y.M.C.A. may say, but it's passable anyway.

My appointment with the dentist came around today, and I had three small fillings added. He said to come back in twelve months, but I don't figure on it.

I still haven't received any mail but hope to very soon. You know it has almost been six months since I last heard from civilization.

Wednesday 9

Postcard excerpt
to Butlers

I haven't received any mail yet but am looking for some any time now. The weather has been surprisingly mild for about six weeks now.

Monday 14

Letter excerpts

I hold my breath every day now until the mail and parcels are brought in. I haven't been on the list yet, but I have a feeling. Three of the boys that I met in Italy received parcels yesterday, so it can't be long before my turn comes, I keep telling myself.[1]

We're trying to have a little winter now. It has snowed about six inches and is a little colder than usual but not half bad yet.

Tuesday 15

Four months to the day since I arrived here. My first communication from home, Nov to Jan parcel.[2]

Thursday 17

Card

I'm a new man tonight. I received my first parcel today. It had the billfold and your picture in it. No letters yet but I'm satisfied—for a while. I at least know that you've heard from me. Everything came thro' swell. A well-selected parcel.

---

1. "I recall someone asked Dick what his initial M meant. He wouldn't tell us. So we found out. *Marsh.* So just for meanness we changed his nickname from 'The Panda' to 'Swampy.' He was called Panda because he appeared to be so far from the mainstream at times with his quiet composure—hands folded & etc. Unlike the rest of us, Dick got on his knee every eve by his bed, short prayer. Dick was not too out-going, but 'rolled with the punch' & admired by everyone. Congenial." (Corson letter)

"Panda" stuck. Combine G inmate Stan Sands uses that nickname in his 1946 Christmas letter and Corson does so in his 1947 Christmas card.

2. This parcel from Geneil preceded by six weeks the first letters Richard received in camp; those had been mailed slightly ahead of the parcel. Contents: 1 pair mittens, 1 wool underwear, 6 pair stockings, 12 handkerchieves, 2 decks playing cards, 4 pkgs. gum, 1 razor, 5 razor blades (pkg.), 1 sewing kit, 1 toothbrush, 1 shaving brush, 1 shaving soap, 1 tooth powder, 1 talcum powder, 1 mirror 1 wallet, 2 pair wrist lits [*sic*], 3 underwear (cotton), 2 Bibles, 1 pkg. vitamin tablets, 1 trousers, 1 shirt, 2 bars soap.

Saturday 26

Letter

I just received what I've been waiting for six months for. I received my first parcel from you on the 15th, just four months to the day after I arrived here. I always thought that I'd rather have a letter, but this is one of those exceptions. Several of the boys here remarked about how good a parcel it was. (You know when something new comes in it has a good audience.) It had everything in it that I really needed, including the picture and pennies & tokens. I think that I have about everything that I really need, except letters. They're pretty scarce, in fact "hardly ever."

According to the picture, you seem to be getting around now & then. I was in Rome, by the way, when it was taken. (I don't think they'll mind my telling that.) Get around a little myself, don't I?

The weather has been chilly for a week or so now but is looking better. After all, this isn't California.

Sunday 27

Postcard excerpt
to Butlers

I thought that by now I'd have a pile of letters, but the parcel is the only thing that's come thru. At least I've heard from you. It was a swell parcel, tho.'

March

Sunday 5

Letter excerpts

I swore that I wouldn't write again until I got a letter, but I guess it isn't coming. It may help out if you sent an occasional letter by "Clipper Mail." They come pretty fast that way. Don't worry tho.' The mail is just beginning to come in for us from down South. I'm just impatient—with just cause, of course.

After being away so long, your picture is almost like having you here in person. It really is wonderful. I hope you don't expect too much from my letters. I'm still not used to writing to so many different people at one time. . . . please send a thin lead eversharp (no pen) and a bunch of candy bars.

Protecting Power and International Aid Groups

Protecting Power

The government of Switzerland acted with the German government (Detaining Power)—specifically with the military officials running the prisoner of war camps—in behalf of American prisoners of war in all serious matters. In particular and most frequently these involved potential violations of the Geneva Convention and included everything from mistreatment of individual prisoners to inappropriate camp locations to inadequate food, housing or clothing.

International Committee of the Red Cross

Based in Geneva, the ICRC packaged and delivered to the POWs food, clothing and medical supplies to bridge the gap between bare necessity and what the Germans provided. With particular reference to their food parcels, the ICRC were responsible for Kriegies' survival under what would otherwise have been conditions of slow starvation.

The International YMCA and Henry Soderberg

The YMCA was responsible for prisoners' "intellectual, recreational and spiritual needs (excluding the pastoral work . . .)." (Soderberg 1) In practice this meant everything from musical instruments to sports equipment to books filling the shelves of camp libraries.

Henry Soderberg, a Swede, was one of six representatives of the International YMCA's War Prisoners' Aid group working in Nazi Germany. Stalag Luft III was the largest and highest-profile camp for which he was responsible. "I regarded it as a real privilege to have Stalag Luft III within my geographical areas of responsibility. . . . I had the feeling of being among friends when I walked through the barracks and crossed the camp grounds." (Soderberg 2)

Shortly before Richard arrived in Sagan, the YMCA moved its German headquarters there from Berlin. The move from the increasingly dangerous capitol placed Soderberg within a few kilometers of the camp. ". . . as its only regular visitor from the outside, [he] was to go back to it time after time.[1] He was, in fact, the only non-German the Americans saw except for a few visits by a Red Cross and Protecting Power representative." (Diggs 48)

"Representatives of all three of these organizations visited our camps regularly, listened to our complaints, took note of our needs, undertook to alleviate our problems through negotiations with the German authorities, and sent us prodigious amounts of food, equipment and supplies throughout the war." (Clark 45)

---

1. A total of some 30 visits by his estimate.

Tuesday 7

Postcard
to Butlers

Another Sunday evening. I just came back from the concert (in cans).[3] It is pretty nice considering everything. Everything is going nicely, and I'm enjoying real good health. I'm sure to have a letter this week—I hope. Write as often as you like & send pictures.

Tuesday 14

Letter excerpts

Sunday evening again. I just got back from the concert, which we have each week. The "powers that be" supply us with a different set of records each time. It kills a lot of monotony & helps out on a few choice day-dreams.

Those of us who haven't heard from home in three months were allowed to send a hurry-up letter thro' the Red Cross. I may have given you the wrong idea when I asked for food. I meant stuff like: onion flakes and a few other things that may "help" our cooking. . . . How about book parcels? I read quite a bit more now, for some reason, than I used to.

During the other time I was without mail I must have gotten used to it 'cause it doesn't bother me too much. . . . After I start getting mail I suppose I'll meet it at the gate from then on.

We're going to start taking walks around the nearby country pretty soon. . . .

Keep on sending pictures. The one I have is only a beginner.

Friday 24

[On the night of 24–25 March, 76 men left the camp's North Compound in the legendary mass escape from Stalag Luft III.]

[Beyond this point, Richard's records include the 1944 YMCA *Kalender* pocket calendar; presumably, the Kriegies did not receive them until this point in the year. Richard's first *Kalender* entry on 25 March records the inaptly-named Great Escape.

The unused 1944 pages (along with the endpapers and expense register) later provided space for supplementary entries in the ten days just prior to the winter march and for recordkeeping after he set out in the early hours of 28 January 1945 with the *Log* protectively packed and stowed away.]

---

3. I believe he means "canned music," records.

Saturday 25

Kalender

A.M. appel was pretty late today. There was a mass breakout of the N. camp (82 men). The whole country was alerted. No mail came in at all. (Air raid last night.)

Sunday 26

Kalender

A lovely morning after 2 weeks of rain & snow. The Goons are rather on edge today. Lockup at 7:00 instead of 10:00 tonight. (Raid last night.)

Monday 27

Kalender

The Goons are still rather unhappy for some reason or other. We've had 5 appels today.[4] They're trying to cook our food for us. We're refusing it.

No R.C. parcel. No lights after 20:00.

Tuesday 28

Kalender

Dulag[5] at Frankfurt bombed & coming here. (1 American killed/7 injured.)

3 fast laps.[6]

Wednesday 29

Log

Received my first mail from home. One from Geneil and one from "Mom & Dad." Very! welcome.

Letter excerpts

Gee! Am I ever tickled tonight. I just received two letters, one from you & one from Dad & Mother. They were both [your] first to the 3rd Reich. For some reason they seldom arrive in the order written, but these did.

---

4. Hopewell speaks of only one retaliatory appell per day in South Compound, but they continued. "It might be between the regular appels, or it might be at odd hours during the night. Regardless of day or night, the Goons were always heavily armed." (146)

5. Dulag Luft was the central processing center through which all downed airmen were theoretically sent for sometimes intense interrogation before being sent to their assigned camp. Richard and his group coming out of Italy bypassed Dulag because the German processing system was overwhelmed with the rapidly increased influx of POWs.

6. Around the compound walking circuit.

You knew just what I've been waiting for 'cause all the news was there.

I could tell by your picture that you had either been sick or worrying too much. That was before I read the letter.[7]

Postcard excerpt
to Butlers

Today has been my happiest in years. I received my first letters in you know how long. They were the first ones you sent after my address arrived. Unusual because letters don't very often arrive in the order they were intended.

Kalender

The boys are coming in from Dulag.[8]

Yipe!! Two letters. & pictures.

The Goons gave in. We're getting our boxes.

1 Letter to "Gen," card to folks.

Thursday 30

Kalender

Corson left his blankets out tonight; he's trying to flag a goon down now. Trouble Buddy?

Saw "Meet the Band" show today. 2 laps.

Friday 31

Kalender

Timoshenko had kittens.[9]

April

Saturday 1

Kalender

Church finally got his first letters.

---

7. Geneil had had an appendectomy on 29 July 1943. Grandma Butler had written Richard to give him that news, but her letter of 30 July arrived after he went down and was returned to her.

8. This presumably included Sands and Perle, who brought the contingent in Combine G to 8 men.

9. It's unclear whether this cat, named for a prominent Soviet army marshall, was particularly attached to Richard's combine or had wider circulation. This isn't the last we hear of her.

Sunday 2

Kalender

The boy from Bl[ock]-39 rolled the potato with his nose (invasion bet).
   I made a cake today (Sehr Güt).
   1 letter Gen, 1 card home.

Monday 3

Kalender

The news we hear about the German prisoners in the U.S. doesn't make us a bit happy—Likewise what you seem to be getting from the R.C. about our welfare & recreation doesn't help our morale. I know you're not as gullible as some tho!

Tuesday 4

Kalender

Bath.

Letter excerpts

I've been sending all three of my letter forms to you in the post, but I'm going to keep one out for Dad & Mom this month. OK? I'm afraid they feel a bit slighted and with good cause.

   It's a bit late for Xmas but I'm used to that. Besides, they were that much better for the waiting. My morale is miles higher than it was. I thank you for that from the bottom of my heart. Those pictures were swell; please send lots more of them.

   I'm glad to hear that my uniform is back where it belongs. That yellow ribbon has company now, I suppose. You might put an imaginary purple one there, too.

Postcard excerpt
to Butlers

Received your first letter, and it (or they) really did me good. I was especially tickled to hear from Dad.

Wednesday 5

Kalender

A beautiful day—played ball—some parcels came in.

Thursday 6

Kalender

April weather.

Col. Spivey says 41 escapees killed, 14 Gestapo recaptured. We think—Hitler youth (fanatical) got hold of them. (Experience says they're spoiled brats.) Warned to be careful with "Goons." Retaliations.

Friday 7

Kalender

Haircut.

Saturday 8

Kalender

"August" is breaking in some new Ferrets—some of them we think are "Gestapo."
Rumor: Himmler ordered those boys shot as reprisal.

Sunday 9

Kalender

EASTER.
Air Raid just before church. Sgt in S[outh] camp was shot for being outside the building during raid.
Hope the Russians hurry.

Monday 10

Kalender

Luftgangsters over Deutschland 1h15 afternoon.[10] Played softball. Cooking again. Announced Odessa's fall.

Tuesday 11

Kalender

Goons pulled a search on us this A.M. Air Raid at 1:00 coming straight at [us]. They hit Sorau.[11] The smoke is really coming over here. 30 mi away.

Log

The town of Sorau (not far from here) was hit. They were coming directly toward us on the bomb run. Quite a fire. Saw them again on May 29 and June 21.

---

10. For "luftgangsters" read Allied airmen.
11. Sorau (now Żary, Poland) was only about 10 kilometers west of Sagan. A branch of the Focke-Wulf factory had been moved to an underground facility in Sorau during the war and was presumably the target of this raid. A portion of the historic old town was reduced to rubble in the attack of this date.

Center Compound Library

As Spivey took command and Center became an American compound, an "existing library was cleaned up and enlarged with the arrival of some American books from Geneva." (Mulligan, Burbank and Brunn 250) Thereafter, books requested arrived in about two months. (256)

"The fiction library was located in a small room in the east kitchen and was probably the greatest morale factor in the camp next to the Red Army. By evacuation day the books in the library were literally in shreds and were rebound as quickly as possible with binding material received from Geneva." (Mulligan, Burbank and Brunn 120)

"The reference library was also in the east kitchen in a large tiled room adequately heated by two stoves. In the winter it was filled to capacity and was the only place in the camp where a man could go for quiet reading and study and as such was a haven for the more sensitive and highly strung. The room was also a refuge for those [men whose] barracks which were locked . . . by the Germans during the winter. The men were able to stay in the library room while the Germans searched their quarters." (Mulligan, Burbank and Brunn 123) "The [reference and technical] library was fortunate in having a good-sized room, used both for reading and studying as well as a storage place for the books. Tables and benches were nearly adequate, taking care of 60–70 men." (Mulligan, Burbank and Brunn 124)

"The library was open four hours each day of the week, Sundays excepted, and for each hour that the library was open, three men were on duty—two for the checking in and out of books, the third to act as a sort of floor supervisor and to replace books. . . . The staff was composed of twenty-one men and arranged in such a way that three men worked during a certain hour—worked three weeks and off two." (Mulligan, Burbank and Brunn 121–2)

In a postwar interview for recovered personnel, when asked what duties he had performed while in POW camp Richard replied "Librarian for 14 months."

THE REFERENCE LIBRARY
Sagan Germany

From the Wartime Log *(Richard M. Butler papers MSS 8849, L. Tom Perry Special Collections, Harold B. Lee Library, Brigham Young University)*

Wednesday 12

Kalender

Bombers all over Germany today.

Thursday 13

Kalender

I've been working in the library again this week.
    Raid again.
    Moved the door & changed the combine.

Friday 14

Kalender

Air Raid. 3 one-act plays this evening. A bunch of mail came in today.

Saturday 15

Kalender

More mail but none to me. The Col. pulled another insp[ection]. (Air raid.) (Ping pong.)
    Signing up for West Camp.

Sunday 16

Kalender

Ballgame this afternoon. I was catcher, 4 hits.

Monday 17

Kalender

We hear a raid every night or so.

Tuesday 18

Kalender

Air Raid while I was in the library. Having a little rainy & cold weather.

Wednesday 19

Kalender

Two more letters from Gen. Dec 23 & Jan 4. I wrote a letter & card.
    (Sgt from Italy in today.)
    Cold today but is warmer this eve.

Thursday 20

Kalender

Starting to do a little gardening.

Friday 21

Kalender

Big hot rumor going around.

Letter excerpts

I hit again today. Two more letters and both from you. One was written just before Xmas & the other on New Years. . . . Each letter I receive makes me feel just that much better. You know, funny as it may seem, my biggest worry has been there at home, wondering how you were all taking it. It hasn't been hard on me at all. In fact it has done me a lot of good in many ways.

I never have mentioned Heber before this, but I know he understands my reasons. Just the same, I'm up there with him every day.

Tell everyone hello and give them my love. I am living for that alone when we shall meet again.

Postcard
to Butlers

I just received two more letters today and am mighty tickled. Am expected to get my second parcel, which is from you, any day now. Thank Mr. & Mrs. Mann for the Xmas card. It came today, too. We've been having swell weather for the past week or two. Playing softball, etc., which passes the time much faster. Am well & healthy.

Saturday 22

Kalender

Corson & I worked in the garden & missed the S.M.I. Finished two weeks more in the library.

Sunday 23

Kalender

Nice morning but clouded over later.
   Air Raids last night.
   Music tonight was good. It really took me back. Read my letters again.

Monday 24

Kalender

Traded 2½ lbs of sugar for 9 "C" ration bars.

Tuesday 25

Kalender

Cooking today. I made a prune whip with caramel dessert.

Wednesday 26

Kalender

2 letters from Gen (dated Dec 22–29 '43) & 1 from Dad & Mom (Jan 10 '44).
Played ball all afternoon.
My mail has all come in on Wednesdays. Wrote 1 letter, 1 card

Thursday 27

Kalender

'Doc' Rose cut my hair. The band put on an open air show for the East camp.
[Wrote] 1 card

Friday 28

Kalender

Planted some garden. We mopped the floor for S.M.I.

Letter excerpts
to Butlers

Today has been a big day for me again. I received three more letters. Two from
Geneil and the one of yours & Joe's combined. It was the latest letter I've had. It's
really wonderful to have mail again, as you can readily understand.

I'm looking forward to a Christmas at home for a change. It will be a change,
won't it? It's awful to waste all of this time when there's so much to be done. But
the best I can do is keep busy, doing very little, until that wonderful day.

Saturday 29

Kalender

SMI Col. Jenkins.
Some mail came in.
Rumor: personal parcels in the Vorlager. Planted some peas.

Card excerpt

I received two more letters from you yesterday. They were swell. None yet have mentioned any mail from me, but I'm certain you've had some from the things you've said.

Sunday 30

Kalender

A dull day.

   Eating late so I missed the music.

May

Monday 1

Kalender

Finished a story on the UPRR.

   We hear rumors of broadcasts from the States for our benefit. Tough luck.

Tuesday 2

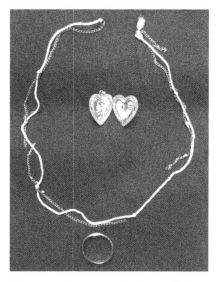

Kalender

Mayday. Parcels didn't come in til today. Changing sheets this AM. Personal parcels coming in

Wednesday 3

Kalender

Parcels coming in today. Haven't hit yet. The wind's blowing to beat the devil. More personal parcels.

Thursday 4

Kalender

Sun came up this morning for a change. RC. parcels.
   Starting training for track meet.
   I stopped wearing my locket a couple of weeks ago. The silk string is wearing out.

The 1942 Christmas locket and the 1943 birthday wedding band, both fiercely guarded in captivity. Also shown is the original locket chain with Richard's POW string repair. (Butler family collection)

Friday 5

Kalender

Six Letters, all [written] in Dec. Received My Oct mail.
   Wrote 1 letter.

Saturday 6

Kalender

SMI.

Sunday 7

Kalender

Cold & dreary for May.

Letter excerpts

I received six more letters today, which brings my total up to fifteen. The main thing I'm glad to hear is that you've been getting my letters. And in comparison they aren't taking so very long getting there.

I got quite a kick out of it in general. All of the amusements and so on. Life seems to be going on there as usual. I see that people are thinking of me even tho' they don't envy my position.

A lot of parcels have been coming in lately. I hope my second one is in the bunch. Things from home are really looked forward to here.

You asked me to tell someone here hello. The boys got quite a kick out of it. I was surprised to see it come thro'. You know some things don't.

Letters are coming thru now a lot faster than they were, so I'm looking forward to some pretty late ones.

Monday 8

Kalender

Bath. I saw a load of parcels come in.[12]
   Nice & sunny.

Tuesday 9

Kalender

Sunny for a change.
   Gestapo still out front. Goons are pretty jumpy.
   Sunny day.

---

12. Richard would have had to go to the Vorlager to bathe and could have seen the parcels arrive at the nearby Vorlager building where they were stored.

Photo in Kommandantur appears to show Adjutant Simoleit, left; Kommandant von Lindeiner, right; with Gestapo. (Thomas E. Mulligan Collection SMS 603, Clark Special Collections Branch, McDermott Library, US Air Force Academy)

Wednesday 10

Kalender

I've been training pretty hard for the mile.
   Nice day.

Friday 12

Kalender

Letter from Wm,[13] Dec. 1.

Monday 15

Kalender

The weather is bad again. Wrote a card to Wm.

Tuesday 16

Kalender

The fronts seem to be getting ready to move.

My legs are bothering me. Lost a filling from a tooth.

Wednesday 17

Kalender

Parcels coming in again. "Curt" got one.
   "Ite" front looks good. Raining.[14]

Thursday 18

Kalender

'Goons' are taking the raisins & dried fruit out of our parcels.
   ([Monte] Cassino fell.) They say Forts over again.
   No mail today. Bath.

---

13. William, his oldest brother.
14. "Curt" refers to Combine-mate Church. "Ite" is shorthand for Italian.

Friday 19

Kalender

Two letters, Lester & Theron (Dec 8 & 10).
   A letter home.

Saturday 20

Kalender

I found out that I have a parcel out front.

Sunday 21

Kalender

Air Raid. Am writing a letter dated May 23. Dentist appointment.
   1 card to folks.

Monday 22

Kalender

RC Rep took our pictures. Took in the concert—new PA system.

Postcard
to Butlers

Just received a letter each from Lester & Theron. Were very nice—thank them. Theron certainly has been swell about writing. Would like to get a short letter or two from some of the other kids, too. Have them drop a line or two in with your regular letters so as not to overcrowd the mails. I'm certainly not getting too many, but some are. All is well here. Am well & healthy & enjoying the sunshine.

Tuesday 23

Kalender

Got my Jan–Mar parcel.[15] Cooking again. Talked to Jack King about RC work. Turned shoes in.

---

15. From Geneil. 1 shirt, 2 blades, 3 pencils, laces, comb, soap, raisins, rice, flour, salt, 4 face cloths, 6 hankies, tie, 3 socks.

Postcard
to Butlers

Maybe we'll have spring here yet. Today, Sunday, is a very pretty day. The kind that makes a guy feel as tho' he could take most anything. Have been receiving my mail pretty regularly of late and my next parcel is out front—I was told. Probably get it tomorrow—but more on that later. Playing a lot of base- & basketball, also track, so I'm in good shape. Hello & love to all.

Thursday 25

Kalender

1 letter & 1 card, Mother & "Sis" Manning.
    3 act play "John & the Paycock."
    Goons pulled late count after lights out.

Friday 26

Kalender

We hear that Larry Allen has been repat[riat]ed.

Saturday 27

Kalender

S.M.I. Cooked a big meal today & "Goat" Baker ate with us.
    The Ite front is doing nicely.
    No more mail 'til next Wed.

Sunday 28

Kalender

Nice day. Big ballgame. RC. ball uniforms. Air Raid at 14:40.

Monday 29

Kalender

Nice day. 1400 Air Raid. We saw them again. They really look good as long as they come no closer. B-17. That's the 2nd time they've come in sight.

Tuesday 30

Kalender

Air Raid again.

I was just starting my last letter to you this mo[n]th.[16] Dated May 31. Some mail came in.

Wednesday 31

Kalender

No air raid today. A few parcels came in. I'm getting sunburned slightly.

June

Thursday 1

Kalender

No raid.
    Some mail came in. Have been running around in shorts all week.
    The Gooses '65 Club has a ball team. I'm catcher.

Friday 2

Kalender

Well, the good weather is over. It's rainy & bad all day. Some mail.
    I'm entered in the track meet for the 600 yd & 1000 yd runs.
    Gen's birthday 1 month.

Saturday 3

Kalender

Another rainy day.
    Haircut & washed my hair.
    Haven't heard from Gen for over a month now.

Sunday 4

Kalender

56 played the Sgt's. Beat 'em. Broach's team played "Coon Dogs."
    I ran the 1080 yd. in 3 min 3 sec.
    1 letter to Gen.
    [Margin:] One more Goon on my list.

---

16. The Germans limited the number of mail items each Kriegie could send per month.

6 June 1944

"After noon the men went into the barracks and lay on their bunks reading. It was just another gloomy day. The German loud speaker was blaring military marches. A few studious POWs walked past the water hole on the way to class with stools under one arm and pads and books under the other. Months of waiting, false alarms, no news, confinement weighed heavily. All were reflected in a slouching gait.

"At 1330, the persistent news translator ventured out in the drizzle to take refuge under the veranda of the West Cookhouse just below the cloth-covered speaker. A few serious, uninterested POWs hovered under the roof. A German ferret with hands behind his back and the ever-present look of apathy on his face cocked his ear as the music stopped blaring, the radio went dead and then the OKW gongs signalled the news broadcast.

"The well-camouflaged sentences at first did not cause alarm, but then their meaning dawned on the handful of listeners. 'The long-promised and long-expected for the Germans, attack from the West began last night. The enemy made attempts to land at the mouth of the Seine, le Havre. Other landings were made. Paratroopers and airborne troops were beaten off.' A wild yell went up immediately. They had heard enough. The cry of INVASION went through the whole camp in less than 15 seconds. Some men began to doubt the news as another joke, a false alarm. Voices echoed through the camp. There were too many yelling. It was true. It had come.

"A group of British leaning from their windows in the East Camp noticed the sudden flare of life and yelled across the fence for an explanation. At the word 'Invasion' they scrambled through the windows and disappeared to spread the news. Some of those men had waited five years for this day.

"Near hysteria mounted as the whole camp of 1079 men gathered between the two cookhouses for more details. . . . There was a flare of cheering, but Colonel Spivey ran to the center of the crowd and warned them to be calm. There was handshaking, grins. There were fantastic predictions about getting home in a month—the older men and particularly prisoners from Italy raised the question 'what next?' 'Where do we stand now?'

"After the initial hysteria subsided, the men tried to resume their activity. Meal schedules and stove schedules were confused. The blackboards in all classrooms had 'Kein classes—The Invasion.'" (Mulligan, Burbank and Brunn 317–18)

Monday 5

Kalender

Saw Col. Puritan [Purinton].
  Cooking this week. The "Goons" gave us some good tomato plants.
  Rome fell. Things should start.

Tuesday 6

Log

Invasion by the Allies at the mouth of the Seine and west toward Cherbourg.

Kalender

INVASION: Mouth of Seine River N. of Paris.
  Ran 1000 yd in 2:50 & 600 almost immediately after in 1:37.

Wednesday 7

Kalender

A lot more talk about going home already.
  Rainy all day.

Letter excerpt

It has been another swell Sunday. The weather is fine most of the time now, and that means a lot. I have quite a lot to keep me busy now. For one thing we have a ball team from which we get a lot of fun, although it's not the best by far. The track meet is coming off in about a week, and I'm getting in shape for the half mile. It takes time and is quite a bit of fun besides keeping "the body beautiful." We caught a mouse this afternoon and some of the guys are fooling around with it. I suppose they'll build a cage & have it doing tricks next.

Thursday 8

Kalender

On D.P. today.
  Ran the 600 yd. in 1:33.
  Operations seem to be doing all right.

Friday 9

Kalender

Didn't run at all today.

A compound war status room (Lt. Gen. Albert P Clark Collection SMS 329, Clark Special Collections Branch, McDermott Library, US Air Force Academy)

Saturday 10

Log

Kriegie Track Meet. I ran the 600 yd. & 1080 yds.

Kalender

SMI.

  Track Meet. I ran the 600 yd. Placed 5th. Placed fourth in the 1000 yd. Two races are just too much. Another meet July 4th. [Margin:] 600 > 1:16, 1000 > 2:43.

Sunday 11

Kalender

[Margin:] Orel's accident

Anniversary of Jerry drive EAST. Russians should start back today. News comes in pretty regularly now. Wish the mail would. Rain all week. [Margin:] 7th day.

Monday 12

Kalender

Doing OK still in the west & E. Worked in the library. No mail for me. Concert tonight.

Getting the Gen

Kriegies received OKW (German Army High Command) broadcasts via speakers in the camp; these were often considered surprisingly honest. "The political news was broadcast in the early afternoon. The Army communique usually came at 4:00 P.M. and was immediately translated and posted on the bulletin board." (Burbank 30)

  They also got news from the BBC. We "had a radio in the camp. I never saw it, didn't know where it was, but we had a radio." A courier would rotate through the combines. "The guy would walk in the door, and he'd say, 'Johnny Walker time,' and he'd pull a little piece of paper out of his pocket, and he'd read from the BBC." (Corson/ Thobaben 156) Spivey describes it this way: After receiving his clearance, a copy of the "gen" (news) was delivered to each barrack's security office. After lock-down, copies were circulated and read to each combine before being destroyed. (Spivey, 105) One of the surviving examples from Spring 1945 is included on page 340.

Tuesday 13

Kalender

Library. Ran two laps. Listened to the Kriegie News broadcast.

Wednesday 14

Kalender

Goons pulled a general search of the camp. Seven weeks since I heard from Gen. This damn system.

Thursday 15

Kalender

Working in the library all week.

Friday 16

Kalender

Doing a little more work on my war log. Did one lap in 2:28. No mail came in today.

Letter excerpts

The mail situation is rather slow, but that's to be expected considering the way other things are speeding up.

. . . I've been reading my mail over again. The average "Kriegie" usually does too much reading, and I suppose I'm about average—but that's about all there is to do most of the time. I've cut down now to the works of Mark Twain, Essentials of Business Law and stuff like that with a best seller thrown in occasionally to kill monotony. Some days tho', when the sun shines, I just spend all day getting a tan. I don't have much of a tan, yet.

You may sometimes wonder what kind of life we live here. It's amusing, to say the least.

Saturday 17

Kalender

SMI. Another dull rainy day.

Postcard
to Butlers

Although big things are happening elsewhere, life goes on at Stalag III much the same as before. We held the first track meet of the season on Sat. last, and our barracks came in 4th place in all around events. We're holding another on July 4th, so you can see that in one way or another we keep busy.—Wish Margaret a happy birthday—a bit later, what?

Sunday 18

Kalender

The show "Orchestra Wives" coming up.[17] Second since Nov.

Wednesday 21

Kalender

Theron. [Source of mail received.]
    Air raid 12:00. Extra long. The bombers flew right over here in 4 separate waves. Went out over EAST Germany.

Thursday 22

Log

I organized a block soccer team, and we played our first game.[18]

Kalender

Cooking today
    My soccer team played first game today. 1 to 1.
    [Margin:] Skinned a knee & cut my foot

Friday 23

Kalender

Played our 2nd game at 13:30 with Bl. 52. Score 1-1.
    RC. Boxes. "Uncle Joe" is moving.
    3 years ago today Russians entered the war.

Saturday 24

Kalender

My team played another practice game. Score 0-0. I didn't play; my foot is pretty bad.

---

17. This was a 1942 American movie musical.
    18. "The Roman Catholic Chaplain in our compound, Father Wilfred Coates of England, was by far the best soccer player. Not only did he play well but also he was the rallying person around whom the Americans learned to play." (Daniel 81)

Sunday 25

Kalender

The team did some kicking practice. I'm stirring up a lot of interest in the game. 1st league game: 43-46 = 43.

Monday 26

Kalender

The Goons kicked us out at 08:00 for a search.

Reading: *My Days of Anger,* J.T. Farrell. Concert tonight was very good.

My foot is a little better. 42-51 = 42

[Margin:] Nice day

Tuesday 27

Kalender

Big Band show outside. No mail. Clothing requisition.

Kicked the ball a little. 3-0.

Still in Cherbourg.

Foot still sore. 44 vs 39 = 39.

[Margin:] 1 card home & 1 to Theron.

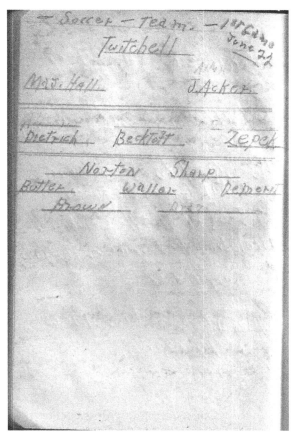

Soccer line-up from Kalender *(Butler family collection)*

Wednesday 28

Kalender

Reading *Stately Timber,* Rupert Hughes.

1 card home 1 letter Gen.

Soccer: 56 vs 41 N Sgts: 0-0. Play-off tomorrow.

Thursday 29

Kalender

No Mail.

We played 41 N again. Beat 'em 3-1.

Soccer game, apparently in Center Compound looking across East Compound to the granary. Hut 56 would be to the left and behind the viewer. (Courtesy of International Committee of the Red Cross)

Friday 30

Kalender

No Mail.

One more game with 55 decides the final. We played 52. Beat 'em 2-0.

Postcard 1 excerpts
to Butlers

We have a new speaker system in camp, which helps out in the theater productions, also in the daily newscasts which are taken from the German papers. We had another movie last week, *Orchestra Wives*. . . . Except for a skinned knee (soccer), I'm well.

Postcard 2 excerpt
to Butlers

Things get pretty dull around here, as you can very readily understand. Even I can get my fill of playing basketball, running, & reading books. That reminds me. Have you sent me any books yet? If I'm not mistaken, you can send one each month. It isn't necessary that often, tho'.

July

Saturday 1

Kalender

SMI. No Mail
　The war is looking better.
　No game tonight. My team is winner of the semi-finals.

Sunday 2

Kalender

Two men came into our combine: Re[a]ding & Williams.[19]
　My soccer team played 55. Score 1-0; they made a free kick.

Monday 3

Kalender

Took a hot Bath this A.M.
　Soccer: 40 beat 39.

Tuesday 4

Log

Big band & athletic parade, track meet and ball games all day.

Kalender

Band Parade, track meet, ballgames. (Soccer: 55 40 tie: 1-1/a goal & a free kick).
[Margin:] 1 card to Gen.

Wednesday 5

Kalender

Play 46 soccer. Beat 'em 3-0.
　Mar. to May parcel.[20]

---

　19. Both went down over Berlin on 21 June (B-24 navigator and pilot respectively). They brought the total in the combine to 10 men.

　20. From Geneil. Contents: 3 socks, 4 [hankies], 1 towel, 3 face cloths, soap, laces (B[uck] skin), blades (1 carton), 1 box gum, 1 raisins, 1 prunes, 2 candy (mix), gum, pencils (confiscated), talcum powder, tooth powder, toothbrush.

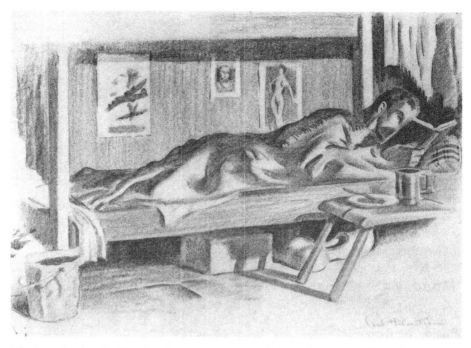

The Kriegie's bunk offered unique privacy as well as a place to read and keep warm. (© C.H. Holmstrom 1946. Published by permission of the Carl Holmstrom estate. © 2018, by John Holmstrom, Liz Holmstrom, Susan Kohnowich and Anne Shumate)

Thursday 6

Log

I received sixteen letters today. The whole camp was given typhoid shots.

Kalender

16 Letters (8 from Gen), 1 Heber
  Typhoid shot. A lot of food coming in from the Goons lately. Why?

Friday 7

Kalender

No mail! Goon rations keep coming in. Those onions were the first given Kriegies—say the English.

Card excerpts

Independence day today, also our anniversary. . . . We started the day out with a parade of the band and the ball teams & other athletes. Then the games started & have been going all day.

Saturday 8

Kalender

SMI.

Letter excerpt

It never rains but what it pours, does it? In short, I'm a mighty happy Kriegie. You know after two months without a letter from you even I start to wonder if everything's OK. Yesterday I received my Mar-May parcel (which was swell), then today the mailman came thro with sixteen letters, half of which were from you. They were all written between Jan 12 & Mar 16 '44. Gee, it was swell. Nineteen pictures all at once. You know I appreciate pictures almost as much as I do letters—almost. . . . Those pictures were really swell.

I received [Heber's] letter of Jan 26, which was probably the first he'd written.

Monday 10

Kalender

Working on my War Log again.
My week in the Library.

Wednesday 12

Kalender

Soccer: 56 played 41S (Sgt). Score 0-0.
We should have beat 'em.

Thursday 13

Kalender

Sands' & Bongo's birthday.[21] We had a big toothpowder cake.[22] (Pykopé)[23]

Saturday 15

Kalender

SMI. NEW Purges.[24]

---

21. In the Log Richard includes a registry of Kriegies which gives the nicknames of some of the men. "Bongo" was Perle's; at the end of his entry he wrote "'Bongo'—round the bend in a parachute!" He and Sands were members of Combine G.

22. On his "Desserts!" page Richard lists the following ingredients for this cake: Crackers, milk, sugar, raisins, margarine, Pycopé toothpowder.

23. Pycopay was a brand of toothpowder. Richard apparently is making a joke of the spelling.

24. "Purge" was the term for a group of incoming Kriegies.

Soccer: 56-42. Lost 2-1.

Monday 17

Log

Three-act play "The Man"—taken from Woolcott's "the Man Who Came to Dinner."[25] "TIMO"—made a bomb run on block 56—8 & one dud.

Kalender

The play "The Man" from Woolcott. Very good.
    Timoshenko [the cat] makes another bomb—this time 8 & 1 dud. (The new V2.)

Tuesday 18

Kalender

Caught a cold—German weather.
    2 Letters [from] Gen & 1 [from] Theron.
    NEWSROOM REOPENED. Protecting Powers are here.

Log

Visit from the protecting powers.

Wednesday 19

Kalender

1 Letter from Gen. My latest.
    Played 41N. Beat 'em 3-0.

Thursday 20

Kalender

Adolf had a little trouble.[26]
    My eleventh month.

Log

Attempted revolt in Deutschland.

---

25. Kaufman & Hart's 1939 play; author and critic Alexander Woolcott was the inspiration for Sheridan Whiteside, the play's main character.
    26. This was the day of the failed briefcase-bomb attempt on Hitler's life.

Letter excerpts

My mail is really coming in now. At least in comparison to the past. On the 6th I received sixteen letters, half of which were from you, all loaded down with news & pictures. I think I counted twenty-two pictures. Then today I got two more from you & one from Theron. . . . You can't realize just how much you help things out around here. I was certainly tickled to read about your talk with Stahl.[27] I could see that crazy Dutchman just as plainly as I used to. He's really a swell egg. I'm glad to know that they're still together, also the ships they're flying.

Please don't worry about what I think about & do here. A person in my position, considering home front & all, would have to be pretty narrow to remain bitter about the turn of events. Especially after seeing some of the more unlucky people who come in. They're not all as ready as I am to fly again.

Postcard excerpts
to Butlers

Was tickled to get the pictures of you & to hear that Heber has been home again. . . . I think I told you that I'd received a letter from him. It was short, but a little bit can mean a lot sometimes. I now have a total of thirty-nine letters.

Friday 21

Kalender

Started running the track again. Did my laundry. Haircut.
    Going to try for the mile. 4 Rounds.

Saturday 22

Kalender

SMI.
    Rain again.

Sunday 23

Kalender

News looks mighty good in the East.

---

27. One of the Sad Sacks, fellow 97th pilot and tentmate Urban Stahl, was photographed with Richard and Heber beside Richard's P-38 in North Africa. By this time Stahl and Heber had both finished their combat tours and were back in the States. Geneil had made a trip to southern California to see Heber and Martena; there she met Stahl, who was working with Heber at Van Nuys Army Airdrome.

    Urban Stahl was later killed in a flying accident in Hawaii while on his way to a tour of duty in the South Pacific.

May try the 3 mile. Team is going to E. Camp. Made 5 rounds today. (Tired.)

Monday 24

Kalender

Taking it easy today. Big race tomorrow.
　　The concert was wonderful tonight.
　　News sounds better every day.

Tuesday 25

Kalender

My legs were all stoved up with Charlie horse, but I ran 4 times around against 3 other men to see who goes on the track team. I came 2nd. (1080 yds around).

Wednesday 26

Kalender

3 letters from Gen. Nov 19 & Dec 6 in the same envelope & Dec 9. Things here are beginning to look as they did once before.
　　Soccer: 41N-56 Score—0-0.

Thursday 27

Kalender

Spent all morning out in the sun.
　　Worked on my War Log.
　　Things are moving as usual.

Friday 28

Kalender

Big day today! 4 letters from Gen & 1 from Wm.
　　Also four big towns fell in the East.
　　(Wash day.)

Letter excerpts

My mail is coming in pretty regularly now. I received three very good letters from you today, bringing my total up to forty-two. They were dated Nov. 19 & Dec. 4 & 9.
　　I think about the times we used to have maybe more than I should. That's what a Kriegie's life is, tho'. Just living in the past and hoping for the future.
　　Surprise! I do get off my "sack" once in a while. I'm on the track team, running the three-mile. It's a cross-country if there ever was one—in this sand. We're trying to get permission to tour the other camps near here for track meets.

Daily line-up for water to fill the Kein Trinkwasser. Each combine had one of the large pitchers ("Keins") for collecting hot water. (Lt. Gen. Albert P. Clark Collection, SMS 329, Clark Special Collections Branch, McDermott Library, US Air Force Academy)

*Postcard excerpt
to Butlers*

Haven't heard from you for a few weeks but am receiving Geneil's. Everything is swell here and improving. I am glad to know that I am being thot of by those at home.

Saturday 29

Kalender

General VANAMAN came in today.
Tossed the medicine ball.
News is still getting better. May get out of here yet.

Sunday 30

Kalender

They are still coming. Warsaw is having "it."
To be able to see the apparent end only serves to make me more restless than I've been in several months.

Letter excerpt

I'm working on a war log of interesting things I've done. You'll have your fill of wild stories, never fear.

Monday 31

Kalender

Cooking & in the library this week

I get an odd sensation from your [lock of] hair. I guess I won't know how much I've missed you 'til I get back. I'll explain.

August

Tuesday 1

Kalender

Not much news today.

Soccer with 55. Beat us by a free kick again.

Wednesday 2

Kalender

Dreamt I was home & we had the world's cutest baby. The rest of the dream wasn't so good.

Another big day: 8 letters—Gen & 2 from Mom.

Thursday 3

Kalender

Was K.P. today, pretty busy.

Wrote a letter to Gen.

Dell Porter is leaving soon.[28]

Friday 4

Kalender

Porter left this A.M.

Kochen:[29] made a raisin pie.

Picking up in the West. A lot of fighters around here now.

---

28. See Postcard to Butlers below at 8 August. In the Kriegie registry he signs himself as Del; he was a B-17 pilot from Beverly Hills CA who went down over Paris in September 1943.

29. German: to cook.

Saturday 5

Kalender

Moving toward Rennes & Nantes.
 I went on sick call, sore in nose.
 Library today. Worked on Log.

Sunday 6

Kalender

Air raid at meal time.
 Cooked an apricot pie. No more cooking for 3 weeks.
 Good news in the West.
 Movie coming.

Monday 7

Kalender

O.K.W. has been holding back on the news the past few days, it seems.
 I made several laps this afternoon.
 Hope I get a lot of mail Thurs.

Tuesday 8

Kalender

Received Caterpillar order.
 Tooth filled at the dentist (British Sgt).
 Missed the library today.

Postcard excerpt

My fourth movie at Stalag is coming Thurs. so my birthday will be a little different from others—I hope. I received my Caterpillar membership card today. Just
wondering if you had the pin yet. Am receiving some very late mail now. Some
taking just three months.

*Postcard
to Butlers*

Gee! I'll be an old man in a couple more days. . . .[30] You may hear from Dell Porter.
Latest "repat" to leave. He lived in this barracks.

---

30. Richard refers here to his twenty-fifth birthday.

Wednesday 9

Kalender

Listened to part of a biology lecture in S.55 last night.
   Several laps around track
   Brest Peninsula has had it.

Thursday 10 *Richard's 25th Birthday*

Kalender

Wrote 2 cards & 1 letter
   Picture parade at appel.
   Movie was called off. Scrubbed out the Combine.
   Kein Butler post.[31] Lecture.

Log

My first birthday at Stalag Luft III.

*Postcard excerpt
to Butlers*

Today brings back a lot of fond memories. Many a birthday "licking" I've received while working on the harvester. If I could get back to work today, it would be the answer to my prayers. I suppose the day will come, tho'.

Friday 11

Kalender

Letter from Wales. K. Gregory. Answered.
   Soccer: 56 vs 44 (56 4 to 1).
   Not much news from OKW. Any more.

Saturday 12

Kalender

S.M.I. Gen Vanaman & Col. Spivey.
   'L' Combine held anniv. dinner.
   55 vs 39—55 won.
   Library.

---

31. Meaning Richard received no mail on his birthday.

Sunday 13

Kalender

Protestant Service.[32]
   Put Willie Green in War Log.[33]

Monday 14

Kalender

Nothing doing.
   Soccer: 56-52—56 2 to 1/puts us into the finals.

Tuesday 15

Kalender

Soccer: Bl 40—55 & 56. Playing R. Robin for championship. 55 vs 56 tonight: we lost 5 to 0.[34]
   3:00 news: Invasion. S. France. Just 10 months after I arrived here.

Log

At 3:00 P.M. O.K.W. announced an invasion of South France between Toulon and Cannes. Ten months since my arrival here.

Wednesday 16

Canceled the soccer game.
   Big things happening.

Thursday 17

A lot of mail came in.
   Dull & rainy.
   Good advances near Paris.

---

   32. Presumably means Richard attended the service that morning.

   33. "Willie Green's Flying Machine" is a poem by Ray E. Deadman, consisting of 15 stanzas of four rhymed lines (aabb) each. It appears on pages 112–13 of the *Log* and wryly pokes fun at camp life by telling the story of a Kriegie who builds a plane from unlikely elements of their daily hardship.

   34. The first part of this entry is very hard to read. I believe it means to say that Block (barrack) 40 along with Blocks 55 and 56 played in a round robin competition.

   At least some of the sports games carried prizes or bets. This date Block 42 beat 41 in a softball game and took home twenty D-bars and twenty cartons of American cigarettes. (McKee 74)

D-Bars

Officially "D ration bars," these were developed to government specifications by Hershey; they weighed 4 ounces and yielded 600 calories from the following ingredients: chocolate, sugar, skim milk powder, cocoa butter, oat flour, artificial vanilla, 150 I.U. B1. They were constituted so as to withstand high temperatures without melting. The D-Bars were rectangular, measuring approximately 3¾" × 2⅛" × ¾" and were so hard that many found it best to slice them thinly before taking a bite.

They were popular among Kriegies for their high-nutrition value as well as their chocolate content; due to their bitter flavor, however, troops eating a more normal diet often discarded them. D-bars included in K ration meals were smaller, only 1oz or 2 oz. For combat situations, the 4oz size was packaged in threes, providing an infantryman the minimum to sustain him through a day without other food. These 3-packs were also included in USAAF parachute kits.[1]

In July 1944 McKee[2] describes the contents of a standard Red Cross parcel. (49) His description coincides with the photo from the Air Force Academy's Clark Collection illustrating a February 1944 parcel's contents, although McKee lists a much higher amount of chocolate (2.5 lb). Neither list includes a D-bar.

On 14 August McKee makes the earliest reference I've found to D-bars in Stalag Luft III (74); 12 days later he says he has exhausted his supply by eating four in one week.[3] (82) On 13 September he speaks of making a trade for his "ration of D-bars" (90); in late October he refers to them as an item of trade at Foodacco.[4] By 23 November he includes a D-bar as part of each Red Cross parcel (117). Although this could conceivably have been a separate ration delivered with each parcel, at least two other sources list D-bars among the contents of each parcel.[5]

Around this time McKee uses "chocolate" and "D-bar" synonymously, as in his recipe for chocolate pie (118), so by this point Kriegies' only source of chocolate may have been D-bars. The Red Cross lists only "assorted candy" in its 1944 Christmas parcel. At the time of the evacuation, Clark states explicitly that D-bars "were contained in all Red Cross food parcels" (145), but he also speaks of trading with "chocolate" during the march and at Stalag VIIA. Finally, it's noteworthy that Richard mentions D-bars but not chocolate being salvaged from parcels handed out in the Vorlager as the winter march began.

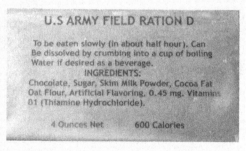

D-Bar box (Butler family collection)

1. http://yankreenactment.nl/rations/d-ration.html

2. Because of his specificity and consistency, I rely on McKee's account throughout the POW chapters.

3. He had received extras as part of the prize from his team's recent softball win. (74)

4. "American D-bars are fifty points on the tobacco side and thirty on the food side." (55)

5. Undated 1944 entry in a *Wartime Log* from Stalag Luft I (phillipsamoore.com) and https://www.med-dept.com/articles/ww2-american-prisoner-of-war-relief-packages/.

Friday 18

Kalender

The three teams in the finals were: 40, 55 & 56. My team took 3rd place anyway. In soccer: 40 vs 56. 40 won 1-0.

Log

In the soccer finals we lost to 40 & 55 to take third place.

Saturday 19

Kalender [star]

SMI Jenkins.
   A letter from Mom.
   West front is doing very well.
   3 act play *Front Page.* Not so good.

Sunday 20

Kalender [circle star]

Letter from Geneil. Mar 2.
   One year ago at this minute I was having a rough time.[35]
   Soccer finals: 40 beat 55 2-1.

Log

My first anniversary in the bag.

Monday-Tuesday 21-22

Log

American Movie: *Dixie Dugan.*[36] III rate.

Monday 21

Kalender

Two New Men this PM.[37] Lunt & Fitzgerald.
   'Dixie Dugan' now showing.
   3 laps around the track.

---

35. Richard refers here to bailing out on 20 August 1943.
36. *Dixie Dugan* is a 1943 comedy based on a comic strip character.
37. This means that the two new men were added to Combine G, bringing the total to 12.

Tuesday 22

Kalender

Saw this movie—Pretty Bad.
    Starting a new soccer league tomorrow with an A & B league.
    Labor Day track meet. Running 2000 yds.

Wednesday 23

Kalender

We've had it! They're bringing in tents.
    New soccer league starting: 51 vs 43, 44 vs 42.

Thursday 24

Kalender

Soccer 56 vs 41 & 46 vs 39. Winners-41.
    Air Raid 12:30. (Hot !!)
    Big adv[ance] thru Bessarabia.[38]

Friday 25

Kalender

Rumania changed horses.[39]

Saturday 26

Kalender

SMI Col. Hatcher.
    I refereed a soccer game, then ran two laps.
    The orchestra put on a program.

Sunday 27

Kalender[40]

Quite a lot has happened since I drew this. 3 weeks ago. Wonder what the next 3 hold.

---

38. Bessarabia, now part of both Moldova and Ukraine, has a long been the object of conquest and division. In 1941 it was occupied by Romania during its alliance with the Nazis; in 1944 Romania lost it due to the Soviet westward advance.

39. The fascist regime was overthrown and the country returned to the Allied camp.

40. The top of this page shows a hand-drawn map which seems to represent a line along the base of France's Normandy Peninsula from Rennes through Caen and beyond to the north. The map is dated 6/8/44.

Monday 28

Kalender

Russians [prisoners] clearing the woods out back.
    Cooking this week.
    I'm representing the West [Camp] in the 2080 yd.

Tuesday 29

Kalender

Corsican Brothers coming. I hope.[41]

Wednesday-Thursday 30-31

Log

American movie: *Corsican Brothers* starring Douglas Fairbanks.

Wednesday 30

Kalender

Soccer: 56 vs East All Stars. 2-0.

Thursday 31

Kalender

April 15 Letter—Gen.
    Got a lesson in lip reading.
    Saw above movie.
    Cooked today: made caramel dessert.

September

Friday 1

Kalender

Soccer: 56 vs 52. Ran 2160 yds 6:47
    Lock-up at 10:00—observing blackout paths now.

---

41. This film is a 1941 swashbuckler starring Douglas Fairbanks, Jr., and loosely based on Dumas père's short novel *les Frères corses.*

Saturday 2

Kalender

SMI.

    Some rainy weather after three weeks of sunshine.

    Track meet for Sept 4.

    Band show with Bl. 51.

Sunday 3

Kalender

Very dull day today.

    No V1[42] mentioned today

Monday 4

Kalender

Labor Day—ANNIVERSARY.[43]

    Going on half R.C. parcel next Mon.

    Finally announced fall of Bucharest.

Log

My second wedding anniversary, both spent in the bag. Labor Day track & field meets.

Tuesday 5

Kalender

Mail is very slow lately.

    Finished reading *Drums Along the Mohawk*, Walter D. Edmonds.

Wednesday 6

Kalender

Doing very well in the West. Russia declared war on Bulgaria. The line in France now runs almost straight North & South along W. Germany.

---

42. It's unclear whether this says VI or V1, but it's most likely a reference to the V1 "buzz bomb."

43. Geneil and Richard's second anniversary.

Log

The [battle front] line runs practically straight north & south along East France. This completes their liberation except in a few scattered places.[44]

Thursday 7

Kalender

Put a sink in the Combine.
Soccer: 2nd team. 1st Team's caput.

Friday 8

Kalender

Lots of mail in today for Holmes.
Whitewashed the combine.

Saturday 9

Kalender

SMI. Hatcher.
Life is terribly dead now days. Wish they'd hurry up.
Letter forms finally came in.

Sunday 10

Kalender

Days certainly are dragging lately.
Thompson is sleep walking again.

Monday 11

Kalender

Half R.C. Rations today. Worked on Foodacco[45] this morning.

---

44. Tucked into the *Log* is a hand-drawn map in Richard's hand, showing major Allied territorial advances; it appears to have been at least partially updated as late as 22 January 1945.

45. Foodacco (Food Account) was a Kriegie-run exchange where commodities could be traded on a point system. In a letter to Geneil of 8 October 1944, Richard tells her "You asked about cigarettes . . . . I do use them for trading materials, but don't worry about sending more." 5 packs equaling 100 cigarettes were included in each Red Cross parcel; Daniel says that, because he no longer smoked, he was a "Rich Kriegie." (83)

McKee records that on 13 September he made a deal to trade his weekly D-bars and sugar for five packs (90) and on 28 October, he says, one D-bar was worth 50 tobacco points at Foodacco. (55)

Soccer: 56 (II) vs 39 (I): 1 to 3.[46]

Log

History repeats itself again. We went on half rations again. It was almost exactly a year ago when we did it before.

Postcard excerpts
to Butlers

I've been cooking this week again. There's nothing like that job to take the monotony out of life. One consolation tho'. We eat better when we fix it ourselves, we think. Your latest letter written Apr. 20 arrived Aug 2. . . . These new letter forms have come thro in six weeks.

Postcard excerpts
to "Mark & All"

I've never heard from you since I got here, but as long as you remember me I'll be satisfied. So much time has passed since I left that by now you kids have most likely grown beyond my recognition. . . . Everything is going swell here. Even the mail comes in now & then. I'm just dreaming of the day when I arrive home and hope it isn't too far into the future.

Tuesday 12

Kalender

Air raid: saw them again.
    Letter to Gen dated 14. Letter to Dad & Mom. Card to C. Vaughan.

Log

Forts [Flying Fortresses, B-17s] over Sagan again today.[47]

Postcard
to Butlers

Time has been hanging pretty heavy lately. It must be that a streak of homesickness has me. What would cause it I don't know unless I've been thinking of home as a reality instead of the usual dream. Some of my letters may need explaining, but don't worry about them. Everything is going very well here. Enough of all except mail, & I could never get enough of that.

---

46. The Roman numerals refer presumably to leagues or divisions of some sort.
47. Sagan was consistently spared bombing because of the prison camps.

Wednesday 13

Kalender

The Goons pulled a search on 51, 52, 55, 56. Looking for tunnels. Etc.

The line has covered Rumania & cut off Bulgaria. [Margin:] H[air] cut.

Log

The Germans pulled another search on this end of camp. The first in a long time. They're doing a little digging on their own under Bk. [block] 55.

Thursday 14

Kalender

3 cards to Dad, Wm & Gen.

Bulgaria fighting with the Russians.

Marching to appel as of tomorrow AM.

Letter excerpts

Butler-post has been practically nil for some time now, and that isn't good. I'm thankful for one thing, tho: I have a lot of good pictures, and they can never grow old from frequent use. . . . the new letter form . . . comes through sometimes as fast as six weeks. . . . Here's hoping mail isn't necessary much longer.

. . . a guy certainly comes to appreciate good music around here. For one reason it's rare and another the popular music is so run to death that I get sick of it. Oh, for a good "quiet" afternoon all by myself (almost) when I can have a nice long talk with someone I care about. You know I hadn't really thought of it that way, but it has been a long time since I was all by myself for more than a few minutes. . . . I received my Caterpillar card—hope you're wearing the pin for me by now. It should have "red eyes."

Letter excerpts
to Butlers

Every time I write I say that all is well and as it should be. I suppose you sometimes wonder if it really is, but there's no need for worry. I have a hard time finding enough to keep me busy, which is true of most all of us here. We have a very good selection of books of most all types. That's good considering the fact that most of our time is spent in reading. I suppose you get the R.C. Bulletin that is sent out, so you know about most of our activities.

The detaining powers are allowing us to go for short walks outside the camp. I haven't been as yet, but they take ten to twenty each week and my turn should come around seeing as how they're going according to time here.

Friday 15

Kalender

Quite a bit happening in the East.
   Soccer: 56 (II) vs 40 (II). Score 1-1.

Saturday 16

Kalender

SMI Spivey.
   Soccer: 1st Team 56 vs 55. 1-3.

Postcard
to Butlers

I suppose by now the harvesting is all finished. If I could only have been there to help, it would mean an awful lot to me. I'm sure you could use me. It seems funny that after so long the farm is finally split up, but that's the best thing that could happen, I'm sure. I can imagine how it must be at home with all of us kids gone. We'll soon be back, tho'.

Sunday 17

Kalender[48]

Church this A.M.
   Called into office about position in sqdn.

Monday 18

Kalender

Cooking again.
   Parachute landing in Holland.
   Soccer: 56-51. 0-1.
Log

Big airborn landing in Holland in the area of Nijmegen and Arnheim.

---

48. The top of the next page of the *Kalender* shows a hand-drawn map which seems to show 2 areas: The first consists of a line, presumably representing the western front, running roughly east-west along the Loire Valley to a point somewhat east of Orleans, then northwest so that it cuts just west of Paris and continues northward. The second shows a tall triangle whose tip is just south of Lyon; its corners are at Marseilles and Cannes; appears to represent the state of progress for Operation Dragoon, the invasion of southern France.

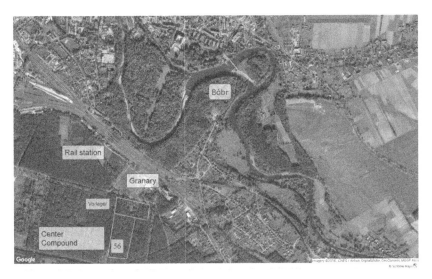

Parole walk satellite view (Courtesy of Google Maps)

Tuesday 19

Kalender

Big day today. I went on a walk around Sagan.

    Soccer: 56 (II) vs 44. 1-2

Log

I went on my first parole walk around Sagan. It's quite a sensation getting out of this place.[49]

Wednesday 20

Kalender

2 form letters from Gen. June 20–21.

---

49. Marek Lazarz, Director of the P.O.W. Camps Museum in Sagan, showed us the probable area of Richard's parole walk. He would have left the camp going eastward, then turned north and crossed the railway. His walk would then have taken him along the river and its canalized portion not far north of the camp and southeast of Sagan. (They would have avoided the center of the town.) He may well have walked on to the east and passed through the nearby villages of Deutsche Machenau and Polische Machenau.

We visited within ten days of the time of year Richard made his first walk and found the temperature very comfortable, though the weather was changeable and we had showers on both ends of the day. The trees are thick and the undergrowth lush; the water is placid. Richard would not have seen any mountains as he was accustomed to at home. It would have been a very pleasant outing under any circumstances, but for Richard it must have felt heavensent. (See his letter excerpts of 26 September.)

Parole Walks

Kriegies who gave their word (parole) not to try to escape, were occasionally allowed excursions outside the camp. In the early days of the camp such walks were common and conducted under relatively relaxed conditions. As time went on and the numbers of men in the camp greatly increased, the walks decreased drastically.

"These walks were supposed to have been put on a medical basis and the older prisoners were supposed to have been the first to take them. This policy did not work satisfactorily at any time and in the history of Center Compound some men had several walks while others had none. The Germans did not help the situation. . . ." (Mulligan, Burbank and Brunn 154)

"Groups of five or ten officers would be accompanied on these strolls by guards, and would return refreshed by having seen something else than barbed wire and dust for a change. . . ." (South History 0983) Several sources say the walks covered about ten miles.

Following is the language of paroles signed by prisoners:

Ausweiss, 2-part Pass for parole walk (Imperial War Museum)

Declaration

I herewith promise not to try to escape on the occasion of the walk outside the camp taking place on (date inserted) 1945, and not to undertake anything that could facilitate or encourage a flight to me or my fellow P.o.Ws.

I particularly engage myself on the occasion of this walk not to undertake anything detrimental in any way to the interests of the German Reich.

Signatures of P.o.Ws.
(Mulligan, Burbank and Brunn 435)

EVERYTHING HAPPENS AT ONCE.
Soccer: 56-40. 0-3.

Thursday 21

Kalender

Goon General in camp.
 All soccer canceled because of dust.

Friday 22

Kalender

Rainy weather.
 Wrote 1 letter to Gen & 1 to Dad & Mom.

Saturday 23

Kalender

SMI Col Smith.
 Air raid. Band show.

Sunday 24

Kalender

Everything is slow today.

Monday 25

Kalender

Form letter from Mother. July 14.

Tuesday 26

Kalender

Russians doing well.
 Rumor: 10,000 personal parcels in Vorlager.

Letter excerpts

I just received my first two form letters from you, written June 20 & 21. Yes, they come thro' in a hurry, don't they? They were six weeks newer than my latest— and especially welcome for several reasons. Mainly because they're my first this month. I still like regular mail, but I hear that you have to send something in them like pictures if you send them at all.

. . . I had a big day Tuesday. Guess what. I got all spruced up and went on a parole walk—outside of the camp, with several other "kriegies." The great out-of-doors is quite a place, isn't it? My first odd impression was seeing the camp from the outside. It was funny, too, surprising as it may seem. We walked out thru the woods, threw rocks in the [Bober[50]] River, then out thru a meadow. Really quite pretty here . . . .

*Letter excerpts
to Butlers*

I went with several other kriegies for a walk around the countryside and enjoyed it no end, as you can readily imagine. It doesn't seem like eleven months since I came in here. That's probably a good thing, too.

Several new men have come in lately that I meant to tell you about before. One from Cedar City, Ut. Quite a guy. I get a lot of fun out of him. His name is Richard Lunt. We're in the same building here.

Another fellow named Schauer[51] is in this camp.[52] He is related to the Taylors.

Keith Conley[53] and the other boys are not in this camp, and I have no way of getting in touch with them—much as I'd like to. Our little campus has quite grown up during the past year. . . .

Wednesday 27

Kalender

Weather still bad.
Finished *Wild Geese Calling.*[54]
Hard fighting in the West.

Postcard excerpts

The only thing that kept this from being a very dull rain day is the mail. Now it's just rainy. I got a July 13 form letter from Mother, and it's really full of news. It

---

50. Today it's the Bóbr (beaver).

51. Harold C. Shauer of Berkeley CA appears on Spivey's camp roster.

52. Here and elsewhere, Richard uses "camp" to mean "compound." This confusing practice was common among Kriegies but is understandable if one remembers that their world was confined to the one compound.

53. Conley was in South Compound and a member of the LDS branch organized there. He appears on the last page of Richard's Kriegie registry and on the LDS list Richard made in Moosburg; he was from Portage UT, a village not far north of Garland. Conley tells the story of his bailout and capture in "Turnabout," collected in Joe Consolmagno's *Through the Eye of the Needle.*

54. This 1940 novel by Stewart Edward White was adapted as the 1941 film starring Henry Fonda and Joan Bennett.

was almost a month later than my last. . . . I'm just waiting impatiently for that day—soon.

Postcard excerpts
to Butlers

Big day today! I got my first letter from you in over a month. . . . These form letters[55] come in in a hurry in comparison to previously. It surely did seem good to hear about Heber and Martena. Apparently, they get along very well without me to torment them. I'll be back before long tho'.

Thursday 28

Kalender

Shower [washed] hair
    Read *Fighting Caravans*—Grey.[56]
    Interviewed for my story.
    Working in Library.

Friday 29

Kalender

Received 4 letters: 1 June 25, 1 Apr 30 from "Gen" & 2 July 16 [from] "Mom." Bad news about Orel.
    Sometimes I wonder if this damn war is ever going to end.

Saturday 30

Kalender

SMI Col. Kennedy.
    Wrote a letter to Gen to be dated on Oct. 8.
    Learning to play bridge.

Letter excerpts

Well, here's the end of another month in Germany, and we're having the kind of weather that you football fans at home know so well. It's about the same way here at the center camp, too. Softball has died out, and the pigskins are taking a beating. I'm spending most of my time playing soccer. A lot of fun except for the nicked-up shins.

_____

55. These were partially pre-addressed aerogram-style folding sheets to be sent to prisoners of war.
56. *Fighting Caravans* is a 1929 novel by Zane Grey.

Postwar Plans: POW Support

"Many inquiries are now reaching the Red Cross about the release and return of prisoners of war on the cessation of hostilities in Europe.

"Relatives can be assured that much thought and planning have already gone into this matter. Even before D-Day a representative of the American Red Cross went from Washington to London to discuss with General Eisenhower and his staff, as well as with the British Red Cross, the collaboration of Red Cross societies in the measures to be taken for the protection and welfare of prisoners of war on the collapse of Germany.

"The military authorities, of course, are looking forward to the protection of the men as soon as they can be reached in Germany; but the Red Cross will assist the military authorities in every way possible. For this purpose, a special representative of the American Red Cross has been assigned to work with the military authorities in Europe and with other Red Cross organizations there which are no less concerned about the welfare of their nationals.

"The stocks of standard prisoner of war food packages now on hand in European warehouses and here in the United States amount to over 5,000,000, and the packaging centers will continue to operate as long as our approximately 45,000 American prisoners in Europe and some 1,000,000 Allied prisoners require aid. There will accordingly be a very large reserve of food packages and other supplies available for the needs of the men until they can be brought out of Germany. Much of the preparation now being made, as far as the Red Cross societies are concerned, deals with getting these supplies to the men. The military authorities will make all the preparations possible for the men's protection and eventual evacuation."[1]

---

1. American National Red Cross *Prisoners of War Bulletin*, Oct. 1944, 1.

I suppose you've been wondering when I was going to mention my May–July parcel. I don't have it yet, but they say there are a lot coming in. Just holding my breath 'til it comes. . . .

I've received two June letters from you and a July letter from Mother this month. A lot of news in them tho.'

October

Sunday 1

Kalender

Finished *The Four Winners*, Knute Rockne.

Good weather is back again.

Damn, this is a miserable hole. I hope we don't have to last the winter out. Especially on half rations as at present.

Monday 2

Kalender

Wrote 1 letter to Gen & 1 to Mom. To be mailed later.

Parcels are coming in. Received a letter from Gen dated Apr. 9. Also pictures.

Tuesday 3

Kalender

No appel this morning. Case of diphtheria in Bl 52.

No show tonight of *Arsenic & Old Lace*.

Log

Case of diphtheria in Bl. 52.

Wednesday 4

Kalender

Cold as H- last night but we're having a beautiful day today.

No parcels in today. I'm hungry for something but don't know what.

Thursday 5

Kalender

Letter from Wales.

Goons aren't satisfied with punching our cans, now they're confiscating boxes & cans OXOXX!!

A few pers[onal] parcels came in.

Log

Germans started confiscating R.C. boxes and cans, putting us to quite a disadvantage in more ways than one.

Friday 6

Kalender

Big batch of mail in this AM.

Air raid 1:00 P.M.

Mail forms came in. I'll mail the letters I've written (2 & 1).[57]

---

57. (2 & 1) as here would generally mean 2 to Geneil and 1 to Butlers.

Saturday 7

Kalender

SMI Col Hatcher.
  2 letter[s] [from] Gen Feb 16—June 1.
  1st form letters written.
  Air raid: 1:30. Something explodin'.
  Indian Summer day.
  Wrote 1 [letter] to Gen, 4 same cards.
  Breslau[58] seems to be catching it. 9:00 PM

Sunday 8

Kalender

Shoes from R.C. yesterday. T. Football in full swing. Caught slight cold.

Letter excerpts

I had a big day on the 29th. Four letters came in, two from you & two from Mother. It looks like my parcel is <u>really</u> going to be a good one this time. I can hardly wait.

One of your letters was a form letter & it really came across in a hurry. It was postmarked N.Y. Aug 5. Not bad time, except it was written June 25. . . . The other was written Apr. 30 and had some pictures. Gee! T'anks!

Gee! I hope all those things you mentioned are in this parcel, especially the records. I get so darn tired of hearing the same old tunes over & over.

I rec'd seven letters in Sept.

Letter excerpts

I received another letter from you today dated Apr. 9. Rather old, but that doesn't matter even a little bit anymore. There were three more pictures in it. I really am lucky on that score, getting quite a collection.

It was really a swell letter, just what I needed for my morale. You know those old familiar days of fall are here again.

The May–July parcels have been coming in all afternoon. Here's hoping there are enough to go around. Things direct from home surely look good. You asked about cigarettes. I couldn't say more than you've found out. I do use them for trading materials, but don't worry about sending more.

---

58. Now Wroclaw, Poland, Breslau was about 160 km southeast of Sagan. Men of the Wehrmacht were besieged there by Soviet forces from mid-February to early May 1945.

Baking powder has never been seen around here to my knowledge, so you can see it would come in handy, if you can send it. Also spices & dehydrated onions, etc.

It won't be long now. I keep telling myself.

Letter excerpts
to Butlers

Your three letters of July 13–16 arrived in that order and within a very few days of each other. (Which is a rare occurrence.) I was pretty worried for a while about Orel, but I'm sure that by now he's perfectly well again. Those two words he wrote meant more to me than he could ever dream. I suppose only a person under these circumstances can understand what I mean.

Mother, in case anyone needs any money or can put it to a better use, I hope you don't hesitate in letting them have what I sent you. I was tickled to hear how well the farm is doing, but I'm sure you could use some help. Namely me. That, I think, is about the hardest part of this. To think of all the good time that is being wasted. . . .

Some parcels from home have been coming in today, and that's good.

Monday 9

Kalender

Rainy all day. May get two more men soon.
Finish[ed] *The Guardian*, Bartlett.[59]

Tuesday 10

Kalender

OKW announced big OFFENSIVE ON ALL FRONTS. Oct will tell a lot.

Bad case of cramps tonight. Be glad to get out of this rat hole. The air is just plain stale at night.

Letter excerpts

What a day! One might be inclined to rave about the "Indian Summer" even here.

In the past two days there has been almost as much mail come in as there was all last month.

I got another letter from Wales (my second) on Thursday, and today two more from you. One was rather old (Feb. 16) but was a very good letter & had pictures, too. The other was your first airmail form June 1. . . .

---

59. This is a 1912 work by Frederick Orin Bartlett, an early "speculative fiction" author.

I've been tracking down a fellow who is supposed to have had the Dutchman for an instructor and knew Heber. I'm not sure about this because I didn't find him in time for the press.

Wednesday 11

Kalender

A lot more private parcels in. June 6 letter from Gen.

Thursday 12

Kalender

[Parcel in] MAY BE EXTRA PARCEL—NOT MAY–JULY.[60]
    MAY 2 letter [from] GEN. JUNE 9 & 23 [from] MOM.
    Moved into 3 deck bunks.

Log

Installed triple-deck bunks.

Postcard
to Butlers

I just ran into one of H's Students. It seems he is very well liked there. . . . It's surprising the boost in morale that I get just from talking to someone like that.

Friday 13

Kalender

Worked on Lunt's bed.

Saturday 14

Kalender

May 14 letter—Gen. May 14, Aug 13 & Sept 13 Mom.
    Made a pie for after band show. Cooking last this week.
    4,000 letters in this morning.

Sunday 15

Kalender

[Note at top of page] Around 9,000 letters Saturday & Mon.
    1 Letter to Mom dated 17.

---

60. Sent by Geneil, this parcel contained Calumet baking powder, cloves, ginger, allspice, cinnamon, waffle flour, jello, rice, pudding mix, soda, raisins, sugar, cookies.

A combine after triple bunk retrofit. (Lt. Gen. Albert P. Clark Collection SMS 329, Clark Special Collections Branch, McDermott Library, US Air Force Academy)

Very heavy fighting.
1 card to Mom dated 18.

Letter excerpts

I've really been doing nicely of late. Yesterday the 11th I got a June 6 letter. Then this A.M. I was busy cooking when my name was called for a personal parcel. You can guess what happened to the cooking—for a while anyhow. Gee! You really did yourself proud on this parcel. I've wished several times that I'd written for some of that stuff, but here it is. This is the May–July parcel, and there are a lot of July–Sept parcels coming so I can still hope for another soon. I baked a cake this afternoon just to see how that baking powder works. . . .

Well, time does fly, doesn't it? The 15th makes one year for me right here. If I'd have known, a year ago, that I'd be here this long—well, I'd probably have gone "around the bend" which, in Kriegie language, means just that. I'm OK tho'. But sometimes I wonder about some of these new boys that come in.[61]

61. From 6 October in the camp history: "A clash between old and new prisoners over the saving of food and fuel. The new men want to eat everything immediately and burn the reserve coal now. The critical state of German transportation seems to mean nothing to them. (Mulligan, Burbank and Brunn 350)

Postcard excerpt
to Butlers

Big day yesterday. In addition to my May–July parcel . . . three letters came in, too. . . . May 2 & June 9th & 23rd.

Monday 16

Kalender

3 letters—Gen: May 11, June 29, July 31. 2 letters Mom: June 2, Aug 8. H[eber] promotion
    Air raid. Came over I think.

Tuesday 17

Kalender

Rainy day. 1500 letters in. Wrote a letter to Gen.
    Fresh attacks by the Russians.

Letter excerpts
to Butlers

The last few days have really been swell for mail. Yesterday brought me four wonderful letters. One from Geneil & three from you dated May 14, Aug 13 & Sept 13. How's that for getting here in a hurry? Thirty-one days isn't bad at all. Your Mother's Day letter is one of them, and it's going into my war log.

    There's a fellow in my barracks who knew Heber back in May. . . . It certainly is swell hearing about him again.

    I'm glad that you've sent books. We can use them. Our fiction library is well stocked (I've worked in it for 8 months.), but I could use a few technical books or anything new otherwise. Oh, yes, I'm waiting breathlessly for the second installment on *The Flower Garden Mystery or Who Duffed the Dahlias?*

    Just got over a cold.

Wednesday 18

Kalender

No mail came in today.
    Worked on a tin pan.[62]

---

    62. Could this be the one pictured on page 266, the one he carried away with him? See Richard's explanation of this craft in his letter excerpts at 15 and 17 November.

Postcard excerpt
to Butlers

Just a few lines this A.M. before I get up. Geneil told me about your visit with Lt. Means. Too bad I didn't happen to speak to him before he left here. You may have heard from some others, tho'.

Thursday 19

Kalender

3 letters Gen + pictures: June 8, July 4, Aug 14. 3 letters Mom + 1 Willard: Jul 23, Aug 20, Sept 3 & Aug 4

Leo's birthday.[63] Tex Shackleford & Hillbilly Band are in. The cigar smoke is thick enough to cut with a knife in here.

Letter excerpt

Well, there's no mail for me today & it's raining, so I'll just stick to the sack & read yesterday's. I received four letters Sat. & five yesterday, so I really can't complain, can I? Three of them, May 11, June 29 & July 31, all regular letters, were from you. The other two from Mom June 2 & Aug 8. One that came Sat 14th was dated Sept 13. Mighty fine!

Friday 20

Kalender

400 parcels in Vorlager. 1 letter for the block. Wrote two cards.
    I WONDER WHAT CIVILIZATION IS LIKE.
    Made a Klim container.

Saturday 21

Kalender

SMI Col. Hatcher.
    Hardly any mail coming in. Making a container for sugar.

"We put the tin together by flattening the cans out and folding the edges back about a half inch on the tin to be joined and putting a U-shaped piece between them and flattening out the seam." (McKee 47)

63. No doubt this is Leo Gladin, one of the original six men in Combine G.

Sunday 22

Kalender

[Note at top of page] TROU-
BLE WITH THE FRONT
OFFICE ABOUT COAL
   News is picking up a little.

*Postcard excerpt
to Butlers*

The past week has really
been swell for incoming
mail. I've received 19 in the
past 10 days. Two dated in
Sept. Dreamed last night
that H— & I were breaking
out of here.

*Tin dish/pan (6½" square × 1") made by Richard
and carried home (Butler family Collection)*

Monday 23

Kalender

(Library week.)
   Air Raid 1:30.
   Reading *Reap the Wild Wind*, Thelma Strabel.
   Saw *Arsenic & Old Lace*. Very good.

Tuesday 24

Kalender

Very little mail.
   Reading: *Tales of Shakespeare* by Lamb.[64]
   Gen[eral] signing logs.[65]

Wednesday 25

Kalender

8 letters [from] Gen, latest July 25. Lots of pictures. 3 other letters, Mom, Wm &
Will[ard]. Bring me up to date pretty well.

---

   64. 1807 children's version of some of Shakespeare's plots by brother-sister team
Charles and Mary Lamb.
   65. General Vanaman's signature and the standard Kriegie registry information are
found on p. 120 of Richard's *Log*.

Thursday 26

Kalender

Library hours 10 til 14:00.
    Cold as H- today inside & out. Stirred up my sack.
    Classical concert.

Friday 27

Kalender

Worked on the stove & roof.

Saturday 28

Kalender

Col. Spivey SMI.
    Book parcel (six books); been in [Block] 55 for several days.[66]
    July 5 letter [from] Mrs. Miller. May 15 & July 3 [from] Mom.

Sunday 29

Kalender

Wrote my last mail [allowed for this month]: 1 to Gen, c[ard] to Mom, Wm.

Monday 30

Kalender

6 letters (2 [from] Gen: May 23, June 11; Sept 24 Lee Andrews; Apr. 30, Sept. 17
& Xmas Card [from] Mom).
    Cooking. Concert this P.M.

Tuesday 31

Kalender

[Letters from] Gen July 12, 20, 27, Aug. 6. Mom Apr. 16, May 28, July 31. Heber's
citation.
    Our recordings are the 1930 era.

---

66. Sent through Deseret Book by Geneil, it contained *The Hunchback of Notre Dame,*
The Maltese Falcon, Pigs is Pigs, Poe's Best Tales, Life with Father, Gulliver's Travels.

Letter excerpts

Here goes for the last letter this month. Hope the end of next will tell a different story. I've really been drawing in the mail this month. I should be pretty near caught up to about July at least.

I received a very nice letter from the Millers yesterday (Sat) along with two from Mother. My first book parcel arrived at the same time. A very good selection of books, too. You've been doing me proud in the picture line. I'm going quite mad pasting them in my log—but good.

My return was slightly delayed and I know that it's been harder on you than it has me, but it can't be too much longer. We have an awful lot of lost time to make up, don't we?

Postcard
to Butlers

I've been doing very well on mail lately. Tot[al] of 38 during Oct. dating anywhere from one in Feb. to Sept. 13. Most of them were written lately, tho'. My first book parcel arrived yesterday, & there are a lot more to come in yet so I'd better get busy. It was a very good selection of books, by the way. Guinea pig must multiply like rabbits.

November

Wednesday 1

Kalender

Not much mail today. All is slow.

My news on furlow [*sic*] hit the paper.

Thursday 2

Kalender

Two new men in combine. Now 14. Juntilla & Prickett. 4 triple bunks in combine now.

Log

Juntilla & Prickett bring the combine up to fourteen men.[67]

---

67. See Richard's entry for 12 October. This addition of another pair of men to the "room" explains why extra bunks had been added.

Friday 3

Kalender

May 28 letter—Gen. "Curt" & Bongo[68] got parcels.
  Rumors of ¼ parcel Nov 15.

Saturday 4

Kalender

Col. Smith SMI.
  Mail forms came in. Rumor: Parcels are being loaded in Genève.

Sunday 5

Kalender

Wrote 1 card to Mom & 1 to Lester. About Heber.

Monday 6

Kalender

Red says I have a parcel outside.
  Schubert's *Unfinished Symphony* at concert.

Tuesday 7

Kalender

1 [letter] to Gen. 1 [card] to Mom.
  Yep! Holmes & I got parcels (May–July).[69] Birthday cake & candy. The one on the 12th [of October] must be extra.
  Finishing a pot for barley.

Postcard
to Butlers

I wrote in Oct that my total was 38 for that month, but in the last two days of the month I got 13 more. My best month yet. Your [censored][70] letter was one of

---

68. Richard refers to fellow Combine G inmates Curtis ("Curt the Angel") Church and Richard Perle.
    69. Contents: soda, baking powder, soup mix, dish rags, shoe brush, cake, toothbrush & powder, shaving & palmolive soap, candy, gun, pencils, blades, socks, hankies & [kleenex].
    70. Presumably, the one word censored here was something sensitive and war-related. And given the level of interest described among the Kriegies, one has to wonder what

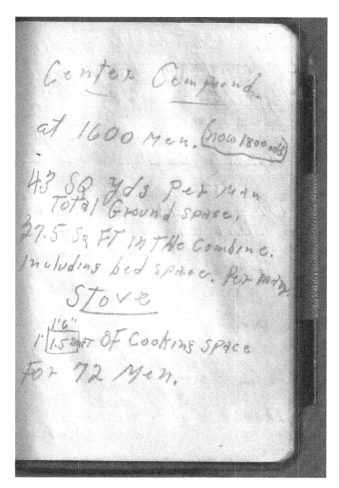

Space computations from Kalender *endpapers (Butler family collection)*

them. That kind of news does me more good than any other I could ask for. A lot of other fellows here were interested, too.

Wednesday 8
Kalender

June 14 & Sept. 24 letters [from] Mom.
    Soldered barley pot.

Thursday 9
Kalender

Worked in my tin shop.
    News is picking up again.

Friday 10
Kalender

Three more men went around the bend.
    S-2. On again tonight.

Letter excerpts

The last letter I wrote in Oct. was a little ahead of time. I received 13 more letters, bringing my total up to 51 in that month. My best yet. My first book parcel arrived about 10 days ago, and my May-July parcel came today. This is the one I thought I'd received on Oct. 12. The date was torn off that one, so I took it to be the next in order. Your mother's parcel had a lot of swell spices, etc, & in this one I was hoping for candy & gum. That's what I got, so I'm well satisfied. . . .

    . . . I've been telling myself for a long time now that it's about over & I'm almost convinced.

---

news squeaked through in that letter. Unfortunately, the surviving letters received in the last days of October 1944 contain no references to anything other family news; we'll never know what was censored.

Postcard
to Butlers

Time is going so fast that it seems a shame to waste so much of it. After being raised the way I was, it was quite a blow for a while—this sort of life. Man can get used to anything, tho'. I received another parcel today. May–July. Two parcels in the last month. Wish that would continue.

Saturday 11

Kalender

Armistice Day.
   No AM appel, no SMI.
   Made a spatula. News is getting better.

Sunday 12

Kalender

11 o'clock appel. Slept in.
   Last of English & Canadian parcels. All American from now on while they last. Rumors of more leaving Geneva.

Log

Ran out of Eng[lish] & Canadian parcels.

Monday 13

Kalender

Snow this AM. Working [on] War Log.

Tuesday 14

Kalender

Pretty cold night.
   Rumor: F/O & 2nds get First at end of E.T.O.
   [Letters received] June 23 Gen; June 21 Willard.

Wednesday 15

Kalender

Another movie *The Spoilers.*
   Snowing. Slushy & miserable.

Letter excerpts

There isn't too much doing around here lately. The weather doesn't permit it. It's been warm but rather wet & miserable. I've taken up a new occupation—building things out of tin cans. A potato peeler-ladle, pans and so on. It's kind of fun and kills a lot of time.

A lot of boys were quite interested in that furlow news you sent. It made front page in the "Gefangenen Gazette" (our camp paper—weekly).

Well do I remember that evening up the canyon July 21, 1940. I hated leaving as much as I'd ever hated anything in my life. Then it happened again two years ago. Will it ever end?

Postcard
to Butlers

Armistice Day is over—almost the same as any other. I'm doing very well on letters & parcels of late. One parcel from Mrs. Miller on Oct 12 & May-July from Geneil on Nov 7. Also my 1st books arrived Oct 28th. I received your letter marked No 10 & was very tickled to get the news. One of us is accomplishing something anyway.[71]

Thursday 16

Kalender

Saw the show this AM.

Read *Tales from Shakespeare*; *Life with Father*, Day.[72]

Friday 17

Kalender

No appel this AM. Sad weather.

News is a little better.

Postcard excerpts

I received two more letters today dated in June. . . . I'm usually busy, but today I took a break & read my mail again. I can always get a kick out of that. Parcels keep coming in a few at a time. Always something to look for.

---

71. Richard refers to Grandpa Butler's departure on another mission for The Church of Jesus Christ of Latter-day Saints.

72. Clarence Day's humorous 1935 autobiographical collection of stories became a long-running Broadway play, 1947 feature film and, later, a television series.

Postcard
to Butlers

Life here has sort of calmed down to the winter schedule—weather & all. Although it's not especially cold. I've set myself up a temporary tin shop making pans & junk. It kills a lot of time and there's really quite a technique to it. You ought to see some of the things these Kriegies make. It's just as well you don't, tho', I guess.

Saturday 18

Kalender

Col. Jenkins [SMI].
    Cold as hell this morn.
    Telegram from Gen dated Sept. 4.

Log

Anniversary telegram (Sept 4) from "Gen."

Sunday 19

Kalender

Warmer this morning.
    Big banana pie tonight.
    Reading: *Of Human Bondage.*

Monday 20

Kalender

Apr. 21 letter—Gen. Book parcel: 3 Church books.[73]
    Made my quilt over.[74]

Tuesday 21

Kalender

Cooking today.
    News in the West moving.
    Protecting Powers have gone.

---

73. Sent from Grandma Butler through Deseret Book. Preston Nibley, *Missionary Experiences*; Mabel Harmer, *Story of the Mormon Pioneers*; Bryant S. Hinckley, *Daniel Hanmer Wells and Events of His Time.*

74. This may refer to creation of a "flea bag" as described by Spivey on page 192.

Wednesday 22

Kalender

So the Goons pulled a little more dirt. [They're] cutting our cans wide open now.

Thursday 23

Kalender

R.C. rep is here. A few more R.C. parcels came in too.

Friday 24

Kalender

Apr. 24 letter—Gen. Only one in the block today.

Saturday 25

Kalender

SMI General Vanaman & Col. Spivey.
   Made some fudge.

Sunday 26

Kalender

Reading *Missionary Experiences* by Nibley.

Monday 27

Kalender

Library this week.

Tuesday 28

Kalender

Cold as - this A M.

Wednesday 29

Kalender

Letter from Wales.
   No appel, stayed in bed all AM. We're on parole tomorrow. No appel.
   Wrote two more cards.

36

Read at appel —

COMITÉ INTERNATIONAL DE LA CROIX-ROUGE
AGENCE CENTRALE DES PRISONNIERS DE GUERRE

Rappeler dans la réponse :

Serv. américain   GENÈVE, Nov.29th 1943
MS/mh

Chèques postaux I. 5527
Téléphone 4 23 05
Télég. "INTERCROIXROUGE"

Letter Nr 14

Col. Delmar T. SPIVEY
American Psow Representative
SAO Central Camp
S T A L A G   L U F T   III
                              Allemagne

GEPRÜFT 43

*ANNOUNCE CHURCH SERVICE AT
8:00 AM CAMP TIME*

Dear Sir,

We should be most grateful if you would
kindly convey to all American Psow in your camp,
the following cabled message which we have been
requested to transmit to them :

"Washington D.C.
Wherever you are, this Christmas message goes
to you with my heartfelt thanks and with my prayers for your well being and safety. God bless
you all. May your Christmas be a cheerful one.

Signed: G.C. MARSHALL
Chief of Staff."

Thanking you for your assistance, we remain,

Yours truly,

Comité International de la Croix-Rouge
Agence centrale des prisonniers de guerre

*South Camp Personal at 1:00
Salzman 7:00*

*Gen. Marshall to American POWs of Center Compound (Thomas E. Mulligan Collection
SMS 603, Clark Special Collections Branch, McDermott Library, US Air Force Academy)*

Fudge Recipe

In a postwar memoir Mrs. Sigrid Hesse, a former Stalag Luft III censor, included a fudge recipe which she had copied from a letter written by one of the Kriegies whose correspondence she had routinely read. Here is the recipe she copied from the letter of a Kriegie whose name began with "D."

Kriegies as Housewives Fudge¹

2 cups sugar
1 cup milk

½ teaspoon salt
2 oz. chocolate
2 tablespoons butter
½ teaspoon vanilla extract

Combine sugar, milk, salt and chocolate and cook until a little dropped in a cup of cold water forms a soft ball. Remove from fire and add butter. Do not stir.

When candy has cooled, beat briskly until a small amount dropped from spoon holds its shape. Pour into a greased pan and let cool. Cut into squares and it's mighty good!

_____

1. Lt. Gen. Albert P. Clark Collection SMS 329, Clark Special Collections Branch, McDermott Library, US Air Force Academy

Card excerpt

We've been saving up for a big spread tomorrow. I suppose we have a lot to be thankful for, but sometimes it's hard to realize. Most holidays make me feel this way because I get to thinking of all I'm missing.

Thursday 30 [Stalag Luft III Thanksgiving]

Kalender

Big football game.
 Fruit cake, apple pie, succotash, spam & dressing, [braised] potatoes.
 Classical concert.

Log

By saving for a few weeks, we turned out a pretty good meal.[75]

Postcard
to Butlers

I received another letter today from our friend in Wales. I'd like to visit them sometime. Having a big holiday tomorrow not[hing to do (erased)] 'til afternoon.

_____

75. According to the 1944 calendar, Thanksgiving was celebrated at home on 23 November; for some reason it was celebrated on 30 November in the camp at Sagan.

Wish I was home eating one of your wonderful meals. I will be before long tho! Have one ready for me when I arrive, will you? The weather is clear & cold—just about like home.

December

Friday 1

Kalender

Traded my jacket. Made a pan for cooking.

Saturday 2

Kalender

Col. Smith [SMI].

Sunday 3-Monday 4

Kalender

Parcels coming in again. Herb [Corson] got a parcel.
   Hasty Raisin Brew in theater.

Monday 4

Letter excerpts
Geneil to Richard (returned due to camp evacuation)

Geneil recounts a visit to Martena and Heber in southern California. "We spen[t] one day out at the field. I nearly went crazy over those beautiful "dirty-eights." Honestly, I did nothing but sit and gasp when they would take off or land."

   "I believe I wrote you before that another parcel had been sent to you. I mailed [it] several weeks ago. I hope it arrives before Christmas. Silly, huh? My July parcel might accidentally get there by then—with luck and a lot of faith."[76]

Tuesday 5

Kalender

Guard in Block 56.

---

76. In the *Log*, Richard kept a register of items received; the register shows receipt of Geneil's May-July parcel on 7 November 1944. The parcel Geneil refers to above (mailed in November 1944) must be the returned parcel Granny Miller refers to in her letter to Geneil of 26 May 1945.

Wednesday 6

Kalender

4 letters Vida's baby. Oct. 8 Gen; Oct 1st & 8th Mom.[77]
 Saw *Night Must Fall.* Ok.[78]

Thursday 7

Kalender

Wrote 1 letter to Gen, 1 card to Mom.
 Bath & haircut. I cut Lunts & Sands, too.
 6 laps.
 Rumor: More R.C. parcels in.

Friday 8

Kalender

1 letter from Gen, Oct. 1.
 Rumor: Enough RCs [Red Cross parcels] to go [back on] full.

Saturday 9

Kalender

SMI. Col. Kennedy.
 Fair news in Hungary.
 Thanksgiving Week concert this eve. Nik. Nagorka conducting.

Log

Thanksgiving Week Concert under the direction of Capt. Nick Nagorka.

Sunday 10

Kalender

Signed a parole for another walk.

Log

Signed parole.

---

77. Several numbers and dates in this entry were later clarified or corrected in ink.
78. The film is a 1937 thriller with Robert Montgomery and Rosalind Russell adapted from the 1935 play of the same name.

Walking the wintry circuit. (Courtesy of Marek Lazarz)

Letter excerpts

It has been three years today (Thurs.) since that fateful Sun. morning. I was at church in Sacramento. I went alone because Heber was busy. From that time on things have really happened—both good & otherwise.

Until yesterday my latest letter from you was dated Aug 14. Received Oct. 19. Didn't do so well in Nov. All 8 letters were pretty old, but this month is looking better. I received four yesterday. Vida's new arrival announcement, two from Mom & one from you, all written Oct. 8. After reading them I got to thinking about how things have changed back there. Everybody's growing up & so on. I won't know anyone when I get back.

The weather has been swell, tho' a little wet, for quite some time now. Hope it lasts. We saved up a little & really had a mess for Thanksgiving. Even the cooking was good for a change. Private parcels from home containing special items of food & spices really help.

Postcard excerpts
to Butlers

Received four letters yesterday written between Oct. 1 & 8. Give Vida & Vay my congratulations. They're lucky, & I'm sure they're very happy. . . . We're getting a very slow start.

Monday 11

Kalender

No walks this week. 10 laps today.
  Made fudge. Organizing a soccer game.

Tuesday 12

Kalender

10 laps. Reading: *Three Harbors*, Mason[79]

Wednesday 13

Kalender

Trouble: Someone's switching food in the parcels. Put in a complaint.

Thursday 14

Kalender

No AM appel. Made a scalloping pan.
  Reading: *Claudia*, Franken.[80]

Friday 15

Kalender

Xmas parcel situation looks good.
  Washed clothes. Built a shelf.

Saturday 16

Kalender

Col. Martin [SMI].
  Parcels came in ok today. Full parcels next week. Xmas.
  Band show.
  New rumor on parcels.

Sunday 17

Kalender

Lieut. Col. Dix to fill questionnaire out.
  Picture parade.

---

79. F. van Wyck Mason's *Three Harbors* is a 1939 historical novel set in colonial America.
  80. *Claudia: The Story of a Marriage* was a 1939 coming-of-age novel by Rose Franken; it was adapted as a play, a radio series, two films and a television series.

Letter excerpts

I've received two letters from you this month & three from "Mom," all written in Oct. 1st to 8th. Much later than any others I've had. I was looking at my pictures again tonight. . . .

You seem to have picked up the idea that I've changed camps. No, I'm still here at the center—just where I came fourteen months ago. Don't get around much any more.

Through our band and new Kriegies, we get to know a lot of the new tunes and other things that are going on back there. . . . I know both of those tunes you mentioned. . . .

Monday 18

Kalender

Cooking this week.
    Interviewed [by] the Goon Doc for my walk.
    More mail in today.

Log[81]

Interviewed by Gr. Dr. [German doctor].

Tuesday 19

Kalender

Aug. 29 letter [from] Gen.
    Went on 2nd parole walk.
    Wrote a letter & card.

Log
    Went for my 2nd walk around Sagan. Quite an experience getting out of here.[82]

Wednesday 20

Kalender

[Letters received:] Aug 22, Mom. Aug 18, Garland Ward.

---

81. In the *Log*, the next two entries are embedded in the December 10 entry with dates in parentheses. I've separated them into separate entries under their dates. There are one or two other similar changes from this point to the end of the *Log*.

82. The route was much the same as in September, but the weather would no doubt have given Richard a foretaste of the march he would begin five weeks later.

Christmas 1944

"Although I never doubted the Allies would eventually win, the Battle of the Bulge was a major set-back in the time table of the Allies and therefore a great disappointment to POWs. Christmas, 1944, and New Year's Day, 1945, were low points in Kriegie morale. We arranged special Christmas services and celebrations. Many barracks had New Year's Eve parties, yet a heavy cloud of frustration and homesickness hung over us." (Daniel 84)

"Soderberg drove through a blinding snow storm to spend Christmas, 1944, at Stalag Luft III. . . . The camp was brightly decorated with garlands, man-made Christmas trees, and shiny stars cut from empty tin cans. . . . That evening Soderberg attended a carol service, and when he looked out the window, he saw dozens of German guards standing in the snow singing along with them to Silent Night." (Walton & Eberhardt 372)

"Christmas: Much eating and an all-out cooking schedule with the small stoves red hot for 36 hours." (Mulligan, Burbank and Brunn 374)

An ice hockey match in North Compound was reported to the entire camp though a loudspeaker system provided by the YMCA. (Soderberg cable)

The general and colonel extended season's greetings to attendees at a 10:00 Center Compound Christmas service which included Kriegie-composed music; Soderberg also greeted them on behalf of the YMCA and their loved ones at home. Following the service Soderberg accompanied the general through the barracks, wishing the men a Merry Christmas. (Soderberg cable)

Richard mentions nothing about that day's food. Conceivably, Combine G had decided to save some or all of the contents of their Christmas parcels despite the threat of confiscation. If not, Richard's Christmas Day meals would have been similar to McKee's.

"For breakfast we had oatmeal with Vienna sausages, toast and jelly, and coffee. For lunch we had two cheese sandwiches and soup. Dinner was *it*! Wow!

"Here is *it*: turkey, mashed potatoes and gravy, peas and carrots, butter beans, bread and a muffin, plum pudding with whip, and coffee. For brew #1, cookies, bread and jam and for brew #2 we had banana pie with whip." (121–2)

Thursday 21

Kalender

1st Xmas parcels are in. Cold as the devil.

Friday 22

Kalender

News in West hasn't been too good this week.[83]

---

83. This is no doubt a reference to the Battle of the Bulge.

*A combine holiday table (Lt. Gen. Albert P. Clark Collection SMS 329,
Clark Special Collections Branch, McDermott Library, US Air Force
Academy)*

Letter excerpts

It seems like only a few days ago that I wrote 1944 for the first time. . . . I never
dreamed I'd write '45 from here but we're crowding it pretty close.

I wrote some time ago that I'd been on a parole walk outside the camp. I went
on another one today to about the same places. You can't imagine what it's like
to hear an occasional car whiz by, to see people, and especially to look just as far
as eye can see with no obstruction to the view.

I received another letter from you today dated Aug. 29, still no Sept. mail.

Saturday 23

Kalender

Aug. 21 letter [from] Gen.

Sunday 24

Kalender

Xmas Eve!! What a H— of a place to spend it. I'm homesick.

Monday 25

Kalender

YMCA Rep [Henry Soderberg] was in with the General.
  Big dinner.

Log

Full parcels for Xmas week.[84]

Wednesday 27

Kalender

Ice rink opened this A.M. Not much mail in.

Log

Ice rink opened this morning. Hockey games coming up.

Thursday 28

Kalender

Went skating again. Wrote 1 letter to Gen.

Friday 29

Kalender

Went skating before appel. I'm getting the touch again.
  Wrote a card to Mom.

Saturday 30

Kalender

Went skating early.
  SMI Col. Jenkins, then went skating again. Pretty tired.

---

84. On his 1947 Christmas card Herb Corson included this note above his signature:
"Got your RX [Red Cross] parcel, Panda?" (Card in author's possession.)

Letter excerpts[85]

We opened our ice rink yesterday morning, and I found out how weak my ankles are. Had quite a lot of fun while it lasted. It's snowing now, so I'm afraid we've had it for a while. . . .

We're having another movie tonight: "The Male Animal." Henry Fonda, etc. Our seventh one already. The last one was "The Spoilers." John Wayne. I'll be kind of glad to see this one for the second time. It's a comedy, just what we need.

I'd rather be watching snow fall on the Rockies instead of here. . . .

Sunday 31

Kalender

Skated before appel. Not feeling so good tonight.

New Year's Eve in a few minutes.

It's now 1945, one more year shot!! Hitler is going to speak at 1:15 (12:15 Goon Time).

---

85. This 30 December letter is the last mail we have from Stalag Luft III. The next correspondence we have from Richard is his 13 February 1945 card to Geneil from Stalag VIIA. Letters and cards sent during January appear not to have gotten out of Germany.

This isn't surprising, given how chaotic conditions had become. Furthermore, Richard was likely distracted by preparations for the march. In the *Kalender* for 13 January he records sending a letter each to Geneil and Grandma Butler; on the 27th he wrote a letter to Geneil and a card to Grandma Butler. He records receipt of only one letter each from Geneil (on the 25th) and Grandma Butler (on the 27th).

5

PRISONER
OF WAR
1945

January 1945
Preparing for the March

"When 1945 arrived all of us knew that the war was drawing to a close, although we did not realize how much hard fighting still lay ahead. We also suspected that we might be in mortal danger. The 10,000 or more Allied Air Force officers at Stalag Luft III constituted one of the most valuable groups of hostages held by the Germans. As the Russians neared Sagan, the Germans warned us that we might be evacuated to the West. Led by our senior officers, we began to make preparation to march out of the camp if necessary. . . ." (Daniel 85)

". . . the Stalag Luft III prisoners busied themselves making foot protection, putting linings in coats, making mittens, and improvising packs of all sorts. They spent hours sewing the packs, making scarves, and stitching *Allgemeine Zeitung* German propaganda newspapers between blankets for added warmth." (Walton & Eberhardt 468)

"Kriegie tailors created every conceivable type of knapsack and 'carry-all.' Some men had to make their kits over and over before approved by Colonel Spivey's staff, who stressed the importance of traveling light." (Mulligan, Burbank and Brunn 387)

"Each Kriegie had his own plan. Some joined into groups to build sleds to carry food, clothing, or other things deemed valuable, but most men tried to figure how they could carry these things on their person.

"I cut up a towel and sewed the pieces on my blanket to make pockets. The pockets were tailored to hold specific items of food or value . . . each morning when I arose, I packed the pockets as I would if I were leaving on foot. The blanket was then folded and rolled into a package, secured at each end with a piece of rope (obtained by trade) long enough to pass over my shoulder. A classical "blanket roll." (Petersen) Some made shirt bags to hang over one shoulder, across the back and under the opposite arm. "We all had some sort of bag or case to carry what precious little we had. . . ." (Keefe 281) Some men carried two.

"Each man . . . was also to see to it that his shoes were in the best possible condition for a forced march. Available Red Cross clothing was distributed to those who needed it and other preparations were carried on. . . . Lists of the minimum amount of food to be carried by each man were issued and Dr. Robertson interviewed all prisoners to obtain the names of those who were incapable of marching." (Burbank 31)

One Kriegie says ". . . I made overshoes out of a pair of wool socks with Klim (milk cans) tin soles, which I could tie over my shoes. I made heavy mittens by stuffing German toilet paper between layers of cloth and insulating my blankets with layers of toilet paper. A backpack was made by sewing one stocking on the top of a bag and one on the bottom and putting a belt as a strap between them." (Burda) In another example of Kriegie ingenuity in this regard, Robert Buckham created a tube of soldered klim cans in which he carried some of his drawings and paintings. (6)

"Kriegies started making emergency candy bar rations similar to the ones the escape artists had been provided with. Whatever the combine had in the way of energy-giving proteins—chocolate, prunes, dry oats, raisins, sugar—it was all made

1945

January

Monday 1[1]

Kalender (Januar)

Warm spell/ice pretty soft.

Tuesday 2

Kalender (Januar)

Read: *Claudia & David*—Franken.[2]

Wednesday 3

Kalender (Januar)

Started allot[ments] again. Very little mail in. Hair cut. Also Lunt & Sandy [Sands].[3]

Thursday 4

Kalender (Januar)

Working on a mixing bowl.

Friday 5

Kalender (Januar)

A little colder. Some skating today. Reading: *Am. Drs Odyssey.*[4]

---

1. From 1 January through 23 March 1945 Richard was now keeping his record in the unused 1944 section of the *Kalender*, changing the dates to match the correct day of the week. A few longer entries from this period were entered on blank endpapers and in the Kasa section; the same is true for all entries beyond 23 March.

2. Another in Franken's Claudia series.

3. Both of Combine G.

4. This was *An American Doctor's Odyssey: Adventures in Forty-five Countries*, a 1936 autobiography of Victor Heiser, an international public health doctor of the late 19th and early 20th centuries.

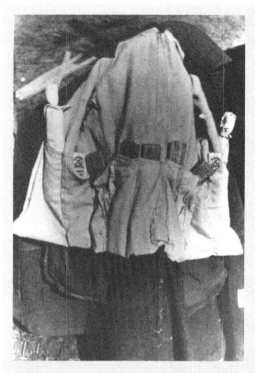

This vest, its pockets stuffed with D Bars and cigarettes, was worn inside the over-coat. Note also what seems to be a set of shoulder-holster pockets and that the coat's rear flap appears to have been stitched shut. Clark notes this as escape kit, but it would certainly have served as a model in preparations for the winter march. (Lt. Gen. Albert P. Clark Collection, SMS 329, Clark Special Collections Branch, McDermott Library, US Air Force Academy)

into bars to help carry us through the tough times we foresaw ahead of us.[1]

"Everything we owned of value that could come in handy was put in the backpacks or in our pockets as we had to carry toilet articles, soap, extra socks, cigarettes, matches, handkerchiefs, toothbrushes . . . and other items we considered necessary. Frying pans, coffee pots, knives, forks and spoons and other utensils were definitely necessary and room had to be found for them. . . .

"In preparation for the anticipated march, kriegies washed all their clothes and with needle and thread repaired any holes they might have in their shirts, socks and trousers, and underwear." (Hopewell 195)

"At 1500 hours on January 17, 1945, the German news broadcast announced unprecedented Russian advances toward the camp. That same day, the prisoners heard that shipments of Red Cross food parcels had arrived from Lübeck. . . .

"The news electrified the men and gave everyone much to think about. They had heard that prisoner of war camps farther east already had been evacuated and on very short notice. Clearly their own preparations had to be speeded up. . . .

"For a few days the camp seemed to be in limbo. Prisoners tried to carry on normally in the theater and outdoors, but their attention was glued to events outside the camp." (Durand 326)

---

1. The original "special food concentrate . . . consisted of Red Cross food with high nutritional value, such as milk powder, [H]orlicks powder or tablets, vitamin pills, oatmeal, crushed biscuits, Ovaltine, raisins, glucose, and chocolate. These items were boiled together until they formed a fudgelike substance." (Durand 292)

Saturday 6

Kalender (Januar)

Lunt's moving out. Have had quite a warm spell for the past week but cold again last night.

Sunday 7

Kalender (Januar)

Extra cold this A.M. Goat Baker moving in.

Monday 8

Kalender (Januar)

Skated this A.M. On cooking again. Hockey practice tomorrow morning.

Tuesday 9

Kalender (Januar)

Cut Fitz' hair—"shorty." A few personal parcels came over. Awful cold last night.

Wednesday 10

Kalender (Januar)

Skated yesterday & today. Warmer today. Parcels came in: nix mail.

Thursday 11

Kalender (Januar)

Too warm to skate. Russians starting to move again!!![5]

Log

New Russian drive starting. If things develop far enough, we may have to evacuate.

Friday 12

Kalender (Januar)

No skating. Saw the New Years show at theater.

---

5. "On January 12th, 250 Russian divisions with numerous tanks, covered by an unbroken line of artillery and supported by 7,500 tactical aircraft, emerged from the eastern bridgeheads and swept across Poland in a little more than two weeks. Altogether, there were two-and-a-half million Russians." (Walton & Eberhardt 467)

January 1945
Events in Camp

Monday 1

"The granary—only landmark above the pine fringe—is now used for storing Red Cross food parcels." (Mulligan, Burbank and Brunn 376)

Thursday 11

"There was measurable tension in the camp, yet an exhilarating air of anticipation at the thought of being outside the wire. . . ." (Walton & Eberhardt 467)

Monday 15

"Germans working in the camp kitchen are hungry. . . . It is predicted that March and April of this year will be critical months. All German food issues running two to four days late. . . . The coal ration is very small. . . . All barracks are on a strict coal ration program. Prisoners are wearing coats all day and more than half remain in bed due to lack of combine space and heat. . . ."

"Many men are 'very peaked, drawn, pale, underweight, apathetic empty eyes, living for something to happen.'" (Mulligan, Burbank and Brunn 379–80)

Wednesday 17

"Announcement of full parcels at evening appell cheered as the announcement read to each Block. . . .

"Explanation: 'The German Kommandant states that he has received a notice from Lübeck, the port of entry for our parcels from Sweden, that a great stock of parcels is on hand there. . . . In the light of this information the general has decided to go on full parcels until the stock on hand diminishes to a six-week supply of one-half

parcels.'—This notice was later read to the whole camp under security. The time has come to 'fatten up' and get ready for any eventuality." (Mulligan, Burbank and Brunn 381)

On the same day at 3pm "the German news broadcast announced unprecedented Russian advances toward the camp." This news "electrified the men and gave everyone much to think about." (Durand 326)

Thursday 18

"Another good thing—this is D-bar day, and we got another barley issue, along with one-third of a British Christmas parcel, which contained as follows: 16oz. steak can, 16 oz. pork, three puddings[,] one custard, one can of honey, one can of butter, one can milk, one cake, one can of Boston baked beans." (McKee 125)

Saturday 20

"Increased cooperation and obedience to orders in spirit and letter as the Russians advance." (Mulligan, Burbank and Brunn 383)

"Many of the men, notably the old 'sack' artists, are walking the perimeter. There are still some who scoff at the advice to get exercise and in shape." (Mulligan, Burbank and Brunn 384)

"The prisoners were getting reports on the advance over the loudspeaker system in the camp and in other ways. They knew that the refugee traffic through Sagan was heavy, that the railroads had broken down, and that there was a strong possibility of an evacuation. Returning medical cases from Breslau reported near panic there." (Walton & Eberhardt 468)

Saturday 13

Kalender (Januar)

Froze a little last night. Wrote 1 letter to Gen & 1 to Mom.

Sunday 14

Kalender (Januar)

Big hockey game. Air Raid late in PM.

Monday 15

Kalender (Januar)

Finished cooking. (I do KP Tues.) Did laundry & skated. Rumor of a lot of mail coming.

Tuesday 16

Kalender (Januar)

Went skating. Air Raid. Since Russian drive more rumors on us moving out.

[Beyond this point, because the *Kalender* contains some double entries for the same day, each entry is labeled to show in what part of the *Kalender* it was made.]

Wednesday 17

Kalender (Kassa)

Big day for all Kriegies. Since the Russian drive started on the 11th our morale has taken a turn for the better. Today the mail was a little better with promise of

O.K. ON INTER-CAMP GAME
TWO GAMES TO COVER THREE CAMPS

For the first time in almost a year, permission has been granted by the German Kommandant for inter-compound sporting contests. This permission was granted to permit two hockey matches to be played among the three American camps in the area. Camp authorities were notified of this fact Tuesday, and the contests will be arranged for within a few days as to number of men and camps included.

Gefangenen Gazette, *17 January 1945 (Arthur A. Durand Collection SMS 792, Clark Special Collections Branch, McDermott Library, US Air Force Academy)*

21 January

"Colonel Spivey to the staff: ". . . a 'state of emergency' exists in camp. . . . The camp was instructed to prepare for a move on foot. Much excitement—packing bedrolls—no knapsacks—Germans still calm." (Mulligan, Burbank and Brunn 384)

Monday 22

". . . the men stood a back-pack or blanket-roll inspection by the Senior Officers. Late into the night men were busy preparing knapsacks or blanket-rolls of the Spanish-War type." (Burbank 30) ". . . the opinion is that the Kriegies 'will look like a gypsy army on the move.'" (Mulligan, Burbank and Brunn 384)

"'Popeye,' asking questions, scoffs at idea of move, and remarks that the 'Abwehr' will be displeased with the POWs for doing this (making packs)—and then showed the men how to do a better job." (Mulligan, Burbank and Brunn 385)

". . . the compound received a large supply of winter uniforms and overcoats [delivered] by the Red Cross. These, of course, were new and of excellent quality. They were very welcome and during the lengthy cold German winters, the G.I. overcoat was the best blanket we had." (Hopewell 105)

". . . some rotten potatoes were available. . . . After thawing, they were scrubbed and peeled. The pulp was inedible, but the peelings, when salted and fried in margarine, were surprisingly tasty." (Buckham 13)

Tuesday 23

"The population of Sagan, normally about 20,000, has swollen to more than 100,000 as hordes of civilians move west away from the Russian offensive. The winter weather is severe; snow lies deep on the ground and below-zero temperatures are commonplace." (Buckham 9)

"On all sides of the prison camp . . . the roads were congested with evacuees from the Breslau area. . . . thousands of old men, women and children were shunted through the threatened area without a stopover at Sagan for food or warmth. Endless lines of boxcars and flat-tops were congested with humanity." (Mulligan, Burbank and Brunn 385)

24 January

A German officer spoke to a contact man frankly about the possible move. ". . . he volunteered information (in confidence) that greatly helped camp S-2 in reaching a decision. The truppenlager, outwardly calm, nervously made preparations, but no one in the German camp would encourage the prisoners' preparations." (Mulligan, Burbank and Brunn 387)

"Feeding of evacuees was a serious problem and bread consigned to the men in Stalag Luft III was confiscated and used by the German Red Cross to feed the hungry as they passed through." (Mulligan, Burbank and Brunn 387-8)

"Colonel Spivey told the camp historians to start packing the camp records and files." (Mulligan, Burbank and Brunn 388)

Thursday 25

German camp officials "told the men they were being 'foolish and over-cautious.' 'The other compounds are doing nothing like this,' they added. In keeping with the abwehr policy, the Germans wanted to confiscate all the kit bags made by the Kriegies, but Col. Spivey argued the point and then they compromised and wanted a parole signed, the equipment stored in a room, and a full assurance from the SAO that there would

tomorrow being [better]. A lot. The Russians made an extra large move today & last but far from least we are to go on full parcels next Mon. for a period of two weeks.

Kalender (Januar)

56 [Richard's block] hockey this AM & 52. Cold wind. Another rumor: at full parcels. 1000 parcels coming in tomorrow.

Thursday 18

Kalender (Kassa)

Was chosen to try out for all star hockey game Saturday. English Xmas parcels coming in. Something odd is going on—all this food & stuff coming in. Russians are giving the "Goons" hell.

Kalender (Januar)

Hockey with 40 this A.M. Extra parcels.

Log

A few Eng. Xmas parcels came in. Also notice that we go on full R.C. parcels Mon. 22 for a period of two weeks at least.

Friday 19

Kalender (Januar)

Good news but not as sensational as yesterday.

Saturday 20

Kalender (Kassa)

Russians are still going all out. Warsaw—Littsmannstadt[6] Krakow Etc. have fallen. They're 30 mi from Breslau. About 130 from here.

    Rumors of our moving (another—from Bres[lau]—here.)

Kalender (Januar)

Postponed our Hockey game until tomorrow. I'm a sub.

---

6. Litzmannstadt (now Lódz), about 250 km due east of Sagan, was the site of an infamous ghetto established for Jews and Roma after the 1939 invasion of Poland.

not be a 'mass insurrection.' After discussing the parole, the staff agreed with Col. Spivey and at 1100 hours the Germans agreed to the storing of all kit-bags in the B[lock] C[ommander]'s room in each barracks." (Mulligan, Burbank and Brunn 388)

"All the Germans and the prisoners could do . . . was wait and try to carry on as usual." (Durand 327)

"A near-panic was caused tonight by an unconfirmed rumour that the goons were actually pulling out and leaving us behind. There are an estimated 15,000 to 20,000 Allied Airforce POWs in the several compounds in this area. . . ." (Buckham 15)

Friday 26

"When the Russians were some 25 kilometers away, our preparations were almost complete. Every man had either an approved shoulder roll or some kind of knapsack. These were packed with the required minimum stock of provisions. All had to pass inspection." (Spivey 116)

Always in the background was the possibility—known and fully understood by the camp's Allied leaders—that the Germans would decide to liquidate the prisoners. "There was a great air of expectancy throughout the camp; morale was extremely high. Most of the boys did not realize that there was the slightest possibility that our plans could go wrong or that the SS might come in and carry out the grim orders of some of their sadistic leaders." (Spivey 117)

Saturday 27–Sunday 28

"From midnight until approximately 0300 hours, many of the prisoners were busy building sleds, and when evacuation started, with Block 39 leading the way, approximately one-third of the prisoners were pulling sleds of all sorts while the other two-thirds had blanket rolls or knapsacks." (Mulligan, Burbank and Brunn 398)

Sunday 21

Kalender (Januar)

Hockey game/my first rink game. Pretty cold last night.

Letter excerpt
Granny Miller to Geneil

We are listening every day to the radio to see how fast those Russians are driving toward Berlin. . . . They will soon be to Richard if he hasn't been moved. From what this last Red Cross Bulletin says, he hasn't been moved.

Monday 22

Kalender (Kassa)

Big explosion this A.M. Duffel inspection at 1:00 in prep. for possible move.

Richard's hand-drawn map of war progress. Latest update is 22 January. (Richard M. Butler papers MSS 8849, L. Tom Perry Special Collections, Harold B. Lee Library, Brigham Young University)

SHOE REPAIRS GO FULL BLAST

Working again on a full-time schedule in order to make what repairs it can in the possible time, the camp shoe repair shop Tuesday night had taken care of the needs of three of the 10 blocks.

Remainder of the blocks are expected to be finished before the week is out.

The only materials on hand are the rubber stick-on soles that recently arrived. These, however, are being affixed both with glue and nails in order to assure longer wear. It was announced that as long as the present emergency exists--or until all outstanding needs are filled--no more soles will be issued to individuals. The materials--must be affixed by workers.

The shop now works from appel to appel daily ecept Saturday when it is open only in the afternoon.

As a word of caution in the interests of preserving the present footwear, Lt. G. Hodges,-warned against placing damp shoes atop stoves. "More shoes are burned out here than are worn out," Hodges said. He explained that sudden heating and drying causes the undersoles to crack and rot to the point that is beyond repair............

Gefangenen Gazette, *24 January 1945 (Arthur A. Durand Collection SMS 792, Clark Special Collections Branch, McDermott Library, US Air Force Academy)*

All goon manpower called to Breslau. Can't get our parcels censored. Russians still moving. Good chance that we'll move but I hope not. Bread room is locked. Nasty rumor that food is frozen.

Kalender (Januar)

The parcels didn't come in. Skated on the big rink this AM.

Tuesday 23

Kalender (Kassa)

For the past week everything with wings has been going west. Today the air has been full of 190s & 109s. It's coming to a head.

Kalender (Januar)

Goons hauled our bread out. Big adv[ance] again today. Rumor: Sagan full of refugees.

Wednesday 24

Kalender (Januar)

Refugees passing all day. Russians heading for Danzig. -25° C. -15° F this AM.[7]

Log

Last night was the coldest yet: -25° Cent. We've been hearing Russian shellfire in the east.

Thursday 25

Kalender (Kassa)

Talk about nervous tension. These kriegies really have it. Mostly worry as to whether we'll move out or whether the Russians

---

7. "The Silesian winter had gathered more fury. Defying the coldest winter on record in fifty years, the men walked the one-and-a-quarter-mile circuit, trying to get in ten laps daily as they prepared for a possible march." (Walton & Eberhardt 468)

will stage a fight around us. The next few days will mean an awful lot one way or another. I don't think that any important crisis will excite me much after this.

Kalender (Januar)

Sept. 17, '44 [letter from] Geneil. Worked on the rink. Russians have reached the Oder [Odra]. Just 45 miles away. Yike!!

Hockey game at Stalag Luft III. (Courtesy of Marilyn Walton)

Friday 26

Kalender (Kassa)

Not much news came in today. The camp has settled down somewhat. Big hockey game with the west camp.

Kalender (Januar)

A lot of shell-fire in the distance.

Log

Inter-compound hockey games with the South Camp yesterday & the West Camp today. We lost.

Editor's Note: In both the *Kalender* (*Kassa*) and *Log* entries, events of 27–28 January are conflated; I've split and slightly reformatted entries from both sources for the sake of chronological clarity. Note also that Richard indicates that *Kalender (Kassa)* entries for 27–31 January were made on 2 February.

Saturday 27[8]

Kalender (Januar)

Nov. 19 letter 'Mom'[9]/wrote 1 letter to Gen & 1 card to Mom. News still pretty good/went Skating. [All caps in box:] ALERT

---

8. "The men of Center and West Compounds had enjoyed a spirited hockey game that day, and the Germans conducted a routine search of the barracks in Center Compound. By evening, most men were enjoying presentations in the camp theaters." (Walton & Eberhardt 470)

9. Grandma Butler's letter of 19 November 1944 was the last home mail Richard received in Sagan; it came in just over 2 months and reached him only hours before he

What Richard Wore & Carried from the Camp

*High-value personal items:

    Christmas locket and chain repaired with string.

    His journals (2lb): The *Wartime Log* (7.75" × 9.75" × 1.5"). Of similar dimensions but much thinner, the Italian *Quaderno* was likely packaged with the *Log.* The pocket-size *Kalender* was carried in a protected but accessible niche, since it was updated along the march. None of these shows any sign of weather damage.

    Some of his mail (12oz): We have 45 pieces of mail received by Richard in Stalag Luft III; four were permanently affixed in the *Log.*[1] When he left the camp, Richard carried the other 41 letters separate from but possibly packaged with the *Log.* The bundled letters weigh about 12 oz and form a compressed, uncovered packet 7.5" × 3.75" × 1.1".

*Clothing worn: We know Richard had wool underwear (presumptive long johns).[2] I also assume he wore 1 pair of wool pants, 2 long-sleeve shirts (wool and cotton), a sweater or jacket;[3] socks and boots (lightweight if he hadn't replaced his shot-down footgear); over-coat/cap/gloves, a blanket poncho/wrap, and a scarf covering head and ears. Perhaps a Kriegie form of "overshoes."

*Supplies previously saved: I assume that Richard had saved the equivalent of one Red Cross parcel[4] along with three 4oz D-bars from Spivey's special distribution.

    Packed in coat: 4 D-bars (16oz), sugar (8oz), Vitamin C tabs, cheese (8oz), biscuits (6oz), salmon (8oz), paté (6oz), jam (6oz), soap bar (2 oz). I assume he had also saved 4 oz of additional chocolate and kept one pack of cigarettes easily accessible.

    Carried in pack: corned beef (12oz), prunes (16oz), paté (6oz), powdered milk (16oz), margarine (16oz), pork (12oz), salmon (8oz), jam (6oz).

*Miscellaneous necessities: Richard carried out of the camp and brought home a small towel/washcloth set, his Klim-can tin dish (6.5" square × 1") and sewing kit. I assume he wore his second blanket if it wasn't used as a pack (2.5 lb.) and that he carried rope for a hammock (10'), a bath towel, soap, toothbrush & powder, toilet paper, cooking & eating utensils and 2 handkerchieves. For trade I allot him the extra bar of soap and 200 more cigarettes (10 packs, 20 oz); if compressed, 10 packs would have required a spot roughly 3" × 2" × 5".

---

    1. Based on Richard's record of mail received, nearly 100 letters were destroyed or left behind.

    2. In February 1944 he received "wool underwear" and "wrist lits" (short gloves or wrist warmers) in a parcel from home; he also received a shirt in that parcel and another shirt in a later one. As a nonsmoking "rich Kriegie," Richard may also have enlarged his wardrobe through trades; one source says a shirt was worth 80 cigarettes.

    3. I'm assuming that he got at least one of these via the Spivey clothing wish list.

    4. The first full parcels were received Christmas week. The full-parcel flow slowed early in the year, then resumed a week before the evacuation. There was also the special Christmas parcel (much or all of which may have been "bashed") and the 1/3 British Christmas parcel on 18 January.

*Food added in the Vorlager: As he passed the storage shed, Richard was tossed one Red Cross parcel; he likely pitched the coffee.[5] Even if he had to stuff them inside his shirts, he could have found space for the Vitamin C tabs, jam/honey (6oz), two D-bars (8oz), the smaller cans of salmon (8oz) and pâté (6oz) along with the cheese (8oz) and 2 bars of soap (4oz).

(I imagine him eating prunes (16oz) as he walked, and perhaps he found pocket space for sugar (8oz), biscuits (6oz) and cigarettes (2oz). If his arms were free, he might have tried to carry the bulkier parcel items—larger canned meats (24oz), margarine (16oz), powdered milk (16oz)—in the box itself, but none of these is counted in the weight totals below.)

What We Can Surmise He Also Carried

*Extra clothing: 1 set khaki cotton long sleeve shirt and pants,[6] 4 pairs cotton underwear, 3 pairs socks.

Sundries such as matches.

How He Carried His "Equipment"

Richard may have used a blanket-roll, but the journals and mail clearly had special protection. He may have sewn a carry-all from a towel, shirt or blanket. I think it most likely that he made a Canadian style front-&-back pack, which would have given two well-protected spaces against the body. It's also possible he had one of the suitcases available from the canteen in PG 21 (Chieti).

On the first leg of the march, he carried or wore everything. In Halbau he bought a sled; in Bad Muskau, with warmer weather, he made from the sled a travois to transport his remaining possessions to Spremberg. Along with the extra clothing, the posited miscellaneous necessities and supplies not carried in his clothing can be crammed into a backpack 13" × 18" × 10" (2.5lb).

Weight carried and/or pulled	lb	oz
Clothing worn/items carried in clothing		
Journals, mail & locket/chain	2	13.5
Food, cigarettes	4	14
Clothing worn	11	
Backpack[7]	17	
Total worn or carried	35	11.5
Sled/travois	5-7	

5. Of this, Keefe says "I threw away the cigarettes and the soap. I didn't want to carry the Klim powdered milk, so I pitched that also. I kept the Spam, the prunes, the corned beef, and the D-bar and crammed those into my coat pockets. I also threw away the coffee mixture and a few other items." (282)

6. He is wearing these in post-liberation photos at VIIA. I believe these may be his bail-out "suntans," which he probably wore in the camps during warm weather.

7. Containing previously-saved Red Cross cigarettes and bulky food items not carried in what he wore, miscellaneous necessities (including the second blanket) and extra clothing.

The Winter March

Once outside the camp, different compounds followed varying routes. The accounts and times given here reflect the experience of Center Compound men.

"At his 4:30 staff meeting in Berlin on the afternoon of January 27, 1945, Adolf Hitler issued the order to evacuate Stalag Luft III. He was fearful that the 10,000 Allied airmen at the camp would be liberated by the Russians. A spearhead of Soviet Marshal Ivan Konev's southern army had already pierced to within 20 kilometers of the camp." (Consolmagno)

"It had snowed for several days and the weather was bitterly cold. We were having trouble keeping warm. We were having even more trouble keeping sane. . . . Rumors were so thick among the Germans that they frequently tried to verify them by talking with us. . . . General Vanaman, Colonel Jenkins, Colonel Hatcher, and I were having a lively game of bridge when, about nine o-clock, our camp officer rushed into the room and told us that we would have to leave within 30 minutes. This was the moment we had been anticipating for the past two years." (Spivey 118)

"Under the bright fence lights, Col. Delmar Spivey, SAO [Senior American Officer] of Center Compound, moved about the camp to notify the block commanders of an imminent departure. . . . The night was cold, but by ten o-clock the snow stopped falling." (Walton & Eberhardt 470)

"Throughout the camp there was a mad rush, excitement, and confusion, in kriegie jargon a gigantic 'flap.' Bedrolls were repacked, and men cleaned out cupboards. . . . The men scrambled to their blocks to put on clean, warm clothing, and food that could not be carried was bashed [binged]. Most marchers packed the most nutritious and lighest of foods—raisins, sugar, cheese, coffee, cocoa powder, prunes, and chocolate instead of the heavier cans of Spam and powdered milk. The men, dependent on each other, helped one another into greatcoats and packs. Blankets were tied around shoulders. . . . There were plenty of cigarettes, and they would be used for barter, easily traded for food and favors." (Walton & Eberhardt 472)

"A mass assault was made on the prison grounds to dig up three million cigarets [*sic*], and chocolate bars, maps, money and compasses that had all been hidden for this day." (Spivey/Halvorsen 7) "Joe Doherty ran to the kitchen and started making a huge batch of fudge. . . . At the last moment, I decided to make a sled and Schauer and I took four bedboards—used two as runners and two for the platform and put tin on the runners." (Burda)

Presumably because they were closest to the road running southwest out of Sagan, South Compound led out, breaking trail over the snow-covered cobbles. The first men to march out onto the road found 6" of snow there; more fell as they marched, sometimes in blizzard conditions. Temperatures that night and the next day were between 10 and 20 degrees Farenheit below zero. The Germans had made "little or no provision for their care on the journey." (Durand 329–31)

March Route of Center Compound[1]

Overnight stops are in bold and current Polish names are in parentheses.

Sunday 28 January	Stalag Luft III
	Hermsdorf (Zaganiec)
	Hammerfeld (Czerna)
	Zehrbeutel (Dolany/Ilowa)
	Halbau (Ilowa)
Monday 29 January	Burau (Borowe)
	Freiwaldau (Gozdnica)
	Selingersrüh (Lipna)
Wednesday 31 January	Priebus (Przewoz)
	Pattag (Potok)
	Jamnitz (Jamnica)
	Lichtenberg (Letow)
	Neissebruck
	Birkfahre
	Schrothammer (Straszów)
	Hermsdorf (Przewozniki)
	Bad Muskau
Saturday 3 February	**Graustein**
Sunday 4 February	Spremberg

---

1. In addition to Richard's account, this itinerary was compiled by consulting a variety of maps and sources including Walton & Eberhardt and Marek Lazarz of the POW Muzeum in Zagan; Keefe's memoir adds two places not listed elsewhere and Roessler's another. Several of the villages no longer exist.

The March begins. Note sleds and packs. (Lt. Gen. Albert P. Clark Collection SMS 329, Clark Special Collections Branch, McDermott Library, US Air Force Academy)

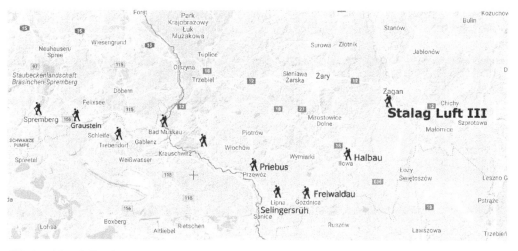

Winter March Route

The struggle to keep moving. Note discards at roadside (Lt. Gen. Albert P. Clark Collection SMS 329, Clark Special Collections Branch, McDermott Library, US Air Force Academy)

Kalender (Kassa)

We were alerted at about 8:30 PM & told to prepare for evacuation by 10:00.[10] After a mad scramble we went out for appel. (Just a dry run) Told to go back & fall out on the next bugle.

Log

Our worries haven't been without basis. We were alerted at 8:45 P.M. & told to be ready for evacuation at 10:00. At that time we fell out with all equipment, but they weren't ready for us, so we were told to wait for the next bugle. We returned to the barracks & tried to eat up all the food we'd saved. A lot of men were sick from the attempt, too.

---

marched into the bitterly cold night. Along with some of his previous mail, Richard carried it out of the camp and eventually all the way home.

10. "... the commandant received an order from Berlin [this morning that] the prisoners were not to be moved. ... That evening the order was countermanded." (Durand 327)

"The evacuation order came very suddenly from the Lager Officer at approximately 2100 hours. ..." (Mulligan, Burbank and Brunn 397)

Sunday 28 January

Center Compound left Stalag Luft III behind South, West and North;[2] their precise departure time varies from writer to writer, though we have what is probably the closest to a dispassionate recollection in Spivey's postwar G-2 interview: "Leaving the camp at 0400 hours in the morning, they first marched to HALBAU, arriving there 10 hours later. . . ." (Spivey G-2 2) Richard himself gives two different times, but we can be sure he began the ordeal in the early morning hours of Sunday 28 January.

Spivey says there were 150 German guards to oversee the 2,000 Kriegies of Center. (Spivey/Halvorsen 4) The gates of both Center and East Compounds opened into the same Vorlager to their north; the Vorlager in turn exited to the west into the Truppenlager, the German Kommandantur headquarters and billeting compound.

The building where Red Cross parcels were stored was in the northwest end of the Vorlager; the men of Center filed out through the compound's north gate and turned left to catch the parcels tossed to them as they passed the storage building near the Vorlager's outer gate. On the fly, they salvaged what items they could most profitably and comfortably add to their loads.

Richard would then have moved on westward into the German compound and to his right out onto the camp perimeter road.

---

2. Spivey says "My compound was the last to leave, having been preceded by North, West, South, and East Compounds and by the prison camp at Baleria [*sic*]" (121), but Durand carefully recounts that "East brought up the rear at about 6:00 Sunday morning. The prisoners in Belaria did not leave until late that evening." In a lengthy footnote, Durand gives his explanation of the discrepancy. (328)

A left/westward turn would have taken him a little over a kilometer to what Keefe calls "a narrow little highway" (283) where he would have followed the file of Kriegies in a turn to the left/southwestward onto the icy and snow-covered cobbles, joining the crush of refugees fleeing the approaching Soviets. "They marched west through disturbed villages and towns and through silent dark woods." (Simoleit 25)

Spivey says they left 55,000 parcels untouched in the Vorlager. "Along the route we saw discarded improvised sleds, clothing, and food which had been abandoned by the Kriegies marching ahead of us. We at the rear did have the advantage of having the snow packed down for us." They marched three abreast. (Spivey 120–1)

"Their common enemy was the bone-crushing cold. . . . The pervasive frost was their constant companion and snow drove hard into their faces which were lowered and angled to brace against the fury of its force. Gums soon bled and blackened. Hands dipped further into pockets to retrieve sugar cubes or raisins. The brutal force of the driving snow bore down on the marching columns. . . ." (Walton & Eberhardt 477)

"We were all happy to be outside our cage, outside the camp. But it wasn't a pleasant experience. We didn't know where we were going, and we didn't know how long we'd be marching like this; we'd been given no information. We were just brought out into the snow, counted, and marched off." (Keefe 284)

"Most of our boys were exhilarated by being outside of the barbed wire. They were thoroughly enjoying the trek through the snow, but this state of exuberance did not last long. Before noontime of January 28 nearly everyone had sobered up to the point where he realized that his very existence

A pause to rest and find reserves of strength. (Lt. Gen. Albert P. Clark Collection SMS 329, Clark Special Collections Branch, McDermott Library, US Air Force Academy)

Sunday 28
Kalender (Januar)

Left Camp at 7:00 & received 1 Box of food (RC). Too bad we can't take mail. We marched to Halbau. 17 Kilometers. Slept in a church.

Log

At about 5:30 A.M. Sun. Jan. 28 we started out on the real thing. At the Vorlager we filed past the parcel room & received a R.C. parcel each, more if we could carry them. We were already loaded to capacity so most of them were just rifled for the "D" Bars & other concentrated items, then discarded. It'll be a long time before I get over the sight of all that food thrown into the snow. One may not realize what it's like 'til he's existed this way for a year or so. (Man lives just a few days short of starvation. "Kriegies" run into the hours.) The Germans, both officer & other rank, were running back & forth like madmen picking it up.[11] That

_____

11. The German guards, too, were short of food; moreover, they knew very well that far worse was shortly to come, and some of them may still have had nearby families to care for.

depended upon many things, including the whim of the Germans and upon keeping his wits about him every moment." (Spivey 122) Throughout the march Spivey moved up and down the column, encouraging and urging the men; in this way he added considerable mileage to his own trek. During this early stage of the march, the road passed through thick forest which would have provided at least some protection from the wind.

"The feet of marching men melted the ice on the road and then it froze over by the time the next compound came along. There was much slipping, sliding, and falling. German civilians were on the road with us. . . . They were in worse condition, for the most part, than the POWs—many old people, mothers, and small children. . . .

"We marched from before dawn . . . under these extreme conditions. . . . A few strong men who made the march will tell you that it wasn't too bad, but for most of us it was just about all we could take." (Daniel 86–7) "Along the highway . . . we met the once mighty WERMACHT SKI TROOPERS, all in white—and these 'supermen' were begging cigarettes from us as we passed. They were either about 40 or 50 years old or young kids—headed for the front." (Burda)

The column passed through Hermsdorf and, not long before Halbau, the marchers came to a snowy rise which was not a hill, after all, but an overpass crossing the autobahn running eastward from Berlin. "We had no idea where we were bound or how long we would be on the road. . . . Items were slowly discarded by kriegies who decided they must lighten their loads of cherished possessions, things they'd hoped to take home. Musical instruments, beautiful models of boats and airplanes, books, and even food and clothing were strewn along in the dirt." (Clark 142)

Popeye (Herr Wilhelm Stranghoner), 1965. (Arthur A. Durand Collection SMS 792, Clark Special Collections Branch, McDermott Library, US Air Force Academy)

The German contingent of guards with them was headed by "Popeye," whom Spivey calls a "trusted, sensible, elderly German sergeant." (Spivey 118) When they reached Halbau, the men had to stand waiting in the cold. "Popeye and a German major sought out the mayor. He said the Americans could not stay in the town. But the mayor was overruled by Popeye, who then went in search of lodging." (Spivey/Halvorsen 4) What he found was a nearby Lutheran church.

"Cold, miserable Kriegies jammed every nook and corner. No one was allowed to lie down since he would occupy too much space. The pews were crowded as tightly as possible with men in sitting or standing

didn't set very well with us either. The march began west out of camp to the road out of Sagan, then southwest. (That was a perfect scene for the movies. The early hours of dawn showing thousands of evacuees, and in the background part of the camp was burning to add a touch of eerie color to the scene.) We would walk for twenty minutes, then rest five.[12] By 3:30 P.M. we reached Halbau [Ilowa, Poland], seventeen kms distance, where we bought sleds for "cig's" from the French arbeiters.[13] Just before dark, eighteen hundred of us were crowded into the Lutheran [church]. It looked like a very beautiful building & grounds with the cemetery also inside the walls. I shudder to think of what it looks like now. Nature will run its course. Just one of the horrors of war, I suppose. A very uncomfortable night was spent sitting up against the wall.

Halbau church today (Butler family collection)

12. After all Kriegies but the sick had gone, the censors were allowed to help themselves to the discarded Red Cross parcels as they "trekked towards the train station in the freezing night." One of them, Lisa Knüppel, describes passing the Kriegies in the train.

". . . after we had been on the train half an hour, we saw them on the side of the road. You could see that they were so tired. It was cold, and they would huddle together. I can remember that sometimes the prisoners would carry the guns because many of the guards were so weak and were limping, so they helped each other." (Walton & Eberhardt/ Lindeiner 358) This was probably near the eastern edge of Freiwaldau or east of Priebus, where the rail line passes near the march route.

13. Forced laborers.

positions. The balconies, steps, and every place was full of humanity." Of the 2,000 or so men from the Compound who sought shelter there that night, Spivey estimates that 1200–1300 sheltered in the morgue, crypts and schoolroom or improvised shelters rigged against the church's exterior upwind wall. (Spivey 123)

"The sanctuary would have normally seated 200 or 300 persons. . . . Every pew was filled. Even the space under the pews was filled. All aisles were crowded, as were the chancel, the stairs, the balcony, the narthex, and every other inch of the church. Men were shoving, pushing, cursing, whining, complaining, and were generally miserable, although glad to be out of the weather. Many were ill and had to go out in the cold to vomit and relieve themselves. Some relieved themselves where they were. The misery of these men caused some of them to act as they would never have acted under less trying circumstances." (Daniel 88)

Keefe says the kindly Lutheran pastor turned on the boiler, but it did little good since the doors were constantly opening all night to facilitate Kriegies' urgent needs. (288) The boiler's warmth wouldn't have reached Richard out in the vestibule in any case.

Monday 29 January

". . . after a night in which very few people were able to secure adequate rest, the column formed, amid the hostile civilian population, and marched 17 kms. in a driving snow storm. . . ." (Mulligan, Burbank and Brunn 399–400)

Spivey notes the great difficulty experienced this morning in finding and organizing his 2,000 scattered men. He also mentions that "Popeye was concerned that the men could not survive many nights like the last one and set off with one of his men on confiscated bicycles to scout shelters for the coming night.

"I was delighted to see that all the men were able to march. . . . Some were limping from frostbitten feet and blisters, but everybody was able to move." (Spivey 124)

"Dawn arrived, and with it the icy gut-ache of reality. Our line of march was revealed ahead of us winding to the horizon. The wind in our faces was now mingled with driving snow. . . . we marched in below-zero temperatures. Food froze in tins. Bread snapped into granular chunks." (Buckham 20) As the men of Center made their way out of Halbau that morning "some citizens cursed and threatened us but none of us was hurt." (Daniel 88)

"We left Halbau at dawn, cold and stiff and hungry. We walked past Freiwaldau. It had a long hill in town and we were all so weak we had trouble making it. From there on, we hit flat farmland and the wind and cold blew right through us. We finally came to a small village [Selingersrüh] where we put up in [a complex of three] one-story barns, about 500 men to one barn." (Burda)

"By three o'clock in the afternoon we had reached our destination . . . a tremendous farm run by a German count and his hundreds of slave laborers. We were put up in three huge barns filled with hay. Popeye had arranged for the big kitchen serving the chateau to furnish hot water for the boys. . . ." The "second night . . . was bitter cold, but the hay was an excellent place to keep warm." (Spivey 125)

"It was so crowded that all of us could not sleep at the same time, so some would walk around while others slept. . . .

"The General talked the Germans into letting us stay here for one extra day, in order to dry out socks and shoes and rest up. We would dry out our socks by putting

Kalender (Kassa)

Left & marched to Halbau where we bought sleds for ciga-rettes[14] & were quar-tered (1800 men) in a Lutheran cathedral. What a mess that was! I slept (?) in the vesti-bule with Fitz.—Sandy & Juntilla. A bigger bunch of hipocrites [*sic*] I've never seen. The horrors of war in that church yard.[15]

The church vestibule where Richard sheltered (Butler family collection)

Monday 29

Kalender (Kassa)

18 kms to Seling[er]srüh [Lipna, Poland], a small hamlet where we stayed in a barn for two nights.

Kalender (Januar)

Marched 18 Kms. 340 men in a barn the size of ours at home. Slept on straw.

Log

Left at 8:30 & marched eighteen kms. to Seling[er]srüh, a small hamlet, where 340 men were quartered in a barn. Not good but more comfortable than the last.

---

14. Next morning Spivey "noticed that somehow during the night and during our wait in the street the previous afternoon that many of the boys had acquired small sleds. There must have been 500 of them." He also gives us a hint of the approximate cost of the sleds: "... for the price of two cigarettes I bought myself a beautiful knife...." (Spivey 124)

15. By Spivey's count, Richard was among approximately one-third of Center Com-pound men who actually got inside the church that night, which likely indicates that he had been marching somewhere in the first third of the column. Since Richard tells us that he and 3 others of his combine sheltered in the vestibule, it also seems probable that they were among the last to fit into the church.

Though Richard doesn't mention marching with Herb Corson, in a card dated 10 January 1946 Herb refers to "our cross-country hike with sleds & etc." (Card in author's possession.)

them next to our bodies while we slept. We fixed our shoes, packs and mittens here. We also did a little trading with the German civilians for onions, hot water and brew, in exchange for cigarettes and soap." (Burda)

Tuesday 30 January

"We remained here in the barn today because the road ahead is crowded with those Kriegies who left Sagan before us. . . . Still no Goon food." (Keefe 289)

"The hay is ass deep and it is dark as pitch in here. It is warm and dry, and the sleeping is sure good." (McKee 127)

"We were all extremely tired and God-awful cold, but I think the German guards were worse off than most of us Kriegies. We were all fairly young, in our twenties and thirties. Most of the regular guards were, I'm sure, in their late forties and fifties. We had been warned and encouraged for several weeks to get in shape and be ready to go, but the guards had not. Most of them were WWI soldiers, or soldiers of the current war who'd been wounded, or they were farmers and not in very good condition. They were having a real tough time carrying their heavy rifles and rucksacks.

"A couple of guards asked the Kriegies marching next to them to carry their rifles for a while." (Keefe 285–6)

Wednesday 31 January

". . . was a long, long day. We walked and walked and walked. 29 kilometers to Muskau. What made it so bad was the fact that the country was very hilly and the weather was so uncertain . . . it would snow one minute and then it would rain the next minute—we even had hail. Sled was still working okay, although it was tough pulling it up some of these hills." (Burda) The winding, cobbled route here passes through farmland mixed with stands of trees, which would have provided only brief and temporary respite from the weather.

". . . the roads really got miserable for the sleds—soft and rutty. . . . scrounging on the road was bad—did manage an apple . . . and a small piece of bread . . . these poor old men we have for guards are really having it tough—two had frozen hands after the second day and most of the others have just about had it. . . ." (Roessler 2)

After crossing the Neisse River on an icy bridge, the Kriegies climbed a steep hill to reach the center of Muskau. Soon they found themselves in a pottery factory, "a long sprawled-out two-story building" where Chiesl says "pottery conduits, spigots and couplers were manufactured" (Kimball at "Evacuation"); Spivey's G-2 interview suggests some of the men may have been housed in a nearby battery factory. In any case, they were warm and dry for 3 nights. They had hot water and could wash, shave and sleep—on the bare concrete floor.

Thursday 1 February and Friday 2 February

"The Germans kept low fires going, and we thawed out on the racks which had been used to bake the wares. This was a real boon, for we had access not only to heat but also water." (Daniel 88)

A brisk trading business was done here and all along the way using the Kriegies' precious cigarettes and soap to supplement their meager food supplies.

The Germans had sent a truck back to Sagan to pick up more of the Red Cross parcels left there. "The supply brought in was entirely inadequate and provided approximately one parcel for every five men. Much of our food supply began to come from

Barns at Selingersrüh (Courtesy of Marek Lazarz)

Interior of Selingersrüh barn (Courtesy of Marek Lazarz)

trading with the French and Polish workers. It was cut-throat competition because some of the men had hundreds and hundreds of cigarettes while others had very few." (Mulligan, Burbank and Brunn 401)

Saturday 3 February

". . . we got up at 4:30 A.M.—raining out and thawing, so broke up the sled. I was really loaded down now, but I was determined not to throw away any of my blankets or food or clothes." (Burda) "It was warm, and all of the snow was gone, so the sleds were no good. The day was just like spring." (McKee 131) A stretch of autobahn ran between Bad Muskau and Spremberg but, as the following passage makes clear, the Kriegies were routed on backroads.

After Muskau the columns "twisted over the hills and along the banks of frozen streams past frosted white-shrouded estates. Along the road, they saw one-man fox holes, freshly dug, and roadblocks and tank emplacements impeded their progress. . . .

"The side roads cut through forests and small towns, where they bartered with the inhabitants, swapping cigarettes and soap for apples or eggs." (Walton & Eberhardt 503)

"Blisters, stiffened backs and legs, and the pain of frostbitten feet and hands still plagued many men. With the slight thaw, the cobblestones were uncovered, and visibility was much better. After a rest and change of weather, some measure of good spirits was restored." (Walton & Eberhardt 504)

"It was mid-afternoon on the march from Muskau to [Graustein] when one of those freaks of nature occurred. As if by a miracle, the wind stopped blowing; the drab, cold grey disappeared: and the blue cloudless sky was everywhere. The sun danced along the snow-covered fields and among the snow-covered trees, turning everything into a wonderland of gold and white.

"It was during a halt for a brief period of rest that Vince Shank played his trumpet.

"The beautiful, vibrant tones of Vince's horn bit softly into the azure sky. Like warming slivers of sun those notes danced from the rear of the column to the front, touching everyone with their upbeat life. It didn't last long, but it lasted long enough so that the melody 'When Johnny Comes Marching Home' came through loud and clear.

"When the prisoners resumed their march they stepped a little smarter and held their heads a little higher. Vince Shank and his horn lifted all their spirits and left a warm memory that has lasted a lifetime." (Cullen)

At Graustein ". . . several small barns were utilized as quarters. . . ." (Spivey G-2 3)

Sunday 4 February

The Kriegies marched on to Spremberg with "little or no snow." (Daniel 89) They were welcomed to an impressive Panzer training facility on the outskirts of town.

"The Germans were most cordial on this day. They had prepared for us about 500 gallons of barley broth, extremely nourishing and good. Many of us had the opportunity to wash up and shave for the first time in well over a week. It was here that we were told that in the evening we would embark for southern Germany, where our permanent camp was located. Rumors had it that we were going to Munich to the big POW camp at Moosburg." (Spivey 131)

"Late in the afternoon we were rousted up and moved out. . . . It was almost dark and a misty wet fog had settled in. . . . This is one of those images that are forever

Here we stayed over a day & rested up. We were still eating R.C. food & cold, but they did let us heat water for drinks. The only food they brought along for us was bread & B. [blood] sausage which we received on the train [nearly a week later].

Tuesday 30

Kalender (Januar)

Stayed here in this good cool barn all day preparing for a long march tomorrow.[16]

Wednesday 31

Kalender (Januar)

Marched 28 Kms to Muskau[17] & stayed in a nice warm brick factory.

Kalender (Kassa)

Marched to Muskau 28 kms & stayed two days in a brick factory. Nice & warm. Had a chance to clean up & make a travis [travois] to carry my equipment. Received a cup of cooked barley & a tablespoon full of soup. We were scheduled to get Boxcars out of here but really didn't expect them.

Log

Marched twenty-eight kms. to Muskau, where we are supposed to get the train. They quartered us in a brick factory &, surprising enough, it was plenty warm. The heat came from the drying ovens & was hot enough for cooking, but the food we'd carried was getting short so cooking was limited.

February

Thursday 1

Kalender (Februar)

Going to stay [in Bad Muskau] today & tomorrow. Got up, shaved & took a sponge bath. This is hell but it's warm. [In margin:] Raining.

---

16. By this time the weather was warming; the wind dropped and the snow on the roads turned to slush. This explains Richard's mention below that he constructed a travois while in Muskau (evidently abandoning and/or repurposing the sled bartered for in Halbau).

17. That long day's march ended in a steep quarter-mile climb on icy cobblestones from lower Bad Muskau at the Neisse bridge crossing to the upper part of town where the factory was located.

impressed upon my memory: the sounds of many men moving through the dark, no voices, just the rustling of clothing and the scrape of boots on the ground, wrapped in near darkness but with a slight glow reflecting through wet fog. . . ." (Keefe 294–5)

Spivey and Vanaman were pulled aside and told they were being taken to Berlin. "As I stood there on the sidewalk and watched my 2,000 men march toward the station, I wanted to curse and kill every German I could find and to take my men and head for home." (Spivey/Halvorsen 5)

The culminating effort of that week of cold and hunger and painful endurance was the climb up a steep hill to the Spremberg rail station, where the Kriegies boarded boxcars from the loading dock of the freight depot several hundred feet down the tracks from the main station.

"We were put in French cars ("forty and eight"—forty men or eight horses). There were fifty of us in each car and absolutely no room to sit much less to lie." (McKee 133) "There were no windows, and the only light and ventilation came through cracks in the car's wooden sides. The cars were pulled by an old hissing engine leaking steam and hot water. Knowing that the Allies often strafed rail cars was a very real cause for concern." (Walton & Eberhardt 505)

Diorama of Kriegies boarding a French 40 & 8 boxcar at Spremberg (Courtesy of USAF Museum, Wright Patterson Air Force Base)

Log

Spent the day cleaning up. We were issued ½ cup of cooked barley & a R.C. parcel for five men (⅕ ea). We're beginning to think a little about that food at Sagan.

Grampy Miller to Geneil
Letter excerpt[18]

I wonder if you heard the news last night. 5,000 prisoners were turned loose S.E. of B[e]rlin. They only spoke of French men, but if Darling Richard hasn't been moved, he will be loose any time and maybe by now. I don't think they have had time to move them. If Mother heard it, I bet she is just about wild; she has just kept track of the news for weeks, waiting for the time to come when they got to him. She has a good map to follow also.

Friday 2

Kalender (Februar)

Got up & shaved & fooled round all day making a container for water & food. Got a Barley ration & 1 RC parcel for every 5 men. [In margin:] ½ cup Barley/1 spoon of soup.

Saturday 3

Kalender (Kassa)

Marched 18 km to G[r]austein & stayed in another barn but cooking facilities were much better. We had cooked spuds & carrots & cooked a few to take along. We were told that we could get our train at Spremburg.

Log

We marched eighteen kms. to G[r]austein, where we stayed in another barn. The people there had a boiler that they used to cook cull potatoes[19] for the cows. We used the boiler & the potatoes & ate 'til they came out of our ears. I don't know what the heifers are eating now.

Kalender (Februar)

Left Muskau & marched 18 Kilometers to G[r]austein. Leaving for Spremburg (10 Kilo[meter]s) tomorrow. Boxcars for Neuremburg. We're cooking spuds for our first hot meal in a week.

---

18. As this excerpt indicates, the family eagerly tracked Richard's status as best they could. (Granny Miller was away on a family visit.)

19. Potatoes not marketable or usable for human consumption or as seed.

Hell in a Boxcar

"With 50 to 60 men in a car designated to hold 40, even sitting down was a trial. In some cars, men found they could all sit if they did so in lines, toboggan fashion. In others,

A line of 40 & 8 boxcars (Courtesy of Marilyn Walton)

they took turns sitting and standing.... It was a 60-hour ordeal, locked in a moving cell becoming increasingly fetid with the stench of vomit and excrement. Chinks in the wall planks provided the only ventilation. The train lumbered through a frozen countryside and bombed-out cities that could only be observed with an eye to a crack." (Consolmagno)

"The claustrophobic journey in the rocking cars was like no other any of the men had experienced. The cars stopped frequently to let higher priority German troop trains or equipment pass. Cars screeched to a slow

Rare clandestine photo taken inside one of the boxcars (Courtesy of Marilyn Walton)

stop, while bombed-out railroad tracks were repaired, before resuming the journey...." (Walton & Eberhardt 507) "... as was true throughout the march, everyone was exposed to attack by Allied aircraft." (Durand 335)

Accounts and timing are, again, for Center Compound's travel. From the *Kalender* listing and other references, between Spremberg and Moosburg we can construct an itinerary of villages, towns and cities where either Richard's train stopped or Kriegies were able to glimpse station signs in passing.

Burbank (38–9) gives a similar itinerary, leaving out a few places listed by Richard and adding some additional stations (shown in parentheses). Again, Roessler contributes a number of unique additions (shown with asterisks). Departure and arrival times are Burbank's save for Roessler's additions; where they diverge, I have used Burbank's times. I have corrected some spelling errors.[1]

---

1. See pages 320–22 for itinerary and map.

Graustein barns (Butler family collection)

Sunday 4

Kalender (Februar)

Left at 7:00 for Spremburg [*sic*] & had hot Barley soup at 1400 at an army base. At 1600 we walked into the station & loaded on Boxcars. 0.7 loaf of Bread each/ ½ can meat each.

Log

Made seven more kms to Spremburg & received a "Klim" can of cooked barley at a Wehrmacht base. That slop was really good. At 4:00 P.M. we left for the station, which was two more kms, & loaded on box cars. I have quite an allergy to the things, but this time they put a guard in & didn't lock the doors. There were fifty-one of us in the car to begin with & we hardly had room to sit down. Sleep was out of the question in that mess, so I made a hammock with my blanket & some rope & got up out of the debris. The trip was comparatively comfortable. Later a few men were put in another car.

Kalender (Kassa)

7 more kms to Sprem—where we had hot barley soup at a Wehrmacht post. Then made 2 kms to the station & loaded 51 men on a small box car. Half of us could sit down at one time. I made a ham[m]ock with my blanket & rope so I'm pretty comfortable, in comparison. I've written this in my makeshift sack. Last night wasn't half bad. My hammock is the kitchenette. It's the only place with enough room to cut & spread this Goon bread.

Rail Itinerary of Center Compound

Sunday 4 February
    22:30   depart Spremberg[2]
Monday 5 February
    08:00   Schwarzkollm-Lauta[*3]
                   Hohenbocka*
    10:50   Schwarzbach*
    11:15   Ruhland
    12:40   Dolsthaida[*4]
    14:30   Mückenberg [now Lauchhammer Ost]
                   Plessa
                   Elsterwerda*
Tuesday 6 February
    03:40   (Dresden)
    04:30   Chemnitz
    09:15   (Zwickau)
                   Steinpleis*
                   Neumark*
    10:30   (Reichenbach im Vogtland)
                   Netzschkau*
                   Jocketa*
                   Jössnitz*
    12:00   Plauen
    12:30   Syrau[*5]
    13:20   Schönberg*
    14:25   Gutenfürst*
    14:35   Feilitzsch*
    15:00   (Hof)
                   Oberkotzau
    19:00   Kirchenlaibach*
                   [Nürnberg bypass]
                   Weissenburg

---

2. They clearly passed south of the group of lakes to the west of Spremberg, turned westward and traveled through the sizeable town of Hoyerswerda during the night when none of the Kriegies could tell where they were.

3. This was a stop west of Hoyerswerda in the village of Schwarzkollm near the town of Lauta.

4. This seems to have been a village on the east side of Mückenberg; it survives today only as Dolsthaidaerstrasse.

5. Possibly due to the bombing raid that coincided with their arrival in Plauen, the train veered northwest to Syrau, then turned southward again and bypassed Plauen about five kilometers to the west.

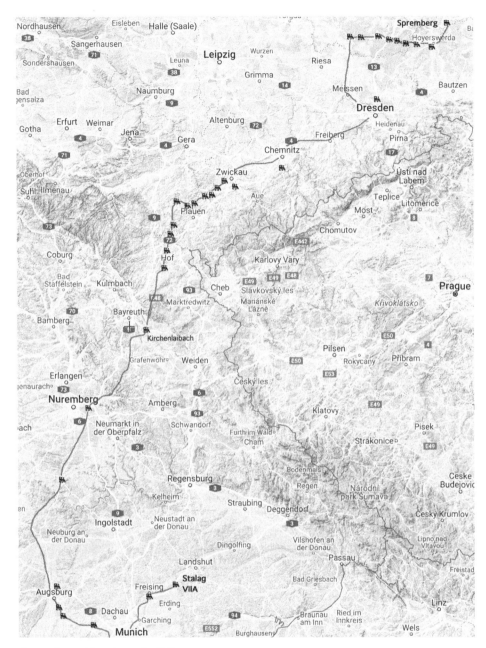

Spremberg-Moosburg Rail Route

Wednesday 7 February

08:00	Augsburg
	Kissing*[6]
	Mering*
	Maisach
10:00	München
14:10	Freising*
15:00	Moosburg/VIIA[7]

Sunday 4 February

"About 10:30, we finally got underway, and traveled approximately nineteen miles that first night. It was raining and the car leaked, it was very cold and to top it off, we were all wet. I really don't know how we made it. The Germans kept promising us hot tea or coffee, but always at the next stop." (McKee 133)

Like his fellow prisoners, Richard obviously gave a good deal of forethought and planning to this journey. His careful preparation well repaid him now, as he could rig with rope and blanket a hammock where he traveled for the next few days.

Monday 5 February

"We finally got a cup of ersatz tea about 8:00 AM on Monday. Between the rain and cold and nothing hot to drink it about got us down. . . . From Monday morn until Wednesday, we had no water (not even cold) and Tuesday night a fellow got sick and the guard would not let him out to throw up. All of this trip has been the most inhumane thing I have ever seen." (McKee 133)

---

6. Roessler records Plissing, but there is no sign of such a place. Kissing, however, is a very common name in that area and Kissing station appears on the rail line at the fringes of Augsburg just 2 km north of Mering station.

7. As of September 2017, most of the stations listed by Richard were still standing, though many had been partially remodeled or were then being remodeled.

Tuesday 6 February

"In Dresden . . . there were a lot of German troops going to the Russian front near Berlin. It seems like they are moving a lot of the troops from the West front to the Russian front." (Burda) Spivey says that 3 cars were added at Zwickau "to relieve the extreme congestion." (Mulligan, Burbank and Brunn 402) They were also finally given something to drink even if it was "lousy" German coffee.

"We spent three nights in the boxcars on that train as it traveled through the country, and still we had absolutely no idea of where we were going. Each one of us was wrapped in our individual, miserable, cold, hungry, lonely world. . . . The miles and hours of constant noise as the boxcars clattered down the rails, the rain leaking down through the cracks in the roof, other just-as-miserable men getting sick on themselves and on others—this all fed into our misery and turned those days into a numb haze." (Keefe 299)

Wednesday 7 February

At Augsburg another dawn passed without water. "We saw the bomb wreckage of Augsburg and München (Munich). What devastation there was! It was unbelievable." (McKee 133) They reached Munich before getting anything else to drink; on arrival there, Burda says men from his car were so thirsty that one of them went to the engine and "got a Trinkwasser of steam water out of the locomotive."

They reached Moosburg in mid-afternoon. Northwest of Stalag VIIA's main gate was the camp's small two-story station.

"They blinked against the sudden light as the boxcar doors were pushed back. With their last ounce of strength, they stumbled down stiffly from the cars, helping down

Monday 5[20]

Log

Most of last night was spent at sidings, so not many miles were covered. We received one quarter of a parcel each, the other quarter to come later.

Kalender (Februar)

Sat around most of the day on sidings. Didn't travel far. ¼ R.C. box each.

Tuesday 6

Kalender (Kassa)

Didn't travel far yesterday. Last evening we were issued ¼ parcel each. Another ¼ coming later. Two air raids, one at 5:30 A.M. & at noon. The engineer stopped us, jumped out & took off out thru the woods. There were Allied planes overhead for quite a while, circling.

Log

Two air raids.[21] One last night at Chemnitz (5:30 A.M.). We pulled out immediately. The other just before we pulled into Plauen (about 12:30). The engineer had evidently "had it," because he stopped the train, jumped out & took off out thro the forest. We could hear aircraft overhead during most of the raid.

Kalender (Februar)

Air Raid at 5:30 AM while we were in Chemnitz. Another at noon near Plauen.

Wednesday 7

Kalender (Kassa)

Nuremburg [Nürnberg] was bombed at 700 last night so we've by-passed it.[22] It's getting light & we just pulled into Augsburg.

---

20. "In some cases the boxcar doors were locked during the night. During the daylight hours, however, the progress of the train was exceedingly slow and during long stops the doors were opened and the men sat beside the railroad tracks." (Mulligan, Burbank and Brunn 401–2)

21. "On the train were several men who, in 1943, had been in boxcars in the railway yards at Bolzano, Italy, during an accurate allied air attack on those yards. The terror which they experienced on this trip cannot be described." (Burbank 38) These men were, of course, Butler, Corson, Church and possibly others of their arrival "purge."

22. "One night we stopped short of a big city that may have been Nürnberg. During the night, the English bombed the hell out of it. We could clearly hear the bomber stream come and go and the explosions of the tons of bombs that fell." (Keefe 297–8)

Stalag VIIA's station, 1956. (Butler family collection)

the weak and sickly. Slowly they made their way down the muddy road between the train track and long barbed wire fences to the rows of green-shuttered, beige, stucco buildings on the other side. They marched through the single gate, bore to the left past a tall wooden watch tower and in a grey mist delivered themselves into the hands of the Wehrmacht—no longer somewhat protected Luftwaffe prisoners." (Walton & Eberhardt 519)

There "they were placed in a temporary compound from which small groups were taken to be searched, deloused, and placed in the main camp. . . . Some of the men were there for a week "living under terrible conditions with no facilities provided for washing, bathing, sanitation and cooking. Nearly one-half of the men had diarrhea and other minor diseases." (Mulligan, Burbank and Brunn 403)

That temporary compound was the infamous "snake pit," where they were housed, one source says, because space for them inside the camp was not ready.

February 1945
Events in the Camp

February

Saturday 10

[Protecting Power representatives visit Stalag VIIA.]

Friday 16

"A long trench was the common open-air latrine giving off a terrible stench and was filled to overflowing. An epidemic seemed inevitable, so the Senior American Officers called a strike. They and their men refused to report for twice daily appels." (Walton & Eberhardt 532)

Friday 23

"The filth & cold & the wet coupled with our run-down condition from the move from Sagan produced considerable illness—espec. pneumonia." (Clark Scrapbook 70)

Stalag VIIA barrack interior (Lt. Gen. Albert P. Clark Collection SMS 329, Clark Special Collections Branch, McDermott Library, US Air Force Academy)

Kalender (Februar)

Passed Nuremburg [Nürnberg] came thru Weissenburg. Stopped in Munich, then to Moosburg.

Friday 9

Kalender (Februar)

Sandy & Church not in yet. My opinion of the Wehrmacht won't look good in print. No fuel at all for cooking. [In margin:] Using marg[arine] for cooking.

Saturday 10

Kalender (Februar)

We're on half parcels again. This soup is terrible. Someone found a mouse in it two days ago. We get ⅙ loaf bread a day & 5 spuds. Also marg[arine]. The Swiss [Protecting Power] were here & heard our story.

Sunday 11

Kalender (Februar)

How about that? Attending church without leaving my sack. We still got that goon tea this AM., but the soup was really an improvement. Other rations are about the same. Some library books came in.

Stalag VIIA Redux

Some of the men spent as much as a week in the processing compound. They "were crowded (crammed) into five barracks—three were small ones, and in ours we have 550 men. It was approximately 30x200 ft. This was a lot worse than the train, as far as space is concerned. . . . About half of the boys took sick last night (urping, GIs, etc.), and the guards made them come back in the barrack. The latrine is a limb built over a ditch. . . . (McKee 133–4)

This was the facility infamously known as "The Snakepit." Richard says he was spared this since he was ill; he doesn't say where he was, but one Kriegie source says that the sick were simply left in the boxcars.

Again Richard was more fortunate than many. Not only did he get to Moosburg relatively quickly and directly, but he reached Stalag VIIA early enough in the POW exodus that he at least had a bed in a barrack,

even if conditions there were barely livable. Some of the Kriegies from Stalag Luft III had to walk all of the way to Moosburg, via long detours through other camps, and arrived at Stalag VIIA barely before being liberated.

"None of the *Lagers* held more than about 1,000 men, so we were broken up into groups scattered among several *Lagers*, making control and communication initially very difficult." (Clark 159)

The men of Stalag Luft III's Center Compound were housed on the south side of the camp's bisecting street toward its eastern end. "Center Compound was placed in five buildings, two of which were separated by two barbed-wire fences from the other three. Outside latrine facilities were provided in both of these areas and a very small open area at the rear of the barracks . . . was available for exercise. . . ." (Mulligan, Burbank and Brunn 403)

VIIA aerial view, Spring 1945. (Annotated detail from photo courtesy of Marilyn Walton)

Monday 12

Kalender (Februar)

They're changing this place for a little permanency. I hope not too much. The Goon rations are much better since Saturday.[23]

Tuesday 13

Kalender (Februar)

Received an extra ½ RC box today.

Card excerpt[24]

The past two weeks seem to have passed as a dream. So much has happened. I wrote just before we left, but it may not get to you. I'm now back at my first stopping place in Germany. A lot has happened since then. I surely am glad that I didn't know I'd be here now. I'm feeling swell & none the worse off for the trip.

Wednesday 14

Kalender (Februar)

Air Raid. They're giving this area lots of attention. Rec'd 1 loaf bread.

Thursday 15

Kalender (Februar)

Air Raids during last night & today. They're really giving 'em h- heck. Received RC box. ([Erasure]).

Friday 16

Kalender (Blank back of Immerwährender Kalender)

What an existence!! We cook over marg[arine] burners. It's against Goon policy to furnish Kriegies fuel. ½ lb of marg[arine] per man per week. There are only five 40 watt lights for 156 men. Not so good, as my writing shows. The Russians have our old home & are still going so there's still a future—I guess.

---

23. The day of the Protecting Power representatives' visit.

24. This is the first mail Richard sent home after the move to Stalag VIIA. It's amazing that the German military managed to keep POW mail flowing from Moosburg as long as we know they did: Though it was dated 31 March, the last letter we have from Richard is postmarked 21 April!

The censors had moved from Sagan to Roth, south of Nürnberg, and continued their work there through the end of March. (Koppenhöfer 9)

"As compared to Sagan, three conditions at Moosburg stood out: extreme overcrowding, the impossibility of proper cleanliness, and the inadequacy of the food supply. With the exception of the food, these conditions became worse as time went on." (South Annexes 1137)

By varying accounts, VIIA was originally designed to house 11,000 or 14,000 inmates and had held 30,000 at its previous peak, but it had custody of about 130,000 POWs by the end of the war, when the Germans had moved prisoners there from all over the Reich. (Durand 351) "The men were packed in like sardines, sleeping on the floors and on the ground outside. Many were quartered in tents or shacks put together with newspaper and wooden planks. Others simply sat on the ground with no roof over their heads." (Diggs 158) The later a Kriegie arrived, the more likely he was to have to take shelter across the surrounding region in sheds, barns and the forest itself.

Conditions were execrable; it's clear that Richard severely restricted his description of life in Stalag VIIA during the late winter and early spring of 1945. The paucity of entries in the *Log* and *Kalender* between 7 February and 29 April is consistent with his reticence to discuss the experience in the following years. The impulse neither to record nor to relive later such a hideous experience is easily understood.

"Our run-down condition on arrival at Moosburg became obvious when we were run through the delousing process on arrival. Clothes went thru a poison defumigation process & we went w/out clothes thru mass showers. We were shocked to see each other in the showers as we had lost much weight & appeared skin & bone." (Clark Scrapbook 82)

"Nearly all of these men needed help of some kind badly. . . . The biggest need was for medicine for the sick and wounded and bandages for people who had injured their feet on the lengthy marches. But the most common complaint was about the presence of body lice. Everyone seemed to have them . . . so [Soderberg, the indefatigable YMCA man] began to carry bags of delousing powder with him, which was more welcome than nectar or ambrosia. . . . Shoes and food parcels came next. . . ." (Diggs 160)

"At Stalag VIIA, the buildings we were to be housed in looked all right from the outside. They had a light brown stucco finish, were one story, and seemed to be about 150 feet long. However, after we were placed inside, we received our biggest shock. They were filthy and crumby. The barracks were divided across the middle by a kitchen and washroom. That made the two main rooms about 40 by 75 feet, each containing about 200 men who had to sleep on 12-bed tiers, which were three bunks high, two deep, and two wide. "We were so crowded that the only way we had of keeping personal stuff was by hanging it from the ceiling." (Burda)

"Bunks in the stucco buildings had filthy vermin-infested burlap palliasses [thin, straw mattresses] on the beds. By filtered light coming through the cracks, the men could see bedbugs, lice, and fleas crawling everywhere. Soon, the men's bodies were livid with welts from insect bites, and many men hung their threadbare blankets out all day in hopes of ridding the fabric of the biting beasts." (Walton & Eberhardt 527)

". . . the men obtained water from one faucet and one hand pump [for 400 men]. Sanitation measures were totally inadequate and with no hot water, the men were left to wallow in the filth of living in severely overcrowded and totally deplorable conditions.

Good weather & lots of bonfires since we got here. Two appels this A.M. there's a reason.

The guards won't let us talk over the wire.

Kalender (Februar)

Raids around noon. Could see Bombers & 38s overhead. Exchanged my overcoat.[25]

Saturday 17

Kalender (Februar)

Another double appel. The weather has been swell for the past week.

Sunday 18

Kalender (Februar)

A very quiet day except for a little wire activity. Mail in Vorlager.

Monday 19

Kalender (Februar)

An inspection this A.M. Some mail came in.

Tuesday 20

Kalender (Februar)

It is pretty warm in here today; we have a fire going. Can't last tho'. Limburger cheese in today. Wow!

Wednesday 21

Kalender (Februar)

A letter to Geneil. 3 inches of snow this A.M.

Grandma Butler
Diary excerpt

In the daily paper Mark read a notice stating that American Prisoners of War were

Yank Prisoners Need More Clothes

NEW YORK—(AP)—Richard F. Allen, vice chairman of the American National Red Cross, says that American prisoners of war in Germany are being marched deeper into the Reich through temperatures as low as 30 degrees below zero without proper clothing.

Allen, in charge of insular and foreign operations for the Red Cross, told members of the organization's Brooklyn branch that "those of you who have someone in the German prison camps must be ready for bad news."

21 February 1945 (Butler family collection)

---

25. This explains why the coat he brought home seems in such good shape.

The German food ration consisted of one-half cup of warm water for breakfast, one cup of thin watery soup for lunch, and a little black bread for supper, with an occasional extra issue of cheese, margarine, and blood sausage." (Walton & Eberhardt 529)

"There are no cooking stoves here and so we use small homemade burners ["blowers"] for cooking. . . . We are able to buy small bundles of wood from the guards for cigarettes. These are used to heat water for coffee and cook any food that we have. Now if we had any food to cook we'd be in." (McKee 134–5)

"In spite of the Germans' best efforts, latrines overflowed and garbage accumulated faster than it could be carried away. The danger of epidemics arose. . . ." (Durand 342)

". . . inadequate rations throughout their marches had sapped the men's strength and detrimentally affected their health, making it all the harder for them to contend with the situations they found themselves in." (Walton & Eberhardt 533) "The filth & cold & the wet coupled with our run-down condition from the move from Sagan produced considerable illness—espec. pneumonia." (Clark Scrapbook 70)

"The main difficulty in February and March was the cold, for no fuel whatever was available for heating the barracks. POWs had arrived in poor physical shape from the march and train ride; and the conditions of Moosburg made matters worse. Fully 30 percent of the prisoners had either diarrhea or a cold during this period." (South Annexes 1138) "There was no coal in the camp so the men burned bed boards for heat, and many stayed under blankets in bed all day to keep warm." (Walton & Eberhardt 525)

"A lot of the fellows had not had their clothes off in four to six weeks, and hadn't washed in just as long. We only had the clothes we wore and no facilities for laundry, and it was too cold to sleep out of your clothes." (Burda)

". . . increasingly, straw was spread over the floors of the barracks to be used as bedding. Dysentery was the norm in the deteriorating makeshift accommodations. Disease ran rampant, and medical treatment was practically non-existent. By the end of February . . . supplies of Red Cross parcels were cut off. . . . There was constant desperate trading among the prisoners with some prisoners assisting others, who had lesser trading skills, and prized possessions such as watches and wedding rings were bartered away in the interest of filling empty stomachs." (Walton & Eberhardt 529)

"Trading over the wire from compound to compound became a major pastime. . . . Our cigarettes, chocolate, and soap gave us real buying power. . . . I wanted a clean sheet and a good pair of scissors with which I could cut tin. I got them very promptly for a reasonable number of cigarettes in a transaction handled by one of our traders." (Clark 159)

"The Germans refused to clean out the outdoor latrines—one latrine for about 2,000 men. It finally filled up and overflowed. As everyone was still sick with the 'runs,' you can imagine the mess it created. We were practically wading in human excrete. It overflowed into the parade ground. . . ." (Burda) "Protests were lodged about housing conditions, the food, the lack of proper bedding, inadequate covers, the lack of cooking facilities, hot water, and sanitation. . . ." (Mulligan, Burbank and Brunn 404)

"Morale was low at Moosburg; for in addition to the above, there was practically no incoming mail, the supply of reading material was inadequate, and little or no exercise being marched farther into Reich through temperatures as low as 30 degrees below zero without proper clothing. . . . Willard, Audria & Joseph came in, also Geneil. I think she had not seen the paper and we did not tell her. I hope she never hears until Richard gets home again. For it is very hard on one to hear these things, and more so when one's own are amongst them.

Thursday 22
Kalender (Februar)

3-hour raid: 38s & 51[s]. RC parcel. There are a lot [of] men sick with colds & flu. I have my first cold this winter.

Friday 23
Kalender (Februar)

5 hrs of raids: 3 in one & 2 in other yesterday. Another today. English band show.

Saturday 24
Kalender (Februar)

A dull day.

Sunday 25
Kalender (Februar)

Another big raid. 51s all over the place. Shooting.

Monday 26
Kalender (Februar)

We're in a compound within a compound within a compound. Now they're restricting our freedom here. Can't go near the gate anymore.

Tuesday 27
Kalender (Februar)

Air Raid 12:30. Bombers going over in a solid stream [scratched out].

Wednesday 28
Kalender (Februar)

This is the last week of parcels even on ½ ration. Very meager German rations.[26]

---

26. "A man's eyes betray his hunger. Watch the eyes recede and narrow as they probe deeply for the taste of remembered meals. Watch them again as the rations are served,

was possible. Even so, the prisoners kept up their balance and their sense of humor at a much higher level than was to be expected." (*South Annexes* 1138)

"I shall never be able to give enough credit to the Swiss for the risks they ran and the magnificent job they did in taking care of the POWs in those hectic days. I do not know whether any of them were ever injured by the Allies or the Germans, but the danger of driving down any highway in Germany at that time was extremely great." (Spivey 165)

March 1945
Events in Camp

Saturday 3

"Today was issued the last of Red Cross Parcels (HARD LUCK)!!" (Kingsbury 39)

Thursday 8

From South Compound record of events for this date: "Swiss train of 84 cars arrives with RC parcels." (South Annexes 1207)

"Inadequate rations throughout the march and during the weeks before the emergency supplies arrived sapped the men's health and strength. Many had become ill and were prostrate by the time the first parcels were delivered." (Durand, 342)

Saturday 10

"¼ parcel per man. Really bashing tonight!" (Kingsbury 39)

Monday 12

"The 'Great White Fleet' of emergency Red Cross provisions finally arrived at Moosburg much to the jubilation of the hungry men. One third parcel per man was all that was allowed, but even a fraction of a parcel was better than none. Intestinal ailments became a reality that evening for men who ate too much after being on reduced rations

for so long. With the arrival of the parcels, the Germans further reduced each man's German ration." (Walton & Eberhardt 529)

"The conspicuously-painted white trucks with large red crosses "traveled on assigned routes known to Allied bomber crews; only once was a convoy mistakenly strafed." By the end of this operation "the trucks had traveled one million miles to deliver 6,600 tons of food and medical supplies. . . ." (Unattributed article in Soderberg Scrapbook 1, Henry Soderberg Collection SMS 25, Clark Special Collections Branch, McDermott Library, US Air Force Academy)

Wednesday 14

"The early thaw that warm spring turned the ground to mud, and the men were ankle deep in it since the camp had been built on a swamp, fostering a constant supply of mosquitoes." (Walton & Eberhardt 529)

Wednesday 21

"In late March, air raids, mostly flown by the 15th Air Force out of Italy, intensified over southern Germany. Prisoners were ordered to stay inside during raids but defiantly watched the exciting action." (Walton & Eberhardt 547)

Thursday 8-Wednesday 28

Log

The place is rather disappointing. At first it was a welcome relief from the cold, but it's really pretty sad.[27]

We have no fuel whatever to cook with, so we use the margarine from the R.C. parcels, 1 lb each week, while on full rations. After two weeks here we're on half parcels again.

The Gr. food issue is: Grass soup, ½ or less loaf of black bread & about 3 to 5 potatoes per day.

The Swiss Rep. was here on the 10th, so we hope to get something done.

They have quite a system here (Black Market). We get a few extra items (luxuries) in our parcel, so the Goons are willing to sell us wood, etc., for these. That's only a beginner.

March

Thursday 1

Kalender (März)

SMIs [inspections] from here on. The weather is changeable.

Friday 2

Kalender (März)

R.C. Reps were here. Maybe our parcels will start coming by truck. Made a small blower.[28]

---

comparing size of portion, measuring width of bread slice." (Buckham 10)

27. One has to imagine that life after arrival at Stalag VIIA was even more difficult and tense than "normal." Richard and his fellow Kriegies were well aware that their remaining time in the camp was limited, but the excitement and anticipation must have been more than outweighed by frustration and the deprivation and indignity of daily life. Added to all that was the uncertainty of Nazi intentions, most notably Hitler's order, issued after the destruction of Dresden, to shoot all American and British POW airmen.

28. "A wooden wheel about eight inches with a handle on it to drive a fan. A shoestring is used as a belt. The fan blows into a small can and this is where the wood is burned." (McKee 135)

"A fire made of cardboard, wood chips, and small pieces of wood would boil water and cook food when kept burning hard by the air forced under it from the blower. It took two men to operate the stove, and clouds of black smoke rose from the hundreds of small cookers. Fires burned in the open air, and smoke hung over the camp all day choking out any chance of breathing clean air but warding off to some degree the onslaught of the

Thursday 22

"We went on half Red Cross rations on March 12 and then full (one parcel per man per week) on the 19th. The goon rations have been cut another four times, but it doesn't matter. . . .

". . . we were only off parcels one week (thank goodness) but we all nearly starved. We got in three weeks of British parcels and went on half rations. We've now been on half rations for a week but are today going on full. (Hurray!) We got a telegram that parcels are being brought in by Red Cross truck." (McKee 136)

Monday 26

". . . decided to bash a full parcel today just to get full once." (Kingsbury 39)

Saturday 3

Kalender (März)

Snowing this A.M. 1 card to Mom. Rec'd part of a Scottish parcel, which they say is the last. Opened the fence a few days ago.

Sunday 4

Kalender (März)

I can't remember any other life. I must have been born here.[29] Shifted some S[outh] Camp [Stalag Luft III] men in here yesterday. Things seem to be looking up again on the fronts.

Monday 5

Kalender (März)

Fitz & I really chowed up this noon. First time I've been full in a month. New Block CO Maj. Hacket[t].

Tuesday 6

Kalender (März)

Letter to Gen dated 8. I'd hate to spend a winter here. It's worse than Sagan & that was bad.

---

flying pests. Wood to feed the burners resulted in the gradual destruction of the flooring, walls, and partitions in the barracks. . . ." (Walton & Eberhardt 529)

29. By now Richard had experienced a full month of life in Stalag VIIA under what were at best marginal conditions. This came on top of the forced winter march made by men already weakened by malnutrition.

Close-up of a blower stove invented at VIIA (Lt. Gen. Albert P. Clark Collection SMS 329, Clark Special Collections Branch, McDermott Library, US Air Force Academy)

Wednesday 7

Kalender (März)

The only heat is body heat, & the only warm place is the sack. We're still eating (a little) but I don't know how long it'll last.

Thursday 8

Kalender (März)

Fitz & I trade our coffee for spuds & soup. (I just found my locket. Thought I'd left it at Sagan.)

Letter excerpts

For the first few weeks after we arrived, the weather was just like May, but now it's back to normal. We have quite a time here. . . .

I haven't heard from you for some time. My last letter was from Mother (Nov. 19). It arrived on Jan 27. It seems like ages since I heard from you and it has been. I'm just about used to it tho'.

The Salvation of VIIA

At Spremberg Col. Spivey and Gen. Vana-man had been removed from the Center Compound column and taken to Berlin. "We knew that no Red Cross food was being delivered to the POW camps in the south and we visualized the misery and sickness which must prevail without this essential assistance. . . . Even in relatively normal times we had relied to a great degree on our Red Cross food for existence. In the confusion and disorganization prevailing during those last weeks of the war, it was a foregone conclusion that POWs would most likely receive no Red Cross food and practically no German rations. We had anticipated this long before the breakdown of German transportation occurred and we had requested not only the Red Cross but also the Protecting Power [Switzerland] to begin making arrangements for the delivery of food to us when the Germans could not or would not be able to perform this function. (Spivey 143)

During their time in Berlin, through "intercession with the S.S. General in charge of all P.O.W.'s [Waffen SS Gen. Gottlob Berger] and with a couple of high-ranking members of Himmler's staff, promises were obtained which made it possible for [the Kriegies] to get some Red Cross food and medical aid during the last days and for [them] to be delivered safely." (Spivey letter)

Fortunately, Allied headquarters had begun planning for the potential POW crisis a year earlier; one result was that food had been stockpiled nearby in Switzerland. With the quiet collaboration of Gen. Berger, on 8 March 1945 massive Red Cross food shipments began crossing the Swiss border for Stalag VIIA in convoys of white-painted trucks and in special trains, thus saving

Richard and many others there from starvation in the last days of the war.

". . . General Berger assured us that he would guarantee safe passage for the trucks and that SS Headquarters had instructed all units of the Luftwaffe and the Wehrmacht to permit the Red Cross trucks to

Convoy loaded with life-saving Red Cross parcels bound for VIIA (Henry Soderberg Collection MS 25, Clark Special Collections Branch, McDermott Library, US Air Force Academy)

We had to leave an awful lot of things at Sagan that could certainly be used now, but "C'est la guerre," as they say. Our theater and concerts are also a thing of the past.

Well, I'll surely be glad when I can write to you alone & say what I want to. It won't be long either—I'll betcha.

Friday 9

Kalender (März)

Big morale boost. A Goon says there are 70 cars of parcels in.

Saturday 10

Kalender (März)

A big rumor ran thru camp about the war being over, but I don't excite very easily. Received one Am[erican] parcel for 4 men.

Card Excerpt

Lately, I've felt sort of like you did about writing. It seems pretty futile and I know my letters show it, too. I'm still hard at it, trying to keep busy in a place where there's absolutely nothing to do. Nice life, eh? Getting by tho' & staying healthy. At present that is most important.

Sunday 11

Kalender (März)

We have parcels enough for two more weeks. Scottish & Eng. (Last week was ¼ ration.)

Monday 12

Kalender (März)

Rumor: trucks with parcels outside—NO JUST THE TRUCKS.

Tuesday 13

Kalender (März)

Eng. Parcel. ½ ration. The sun came out; beautiful this afternoon.

Wednesday 14

Kalender (März)

The weather has taken a turn for the better—not enough wood to cook our rations.

come through. These trucks . . . were to be painted white with a big Red Cross on top and were to be manned by Canadian POWs who were at that time undergoing special training for the purpose. . . ." (Spivey 144)

On 19 April in Konstanz, Col. Spivey encountered a group of Swiss International Red Cross officials escorting a large convoy of food trucks bound for VIIA. He was assured that a trainload of parcels had arrived in Moosburg and "that hundreds of truckloads of parcels were flowing across the border at regular intervals. . . ." (Spivey 165)

"Colonel Purington, the adjutant of Center Compound, later told me that over half the prisoners were flat on their backs with dysentery and malnutrition at the time the food began to arrive. Within two weeks the spirit and will of the POWs were transformed." (Spivey 144)

Spivey credited Berger not only as "a key figure in aiding the POWs to survive" thanks to the food brought in from Switzerland but also with at least partial credit for saving "thousands of them from execution at Hitler's order." (Spivey 175)

April 1945
Events in the Camp

Sunday 1

"By the 1st of April food parcels in sufficient quantity were arriving. The American prisoners, who in March had been extremely weak from hunger and cold, regained weight quite rapidly. (Mulligan, Burbank and Brunn 408)

"During the whole month of April, the prisoners could hear P-47 and P-51 fighter aircraft strafing targets in and around Moosburg." (Walton & Eberhardt 547)

"Conditions became more lax in the camp, and the guards soon began escorting

prisoners outside the camp to barter for food. The kriegies collected what cigarettes and candy they had and followed the guards outside the gate and across the bridge over the Isar River hoping to trade for bread or sugar. With the lax security and futile attempts to control prisoners, as many as seventeen prisoners spread out and agreed to meet their guard at a designated point at a certain time." (Walton & Eberhardt 547)

"Sometime in early April all airmen prisoners were ordered to be ready to depart for the [Alpine] redoubt in two days. Our senior officers had decided, after painful debate, that we should not resist, as it might set off a slaughter in the camp." (Clark 162)

Sunday 7

". . . the YMCA still got into our camp and delivered mail from home to some fortunate kriegie recipients." (Hopewell 223)

Monday 9

"On the 9th, the men looked upward to witness five hundred B-17s from the Third Air Division of the 8th Force, escorted by three hundred forty P-51s, pass overhead just west of Moosburg en route to bomb Munich. The prisoners' spirits were once more raised, and they eagerly plotted the advance of the Allied front on their hidden maps." (Walton & Eberhardt 547)

This date "the entire contingent of Sagan South Compound POWs was moved, bag and baggage, in on top of the Center Compound group. Five large tents had been erected, but the shelter was not sufficient and prisoners slept outside all over the compound. . . . Four thousand POWs now occupied the space which had been inadequate for 2000. All cooking was done outside on 'Kriegie burners.' The pack-in

Thursday 15

Kalender (März)

Col. Smith: Full parcels next week. For how long I don't know. Beautiful day again today. Got a slight sunburn.

Friday 16

Kalender (März)

Air Raid. I've seen more allied a/c since I got here. Beautiful sunny day.

Saturday 17

Kalender (März)

S.I. in ranks. Fitz & I had a big chocolate oatmeal bash. Wrote a letter to Gen.

Sunday 18

Kalender (März)

These fleas are eating me up.

Monday 19

Kalender (März)

News is going great. Parcels in late tonight. ½ parcels.

Tuesday 20

Kalender (März)

Still half parcels, hope to get the other straightened out tomorrow. Received our parcel today.

Wednesday 21

Kalender (März)

Air raid 11 til 3. Dropped a lot of chaff.

Thursday 22

Kalender (März)

Really a beautiful day. We ate outside. Reading: *By Valor & Arms*, James Street.

condition made it next to impossible for the average POW to keep either his clothing or his person clean. . . ." (*South Annexes* 1139)

Wednesday 11

"The air raids continued, and men sat outside and watched. At no time, day or night, was the air free of planes." (Walton & Eberhardt 548)

Thursday 12

". . . the news [of President Roosevelt's death] got through to us almost immediately. We POWs were shocked. . . . Our senior American officers asked the Germans for permission to hold a memorial service. Surprisingly, the Germans granted their request." (Daniel 98)

Saturday 14

Hopewell arrived on foot from Nürnberg this date. "The vast compound looked like a hobo camp with groups of men huddled around fires cooking, or trying to keep warm. The barracks were crude and far more crowded than those we had had in South compound. In addition, there were a number of very large tents . . . that would hold from 300 to 400 men." (219)

Sunday 15

[The memorial service for President Roosevelt was held this date in the camp.]

Wednesday 18

This date "the prisoners were told by the Germans . . . to prepare for another march south that would take place in three days." This would have implemented Hitler's plan to hold them hostage in his Bavarian "last redoubt" in exchange for better truce terms.

Senior American Officers had heard via their clandestine radio that the Swiss Protecting Power had negotiated an agreement between the Allies and the Germans not to move the kriegies and warned the camp kommandantur that they should check

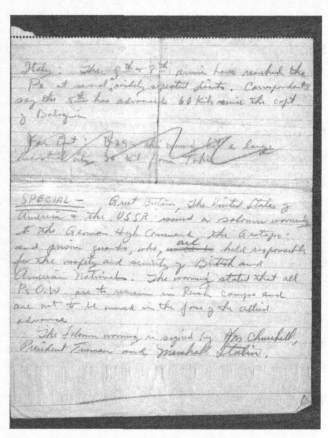

Kriegie news bulletin c. 22 April 1945 (Thomas E. Mulligan Collection SMS 603, Clark Special Collections Branch, McDermott Library, US Air Force Academy)

Friday 23

Kalender (März)

Full parcels started on Wed.

Monday 26

Kalender (Endpapers)

Went on full [parcels] last week, but Goon rations cut down so it's about the same. There's more food in parcels tho'. Thinking of trading my parcel this week for a watch. I'd have to really tighten my belt.

A Guard shot one of the Indian workers (a POW) near the fence.

OKW [news] is really good—near Frankfurt.

Wednesday 28

Kalender (Endpapers)

I bought a watch yesterday for my week's parcel. Now I tighten my belt a little for a week. We have a few cans of food saved so it won't be too bad. I'm used to it anyway.

Boys are doing fine in the West.

Friday 30

Kalender (Endpapers)

Good Friday. Jim Juntilla went to the Hospital this AM.

News is still real hot.

Saturday 31

Kalender (Endpapers)

S.I.

Armies are going wide open all around. These Goons have had it. (P-51s gunnery pattern out here.)

Fitz & I are preparing an Easter bash. Maybe a V------ dinner, too, Goon!!

Wrote 1 letter to Gen & 1 card to Mom.

"A Kriegie hovel—anything to get out of the barracks." (John M. Bennett Collection SMS 500, Clark Special Collections Branch, McDermott Library, US Air Force Academy)

Letter excerpts

If the mail is going through as it should be, I'm sure that by now you know where I am. It was quite a trip. One that I won't forget for a year or two. Things have before trying to move anyone. (Walton & Eberhardt 548)

Henry Soderberg had been reporting on conditions in the camps since early 1943. Today he arrived at Stalag VIIA, describing conditions as follows: "Thousands and thousands of [POWs] live in barns and stables and bombed-out houses and in the small forest around Moosburg. There are new streams of prisoners marching in every day." (Quoted in Durand 351.)

Also on this date, McKee reports that "we were moved out of the barracks into tents. It hasn't been so bad and the fresh air has made some of us feel better." (137)

"Some anxiety was felt in mid and late April that the officer POWs at Moosburg would be moved and held as hostages instead of being allowed to be over[r]un by the advancing allied armies. The solemn warning issued by Supreme Allied Headquarters apparently had its effect, however, for no such move was made." (South Annexes 1140)

Wednesday 25

"By late April, the stench in the camp was overpowering and the multitude of prisoners, riddled with insect bites, picked their way through garbage and overflowing latrines. They lived in filth they had never known before. Hungry men, who had been stalwart in battle and through continual deprivation, became despondent. Without the arrival of emergency Red Cross parcels, many would not have survived at all." (Walton & Eberhardt 541)

"Parts of the camp became unsafe to enter, and a desperate 'every man for himself' air was apparent. Long lines were everywhere and between the unsanitary conditions, lack of adequate nourishment, despair as the war dragged on, and the overcrowding, it was hard to be optimistic." (Walton & Eberhardt 547)

". . . mail had been delivered in camp up to a couple of days prior to liberation. . . ." (Hopewell 232)

settled down now & we're back to the old routine of trying to make our parcel last out the week—and most generally it does. Necessity being the mother of invention, we really throw together some mean concoctions here both in the line of food & cooking utensils. You should see the latest in stoves. Made entirely of tin cans with an oven & two cooking surfaces. Our life here is funny in a way. It's so futile. We're all plenty optimistic tho', especially of late.

I'm just finishing the book *By Valour and Arms*. It's a Civil War story & very good. Our library here is fair but not near as good as at Sagan.

Bye for now & prepare the fatted calf—I can use one.

April

Sunday 1 Easter

Kalender (Endpapers)

9:00 AM appell.

    Big dinner: spam & egg, scalloped potatoes, chocolate pie & milk pie.

Saturday 7

Card excerpt

Received my first mail yesterday since my arrival here. One from you & one from Mother, dated Sept. 10 & Nov 26 resp[ectively]. Glad to know that all is going well at home. It is here, too, for me. About all I can say here is I'm well—& happy about the looks of things. Hope to see you soon.

Sunday 8

Kalender (Endpapers)

Sun[day]. Again they're putting up tents out here. Nurnburg is coming here. They seem to be moving the other ranks[30] out of here.

    Eng[lish] & Indian parcels last week. We had another bash tonight.

    Wrote a card to Gen last night.

    Made a blower for Lunt for 1 D-bar.

    The weather hasn't been so good this week but today was OK.

    Rec'd 1 letter from Gen & 1 from Mom.

Monday 9

Kalender (Endpapers)

South Camp moved into the tents.

Tuesday 10

Kalender (Endpapers)

Met Keith Conley and all of the Mormon Group. Had a long talk with B. Henry [Hinckley].[31]

---

    30. Non-officers.

    31. These were members of the group who comprised the Stalag Luft III Branch that functioned officially in South Compound from 1943–5. Richard was able to meet them because of South Camp's move on 9 April into the area occupied by Center Compound. See *Appendix G.*

Wednesday 11

Kalender (Endpapers)

We had another big air show today. It's a common occurrence.

Thursday 12

Kalender (Endpapers)

Letter from Gen. Oct 22.
    Started Combine mess yesterday. Amer[ican] & Canadian parcels this week.

Friday 13

Kalender (Endpapers)

Another big day in the news. The next 30 days should complete the occupation. Hope they don't move us again.
    The info. keeps coming in on the S. France Hospital for 21 days, then 30 days plus 2 days for ea[ch] month in the bag—furlow.
    Rec. 2 letters from Mom: Oct 29 & Nov 16.

Letter excerpts
Geneil to Richard (unsent)

Time passes quickly and yet eternities have slipped by since I last saw you. Now, I can only remember and pray that you are safe somewhere. . . .
    The reports we get of you and your conditions are most discouraging and heartbreaking. Each day I feel a little more of me die and become useless. My very soul aches and cries at your position. . . . I feel so useless and weak. . . . Just now I seem to be in a daze. I feel nothing except extreme anxiousness. I can take anything but the thoughts of your suffering. If only I could help you or make it all right for you. . . . All I can do is hope and pray for your safety.

Saturday 14

Kalender (Endpapers)

Wrote to Gen.

Sunday 15

Kalender (Endpapers)

This place is really in a 'Flap.' The Kriegies are tearing down all of the partition fences, & the Goons don't seem to care. They did shoot a couple of times, but the harm was already done.

I've come to the conclusion that either the krieg is about over or we're about to make another move.

I went to my first L.D.S. services (at 16:30) since I was in Tallahassee Fla.[32]

Monday 16

Kalender (Endpapers)

1st rumor of the day: They're 30 mi from here. We can hear either bombers or shell-fire. The same as at Sagan.

Big air show south of here.

Tuesday 17

Kalender (Endpapers)

Beautiful day for sun-bathing. Had my hair cut—Holmes.[33]

RAF had a big night west of here last night.

News is good. They say the Russians are moving. We won't be here over a week or two.

It takes a month on full rations to begin eating.

Wednesday 18

Kalender (Endpapers)

Some of the boys came in off the road tonight. They seem to've had quite a picnic. Why couldn't our trip have been that way?

Friday 20

Kalender (Endpapers)

Twenty months.

---

32. Again, this was possible because the Stalag Luft III Branch had moved with the rest of South Compound into Center Compound's area on the previous Monday. Richard met with other LDS men on the two Sundays remaining before Liberation Day.

The Branch minutes record that "Many new faces were present today, due to our move from the South to the Center Camp." They heard "a brief sermon on preparedness," another on "coveting our neighbor's property; especially here where conditions are adverse" and sang "The Spirit of God," "O, My Father" and "God Be With You." They apparently did not take the sacrament (communion), no doubt because of the dreadful conditions in which they were living. (Branch Minutes 34-5) See *Appendix G.*

33. This and other similar references suggest that Combine G had been at least partially reconstituted in Stalag VIIA.

The old Sagan Abwehr personnel have taken over again. We've received spuds 5 days straight now. They've opened our gate, making it one large compound. Did my wash in preparation for our probable move. It'll surely be swell to get home & be my own boss again. At least if I'm bossed around, I won't mind.

Sunday 22

At today's LDS Branch meeting "Brother Arnett, Presiding Elder at the Sagan West Compound, gave us some words of comfort in a short talk reminding us that in conditions such as we have undergone and through trials which we are moving, we can be cheered by noting how others have suffered. He read from Sections 121 and 122 of the Doctrine and Covenants. . . ." (Branch Minutes 35)

Tuesday 24

Kalender (Endpapers)

We're in a big move flap. The Allies are crowding us again, so that's the next thing. This <u>will</u> be the last one tho'.

The tactical A.F. is over here most of the time now, dive bombing & strafing all around.

No mail forms this weekend. The weather has been bad lately.

P.M. The next move is to be to the U.S.A. (It says here.) Large 'flap.'

Wednesday 25

Kalender (Endpapers)

This is the big day of the conference, now what?

We've settled down to wait for the Allies now. They seem to've reached an agreement against moving us.

The war is right in our backyard now. We hear artillery & bombing constantly.

B-26's & fighters & bombers all over.

They strafed the bread train so we received a large cut in the ration.

Munich has really caught it the last two nights.

It's just like Italy over again.

Letter excerpt
Grandpa Butler to Geneil

"I have been wondering about Richard. Do you hear from him? The last letter I have was written before Xmas and that is a long time ago. I am hoping and praying that he has been released, for everything looks like they are about to take over Germany.

"I hope and pray that the day is not far distant for you and him to meet again."

Friday 27

Kalender (Endpapers)

Today has really been quiet. Almost no air activity.

Big 'going home' inspection tomorrow at 10:30.

Surprise!! We got our 2nd hot shower today since leaving Sagan. 59 men & me in the same bath.

Sunday 29[34]

Log

This is the day. Undoubtedly the greatest in my life.

Last night the artillery fire was noticeably drawing nearer.

I was in charge of a platoon of E.M.s [enlisted men] and went over to organize them early this A.M.

At about 9:30 the P-51s came over & started strafing in support of the front lines. We were all outside taking it in until the ground-fire started to sing by. One Kriegie (five in 211) got hit in the leg. The rest of us hit the dirt.

They're really going to town now. Machine-gun fire all around us. The battle for Moosburg is on.

A tank maj[or] came in this A.M. with (Wow! That one shook hell out of the place.) the dope on our move out of here. It's too good to be true.

We're to move within 12 hrs & be completely out within 48 hrs. Go by truck to an airdrome about 60 kms, then by air to Le Havre, where we get identity cards, clothes, pay & a physical. Then if possible by air to the USA. Where we get a 45-day furlow—possibly more.

He also said there was a bill in Congress to advance us one rank, but it hasn't passed yet.

I wonder how much of this will turn out. [Note inserted later: May 23. Aboard SS *Santa Maria* at Southampton: B.S.]

A Cab (observation) just went over.

It's 11:15 & the shellfire seems to be subsiding a little. (I HOPE.)

From here on we eat, sleep & live like white men again.

12:45

What a wonderful sight. The old Stars & Stripes are flying over Moosburg.

The gunfire is receding to the south.

---

34. Richard's next few entries are in large, scrawled handwriting and are disjointed—all for obvious reasons. On 9 May his penmanship returns to more normal size and precision, although even those final entries vary somewhat.

The Battle for Moosburg

"Events began to cascade . . . as Allied forces closed in to surround Stalag VIIA." (Walton & Eberhardt 541)

Friday 27

". . . some kriegies reported seeing tanks at the crest of the hill a mile north of Moosburg." (Walton and Eberhardt 548)

Saturday 28

"During the day . . . firing was heard in the general direction of north and west. The prisoners knew that liberation was not far off." (Mulligan, Burbank and Brunn 409)

". . . it rained all day but American fighters flew over Moosburg and waggled their wings in recognition of the prisoners below. . . . As fighting got even closer, the men were ordered . . . to stay inside the barracks. Closed inside, eager eyes peeped out of holes and saw Allied soldiers in the fields around the camp." (Walton & Eberhardt 548)

"(2000) Goon tanks & equipment have been rolling thru town for the past three hours. Heavy gunfire since noon. Allies reported six kilos away at 1800." (Kingsbury 41)

Sunday 29

Units of Combat Command A of the U.S. Army's 14th Armored Division had been halted the previous night in the region of Mainburg (12–15 miles north of Moosburg) and were to resume the attack at 0600. Just a moment before that time a group including a German major representing the commandant of Stalag VIIA, the senior American and British officers held in Stalag VIIA, a Red Cross representative, and one of the 14th's battalion commanders arrived at headquarters of Combat Command A.

The German major carried a written proposal for creation of a neutral zone around Moosburg; the proposal was rejected and a deadline of 0900 was given for unconditional surrender. The surrender demand was rejected; SS troops set up a line of defense outside Moosburg and opened the battle. (Orsini)

Around 9:30 the P-51s started strafing. "About that time the Germans blew up the two local bridges over the Iser [*sic*] River that ran north and south in front of the camp, and the shooting started." (Clark 173)

"Moosburg sat on a hill, so we could see bits of the action. German machine gunners were firing at the Americans from the bell tower of one church." (Daniel 101)

"Then the shooting stopped, and it was deathly quiet. By 10:30 a.m., the resisting SS troops, the last hold-outs for the Third Reich, were dead on the road and in the fields. Shots of a brief skirmish outside the wire had just died down when the kriegies knew the war was over. For the long-suffering POWs that moment marked when and where Germany's strident goose-stepping finally halted." (Walton & Eberhardt 552)

". . . at approximately 1200 hours, after much firing just outside the camp by small arms, the first jeep rolled up." (Mulligan, Burbank and Brunn 410)

"The excitement in camp was indescribable. As soon as the shooting stopped, men started popping up by the thousands all over camp. They climbed upon the roofs of the huts and even on the wire to get a view of what was going on. . . . Men were hugging each other, crying, praying, screaming, and jumping up and down. Everyone rushed out of the huts, and the crowd grew so large that each man had to do his celebrating in place. The roar was impressive, and the whole scene was very moving." (Clark 174-5)

Many of the Kriegies are said to have faced Moosburg's Cathedral of St. Kastulus, stood at attention and saluted the flag now flying there. In the camp itself, Lt. Martin Allain, a Stalag Luft III security officer, brought out the American flag he'd hidden at Sagan by sewing it between two blankets and which he had carried on the winter march. As thousands of Kriegies looked on, "a dirty malnourished man, clad in rags, scrambled up the camp's flagpole and ripped down the detested Nazi flag. In its place, Allain hung the most beautiful sight the cheering crowd could behold. . . ." (Walton & Eberhardt 589)

Lt. Martin Allain's liberation flag. Note shadows. (Courtesy of Marilyn Walton)

I was just up on top of the barracks. There is a Kriegie flag flying for about every allied nation. I saw some jeeps & tanks, too.

Kalender (Endpapers)

This is the big day. Last night the artillery could be heard very close.

I went over & helped organize the enlisted men this A.M. I have the 3rd platoon of C Company, 6th Batt[ery].

Richard's rooftop Liberation Day photo of Stalag VIIA looking westward toward the main gate. (Butler family collection)

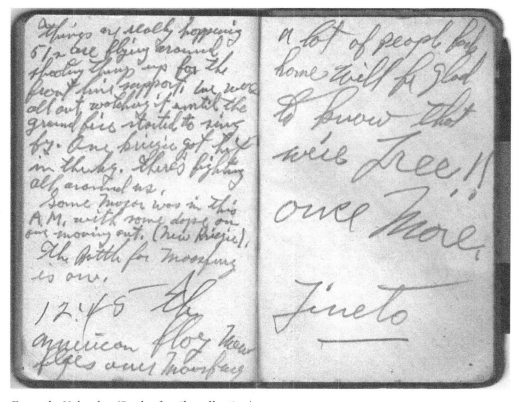

From the Kalender *(Butler family collection)*

Richard's Retrospective Note
c. 1970

It all began on a quiet spring morning on April 29, 1945, when an Allied fighter plane swooped out of the sky to strafe an unknown target.

This began (for those witnesses) what proved to be the most important battle of WWII.

General George Patton began the final phase of the drive to remove all remaining resistance from the State of Bavaria.

The battle ensued for several hours while some 30 thousand POWs watched with apparent detachment for the danger which stood on all sides.

Some hours later the last local resistance was removed by a blast of artillery and the raising of the of the Stars & Stripes (the most beautiful sight one would ever see).

With this sight the air was torn by such a shout of joy that one may never hear again. Within seconds, flags of every Allied nation in the world flew over that enclosure of barbed wire.

But what is freedom/liberty but a state of mind? There was no mass exodus, but rather a deep silence fell over the camp, and God was thanked in word & tear for this newfound freedom. (For a short while the atheist believed and thanked God.)

No, there was no mass exodus. Those thousands who for years had only existed—and at times as animals—stood silently basking in the sheer joy of freedom.

6

FREEDOM, FRUSTRATION, REPATRIATION

After the Liberation

Later in the Day

Sunday 29 April

Through the day events followed each other rapidly. Among other things, the German camp commander formally surrendered and P-51s flew over several times doing celebratory rolls and other aerobatics. The Red Cross quickly brought in a mobile canteen from which female staff began serving doughnuts; their trucks filled with food were lined up to enter the camp.

"Scenes of the wildest rejoicing accompanied the tanks as they crashed through the double 10-foot wire fences of the prison camps. . . . There were men from every nation fighting the Nazis . . . men of every rank and every branch of service. . . . Around the city were thousands of slave laborers, men and women. All combined to give the 14th [Armored Division] the most incredible welcome it ever received. The tanks were finally slowed to five miles an hour as they went through the camps—the press of men was so great. Men, some of them prisoners five years, some American Air Corps men prisoners three years, cried and shouted and patted the tanks. . . . An American Air Corps lieutenant kissed a tank." (Orsini)

"Kriegies enjoying their new-found freedom tore holes in the wire around the camp and walked out into the fields they had seen from afar for so long. . . . A War Crimes room was immediately set up in a barrack." (Walton & Eberhardt 568)

"Loudspeakers were set up and played appropriate and popular songs of the day, "Don't Fence Me In" and "At Last." Movies

Stalag VIIA later on Liberation Day (Lt. Gen. Albert P. Clark Collection SMS 329, Clark Special Collections Branch, McDermott Library, US Air Force Academy)

were set up. . . . Clandestine cameras and others that the Army troops 'liberated' from a German camera factory on the way to Moosburg snapped pictures all over the camp." (Walton & Eberhardt 571)

The Day After

Monday 30 April

"The Goons are still holding a small bridge-head outside of town. The artillery was hitting them all night." (Kingsbury 43)

"I explored the whole German administrative area and found the card files on which the goons meticulously kept our personal POW history. These cards had our photo along with place and date of capture, injuries and wounds, hospitalizations, escape attempts, punishments, and so on. I sent them into camp, and they were distributed to all as a coveted keepsake." (Clark 179–80)

"Shortly after Liberation, one or two congressmen and their entourage came into Stalag VIIA while we were waiting for evacuation. Our senior officers brought them into our tent to see what conditions were like. We were called to attention and stood up as best we could under the low tent.

"The party passed down the aisle between rows of a slightly bent-over ragtag, unimpressed bunch of men, and lines full of

Possibly Combine G after liberation; Richard center front (Richard M. Butler papers MSS 8849, L. Tom Perry Special Collections, Harold B. Lee Library, Brigham Young University)

Liberated Kriegies. Perhaps from Center Compound. (Richard M. Butler papers MSS 8849, L. Tom Perry Special Collections, Harold B. Lee Library, Brigham Young University)

Free again! Presumably men of Center Compound (Richard M. Butler papers MSS 8849, L. Tom Perry Special Collections, Harold B. Lee Library, Brigham Young University)

In Stalag VIIA after liberation; Richard top right (Richard M. Butler papers MSS 8849, L. Tom Perry Special Collections, Harold B. Lee Library, Brigham Young University)

blackened cans and pans. By the time the party passed in front of me they were staring straight ahead, looks frozen on their faces.

"They couldn't wait to escape from the place. Neither could we." (Wick)

"We Americans were divided into battalions and the commanders drew lots to see which group would leave camp first." (Hopewell 232)

"In the evening it was announced that a drawing had been held to determine the order in which the POWs would leave for France, and then home. Our tent was to be in the second group, but we still had no word as to when the evacuation would start. Group departures were announced at a roll call each morning at nine o'clock. . . ." (Bender 334)

It's essential to mention the fabled post-liberation visit of General George Patton to Stalag VIIA; the fable takes many forms. Ex-Kriegies say they saw him 29 April, 30 April and 1 May; arriving by tank, jeep and shiny sedan; greeted by raucous cheers and by resentful silence. However, the Clark Scrapbook has two photos of the general, one of which shows him standing in a jeep. Clark's caption says "Gen. Patton visits Moosberg [*sic*] 30th April, 1945."

The Wait

Tuesday 1 May–Sunday 6 May

"There was no plan as far as we could see, and all the complex but routine operations of running such a huge camp stopped abruptly on liberation. We were not fed. The latrines were not emptied and we were urged to stay in the camp!" (Clark Scrapbook 80)

"It was a heartbreaking sight for me and several other fairly senior officers who were old prisoners when Jeeps started coming in to pick up almost all of our full colonels. . . . Most of them had not been prisoners for long. We old prisoners felt like we'd been forgotten. . . . We bitterly recalled the assurances of that staff weenie who had joined us shortly before the end.[1] He had assured us that the oldest prisoners would go home first. . . . The thousands of junior officers and enlisted men were still there, and most of the senior leadership left them without a concern." (Clark 182–3)

". . . General de Gaulle had prevailed upon General Eisenhower to give first priority to the evacuation of all French prisoners. Since there were several thousand of them out on farms in Bavaria . . . they all had to be brought in, processed, and airlifted back to France." (Clark 182)

"The removal of the French from the camp took several days, and American prisoners resented it. As the days passed, Americans started to disappear and there was no keeping track of where they went." (Walton & Eberhardt 633)

"For the safety of the waiting men, the gates were locked, and they were no longer allowed outside. As the days dragged on, the prisoners became more defiant, and many decided to make their own plans for departure. . . . There was still random fire in the area, and as days passed trash accumulated in the already abysmal camp, making conditions unlivable. Still the Americans waited, starting the delousing process to go home. The first action by the U.S. Army was to powder the Kriegies with DDT to kill lice, fleas, and bedbugs." (Walton & Eberhardt 581)

Waiting for evacuation. "Some of us did not get out for 2 weeks." (Lt. Gen. Albert P. Clark Collection SMS 329, Clark Special Collections Branch, McDermott Library, US Air Force Academy)

1. This is the man Richard referred to on 29 April when he said "It's too good to be true."

"It is difficult to recapture the frustration and disappointment of being required to remain for up to 10 days or two weeks in this filthy camp while we waited for transportation home. . . .

"The artillery BN designated to support us . . . was hopelessly unprepared, untrained for the task & we got C Rations finally & little else." (Clark Scrapbook 83)

"Before they left to return to the fighting war, the army had dropped off many boxes of ten-in-one K rations, and most of us began to put on some needed pounds." (Hopewell 231)

"The only arrangements made to bring recovered Allied POWs (RAMPs) back from our camps to process them for home was 'space available' on C-47 A/C bring[ing] supplies forward & those supporting field evacuation hospitals but not required. . . .

"Also the failure of the evacuation authorities (if there were any) to arrange for priority evac. of older POW's before new POWs was not understood.

"The 10 days to two weeks spent in this repulsive camp while we waited for evacuation was a very unhappy experience for all of us & those of us who were the oldest remaining senior POW's . . . decided to be the last ones out & to see that all our 30,000 Jr. Officer[s] got out of the camp ahead of us.

"When we departed for the evacuation A/ Fields [a day behind Richard] we closed the gate behind us!" (Clark Scrapbook 89)

Evacuation

Monday 7 May

"The first contingent to leave the camp at Moosburg was placed in trucks, and away we drove. Strangely enough, no one looked back toward our former temporary home with any affection. It didn't take very long to reach the flying field at Landschut [*sic*], and we were surprised to find it to be such a small one. . . . The landing strip was . . . pretty crude." (Hopewell 232)

Hopewell maintains that one C-47 loaded with evacuee RAMPs got off the ground before the weather closed in; he, like many others, was stuck there for days.

"Out of the main gate for the last time." 9 May 1945. (Lt. Gen. Albert P. Clark Collection SMS 329, Clark Special Collections Branch, McDermott Library, US Air Force Academy)

1945

April

Monday 30

Log

Since yesterday we've had tanks, jeeps, and about everything in camp, including U.S.O. or R.C. girls. They came in on a jeep just to let us see what people on the outside really look like.[1]

Howard K. Robinette, Richard's "liberator" (Butler family collection)

May

Tuesday 1[2]

Log

What's going to happen next? About 5:30 last eve Howard Robinette drove in in a jeep. (My Liberator.) I went into Moosburg to his room & had the biggest & best dinner I've had since my capture. He also gave me a lot of food (G.I.) to bring back. Boy, was it ever good!

V-Mail

Filling out this first form reminds me of my first one from England twenty-nine months ago. It's been a long time—or did you know.

If I don't beat this to you (I hope), you can prepare to come & meet me. I'll soon be home. The latest dope is we go at least part of the way by air. It can't be soon enough for me. I'll have a bad case of claustrophobia, or something, until I get that Atlantic crossed again.

---

1. This evening Howard Robinette (Aunt Martena's brother-in-law and Richard's friend from Sacramento training days) drove into camp, found Richard and took him back to his billet in Moosburg. Richard's retrospective accounts follow.

2. Geneil didn't hear the news of VIIA's liberation until this morning Salt Lake City time when she arrived at work.

Hey! Guess who liberated me. Not all by himself of course, but Howard K. Robinette drove in in a jeep yesterday afternoon. I don't need to say how glad I was to see him. Just like being home. We went into Moosburg to the room he was staying in & he cooked up the best meal I've eaten since I left home. Then we lay on his bed & talked about everything & everyone. I'll never forget it.

I'll keep writing while here.

Friday 4

V-Mail (postmarked in US 4:30 AM, 23 May 1945)

I'm still here, but the evacuation has begun. We're leaving by air to the coast, then most likely by foot the rest of the way. The fifteenth should see us together once more. I hope—impossible as it may seem.

I'm slowly coming to realize that I'm free. There are jeeps & trucks & GIs all over the place. Even senators have visited us for a look at the place. That should be positive proof.

I took a walk (outside) this

Richard at the Stalag VIIA fence, post-liberation (Richard M. Butler papers MSS 8849, L. Tom Perry Special Collections, Harold B. Lee Library, Brigham Young University)

afternoon all by myself. It's the first time I've been alone in twenty months. Pretty nice, to say the least.

We no longer have to keep our radio hid. There are several of them around & it's really OK.

There are so many things to write about that I don't know where to begin. I just might beat this home anyway.

Guess I'll have some more liberated eggs. I'd forgotten how they taste.

[The following journal entries for May 8–19 have been edited to show events in chronological order. Richard originally wrote some of them retrospectively and, in the original, the order of events gets a bit confusing.]

"Typical boarding group at Landshut," probably 9 May 1945. (Lt. Gen. Albert P. Clark Collection SMS 329, Clark Special Collections Branch, McDermott Library, US Air Force Academy)

Landshut

Tuesday 8 May

"The history of Moosburg prison camp really ended on VE day when the first group was flown from Landshut to Reims." (Mulligan, Burbank and Brunn 412)

Landshut airfield was actually located several kilometers south of Landshut near the village of Ellermühle. Its grass field (1,000 yards × 400 yards) had been used during the war for glider training. There was no infrastructure other than groups of living quarters along the western side at each end of the field.

Clark reached there on 9 May, so the chaos he describes would have been similar to what Richard found there the previous day.

"I arrived at Landshut to see another chaotic scene. Many of the kriegies who had departed Moosburg several days before were still there waiting, without shelter or any amenities, for an aircraft to take them out. Dozens of C-47s were parked on the

field and others were circling, waiting for room to land. The field was a small grass runway marked only by white wooden blocks and badly cut up by deep ruts. When I arrived, an aircraft was burning at one end of the field. It had ground-looped on landing and collided with another parked aircraft. I was told that the copilot had been killed. . . .

"I was appalled when I discover[ed] that there was no airport authority and no radio control of the aircraft landing and taking off." (Clark 186–7)

"Dispersed around the field were more than 30 Nazi planes of different types. Each had had an explosive charge detonated midway between the wings and tail. It was indeed a sorry, wasteful-looking sight to a bunch of flight-starved pilots." (Bender 337)

Richard left VIIA around noon on the 8th; judging from a photo in the Clark Scrapbook, to reach the trucks he had to walk some little distance along the north/south road outside the gate. The distance from the camp to Landshut airfield is only about

By this time the men had a new designation: RAMP, Returned Allied Military Personnel.]

Tuesday 8

Log

After completely giving up hope of ever getting out of Germany (the land of barbed-wire entanglements), the weather cleared and evacuation missions started again. We've been delayed over a week since liberation.

[To]day we were alerted again & it was the real thing. We left VIIA & Moosburg at about noon for Landshut where we watched takeoff & landing for a while, part of which were Gr. [German] aircraft. The first one was a Do[rnier] (or Si[korski]) transport, the second & third Ju[nker] 52's, & later, just before we took off, twenty-three more came in, mostly small trainers. It disgusts me the way these souvenir-mad Americans act. They mobbed most of the ships & took watches & valuables from the passengers, etc.

We finally got off the ground at 20:36 hrs. May 8, 1945.[3]

It's really swell getting back into the air again. We're heading for Reims, France, from there to le Havre.

Butler Family Hoping For News Of Prisoner Son

Mr. and Mrs. H. C. Butler of Garland are in high hopes this week, that they will soon hear from their son, Richard, who was taken prisoner by the Germans in August 1943. Richard was serving as Flight Officer at that time.

According to a card written by him on the 13th of February, he was moved in January to Moosberg 7A, which has been reported liberated recently.

Lt. Keith Conley, son of Mr. and Mrs. Keith Conley was thought to have been in the same prison camp. According to report, they have heard from him, and expect him to be home soon.

Garland Times, *May 1945. (Butler family collection)*

I listened to the radio with a set of earphones & heard King George VI, Pres. Truman, Churchill, & a lot of others speaking in celebration of VE Day.[4] England seems to take this more as a final victory than America does. Our big celebration will come after it's all over. Victory to me seems rather empty, at least as far as any hilarity goes.

---

3. While Richard didn't leave VIIA on the first day of the evacuation, he did manage to get out of Landshut Airfield on the first (full) day of evacuation flights of Americans into France.

4. "It is strange to note that many of the prisoners who landed at Reims on the evening of VE night did not know it was VE night. . . ." (Mulligan, Burbank and Brunn 412)

Richard certainly knew, but how did he come to have those headphones? I wonder if he talked his way into the cockpit!

15km, but because some of the Amper River bridges may have been blown, it could have taken an hour or more to get there. That could have left him as much as 7 hours to observe and explore. The surviving photo he shot there does not begin to capture what Clark describes.

Richard records 2036 as his takeoff time. Given what Clark says of long delays, the field's condition and the lack of traffic control, we should be grateful Richard got out that same day and without incident.

Kriegie evacuation flight over France (Lt. Gen. Albert P. Clark Collection SMS 329, Clark Special Collections Branch, McDermott Library, US Air Force Academy)

Hopewell says "The plane was flying only a few thousand feet above the ground, and it was the best close-up any of us had had at the devastating damage the bombers had inflicted." (234) As we know, Richard could only see the lights winking below but, as he overflew them, he did hear the V-E Day speeches.

Reims

Wednesday 9 May

Richard didn't reach the camp until the early hours of the 9th.

"The camp at Reims was pretty informal. . . . We were told to find an empty cot and sleep in it as long as we wanted. We were on our own EXCEPT we wouldn't get to take the next step on the way home until we were de-loused, had a shower, and got clean clothes. . . . You stripped and stepped into an oversized laundry bag, and an attendant pulled the bag's draw-string around your neck. I could feel that I was standing in some kind of powder. When air was introduced into the sack, the powder went everywhere. Some of the powder was sprayed on your head, you were let out of the sack, and then you were marched into an adjoining area where there were warm showers. Since this was only my fourth shower in over a year, I'd have stayed there the rest of the day if they had let me. . . ." (Bender 338)

". . . we were furnished with an issue of brand-new suntans. . . ." (Hopewell 235) "Eventually, my name was posted on the train assignment bulletin board." (Bender 339) On Hopewell's train there was a brief stop in Paris and a meal in the dining car. (236) Richard traveled on a hospital train, so he probably had few amenities nor would he have necessarily had the same routing. He did pass Reims' cathedral on the way to the train.

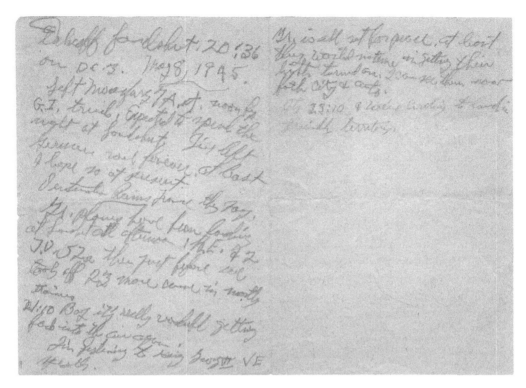

Richard's 8 May in-flight notes (Richard M. Butler papers MSS 8849, L. Tom Perry Special Collections, Harold B. Lee Library, Brigham Young University)

The lights are going on already all across Gross Deutschland.

It's 23:15. We just landed in friendly territory. A field near Reims.[5] [We] stayed up almost all night finding camp.

[From the brief summary Richard added after the war to the back of the *Journal:*] Flew into France 8 May & was almost shot down by our own troops, who were celebrating. No parachute this time.

Wednesday 9

Log

We went by truck to the processing center near Reims & had a bath, clean clothes and a typhus shot at 16:30.

---

5. The base where Richard landed was no doubt Reims-Champagne Air Base, a French Air Force base a few miles north of Reims. After the liberation of France, it was used by Allied forces first as a base for paratroop C-47s, then as a frontline combat base for P-47 fighters; finally, when the front moved eastward, it became a resupply and casualty evacuation base.

Lucky Strike

Thursday 10 May–Saturday 19 May

Richard's train arrived in mid-afternoon at Camp Lucky Strike, one of a conglomeration of "cigarette" camps[2] spread across this part of France. These camps handled homeward rotation of standard troops as well as POWs. According to the account of one nurse who worked in the hospital at Lucky Strike, it was actually located in St. Riquier-en-Caux, about 20 km south of St. Valery and roughly 50 km east-northeast of le Havre.

"Too many POW camps had been liberated ahead of schedule [so] that [Lucky Strike] was full to overflowing. I was in a tent with about six others from Stalag Luft III. . . . Our tent had iron cots, but they had no mattresses, and, of course, we had a dirt floor. The food lines were so long that one was lucky to get one meal a day for the first few days that I was there. . . . we were being fed an especially rich ration. . . . We were issued new uniforms . . . plus all the other necessary

"Lucky Strike was no palace. Dirt floors, iron bunks without mattress." (Lt. Gen. Albert P. Clark Collection SMS 329, Clark Special Collections Branch, McDermott Library, US Air Force Academy)

"Standing in line for one meal per day at Lucky Strike!!" (Lt. Gen. Albert P. Clark Collection SMS 329, Clark Special Collections Branch, McDermott Library, US Air Force Academy)

clothing, toilet articles, and insignia that we needed. There was a medical clinic for those in need. . . ." (Clark 190)

"American POWs, who had been nearly starved, were given several glasses of egg nog for days to prepare their stomachs for

---

2. Camps named for various cigarette brands.

Thursday 10

Log

We pulled out on a hospital train for the Lucky Strike camp near le Havre. Arrived here at about 15:30.

Saturday 12

Log

[We] are now in tents. The weather is fine & I'm the most comfortable I've been in years. They're doing their best to give us the best, but there are an awful lot of us.

I forgot to say that we saw the cathedral at Reims from the outside. It's a very impressing sight. We won't talk about my first night in the place.

We completed our processing at Camp L.S. near St. Valery.

Letter

It has been so long since I wrote a real letter and one that won't be read by every Herman German that I don't know just how to start. At any rate it's really wonderful to be treated like a human being again. They're doing their best here to take care of us & the food is wonderful, but you know how it is when a lot of men get in a group & try to get some action. It naturally comes slow.

I'll be home soon, I keep saying. When, I don't know. I am near le Havre at Camp Lucky Strike, and the processing is progressing. That's about all. I hope to get on a ship within the next week; from there your guess is as good as mine. I don't want to seem casual about it, because I really am anxious to get home; but, well, I guess I've almost learned to be patient. Either that or I don't yet know that I'm free—that could be when I finally see that Statue of Liberty (YOU) I'll be pretty sure I'm there. When I get there, I'll call you, and after I hear your voice you can bet I'll be on the next plane west if there's one going.

They say that we're to be sent in groups to a point in the U.S. near our homes. That may add a few difficulties to our plans, but we will see about that later. I personally intend to get away from this mad mob at the first chance I get. I've been too long now with a man on my neck & one on each toe to take it unnecessarily. You'd think I'd be used to it by now, but no. Come to think of it (if I haven't mentioned it before), I haven't been strictly to myself since a long [time] before I was shot down.

Here I am giving you a sad (& dull) story. I might just as well tell the rest of it. It's legal now, you know.

As you know, I was foolish enough to tangle with an enemy fighter on my last mission. It was a case of see who could put the most lead into the other. Well, I won, but I lost, too. He came apart in front of me, which no doubt kept us from

normal amounts and varieties of food. Uniforms were issued, physicals were given, partial back pay was received, and souvenirs of war registered. War crimes evidence was also collected. . . . The long wait for transportation home began, and impatience was common in the camp. . . ." (Walton & Eberhardt 629)

"They set up a special chow line for us that was open all of the time, because we couldn't eat much at a time, and therefore had to eat many meals in a day. There was a special table full of vitamin pills there, and we were urged to take them." (McKee 141)

Richard's Report of Physical Examination on 16 May shows his weight at 142, so he must have made up for lost time once the emergency Red Cross truck convoys and trains began reaching Stalag VIIA. "This so-called physical was a farce. It consisted of nothing except having our tongues depressed and the usual 'drop the trousers and bend over' routine, following by weighing on the scales. . . . (Hopewell 236)

"Tens of thousands of ex-POWs were now waiting there until transport became available...the waiting was interminable. . . . Discontent among the ex-POWs was intense. Men sent cablegrams to their senators and congressmen telling them of the delay and asking for help. Then authorities caught it from Washington. Finally, General of the Army Eisenhower came down to try his charm on us." (Daniel 105)

Le Havre

Saturday 19 May–Sunday 20 May
At Lucky Strike the repatriates were divided up according to the location of their homes.[3]

Sometime on Saturday 19 May Richard's group were trucked to the outskirts of le Havre and spent that night and the next day and night in a camp there on 30-minute call for boarding. On Monday the trucks took them to the docks.

Boarding the Santa Maria

Monday 21 May–Tuesday 22 May
"As the trucks slowly drove through the city to the docks, it was easy to see a full-scale war had been fought there. . . . This was the first time any of us had seen close-up the damage naval gunfire and bombers could do, and even on the outskirts of the city it was evident the damage had been severe. But that was nothing compared to the damage done to the area surrounding the docks. There were enormous craters where shells had struck, and no buildings at all were standing." (Hopewell 237)

No official ship assignment appears on Richard's Troop Assignment card; it may be that trucks waiting in line to unload the men simply moved farther along the dock as each ship filled up or perhaps the ship assignment was on a form that hasn't survived. In any case, Richard notes in several different places that he boarded the SS *Santa Maria*.

Built in 1942, the *Santa Maria* was a freighter before being converted to a troopship during early 1944. Her history for 1945[4] includes two eastbound departures: from New York to le Havre and Southampton, and from Boston to le Havre respectively on 10 May and 13 June. These bracket her

---

3. The men were required to travel together to their destination, in Richard's case Fort Douglas in Salt Lake City. This disrupted

a plan Geneil and Richard had hatched to meet somewhere along Richard's route from the east coast and spend some time alone together.

4. See Charles, *Troopships of World War II*.

colliding; but I lost the coolant in my left eng[ine] & various & sundry other things, so it caught on fire & forced me out. I pulled up & climbed out.

Heber may be interested in knowing I went between the booms. I wouldn't do it as a regular procedure, tho'. I hit the Gulf of Naples very easy-like after being knocked out by the parachute snap. I had quite a knot on my chin for a few days, caught my leg in the cockpit, too.

Tell you the rest when I get home—if you're interested. Hope to beat this to you, but I know I won't.

Monday 14

[In a May 15 letter to Geneil, her sister Lucile refers to a "message from Richard" which Geneil received during the celebration of Grampy Miller's birthday this date and which caused considerable rejoicing in the family. It seems likely this was the 13 May telegram from Camp Lucky Strike.]

Saturday 19

Log

[We] went by truck to le Havre, where we stayed in a camp at the edge of town for two nights. We were paid 4,000 Francs at L.S., and here we had it exchanged for good old U.S. bills.

Sunday 20

Letter

By now you must think I'm at least in N.Y.C., but no such luck. If present orders work out tho', I'll be loading tomorrow afternoon & will see N.Y. in a week or ten days.

Honestly, this has been the longest three weeks I've spent in my life. There are certain channels that we have to go thru before leaving here, but why does it have to take so long?

We were liberated Apr. 29, as I've already written, but weren't evacuated until May 8. I've almost decided that I'll never get out of this cockeyed country. Maybe I shouldn't say that, because I'm way ahead of most ex-PWs.

Do you know how long it has been since I received your last letter? I think it was written Nov. 27, and it got to me sometime in Mar. or the first part of Apr. I find it hard to believe that I still have a wife. I do, don't I? I hope.

What I'm going to say now isn't so good, but I suppose the main thing is getting me there. We're split up into geographical groups. Ours goes to Fort Douglas S.L.C., Ut., & we have to go almost direct—as a group. It may change a little before I get there. If so, it'll be fine, because I'd sure love to have you come and meet me somewhere. That would be rather difficult if I had to stick with the mob.

Waiting to board, le Havre docks 21 May 1945. (Lt. Gen. Albert P. Clark Collection SMS 329, Clark Special Collections Branch, McDermott Library, US Air Force Academy)

partially-recorded westbound departure on 22 or 23 May carrying Richard from le Havre to Boston via Southampton.

We don't know the time of Richard's arrival on the dock, but the *Santa Maria* remained there at least 24 hours after he boarded her. She apparently left le Havre either late on Tuesday evening or in the first hours of Wednesday. *Santa Maria* clearly arrived in Southampton very early in the day, since some medical cases and returning soldiers had time to join the ship before she sailed again at 8:15 a.m. to join her convoy out in the Channel.

Bound for Home

Wednesday 23 May–Sunday 3 June
From Southampton, Richard crossed in a "very small" convoy; on the second day out, another convoy of similar size merged with his.[5]

On arrival in Boston the RAMPs were taken to Camp Myles Standish in Taunton, Massachusetts. Opened in late 1942, this camp was originally a military staging center and Port of Embarkation for American and Canadian men in transit to the European Theater of Operations; later in the war it housed German POWs. Perhaps during their short stay there, Richard and his fellow RAMPs had a chance to see how their POW experience differed from America's treatment of its prisoners of war.

---

5. We have two addressed but unused V-Mails from Camp Lucky Strike. Richard used one of them to do some figuring and to make a two-word notation: "blackout convoy." I take this to indicate that his convoy traveled in blackout conditions at least part of the way.

Well, if I don't call you on the phone before this arrives you'll know when to expect me, as near as I can tell. If I beat this—That's fine.

I'm in a tent on the outskirts of town waiting for orders to jump aboard (30 min. alert), and it's getting dark so I'd better say adieu.

Be seeing you—not soon but in a little while.

Monday 21

Log

Took truck to the docks & got aboard the SS *Santa Maria* bound for Southampton to pick up hospital patients, then to the U.S.A. (I keep telling myself.)

Wednesday 23

[Richard arrived early this morning at Southampton docks.]

Thursday 24

Log

Docked at S[out]hampton yesterday morning and loaded some patients & the soldiers from Iceland.

Left the dock at 8:15 A.M. to join the convoy in the Channel. Finally pulled out just before noon & have been making good time. We have a very small convoy.

Just 30 months ago today I (Heber, too) pulled out of New York Harbor on board the English SS *Queen Elizabeth* for the limey shore. He beat me back by no small margin of time—thanks to my head-work.

Friday 25

Log

We were joined this afternoon by another convoy about the same size as this.

I ordered some P.X. rations last night (candy, toothbrush, & such). This is the first time I've had to pay for anything in a long time. That green paper is just as good for money as "D" bars.

We've had two movies already & are scheduled for one every other night during the trip. The first one was: *Stormy Weather*—Lena Horne. The one last night was *Keeper of the Flame* (or sumpin')[6] with Spencer Tracy & Katherine Hepburn.

The mess hall is our theater.

---

6. *Keeper of the Flame* is the correct title of the movie referenced above; it's a "dark mystery" made in 1942.

Saturday 26

Log

We set back an hour at midnight last [night]. Movie: *The Hard Way*.[7] Very good!

Someone please stop this darn boat from rocking. The nose (or bow) goes up & down 11 times per minute, 660 times per hour, 15,840 times each day &, if we're lucky enough to make this trip in ten days, 158,400 [total times]. Crossing the Atlantic on a pogo stick. Wow!!

Letter excerpt
Granny Miller to Geneil

"A parcel came back today also. It was returned because it couldn't be delivered, but I don't know which one it was as I didn't open it."[8]

Sunday 27

Log

If we have good luck, we'll see if the lil' gal [Statue of Liberty] still has her hand raised by next Sunday.

The P.X. rations came in today. We had chicken & ice-cream for dinner tonight. We eat, for a change.

I don't want to speak too soon, but I don't feel quite as dizzy as usual. The sea is a little smoother in this latitude, I hope.

Our clocks lost another hour last night.

Monday 28

Log

Clocks dropped back a third hour last night. Something's hay-wire. We're not crossing the ocean that fast. They're probably just getting us on NY time as soon as is possible.

Rumors: (Yes, they're on board ship with us, too.) Blackout is to be lifted tomorrow night. Possibly break up the convoy, too. We're supposed to be in peace-time waters by that time. This is all just hear-say, by the way.

Has this ever been a beautiful day. I was out on deck between lunch & dinner. That wasn't very long, actually. I can't get used to having my meals so close together.

Another movie tonight.

---

7. 1943, starring Ida Lupino.

8. This is presumably the one Geneil mailed in November 1944. See note at 4 December 1944.

The sea is really smooth. Blue almost like the Medit[erranean].

Saw a school of porpoises. They didn't look very studious. Joke.[9]

Tuesday 29

Log

A very dull day today. The sea is quite a bit rougher.

The ship just hit a whale. We passed a whole school of them.

The clock lost its fourth hour last night.

We're beginning to get near white man's country. The weather surely has warmed up.

Wednesday 30

Log

Memorial Day. They held a short service at the No. 3 hatch.

The sea has been real smooth all day & tonight it's just like glass. Beautiful!

I don't realize it, but I'm almost home.

Thursday 31

Log

It's rough as --- out this morning. The clocks lost the fifth hour last night.

The Capt. announced just now that we'd just been assigned our destination. We'll arrive in Boston early Sun. A.M.

Filled out a form telegram to be sent upon arrival.

Journal excerpt
Grandpa Butler

"Received a letter from my wife stating my son Richard, whom we had not heard from for months, had been released as a prisoner of war of the German government."

June

Saturday 2

Log

The past two days have been the roughest I've ever seen it. Guys were sick all over.

---

9. I believe this is a reference to an animated cartoon in which porpoises wore spectacles.

Early Fri A.M. we hit the king of all waves, and the ship raised up & came down with a bang that sounded like we'd hit a mine. The characters started to bail out of their sacks and head for the hatch clad only in their shorts. It was really funny.

Sunday 3

[The *Santa Maria* arrived at Boston's Commonwealth Pier with 1319 RAMPs and 1000 medical patients. They were greeted by Red Cross staff and by a band playing "Roll Out the Barrel" and the Army Air Corps song. Special trains took them to the processing camp.[10]]

Log
Debarked in Boston area & were moved to Camp Myles Standish, where we prepared for the train trip to SLC, arriving 8 June. 11:00 A.M.

Monday 4

[Richard departed Boston at 1500 hours. On his "Map of the Erie Railroad for the Armed Forces" he noted his departure date and time and added New York City at 2130.]

Tuesday 5

[Richard noted Buffalo at 0500 and Chicago at 1930. We have no record beyond Chicago, but he probably traveled from there on the Union Pacific Railroad.]

Wednesday 6

Diary excerpt
Grandma Butler

"Received telephone call from Richard. He was in Dakota. . . . Geneil came and got R. cap so she could take it to Salt Lake along with his uniform when she went to meet him."

Friday 8, 11:00 a.m.

[Richard arrived in Salt Lake City. At that time the city had two different stations: the Denver and Rio Grande Depot and the Union Pacific Depot. Geneil somehow went to the wrong station. Richard couldn't find her, realized there had been a mixup and hurried the three blocks to the other station. There he recognized Geneil in the crowd with her back to him, walked up behind and put his arms around her.]

---

10. *Boston Globe*, 4 June 1945.

Saturday 9

[Richard arrived in Garland.]

Journal excerpt
Grandpa Butler

"Received letters from my wife, stating my son Richard was home. One stated he had arrived in Boston and the other said he was home. This was joyous news for me. My heart was full to overflowing. Words are inadequate to express my feelings. . . ."

Wednesday 13

Diary excerpt
Grandma Butler

". . . at 10 a.m. Leone Miller called[11] to say that Heber was coming our way flying a P-38. By the time we got out of the house, he was here. He flew over the house a few times, did some stunts, gave the neighborhood a thrill, then flew off for Ogden to land at Hill Field. . . .

"Richard, Geneil, Joseph, Vera and myself went down to get him. And oh! what a meeting when R. and Heber met after being separated for 1 year and 9 months. The last time they had seen each other was when they both went out on a flight mission."[12]

Sunday 17

Journal excerpt
Grandpa Butler

"Arrived at Ogden at 3 am. . . . Arrived in Tremonton at 11 am. Mark came with the car. It was a joyous meeting—son and father embraced, also daughter-in-law.

"Sunday night we went to Fielding Ward where Richard related his experiences in a German prison camp for 21 months."

Summer 1945, unknown date

Heber

"Sometime after Richard's return, I took him up in my P-38 in a piggy-back. (Richard was sitting on some part of the cockpit behind my seat with a chest parachute

---

11. From the Miller farm in Penrose, about 15 miles to the southwest.

12. Heber spent most of 14 June with Richard and the family, then took off from Hill Field at about 5:30 p.m. to return to southern California.

Butler Brothers Enjoy Reunion Here Wednesday

Richard Butler Home After Long German Imprisonment

Richard and Heber Butler, P-38 fighter pilots, walked arm in arm in the streets of their home town again Wednesday after a separation of nearly two years which began when Richard's plane was shot down in the Bay of Naples and he bgan his 21 months as a war prisoner. Prior to that event the brothers had been inseparable companions in the same fighter squadron having completed over 50 combat missions together in the Mediterranean area.

Richard arrived at Garland last Saturday after his release from the German camp near Vienna. Heber, serving as a gunnery instructor at a California field, was granted a two-day furlough and a P-38 to come to see his brother, announcing his arrival by jubilantly circling the homestead before landing the plane at Hill Field where the family met him Wednesday forenoon.

Richard reports that treatment of the men in the camps in which he had been held with other American flight officers was fairly satisfactory. Food, however, was very scarce and the weekly Red Cross package was all that sustained life. His observation to friends here is that most of us eat much more than we need. Already 15 pounds heavier than when released, he appears in excellent condition and hopes to get back into a new P-38 right away. He lost his other ship and his freedom in a fight with a German M. E. 109. He downed his opponent but had to bail out when one of his own engines took fire.

on—not exactly comfortable.) I asked if he would like to fly the plane. He said, "Sure!" and we switched places in mid-air, in a cockpit built for a single pilot, flying at 200 miles per hour. Richard flew for the first time since he had had to bail out of his plane and was taken POW—almost two years. What a thrill for him. We flew for an hour and 15–25 minutes and then we switched back, because Richard didn't want to land the plane. It was a lot of fun to fly with my brother. It was the first and only time I ever had the privilege of flying in the same fighter plane with Richard." (Butler 86)

Garland Times, *Friday 15 June 1945 (Richard M. Butler papers MSS 8849, L. Tom Perry Special Collections, Harold B. Lee Library, Brigham Young University)*

A Final Gift of Information

In August of 1984, just months before his passing, Richard completed a VA Former POW Medical History. Dated decades after the war, this document is a final gift of information we would have no other way to know.

Richard was injured during his capture: He got a "cut to left cheek bone," which we can recognize as the scar he bore in that spot.

He experienced intimidation once daily for fourteen days; this was presumably at Nisida and/or Poggio Mirteto. He was once placed in solitary confinement for seven days, probably at Stalag Luft III.

He suffered periods of depression and prolonged periods of feelings of helplessness; he explicitly reported frostbite, presumably on the winter march. He also lists dysentery, pellagra, skipped or missed heartbeats, cavities, sore tongue, diarrhea and fever. Asked if medical treatment was adequate, he responded "Don't know. Never saw it;" the dental treatment was not adequate.

He received news from home "occasionally" and reports his lowest weight in captivity at a surprising 138 pounds, down from 150.

Repatriation physicals were inadequate, and as a RAMP he received no briefing on "events which occurred while you were in captivity." Asked if he was satisfied with his treatment upon repatriation, his answer was "Happy to get moving."

Asked the following questions, his replies were negative.

*Do you feel that you were promoted to the rank you would have been/should have been if you had not been captured?

*Did you receive the medals you believe you deserved?

Richard said he did not find it difficult to adjust to civilian life.

7
HOME, AT LAST

1945-6
Postwar Military

8 June–6 September 1945	Recuperation, Debriefing/Processing
8 September–14 November 1945	Luke Field, Arizona
15 November 1945-4 March 1946	Prin Dy Plt SE & TE
5 March 1946-29 December 1946	Prin Dy Ass't Prep Adjutant Off Supply Officer
30 Dec 1946-11 Feb 1951	Reserve

After reporting at Fort Douglas in Salt Lake City, Richard had a 60-day "period of recuperation" before reporting with Geneil in late August to AAF Redistribution Station #3 in Santa Monica, California. They appear to have spent about a week there, dealing with debriefings, lectures, exams and paperwork while trying to make a bit of a vacation of it.

Richard had a 3-week furlough after their return from California. In October 1945 he was assigned again for several weeks at Luke Field, Arizona, where Geneil accompanied him. While there, he spent 3¼ hours aloft in a P-38.

In mid-November Richard was transferred to Hill Field where he spent the next year as a supply officer and pilot. Richard flew the beloved P-38 for the last time on 5 December 1945 out of Hill Field.

The couple bought a small home at 710 McFarland Street on the west side of Ogden near the base. At long last on 5 March 1946, after being discharged for a second time,

Model of P-38 "Geneil" made by Richard's brother Lester (Butler family collection)

Richard was commissioned a Second Lieutenant. On 18 March baby Richard was born.

During May Richard flew to Montana to participate in an air search for a C-45 lost in "rough
country;" in August he was in Spokane. On 29
December 1946 Richard separated from what
was becoming known as the Army Air Force;
he accepted a reserve appointment. It appears
that the last aircraft Richard flew before his
separation was the P-47.

*Geneil and Richard,
August 1945 (Butler
family collection)*

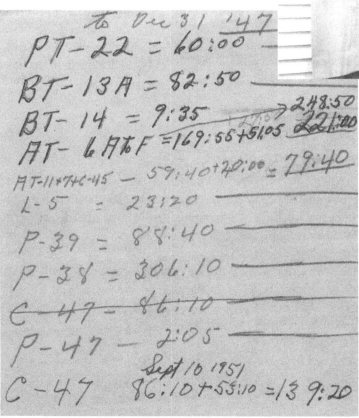

Flight hours per plane (Butler family collection)

1947-50
Home on the Farm

Geneil and Richard sold the McFarland Street bungalow and returned to Garland, where they rented a house on Factory Street while completing their two-story yellow brick dream home on farmland they had bought from Richard's parents. In April 1950 Christine was born, and throughout that year Geneil and Richard also owned and ran Korth Floral in nearby Tremonton. These were halcyon years for them, though they were demanding, hardworking ones.

Garland house, October 1965 (Butler family collection)

Despite his focus on family and farm in the immediate postwar years, Richard received poignant reminders of the war. A deeply moving June 1946 letter from the grieving mother of a missing 82nd Fighter Group pilot asked Richard if he knew anything of her son's fate.

Excerpt from letter of 26 June 1946

"We would indeed be grateful if you could give us any information at all. We can be reconciled to our son's sacrifice if we could only have facts. We had so hoped that he would be rescued as many of you were. If he died in a prison camp we should know it. If he were terribly injured and lies helpless among the fishermen of the islands we should know it. If his grave is somewhere it should be found. But we do realize that if he went down in to the sea we can not know.

"I know that you would rather forget than remember. But if you will remember long enough to help us get this story together we will appreciate it so very, very much. I am grateful for each of you who returned home and hope you will enjoy many useful years in service to humanity."[1]

---

1. Name withheld. (Letter in author's possession.)

Richard had not known the man and could only suggest that his mother contact the 82nd's intelligence officers. In March 1948 the War Department contacted Richard regarding three other P-38 pilots who went down near Naples on 20 August 1943, but again he could be of no help.

Into the 1960s Richard was updated regularly on 97th Squadron survivors by "Uncle Wally" Reyerson, one of two 82nd FG Intelligence Officers, and Richard exchanged Christmas cards with several Combine G members for a few years. But the ever-faithful Herb Corson remained in touch until Richard's death, then corresponded with Geneil, who finally met him a few years before his own death in 2010.

Though we were not then aware of it, Richard's POW memories lived for us in the wartime and especially Kriegie vocabulary he contributed to the family lexicon.

Raus!	Get up (out of bed)! Go! Move!
Klim	Milk
Nix [nicht]	No
Shizen smizer[1]	A heavy bashing tool, a "crap smasher." Also a gun.
The sack	Bed
Hit the sack	Go to bed.
Sack time	Sleep
Flap	Broohaha, fuss
Honey wagon	Farm wagon hauling manure, sump-pumping truck
Cooler	Jail
Verboten	Not permitted
Ruskies	Russians

Language word play was significant in the family, and Richard's mixed-language humor was a part of our everyday conversation; "Kein popcorn!," "Nix understanden," "Was ist los?" (What's that? What's up?), "I want to merçi vous!" and "Mox nix"[2] are a few examples.

---

1. From the German schiessen (to shoot) and Schmeisser (famous German gun maker). I remember the expression being used to mean a gun. Craig recalls helping Richard work on projects by handing him tools; when nothing else worked, a shizen smizer would be called for.

2. Es macht nichts: It makes no diff, doesn't matter.

1951-64
Back in the Service

Lackland AFB, San Antonio, Texas (ATC)

12 Feb 51   Career Proc, 3700th Indoctrination Wing

Lowry AFB, Denver, Colorado (TAC)

22 Mar 51   Stat Svs Crs, 3700th IW

Donaldson AFB, Greenville, South Carolina (TAC)

16 Jun 51   Stat Svs Off, Hq 18th AF

24 Mar 52   Act Ass't Dir of Stat Svs

28 Oct 52   Ch Opns & Mat Div, Div of Stat

23 Jul 53   Ch Machine Svs Div

31 Aug 53   Ch Opns & Mat Div, Div of Stat

In February 1951 as a result of the Korean conflict, Richard was recalled to what had in September 1947 become the United States Air Force. During those first seven years back in the service, Richard's "desk job" consisted of various positions within Statistical Services. Both at Donaldson AFB and in Châteauroux he flew primarily the C-47.

The flower shop was sold and the house was rented to Richard's brother Joseph and his family. Over the decades, there was always the nostalgic dream of returning to the house and farm, but Geneil and Richard would not live in their dream house again, although it was not sold until after Richard's death.

The family did not accompany him to the short training assignment in Texas. The Colorado stay was short, too; I recall glimpses of the geography but primarily the springtime mud surrounding our unlandscaped duplex. In South Carolina we found entirely new topography and countryside and made lifelong friends in church and Air Force circles.

Châteauroux rail station, December 1956 (Butler family collection)

Châteauroux Air Station, Châteauroux, France (USAFE)

10 Nov 53	Stat Svs Div, DCS/Compt, Asst Ch, Compilation Br, Hq 7373d A/DWg
1 Mar 54	Stat Svs Div, DCS/Compt, Asst Ch, Comp Br, Hq CAMA
2 Aug 54	Ch, Con Br, Stat Svs Div w/Compt, Hq CAMA
May–Jun 55	Senior Staff Officer CR
1 Sep 55	Ch, Rps Contr Br, Stat Svs Div, Compt, Hq CAMA

In October 1953 Richard left for France. Dependent family housing was not yet ready, so the rest of the family stayed behind in Salt Lake City. We had a lonely Christmas without him but were soon preparing for our own departure. In February 1954 we got passport photos and Mom sent in the application; she and I shopped for a new '54 Chevrolet and arranged to have it shipped.

We went weekly to Hill Field for immunizations Chris and I dreaded. These were shots from what we called the "shot gun": the nurse pulled from a hook on the wall a pistol-shaped device connected to a long hose, put the barrel against our upper arms & pulled the trigger!

On 12 March we received our Port Call[1] for 2 April; we jumped and danced and hugged and could hardly get to sleep that night. On Wednesday 31 March Geneil, nearly seven months pregnant, started across the country by train with four year-old Chris and eight year-old Dick. We arrived at Fort Hamilton on the morning of our call date and stayed there for a day or two while Geneil waited apprehensively to be cleared for air travel; the next evening we boarded a MATS[2] flight from the New York City area to Paris with refueling stops in Goose Bay, Labrador and Shannon, Ireland. We arrived in Châteauroux by train not long before Easter and were greeted by large chocolate roosters and rabbits in the shop windows. Two months later Marcia joined the family, followed by Craig in February 1956.

When we arrived, Cité de Touvent, the military family housing project, still had not been completed, so we lived for some months "on the economy" in a third floor walk-up apartment at 99 rue des Américains. The family roughed it on GI cots, since our furniture was still somewhere on the high seas, as was the new Chevrolet. But we found many new distractions, like attending church in a quonset hut and hitting the Saturday morning movie matinees on base; once the car arrived, we made up for lost time with frequent country picnics, châteaux visits, first encounters with peacocks and climbing to hilltop *donjon* tower ruins.

---

1. Official notice of date to report at port of overseas departure.
2. Military Air Transport Service

Return to Moosburg, 1956. "Shows the forest where we watched the lib-eration take place. The impossible dream came true." (Butler family collection)

"Christine & friend at Moosburg, Germany, 1956." (Butler family collection)

We made extended jaunts that took us as far away as Denmark. I think Richard would have liked to see Stalag Luft III if we could have reached it, but in the 1950s visiting the camp remains was out of the question. To reach Sagan would have required a serving US Air Force officer and his family to enter Soviet-occupied territory, crossing almost the full length of the German Democratic Republic and passing into Poland.

We spent parts of two summers in Bavaria, and on the 1956 trip we went to see the substantial remnants of Stalag VIIA at Moosburg, where the barracks had been renovated as low-income housing. Most of my memories of the visit consist of retrospective moving-picture versions of the black-and-white photos taken that day. We had parked near the forest, at the eastern end of what is now Sudetenlandstrasse. As we looked westward, a line of barracks on our right held our attention, since Richard had pointed out as his sometime home the fifth barrack on that northern side of the former camp's main street.

Nellis AFB, Las Vegas Nevada (ATC)

4 Feb 57	Statistical Services Officer, Hq 3595th CCr Tng Wg
1 Jul 58	Stat Svs Off, Hq 4520th CCTWg (Tac Ftr)
23 Jul 58	Sq Admin Off w/Admin Sec, 4520th Fld Maint Sq
3 Feb 59	Sq, Commander, 4520th Fld Maint Sq
17 Feb 59	Sq Admin Officer, 4520th Fld Maint Sq
13 Mar 59	TDY: Ft Bragg, N.C., Ex "Dark Cloud, Pine Cone II"
1 May 59	TDY: Ft Bragg, N.C., Ex "Dark Cloud, Pine Cone II"
8 Jun 59	Sq Admin Officer, 4520th CAM Squadron

From Châteauroux, Richard was transferred to Nellis Air Force Base, outside Las Vegas. There he transitioned to squadron administrative duties. We lived in base housing at 20 Wright Street. Geographically, we were closer to grandparents than we'd ever been during the Air Force years and took advantage of that to enjoy many visits to and from them.

March AFB, Riverside, California (SAC)

3 Sep 59	TDY KC-97 Training, Randolph AFB, Texas
7 Dec 59	Pilot, 320th AREFS
1 Feb 60	Acft Cmdr KC-97, 320th AREFS
3 Mar 60	Pilot, KC-97, 320th AREFS
1 Mar 61	Acft Comdr KC-97, 320th AREFS

4030 Watkins Drive (Butler family collection)

Aircraft Flown by Richard in the Army Air Corps and Air Force
(in chronological order within categories)

Single engine	*Twin-Engine*	*Four Engines*
PT-22	P-38G, F, L	(K)C-97E, F, G
BT-13A	C-47A, B, D	C-54
AT-6A-F	AT-11/AT-7/C-45	
P-39D, F, L, M	B-25J	*Other*
BT-14	C-123	H-21 (helicopter)
L-5	T-29/C-131	
P-47		
T-33 (jet)		
L-20		

11 Jun 62	Ops Dy Off, Hq 22nd Cmbt Spt Gp
20 Jul 62	Ops Dy Off, Hq 22nd Bom Wg
25 Jun 63	Ops Dy Off, Hq 22nd Bomb Wg
29 Nov 63	Ch, C-97 Br, Non-Tac Stand Div, Hq 22 Bomb Wg
22 Jan 64	Ch, C-97 Br, Non-Tac Stand Div, Hq 22 Bomb Wg
20 Jul 64	Ch, C-97 Br, Non-Tac Stand Div, Hq 22 Bomb Wg
31 Aug 64	Retired Per SO AC-15805, DAF, Hq 22 Bomb Wg

After Nellis Richard trained on the KC-97 air refueling tanker, which he flew for the next five years out of March. Near the UC Riverside campus in the summer of 1959 we bought our first family house, and everyone settled in happily. For the first time in our Air Force experience, house and community became home—so much so that in 1964, rather than move the family from Riverside, Richard retired from the Air Force.

Richard explains Link Trainer functions, summer 1984 (Butler family collection)

For 46 years it was to 4030 Watkins Drive that we four siblings "went home" from the various places where we had made our lives. In addition to Geneil's loving welcome, we found there during his lifetime Richard's wry wit and constant good humor, his essential selflessness and unfailing generosity, his quiet self-possession and ever-gentle counsel. No doubt the seeds for such qualities were sown at home, but I'm convinced that through that influence which helps us bring good out of evil some of those qualities were reinforced and others generated by his trials as a prisoner of war.

Effective 31 August 1964 Richard was relieved from active duty and retired from the Air Force as a Command Pilot. During his last year in the service, Richard made two significant flights. First, on 9 October 1963 he flew as Instructor Pilot on a four-hour C-97 flight out of March AFB with his wartime companion and brother

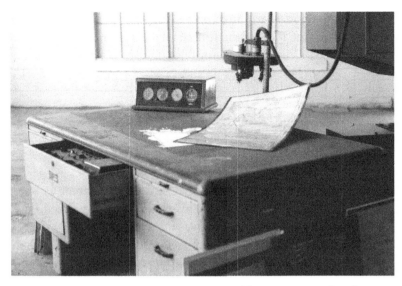

Vintage Link Trainer controls, March Field Air Museum (Butler family collection)

Richard in his office at the hospital (Butler family collection)

Heber as one of two Pilots on board; then on 22 August 1964 he made his last flight in a Gooney Bird (C-47). Richard made his final flight as an Air Force officer 25 August 1964, flying on a C-97 as Instructor Pilot.

1964-84
In Civvies Once Again

Major Richard M. Butler (Ret.) then started a 20-year civilian career as Director of Medical Records at Riverside County Hospital, where he worked on reorganization and digitization until his retirement in August 1984.

In the summer of 1984 we visited the March Field Air Museum with Richard. There we found an important artifact from his wartime days, an old Link Trainer complete with control desk like the one where he had spent many hours training other pilots before his own flight training began. He was thrilled—and spent the next half hour animatedly explaining the system's functions and telling anecdotes about the situations and problems he could set for student pilots.

After retiring from the Air Force, he flew only a few times (on a Commercial Pilot license), but his love of flying was evident in his enthusiasm whenever he spoke of it; and when he did, his hands were as eloquent as his words. To the end of his life Richard was passionate about the P-38, whose qualities he consistently praised and at whose controls he found the ultimate expression of his joy in flight.

On 15 December 1984 Richard succumbed to malignant mesothelioma. Once more we wait behind and eagerly watch for the call to join him.

Richard Marsh Butler on USAF retirement, August 1964 (Butler family collection)

APPENDIXES

Military Abbreviations and Acronyms Appearing in Richard's Orders and Records

Note: Abbreviations in orders and records are not always consistent and seem sometimes to have an idiosyncratic air which could suggest more room for creativity in military service than one might expect. Further, they can sometimes contain local and regional references.

A.B./AB[1]	Air Base	AREFS	Air Refueling Squadron
A.B.A.C.A.F.S.	probable typo[2]		
A.C./AC	Air Corps	Ass't	assistant
A.C.A.F.S.	Air Corps Advance Flying School	ATC	Air Training Command
Acft	aircraft	Avn	aviation
Act(g)	acting		
ACTS	Air Corps Technical School	Br	branch
A/D	Air Depot	CAM	Consolidated Aircraft Maintenance
Adj	adjutant		
Admin	administration/ve	CAMAE	Central Air Materiel Area, Europe
A.F./AF[3]	Air Forces		
AFAFS	Air Forces Advanced Flight School	CCrTng/CCT	Combat Crew Training (Group)
		Ch	chief
AFBFS	Air Forces Basic Flight School	Cmbt	combat
		Cmdr	commander
		Co	company
		Compt	comptroller
		Con/Contr	control
		CR[4]	
		Crs	course

1. Periods after capitalized initial letters were used inconsistently among typists.

2. This should probably have a slash after A.B. (See ACAFS.)

3. This was a transition period during which the name Army "Air Corps" was changing to Army "Air Forces." Again, both AC and AF appear inconsistently.

4. Probably related to the Reports Control Branch.

DAF	Department of the Air Force	**(S)/(SP)**	school and/or special[5]
DCS	Deputy Chief of Staff	**SAC**	Strategic Air Command
Det	detached/ment	**Sch**	school
Dir	director	**SE**	single engine
Div	division/al	**Sec**	section or second
Dy	duty	**SO**	Senior/Staff/Section Officer
ETO	European Theater of Operations	**SP/Sp**	special
		Spt	support
EX	exercise	**Sq**	squadron
		Sta/Stn	station
FG	Fighter Group	**Stand**	standard
Fld	field	**Stn**	station
FS	Fighter Squadron	**Stat**	statistical
		Svs	services
Gp	group		
		TAC	Tactical Air Command
Hq	headquarters		
		Tac Ftr	tactical fighter
IW	Indoctrination Wing	**TDY**	Temporary Duty (assignment)
Mat	materiel	**TE**	twin engine
MATS	Military Air Transport Service	**Tng**	training
Maint	maintenance	**W.C.T.C.**	West Coast Training Command (AAC)
MTO	Mediterranean Theater/ Operations		
		Wg	wing
Off	officer(s)/office(s)		
Opns/Ops	operations		
Plt	pilot		
Prin	principal		
Proc	processing		
Rps	reports		

---

5. These only occur early on and in situations where the entire organization is tasked with training (Air Base squadrons or groups). I can find no firm identification for these abbreviations consistent with the situation and have inferred the meaning(s) from context.

Brief Glossary of Kriegie and Military Slang

Abort	toilet	**Combine**	basic living unit[4]
Night abort		**Compound**	one of five divisions
Appell (appel)	roll call (almost		of Stalag Luft III[5]
	always outdoors)	**Condendo**	sweetened
Arbeiter[1]	forced laborer		condensed milk
		Cooler	jail, detention
Bag	prison		
In the bag	caught, imprisoned	**Ferrett**	German snoop, spy[6]
Bash	eat as in gobble, pig		
	out		
Block	barrack	
Brew[2]	late evening warm	
	drink, often dessert	
C Rations	single, pre-cooked	
	canned, wet ration	
Camp	compound (see	
	below)	
Circuit[3]	route around the	
	warning wire	

walking until dusk. . . ." (Kimball & Chiesl at "Camp Life")

4. The room and the group of men who lived, slept, cooked and ate together in that room defined by bunks and storage lockers within a large open barrack. As time went on, the size of the groups increased; Richard's Combine G, for instance, started with 6 men and ended with 14.

5. This can be confusing; context is often essential to sort out what is meant. For instance, the Germans said *Mitte Lager* (middle camp) to mean Center Compound, one of five separate and independent components of Stalag Luft III, and Kriegies often referred to their compound as their "camp" since they were isolated within that area. But the official and more accurate English term is "compound." The distinction is important because in the wider world "camp" referred to the whole entity of Stalag Luft III.

6. An English-speaking guard who wandered at will through a compound looking and listening for anything of

---

1. From German *arbeit* (work).

2. "Most rooms had their brews after ten. Preparing it was the stooge's final chore for the day. Condendo-pies . . . were served with tea or cocoa." (Kimball & Chiesl at "Camp Life")

3. "If the company or the conversation of his roommates bored, tired or angered him, a man could get out on the circuit and walk it off" until afternoon appell, after which "he could continue his

Flap	crisis, excitement	**Klim**	powdered milk[9]
There's a flap on!		**Kommandantur**	camp headquarters
FoodAcco	commodity exchange	**Kraut**	German
	co-op	**Kriegie**	POW[10]
Forts	Flying-Fortresses		
	(B-17s)	**Lager**	compound[11]
		Truppenlager	"Troop camp"[12]
Gash[7]	surplus, extra	**Luftgangster**	"air gangster"[13]
Gen	news		
Goon	German	**Milk Run**	safe, easy task
Goon box	guard tower		
Goon rations	German-issue food	**Nein**	No!
		Nix	No[14]
Honey Wagon	vehicle into which	**O.K.W.**[15]	German high
	latrines were pum-		command
	ped for disposal		
	outside the camp	**Palliasse**	thin straw-stuffed
			mattress
Ite/Itie	Italian		
Jerry	German		
K Rations	packaged individual		
	daily ration		
Kein	no/none		
Kein Trinkwasser	hot water pitcher[8]		
"Kein"			
Kite	aircraft		

9. According to Clark, it was "very rich powdered milk." (160)

10. Short for *Kriegsgefangener* (war prisoner).

11. Literally, "camp" (See Compound above.)

12. The compound where guards and other German staff lived and where Stalag Luft III headquarters were located.

13. Term used in derogatory propaganda to prejudice the German population against Allied airmen. The German people generally had no idea what devastation their armed forces were aggressively inflicting on other nations, so it was easy to portray Allied pilots and crews as brutal murderers sowing random and hateful death and destruction. As a result, some men were hurt or killed upon capture.

14. "Nein" is the negative reponse in German. Nix is used for "No" in Kriegie usage, but it derives from "nicht," which means "not" or "don't" when used with a verb.

15. Oberkommando der Wehrmacht

interest he could hear or spot: gossip, news, names; something out of place, unusual, new or different, especially as related to escape; someone acting suspiciously or furtively.

7. Thus, to "bash the gash" meant to binge, to use up all the extra at once.

8. Literally, "no drink water" (nonpotable water). This was the name for the large pitchers in which stooges carried hot water for cooking from the central kitchens back to their combines. The pitchers were called "keins" for short.

Some frequently-heard Kriegie expressions from Kimball and Chiesl's
Clipped Wings

Purge in!	I'll bet you a D-Bar.
What's the flap?	Parcels up!
Brew up!	Who's stooge?
What's it worth at Foodaco?	Appel!!! Everybody out.

Purge	group of incoming POWs	**Stooge**	cook's gofer[17]
		Verboten	forbidden
Ruskies	Russians	**Vorlager**	fore- or pre-camp[18]
Sack	bed/bunk	**Whip**	ersatz whipped cream[19]
Sack time			
Hit the sack			
Sack artist			
Sack king			
Psackologist			
Scrubbed	cancelled		
S.M.I.	Saturday morning inspection		
Stalag[16]	prison camp		

16. Short for *stammlager*. Technically, a *stalag* was for nonofficers and *oflag* was a camp for officers; but, as the war ground on and prisoner groups were mixed or substituted, the distinction lost importance.

17. One or two men were assigned per day per combine as runners or helpers for the current cook.

18. Transition area between the high-security compounds and the outside world. It held buildings such as mail and personal parcel shed, Red Cross parcel storage building and showers.

19. According to McKee, this was "similar to Cool Whip" and was "made from goon margarine, powdered milk, sugar and water." (xi)

Appendix C

The P-38

The P-38 is a big fighter plane. It stands almost 10 feet high, spreads out 52 feet, and is over 37½ feet long.

When the impression of size ceases to be a novelty, you notice some rather peculiar looking features. The long slender booms tapering into twin rudders are unique in aircraft design.

A closer inspection from the front quarter shows that the P-38 is a midwing airplane, with 2 liquid-cooled engines and 2 three-bladed propellers. It has a streamlined center section, called a gondola, and stands solidly on a tricycle landing gear. There are four .50-cal machine guns and one 20-mm. cannon in the nose.

Pilot Training Manual for the P-38 Lightning

In February 1937 the Army Air Corps published a request for aircraft designs for "an experimental pursuit having 'the tactical mission of interception and attack of hostile aircraft at high altitude.'" (Ethell 3) This ship would have to meet specifications startling at the time. It must (1) reach an altitude of 20,000 feet above sea level in six minutes and (2) have a minimum cruising speed of 360 mph.

"In essence the Air Corps was asking for a major breakthrough in performance since there were no engines of sufficient power to produce the expected results. . . . One of the solutions envisaged taking two of [GM/Allison's V-1710-C8 engines] and building a fighter around them. . . ." (Ethell 3) Lockheed's design for its Model 22 (XP-38) competed with the Bell XP-39. In June 1938 the Air Corps awarded Lockheed a contract to build the prototype XP-38. "The first service models, the P-38 D, E and F, were delivered to AAF units commencing in August, 1941." (Gurney 12) Lockheed eventually produced nearly 10,000 P-38s.

"From any aspect the P-38[1] was an outstandingly novel concept." It was the first fighter designed by Lockheed's Hall Hibbard and Clarence ("Kelly") Johnson, and into it they "poured many innovations, including the twin booms that bec[a]me so famous, tricycle landing gear, the extremely high wing loading . . . armament concentrated in the nose, and turbo-superchargers hooked to two Allison liquid-cooled engines." (Gurney 7)

---

1. "Lightning" was the name given the P-38 by the British.

"The Lightning's counter-rotating props provided superb stability and negated torque, so there was no need to ride the rudders as in the P-40. Landings were easier because you could actually see the runway. . . . But it was also a more complex aircraft: two throttles, two mixture controls, two prop speed controls."[2]

It's unclear when Richard first became aware of the P-38. Certainly, he had read of it and seen photos by the time it came into production. He would likely have had experiences similar to those Vrilakas describes. "Occasionally we would be 'buzzed' by P-38 pilots. . . . They would come skimming in over the desert at very high speed, leaving us totally in awe as they pulled straight up in a climb to several thousand feet, almost disappearing from view. It was an incredible sight and always left me with the thought that to fly them someday would be the height of my dreams." (47)

The earliest I can document Richard in close proximity to a P-38 is at Atcham Field, but he would almost certainly have been around them at some point during his flight training. We know that he and Heber had already settled on the 38 as their preferred fighter assignment before reaching North Africa.

In his *Journal* entry for 12 March 1943 Richard mentions that he and Heber had been assigned to the Médiouna P-38 squadron and that they both had checked out in the 38 on that day. "I got in two hops with a total of 2:30 hrs. That's really a big airplane, 15,000 lbs., and I had my hands full, no fooling. It sure flies nice. . . ."

Jeff Ethell, whose father also flew the P-38, describes his own first flight in one. "Once I was settled in the cockpit, I was taken with the vast expanse of airplane around me. Sitting deep within the center gondola and wing, I quickly got the impression of being buried in the machine. . . . The cockpit is just about perfect in size . . . and very comfortable. . . .

"The most obvious difference from other wartime fighters . . . is the dual pistol-grip control wheel. Putting both hands on this thing brings a sense of complete authority. . . . The ergonomics of the wheel are also years ahead of their time: the grips are canted inward to the exact position of one's hands when they're relaxed and held out in front of you. Dad absolutely loved the wheel instead of a stick, because he could maneuver and point the four .50s and single 20mm like a fire hose.

"The engine controls sprout from the left pedestal in all directions. . . . The large, red, round throttle knobs are an ideal size for the left hand, completing the sense of total control given by the wheel grips.

"Sitting there with both turbos whirling, feeling and hearing the satisfying, deep-throated growl coming from the top of the booms . . . is absolutely mesmerizing. There is no sound like it. . . .

---

2. R.L. Creighton, "Lightning, Smoke, and Fire," *Air & Space*, August 2007, pp. 16–17.

"During the War, the drill was to go to full power, let the turbos stabilize, see if the props were going to run away, then let go. It must have been like a rocket. . . . The first thing I noticed was absolutely no torque and perfectly straight tracking—heaven with 3000hp screaming into my ears and a wonderful feeling of being pressed back into my seat. . . .

"I was beginning to comprehend why everyone loved the Lightning so much: it flies like a jet with no vibration and light controls. . . .

"The single dominant impression is this thing is *smooth* and effortless to fly. . . .

"Within an hour, something quite astonishing and totally unexpected began to happen. Not only was I more than comfortable, but the airplane also began to 'shrink' around me in my mind. The wings seemed to get smaller, the engines went almost unnoticed, and I was soon flying only the central pod with its guns sticking out front. The sense of power, freedom and effortless control movement is so visceral the machine becomes a part of you. . . ."[3]

Richard flew the P-38G-15-LO. Of the early P-38 models, the "G" was built in highest numbers; nearly 1100 had been delivered by March 1943. Its 1500 hp Allison engines gave it an official maximum speed of 400 mph at 25,000' and took it to 20,000' in 8.5 minutes. A major improvement included on the G model was "improved Fowler flaps that greatly enhanced landing maneuverability." (Maloney 2) Officially, the G had a range of 350 miles at 310 mph, but this is far under what Richard's *Flight Log* shows. As Bodie says, ". . . the C.O. of the 1FG was logging missions of up to 6 hours and more in his P-38G. That translates to somewhere between 1,200 and 1,600 miles! Four-hour missions were common." (161)

"The P-38 was the most versatile fighter of World War II—the only one that served continuously in steadily improved versions from start to finish." (Gurney 21) "It was used in all U.S. Army Air Force combat theaters; it was capable of landing on ice and snow; it could carry and launch torpedoes; and it was by far the most successful allied photo-recon aircraft. The top two U.S. aces of World War II both flew a P-38." (Maloney 5) ". . . the P-38 underwent continual improvements in speed, rate of climb, ceiling, range, endurance, and firepower, to keep abreast of combat requirements. Lockheed built 18 distinct versions to serve dozens of missions at all altitudes." (Gurney 35)

Richard flew the 38 twice after liberation. Later in the summer of '45, probably in late August while he and Geneil were at the Redistribution Station in Santa Monica, he went up with Heber, and the two of them indulged in that joyous, madcap midair seat-swapping flight, which amounted to both celebration and final reprise of their season as brothers who were brothers-in-arms as well. Then on 5 December Richard flew a P-38 out of Hill Field and for an hour made his farewell to the beloved Lightning over the wintry fields of home.

---

3. Jeff Ethell, "Flying the P-38 Lightning," *Flight*, August 1997, pp. 22–9.

With the end of the war, the indispensable P-38 disappeared from the skies seemingly overnight. Richard had requested reassignment to the 38, but those fast, sleek, adaptable and deadly Lightnings became war surplus. Few were spared. But we know where to look for one of them.

P-38 Lightning

German pilots: "Fork-tailed devil"
Japanese pilots: "Two airplanes with one pilot"
American pilots: "Round-trip ticket"
                            (Gurney 21)

The business end of a Lightning (From Pilot Training Manual for the P-38 Lightning*)*

Appendix D

The Sad Sacks: Exclusive 67

When Richard passed away, Geneil handed his wallet to Craig and asked him to take it home. Just couple of years ago, his wife found the wallet and looked inside; among other things, she found a $1 bill with 46 signatures. Those names were headed in Richard's hand with the words "Sad Sacks/Excl 67."

I have confidently identified all but one of the signatures. Some were obvious and clear, some yielded enough letters in the right places to be matched with known names, one located on the central fold is largely indecipherable. Working with the list of transcribed names, I began trying to discover the common factor.

That process was complicated by an 11 June 1943 article in *Yank* Magazine. The author, Sgt. Pete Paris, had met some Sad Sacks at an airfield in Tunisia. Paris featured six men in the article and says that the group "graduated in a body from Luke Field, Ariz., and studied low-level strafing together at Tallahassee, Fla., before being shipped to England last December as flying sergeants. That was when they formed their Sad Sack Society with Jack Middaugh . . . as 'head bag' to lead their mourning over not having shiny bars like other pilots." (Paris)

Paris states that all 67 Sad Sacks had graduated from Luke and gone to Tallahassee. Because the men featured in the article were all 42H Luke graduates who went on to Dale Mabry Field, I at first thought this was simply an overgeneralization on Paris' part. After more careful analysis, I believe that Richard's Luke/Tallahassee contingent had already created their own Sad Sack culture[1] and probably provided the pattern for development of the larger group. It's clear, however, that the "67" Sad Sacks assumed their more definitive form with insignia and motto and that the $1 Bill was signed some 4-5 months later on another continent.[2] What follows is the history I have pieced together for that group.

On 18 November 1942 two groups of Sergeant Pilots left fighter training bases in Florida on short notice; both had orders to report to Fort Hamilton, New York

---

1. Richard's later references to men from the Luke/Tallahassee group who were not members of the "Exclusive 67" suggest that he thought of them, too, as Sad Sacks.

2. There could well have been several groups using the Sad Sack name; Sad Sack was a popular cartoon character of the day, and several thousand enlisted pilots had had the same unpleasant and demeaning experiences.

no later than 0400 Z[3] on 21 November. One group of 24, including Richard and Heber Butler, had trained at Daly Mabry Field; they quietly boarded a train and left Tallahassee in the dark early hours of that morning. The other group of about 70 men, including Robert Hoover, did their training at Drew Field in Tampa; they, too, traveled by train but, by Hoover's account, did not depart with similar secrecy. (Hoover 30)

Men from the two groups may have met while at Fort Hamilton, but we know they became well acquainted in the cramped confines of HMT *Queen Elizabeth*'s gymnasium. Individuals came and went, but the core of the combined group seems to have remained constant at Yarnfield and Atcham (where they were shufffled around for no obvious reason), on the voyage to Oran in January 1943 and during their early time in North Africa.

"The Air Forces didn't know what to do with . . . the sixty-odd . . . unassigned pilots who landed [in the UK]. . . .

"Again, more than three score trained pilots were allowed to languish in Algeria [and Morocco] while operational USAAF units were sometimes desperately short of them." (Blake & Stanaway 60)

In North Africa, after some brief moves here and there in both Algeria and Morocco, rather than being assigned directly to combat, the same group of men were disgruntled to find themselves stuck at another "Fighter School and Replacement Center." They were now in Médiouna, Morocco, not far from Casablanca; Richard says the move there was made on 9 February, though the official order is dated 17 February 1943. That transfer order included the names of 68 men; an elaborating follow-up order of 25 February lists only 67.[4]

"When we arrived at Médiouna, all of the pilots were disappointed to learn we had been assigned to a replacement pilots' pool. One of the men decided we should rename the group the Sad Sacks to show our displeasure with not being ordered into combat." (Hoover 38) Hoover quotes Tom Watts on what happened next. "'[Howell] Coates had the idea that the 67 of us should get an insignia for ourselves on the basis that we were somewhat of a rare collection. We [learned] we were not supposed to have been sent to England in the first place. We had gone to different places there, and they had no idea what to do with us.[5]

---

3. Zulu, the military equialent then of Greenwich Mean Time (now UTC, Coordinated Universal Time).

4. 2nd Lt. Jerome Ennis had apparently been transferred elsewhere.

5. An unspoken element in their sense of grievance was their ill-defined status as quasi-officers and the shabby and discriminatory treatment they had experienced as "sergeant pilots." While in the UK they had been discharged from the Army and sworn in as Flight Officers, and at least some of them had received the misapprehension of having been commissioned in that process.

"'We were sent to five places in Africa, being received the same way we were in England. . . . Everyone agreed to Coates' proposal that we should be the 67 SAD SACKS, with the group title of SNAFU (Situation Normal All Fouled Up). Immediately, we donned our insignia, which, painted on leather, had the large numbers 67 with a face in the background of a sack weeping sadly; below was SAD SACKS, on top was SNAFU.'" (Hoover 38)

The organization and insignia design and production must have happened sometime in late February; the bill-signing took place 3 March 1943,[6] probably with some amount of ceremony. Over the following weeks, Richard says, they managed to get in a fair bit of flying time in an AT-6-C and P-39-L and that by 12 March they had been divided into three squadrons, one each for P-38, P-39 and P-40. (To at least some degree, this division seems to have held when they eventually received their combat assignments.)

Within a couple of weeks, transfers began; one contingent moved slightly southward in Morocco to Berrechid. According to Richard this group was comprised of the Médiouna P-39 and P-40 squadrons; the P-38 squadron remained at Médiouna.[7]

Among those at Berrechid was Robert Congdon, who with "his fellow Sad Sack Russ Williams began ferrying P-38s to various bases in North Africa. When he returned from a ferry flight on April 27, Congdon was told that he and some other Sad Sacks would meet a pilot from the 82nd Fighter Group the next day and then fly back with him to begin a combat tour with that unit. . . .

"The following morning the chosen Sad Sacks met in Casablanca with 97th [Squadron] pilot Phil Taback; a few hours later they arrived at Berteaux, their new home." (Blake & Stanaway 61) A number of Sad Sacks from the Médiouna P-38 squadron had been there since early April: Netzer in the 95th Squadron; Solem, Rawson, Hurlbut, Drayton and Mackey in the 96th; Bentzlin, Stahl, Les Carpenter, Gray and the Butler brothers in the 97th.

On 16 April Conrad Bentzlin had gone down at sea.[8] On the same day, Richard recorded that he "landed at Bône [on the eastern Algerian coast] to refuel and ran into Gimblin and a lot of the other guys, 'Sad Sacks.'" Upon arrival in Berteaux 28 April, Congdon, Williams, Fuller and Shannon joined the others in the 97th. 30 April, on his first mission, Congdon scored a victory. Richard later mentions visiting a group of friends assigned as P-40 training pilots somewhere north of

---

6. My early assumption that other Sad Sacks possessed their own signed bills was confirmed by John Netzer Parliman, whose father John J. Netzer left such a bill which also carries the signature date.

7. See Richard's *Journal* entries and Letter excerpts for 12–24 March for the rivalry and mock attacks between Sad Sacks at the two fields.

8. He bailed out and landed in the water apparently unharmed; a day later he was seen waving from his yellow liferaft. He did not survive. (See Makos 105–7.)

Grombalia; that group may have included members of the 67 Sad Sacks, but Richard does not say so explicitly.[9]

Beyond that time, there are no references to the 67 or to Sad Sacks in Richard's records, nor have I found any relevant artifacts or postwar correspondence. For several decades after the war Richard apparently belonged to the Army Air Corps Enlisted Pilots Association.

In his Epilogue Arbon quotes from a USAF report on the enlisted pilot program. "The program's success . . . lay with the motivation and spirit of the enlisted men it trained. These men made the program. They had been given an opportunity of a lifetime, to fly. They wanted to fulfill their dreams and be a success. They wouldn't—and didn't—fail." (Mamaux 30) Arbon then goes on to ask, "What motivated them so much? They were younger, more impressionable, and highly grateful for the legislative miracle that enabled them to become pilots. They were also aware that the 'system' accepted them with reluctance. Finding themselves cast in the role of underdog, it was only natural that they tried harder to prove themselves." (154)

---

9. Those men were probably based at either El Haouaria airfield (80 km north-northeast of Grombalia at the tip of Cap Bon) or Mezel Heurr airfield (55 km northeast on the eastern coast). See V-Mail excerpts at 9 August and Letter excerpts at 11 August.

The $1 Bill

Front

		Back
Richard M. Butler	Walter J. Mackey	Darell E. Nance
Joseph L. Shannon	Alfred F. Hirsch	Robert C. Congdon
Neil F. Washer	HE Lafferty	Clinton B. Barton
Bob Barnett	Charles A. Garrett	Bill Manke
Conrad F. Bentzlin	Kenneth B. Smith	Caylos W. Chapman
(George) Fitz Gibbon	Garret B. Fuller	Warren Goldstein
John S. Gimblin		Fred N. Smith Jr.
CD Andrews		Robert A. Nicholson
Paul E. Crosier		H.W. Baldwin
Ervin H. Bucher		J.M. McPhee
Kirby E. Smith		RT Carter
George Q. Morscher		Heber M. Butler
TK Johnson		Richard J. Drayton
(Frank D. Hurlbut)		H. S. Solem
Clinton C (Legg)		John J. Netzer
Tom Collins		John R. Rawson
Shorty Joffrion		(Fred) N. Smith, Jr.
Henry N. Durrett		RA Hoover
Richard W. Cornell		WO West
Harlan G. Chase		Urban F. Stahl

Sad Sack $1 Bill (Butler family collection)

Sad Sacks: The Exclusive 67 plus a few[10]

	Name	AFAFS	Fighter	Rank[11]
O	ALLEN, Robert C.	42-H Spence	Drew	F/O
$O	ANDREWS, Charles D.	42-H Luke	Dale Mabry	F/O
$O	BALDWIN, Harry W.		Drew	2Lt
$O	BARNETT, Robert N.		Drew	2Lt
$O	BARTON, CLINTON B.	42-H Luke	Dale Mabry	F/O
$O	BENTZLIN, Conrad F.			2Lt
O	BOLGER, George A.	42-H Dothan	Drew	F/O
O	BOWMAN, Vere M.		Drew	2Lt
$O	BUCHER, Ervin H.			2Lt
$O	BUTLER, Heber M.	42-H Luke	Dale Mabry	F/O
$O	BUTLER, Richard M.	42-H Luke	Dale Mabry	F/O
OY	CARPENTER, Howard G.	42-H Luke	Dale Mabry	F/O
O	CARPENTER, Leslie M. Jr.	42-H Columbus	Drew	F/O
$O	CARTER, Roy T. Jr.	42-H Spence	Drew	F/O
O	CECIL, Robert C.	42-H		2Lt
$O	CHAPMAN, Caylos W.			2Lt
$O	CHASE, Harlan G.	42-H Luke	Dale Mabry	F/O
O	COATES, Howell B.		Drew	2Lt
$O	COLLINS, Gene A.	42-H Luke	Dale Mabry	F/O
O	CONGDON, Robert C.		Drew	2Lt
$O	CORNELL, Richard W.	42-H Luke	Dale Mabry	F/O
$O	CROSIER, Paul E.			2Lt
O	CRUM, David C.		Drew	2Lt
$O	DRAYTON, Richard J.		Drew	2Lt
$O	DURRETT, Henry N. Jr.	42-H Luke	Dale Mabry	F/O

---

10. This list includes all 67 names on the Médiouna Transfer Order as well as names of seven men who in other ways might claim membership in the group (Walter West and the men featured in *Yank*). Note, however, that none of the six men in the *Yank* article signed the $1 Bill, although they clearly wore the insignia devised among the 67 group; note also that Fred Smith appears to have signed twice.

11. As of 25 February 1943.

O	DYE, Lawrence W.	42-I Spence	Drew	F/O
$O	FITZ GIBBON, George T.		Drew	2Lt
Yo	FRAIN, MARTIN D.	42-H Luke	Dale Mabry 1	F/O
O	FUGAZI, John O.	42-H Luke	Dale Mabry	F/O
$O	FULLER, Garrett B.			2Lt
$O	GARRETT, Charles A.	42-H Dothan	Drew	F/O
$O	GIMBLIN, JOHN S.	42-H Luke	Dale Mabry	F/O
$o	GOLDSTEIN, Warren	42-H Dothan		S/Sgt
O	GOSSETT, Dewey L.	42-H Dothan	Drew	F/O
O	GRAY, Thomas W.	42-H Columbus	Drew	F/O
O	HAND, Stanley S.		Drew	2Lt
$O	HIRSCH, Alfred F. Jr.	42-H Luke	Dale Mabry	F/O
$O	HOOVER, Robert A.	42-H Columbus	Drew	F/O
($)O	HURLBUT, Frank D.	42-H Luke	Dale Mabry	F/O
Yo	IRVINE, Robert E.S.	42-H Luke	Dale Mabry 1	F/O
$O	JOFFRION, Leonard M. Jr.	42-I Spence	Drew	F/O
OY	JOHNSON, Charles I.	42-H Luke	Dale Mabry	F/O
$O	JOHNSON, Thad K. Jr.	42-H Dothan	Drew	F/O
O	JORDAN, Hubert W.	42-H Luke	Dale Mabry	F/O
O	JOY, William R.	42-H Dothan	Drew	F/O
O	KNIGHT, Gene C.	42-H Luke	Dale Mabry	F/O
$O	LAFFERTY, Harold E.	42-H Luke	Dale Mabry	F/O
$O	LEGG, Clinton C.	42-H Luke	Dale Mabry	F/O
$O	MACKEY, Walter J.	42-H Ellington	Drew	F/O
O	MALONE, Taylor Jr.		Drew	2Lt
$O	MANKE, William H.		Drew	F/O
O	McCARTHY, Kenneth W.	42-I Spence	Drew	F/O
$O	McPHEE, John M.	42-H Luke	Dale Mabry	F/O
OY	MIDDAUGH, Jack E.	42-H Luke	Dale Mabry	F/O
O	MILLER, Wendell D.	42-I Craig	Dale Mabry	F/O
$O	MORSCHER, George Q.	42-H Spence	Drew	F/O
$O	NANCE, Darell E.	42-H Luke	Dale Mabry	F/O

$O	NETZER, John J.	42-I Dothan	Dale Mabry	F/O
$O	NICHOLSON, Robert A.	42-I Dothan	Drew	F/O
Y	PATTERSON, James H.	42-H Luke	Dale Mabry 1	F/O
$O	RAWSON, John R.	42-I Dothan	Dale Mabry	F/O
$O	SHANNON, Joseph L.	42-I Dothan	Drew	F/O
O	SIMMONDS, Harold M.	42-I Dothan	Dale Mabry	F/O
$O	SMITH, Frederick N. Jr.	42-I Dothan	Drew	F/O
$O	SMITH, Kenneth B.	42-I Dothan	Drew	F/O
$O	SMITH, Kirby E.	42-I Dothan	Drew	F/O
$O	SOLEM, Herman S.		Drew	2Lt
O	SORTERE, Arthur E Jr.		Drew	2Lt
$O	STAHL, Urban F.	42-H Columbus	Drew	F/O
$O	WASHER, Neil F.		Drew	2Lt
O	WATTS, Thomas E.	42-H Ellington	Drew	F/O
$o	WEST, Walter O.[12]		Drew	2Lt
Bo	WILLIAMS, Russell C.			2Lt

Legend

$	Signatory of the $1 bill
O	Listed on the Médiouna transfer order
o	Listed on another relevant order
Y	Referenced in the *Yank* article
B	Referenced in Blake & Stanaway, *Adorimini*
Dale Mabry	Departed 18 November 1942; they met Hoover's Drew group aboard HMT *Queen Elizabeth*.
Dale Mabry 1	Departed 22 October; their ship was torpedoed 650 miles off Ireland. Some of them spent nine days, others more, drifting in lifeboats before being rescued; they had just come out of hospital when Richard and Heber met them in London at Christmas 1942.

---

12. West appears on the order transferring the Drew group overseas. He appears on no other orders of which I have copies, but I am convinced he was present at the formation of the Exclusive 67 Sad Sacks. Until I was reminded of him when reviewing related notes, I could find no match for one signature with any name on the Sad Sack orders. One of the two partially-obscured signatures I was long unable to match starts with the initials WO; the last name is short, begins with either W or M and ends with a tall letter. I'm sufficiently certain it must be West's signature that I have included him on both the Sad Sack and $1 Bill signatory lists. One signature remains uncertain but may be that of Frank D. Hurlbut.

Advanced Flight Training Airfields

Columbus	Advanced pilot training field for for twin-engine bombers and transports near Columbus MS.
Craig	Established near Selma AL as a pilot training facility, it later became Craig Air Force Base.
Dothan	Significant auxiliary field for advanced single-engine training, attached to Napier Army Airfield near Dothan AL.
Ellington	World War I airfield near Houston TX reopened in 1940 as an advanced training facility intended for bomber pilots.
Luke	Advanced single-engine flying school south of Phoenix AZ.
Spence	Airfield built near Moultrie GA for advanced single-engine flight training.

Sources

AFAFS (Air Forces Advanced Flight School) venues for 42-H Luke are from Army Air Forces orders; all others are from Arbon's Appendix L. Fighter School venues are from relevant Army Air Forces orders.

Memorial

On 24 January 1944, Tom Watts went down off Calvi, Corsica. Bob Hoover's description of the event combined with one of Watts' journal entries form a fitting memorial to Sad Sacks and others who gave their all.

"He had successfully bailed out . . . but the force of the high winds dragged him into a reef of rocks offshore.

"I . . . could see his body and parachute in the crystal clear water. He had been such a part of my life that I could almost feel the impact of the reef on his body as I flew away. It only deepened my grief.

"I remember the day Tom and I sailed together for England past the Statue of Liberty. I think it was my fondest memory of our time together. . . . He'd recorded it in his journal:

> . . . I leaned on the rail and took a gander at New York harbor for the first time and definitely not the last, I HOPED. . . .
>
> Finally . . . was singled out one sight I had been hoping for—the Statue of Liberty. When people raved about her beauty, I thought they were just patriotic. When I saw it, though, it was quite different. There was a new kind of thrill in it for me; one that was deep, and I began thinking of my folks at home.

"Tom would never see the harbor, the Statue of Liberty, his home, or his folks again. But, Tom died doing what he loved most—being a fighter pilot." (Hoover 62–3)

Appendix E

Combine G[1]

Barrack 56, Center Compound, Stalag Luft III

15 October 1943

F/O Richard M. Butler, "Panda" (Garland UT); P-38 Pilot, downed 20 August 1943

1Lt Curtis S. Church, "Curt the Angel" (San Francisco CA); B-26 Pilot, downed 21 August 1943

2Lt Herbert F. Corson, "Remember Bolzano" (Dayton OH); B-26 Bombardier, downed 21 August 1943[2]

2Lt Leo L. Gladin (Toledo OH); B-17 Navigator, downed 25 June 1943[3]

F/O William R. Griffith, "Willie the Wabbit" (Canoga Park CA); B-17 Co-Pilot, downed 25 June 1943

1Lt Weldon F. Holmes, "Sacktime" (Brockton MA); B-17 Pilot, downed 25 June 1943[4]

29 March 1944

2Lt Richard Perle, "'Bongo'—round the bend in a parachute!" (Forest Hills NY); B-17 Navigator, downed 18 March 1944

1Lt Stanley M. Sands, "Sandy" (McGill NV); B-17 Navigator, downed 16 March 1944

2 July 1944

1Lt Daniel J. Reading (Alameda CA); B-24 Navigator, downed 21 June 1944

1Lt Melvin H. Williams (Cope CO); B-24 Pilot, downed 21 June 1944[5]

---

1. See Combine G escutcheon on page 193.

2. Church and Corson were not members of the same crew but were flying in the same formation.

3. Gladin had transferred from South Compound before Richard's arrival.

4. Griffith and Holmes were both from the crew of the "LaKanuKi."

5. Again, they were members of the same crew.

21 August 1944

1Lt James T. FitzGerald, "Fitz" (So. Pittsburg TN); P-47 Pilot, downed 3 August 1944

2Lt Richard C. Lunt (Cedar City UT); B-17 Co-Pilot, downed 20 July 1944

2 November 1944

1Lt James O. Juntilla (Minneapolis MN); P-51 Pilot, downed 5 October 1944

1Lt Vernon C. Prickett (Atlanta GA); P-51 Pilot, downed 17 October 1944

6-7 January 1945

Lunt moved out of Combine G on 6 January 1945 and was replaced the next day by 2Lt Luther H. Baker, "The Goat" (Wooster OH); B-17 Navigator, downed 12 August 1943

Appendix F

Other Kriegies

Scans from Richard's Kriegie Registries
in the *Quaderno* and the *Wartime Log*

Notes

• Men included are primarily but not exclusively internees of Center Compound.

• In the *Quaderno* listings:

*The first five on p. 1 are men Richard encountered on Nisida. From there through the second entry on p. 2 they appear to be others he met in Italy (probably Chieti).

*Entries made in Stalag Luft III begin with the third one on page 2; small letters at left margin designate residents of Block 56 combines near Combine G.

• In the *Wartime Log* listings:

*Page 74 copies some entries from the first two pages of the *Quaderno*. Men who joined Combine G up through 2 July 1944 appear on pages 74–6.

*On Page 117 some of the last entries were made in Stalag VIIA and include South Compound men; at least one other entry there is from Camp Lucky Strike.

*Page 120 begins with General Vanaman's entry (made, according to the *Kalender*, on 24 October 1944). I believe the others on that page were entered at Stalag VIIA.

• All *Quaderno* scans are from the Butler family collection.

• All *Wartime Log* scans are from the Richard M. Butler papers MSS 8849, L. Tom Perry Special Collections, Harold B. Lee Library, Brigham Young University.

HERBERT F. CORSON 2nd Lt. O-663595 617 Wilfred Ave
Dayton, Ohio. Hit by flak — Finished by fighters on raid
near Capua, Italy. 21-8-43. – 1131?5
Story: Rear group briefed to continue on past target to air-
drome + drop hung-bombs. This separated the two, so fighters
couldn't cover them.
HAROLD W. DOBNEY 1st Lt. Norfolk Nebraska (B-26) pilot
of above ship. Got sick + stayed in Italy. Later escaped.
PAUL J. HEINBERG 2nd Lt. 1415 Commerce St. Dallas, Texas.
(C.P. in above ship).
CURTIS S. CHURCH 1st Lt. 461 Urbano Dr. San Fran. Calif.
Tel. Delaware 5688 (B-26 P) (above formation)
MAX RICKLESS 1st Lt. 19 Eittel Place Rochester N.Y. (N)
(Nav. in above ship).
THOMAS F. ELLZEY 2nd Lt. 20 Spencer St.
St Augustine Fla. 24-8-43. Retaken after escape
in N. Italy. Esc. again at Sulmona.
ROGER D. MILLER 2nd Lt. 10605 Langmuir Ave. Sunland Calif.
12-8-43 Naples, Italy P-38 "
E. F. PHILLIPS – P-38 Plymouth Ohio – Foggia Italy.
Sq strafing mission. Downed by fighters 25? 8-43

George T. Fitzgibbon   Staten Island. N.Y.
   Castelvetrano, Sicily. 10-7-43. Fighter Sweep.
Paul. K. VanOordt O-737906 Ferrysburg, Mich.
   P-38 Naples, Italy 20-5-43 Same as mine.

-E-Bruce L. Campbell.   Trapani, Sicily   June 18, 1943
   Belgrade, Nebraska.   Escorting Dive Bombers.
                                 P-38   18 Missions.
Was in a squadron escorting another squadron
of dive bombers on the airdrome at Trapani.
As we came into the target area we
encountered light flak. Turning away, my
ship received a direct hit on the tail plane.
Bailed out at about 4000 ft. over the
bay and was in the dingy about 1 hr.
before I reached shore & was captured
by the Italian Carabinieri

1 James H. Goff
   Minatare Nebr
Shot down May 16, 1943 Off Sicily
Escorting it's Spent one night in dingy, Killed
as

a shark with hunting knife. Picked up by
Swedish Red Cross ship "Bardaland." Italians
took charge of me at Messina. 3 weeks in
hospital there. Ended up in Germany same
way you did.   James N. Goff P-38 - 4$\frac{a}{}$M

1 Lt. Alvah Allen

  Bombardier B-17 - "Stormy Weather."
Home – 149 Howard St. Keene, N.H.
Destroyed by fighters. Plane first
knocked out of formation by M.E. 109
#1 on fire #3 out. Later lose rudder.
Fire spread rapidly. Bailed out
at 10,000 ft. Captured by Danish
farmer and "Jerry" troops. Five of
crew killed. Oct. 9th, 1943 Anklam,
Germany.

1 Lt. Richard F. Hull
 847 E. Colfax Ave – Denver, Colorado
Bombardier B-17 "Rebels Revenge"
 Shot down by fighters over Emden,
Germany on the 27th day of Sept.

Bailed out at 19,000' and landed
in the North Sea. Had six
missions before being shot down.
So to Ger. and Stalag III
                3/23/44 Richard Hull

I Samuel D. Rose - 1st Lt.
Rt. 2 - Box 864; Visalia - Calif.
Shot down by ME-109s on the
16th of July - 43 while on a bombing
mission on the Bari air field.
Engine shot out and wing set on fire
was enough for me. I taken prisoner
until Oct. 15-43. Pilot - B-24-D.

I Millard Bitzler - 1st Lt. Navigator
on same ship as Sam Rose. Home in
Hillsboro, Ohio. Like Rose, I believe
a B24 burns too fast for safety. Bailed out without a scratch and still
got my appetite. Mission 27 for me.

I Charles H. Midgley, 633 Turrentine Ave., (B)
Gadsden, Alabama. Shot down on a Milk run?
(5 planes lost over Bari, Italy July 16, 1943
But yours is a much sadder tale, Panda!

I   Lt. Albert J. Chudoba ✓⁴⁰
Shot down by ME-109 just after dropping
bombs on Schweinfurt, Germany. Bailed
out in unconscious state, awoke in time to
pull ripcord (I guess). Attacked by peasants
upon alighting on ground. Was taken prisoner
immediately. Date - Oct 14, 1943. Live at
1012 Brown st, Akron, Ohio

11. WILLIAM S. DAVIDSON 1ST/LT
     Hazard Kentucky Co-Pilot B-17 Shot down
Oct 14, 1943 Immediately after dropping bombs on
Schweinfurt, Germany. 18ᵗʰ mission

N. Henry H. Farmer — Second Lieutenant — Bombardier — Memphis, Tennessee. Shot down Oct.
14, about 20 miles south of Frankfort, Ger.
mission: to bomb ball-bearing plant at
Schweinfurt, Ger. Ship riddled by 20 mm.
shells and "Flak". Bailed out at 26,000
ft. There were four survivors from
a crew of 10. Captured immediately
upon landing. address: 1557
Monroe avenue.

-H. Donald G. Smith - 19 North 33 st. - Billings, Mont
Co-Pilot B-17 - Shot down over Paris
Sept 13, 1943   2 Engines Lost over
Target, Attach by 2 Focke Wolfs.
Bailed out at 4,000 Ft. Loose 5
days.

-H. Gordon D. Seibert - Nav. - Minneapolis, Minn.
2815 Bryant Ave. N. - Left Tunis with the
"GI's". Should have stayed in my sack. Had
the balance shot out me over Weiner-
Neustadt, Austria on the second run over
the target. Left my string at 32½ missions.

-H. 2nd. Lt. J.V. Lilly - 13407 Sussex - Detroit Mich.
Navigator on the "Thunderbird" B-17F. It
Looked like a "Milk Run". Till we learned
we were "Tail End Charlie." Over the
target FW 190's decided they wanted
us. The wing burned off and we had
had it. All but pilot safe and sound
in the bag. Happier landings next time
"Panda"

-H. ROBERT BERGHOLZ NW 2276 ₤. 28th Ave
    PORTLAND, OREGON B-17 GROUP - ENG.
CALLED 'ER "THE DEVILS DAUGHTER" AND HER LAST
TRIP OVER BREMEN WE PARTED COMPANY AS RESULT
OF A PRETTY ROUGH RECEPTION.
JOHN H. WHITE , BOMB , B-17 , ENGLAND
    242 DENTON AVE. , LYNBROOK, L.I., N.Y.
WE HAD IT OVER EMDEN GERMANY
MONDAY, SEPT 27, 1943 IN THE "THUNDERBIRD"
TOURED GERMANY FOR 4½ HRS UNESCOURTED.
HOLLAND AIN'T SO HOT

#. Wendell O. Morris - Co-Pilot - B-17
122 East 16th St - Cheyenne, Wyoming
My luck changed on Sept. 27, 1943
Our target - Emden, Germany
We were tail End Charlie, flying
at 22000 ft - On I P fighters
coming up at two O'clock it
all happened quick - our left wing was
burning fast - dropped out of formation
with FW's coming in on the tail
all bailed out - to left the ship at 5000 ft
hit the water about a mile off shore - I have
now had it ___   Windy Morris

Comk,   H. BECKERMAN   Nav-Bomb B17
727 E. 158 St Bronx, New York City
Our ship was named "Saboteur"
and its last trip was to Anklam,
Germany on Oct 9, 1943. Our altitude was 13000 so you can imagine the reception flak and
fighters gave us. Leading second element in low squadron.
Attacked by hordes of Me 110^s.
Flak put large hole in left
wing near "tokio" tanks. Near
Flensburg, fire started and
we bailed out. Left ship at
13000 feet and was captured
immediately upon hitting terra
firma. Tail gunner & radio operator were killed. Good Luck
"Pardo" - Hy. 11 missions

A   John S. Acken
111-27 115 Street
Richmond Hill L. I. N. Y.

Virginia 3-4511

Shot down on Bremen
Raid Oct. 8, 1943 "T.S."
I need a silver punch
to make me feel better.

* Clarence R. Waller
Benson Tenns. - Benson Wisconsin
Bremen - Oct 8-43 - C.P.
B-24
1st and last

* Joe P. Chenault Jr. 2nd Lt.
302 High St. Richmond, Ky.
Bremen Oct. 4 - Bomb. B-17

* Norman J. Sansom
6829 N. Wayne Av. Chicago Ill.
Bremen Oct 8 - Bomb B-17.
" how know how or why! But
here I am." —

James H. Foster Capt
Erram, Okla.
Hamburg June 25, 1943

K E. D. Norton 2nd Lt.
4629 W. 159th St.   Nav. B17
Lawndale, Calif.
Shot down Oct 8, 1944, Bremen

Shot down 30 miles south
of Bremen after dropping
our bombs. I spilled my
chute inside the plane
so had to bundle
the silk in my arms
to jump out. All of the
officers on our crew
got out alive but 3
enlisted men were killed.
Jerome & Chevault were
on the same crew that
I was. Met the Panda
and the other boys after
coming to Stalag Oct 21.
Come and see my wife and
I sometime. Lawndale is
near Inglewood, Cal., which
in turn is near Los Angeles.

J.L. LOFTIN 1ST LT.   PILOT B-17

SOUR LAKE TEXAS

SHOT DOWN OCT. 9, 1943   ANKLAM, GERMANY

Shot down near Flensburg, Germany –
few miles from Border Denmark – after
dropping bombs on target in Anklam, which
is north of Berlin. Diversion wing at
13000 ft. Flak hit on bombing run –
harassed by fighters on way out – shells
from fighter hit the same spot as the
flak hole – fire started near wing
tank – gave orders to bail out –
jumped with spilled chute due to
bullet embedded in pack. Tail-
gunner and radio operator killed.
So here I am. Arrived Stalag Oct. 21,
where I met the luckiest kriegie in
camp – the Panda. Good luck with a
safe and speedy return to Utah, Panda

                              James L. Loftin

Left formation after dropping
load on the Wreckland, full of
holes and spinning like hell.
Fire on left wing, holes in right
wing and in a general played
out condition I myself can
hardly explain just exactly what
happened. However I am sure
it wasn't conventional. Out
through the skin in the nose
on the right wing, and then
Silence. "God How quiet it was.
Ridiculously hanging in a flimsy
chute at 1100 ft, and then far
too damn far away Looking up
I saw my ship going to pieces
about 1,000 ft above me. That
was the last I saw of her, but
a tall column of black smoke
over the tree tops that bordered the
field in which I landed. Oddly

enough I was greeted with
full honors. The committee consisting
of one landed gentry with shot gun,
a German soldier, and a gentleman
in blue (guess who?). How nice! This is I
hope a fair enough picture of how
I arrived in this beautiful country
and to make a long story short
to hospital and then to this
lovely winter resort (Stalg VII) where
fortunately I met a gentleman
by the name of Panda, alias
Butler, whose a vegetarian
(bean spirits) by nature and a
grave digger by profession. So
till the day we leave here together
and the days after "Good Luck"
and Happy landings. Kadoring.
                        alias
            N. Norman J Lawson.

A/o Geo. W. Davis, Jr. or Wm F. Okeefe
329 Shelton Ave   Box 95   Park City, Utah,
Brownsville Pa.

Flying "Sylvia II" B17F to target in Rhur
Valley. Aug. 13, 1943. Engine failure + hit of "flak"
in left wing causing fire in #2 #1 useless.
Admittedly cold at altitude but thought it
warmer on the ground that setting by #2
Won't fly on one engine anyhow so here I
am. Crew Safe. Happy landing, Parola
                    Geo W. Davis Jr.

Michael Couzzi, Lt.
807 So. 9th St,   "The Delta Rebel"
Hamilton, Ohio
B-17 (D) Aug. 17/43. Gelsenkirken
        Struck by flak and fighters at the I.P.
No 1 was already feathered—due to mechanical
failure. No. 3 knocked out of commission by
flak or 20 MMs. Bailed-out. Fell appro. 20,000
ft. After chute opened another man about 200ft
off and below had his 'chute billow up in fire by

friction from shroud lines. My chute had 4 to 6
panels ripped out while the rest was in flak
holes. Rate of descent was faster than usual
luckily I was facing downwind when I landed in
the town of Dortmund. Hit hard. Was immediately picked up by German populace who
turned me over to the German Soldat.
     "Good luck to you Yanks" — Mike

Sergie Klimkow
1630 S. Millard Ave.   "the Delta Rebel"
Chicago, Illinois
B-17 (c. Pilot) Aug. 17, 1943.
     Struck by flak & fighters at the I.P. No I
was already feathered – due to mechanical
failure. No 3 knocked out of commission by
flak & set ship on fire. Bailed out about
29,000 ft. When chute opened I almost snapped
out of it. Landed near Dortmund. Picked by
populace who turned me over to flak soldiers
who in turn turned me to village police
who inturn turned me to the Luft

GEORGE "SHORTY" LAUSTED   "THE
    125 MACAMLEY ST,   DELTA
        BUFFALO, NEW YORK   REBEL"
B-17 - NAV - AUG. 12 '43 - "RHUR VALLEY.
        KNOCKED DOWN BY FLAK + FIGHTERS
AT I.P. - N₀ 1 FEATHERED + N₀ 3 ON
FIRE - FLAMES SPREAD TO WING
AND NOSE - SECOND ONE TO BAIL
OUT AT 27000 - DELAYED TO ABOUT
10000 - LANDED AT DORTMUND -
PICKED UP BY LUFTWAFE - TAKEN TO
HOSPITAL TO TREAT FLAK WOUND -
THEN TO DULAG. EXPECTED FLAK
TO HIT ME ON DESCENT. THATS ALL -
                    LUCK,
                        Shorty

Jay R. Overman   "Devils Mistress"   B-17
Wolf Creek, Montana
Bombardier - Ahu Valley 9, 12, 43.
    Hit by flak at bomb
release, No 1 ran away, N 2
leaking oil and three in
bad shape. Hid for clouds
under fighter attack, but
were struck again by light
flak. Crash landed at Ahaus
Germany and were picked up
immidiatly, The plane was
burning when we landed and
spread rapidly all over, no one
was injured badly.
    We were the ones who
brought the S17O., Col. Spivey
here, but I still say it wasn't
our fault.
    My regards from one Westerner
to another
                            Jay

A-36 - Winford A. Gaines 1st Lt
O-66 2912 - Route 3, Elberton Ga.
Oil line shot out over
Messina. Tried to make it
back to friendly lines, crash
landed at base of Mt. Etna
Sicily aug, 2, 1943

B-17 - Frank M. Bigelow - 2nd Lt. O-734724
Bombardier, - Direct flak hit over
Naples - Blew right wing off at no.1.
Bailed out at 22,000 - Delayed jump
to 6,000 landed in tree - aug. 1, 1943.
208 Chintan St. Fayetteville - N. Y.

P-39 - Harold D. McGhie 1st Lt.
O-726286 - Tunisia - March 28, 43
address Edgar, Nebraska.

L. Oliver Morton - 2nd Lt. a.c. Navigator B-17
23 West 28th St., Covington, Kentucky
                        (Happy Valley)
August 12th, 1943 Gilsen-Kirchen, Germany

Not an exciting story but here goes my Sad Tale - Hit by flak a few seconds after Bombs away. #3 Engine on fire, two others knocked out, so had to abandon ship at about 17,000'. Fell quite a ways then pulled rip cord. For awhile was drifting in direction of Billon Barrage. Had visions of being spread all over Germany (Explan. Had read about time that dynamite charges were connected to them). Slipped chute + with luck (or wind) stayed away. Hung up in a tree after making choice of landing in trees or a railroad. Kindly assisted on to German soil by soldiers after hanging a couple feet off the ground, as I was unable to release chute fastening.

Here's hoping Panda, you aren't thrown in a brace by the Kid Brother. Seriously my sincere admiration for a job well done. You deserved a few more decent breaks.

"Mork."

74

1st Lt. Curtis S. Church
461 Urbano Dr.
— San Francisco, Calif.
30 Raids. B-26 'P' Capua, Italy.
"Cort the Angel."

Harold W. Dobro 9. 1 Lt.
Norfolk
— — Nebraska
B-26 P. 27 Raids. Capua Italy.
Got Sick & Stayed in
India. Got To Our lines

Paul J. Heinberg 2 Lt.
1415 Commerce St.
— Dallas, Texas—
B-26 'CP' Capua, Italy.
"For The Best In Shoes."

Roger D. Miller 2 Lt.
10605 Langmuir Ave.
— Sunland Calif.—
P-38 Naples. Italy. 12.8.43.
"Jumped The Truth."

E.A. Phillips 2 Lt.
Plymouth
— Ohio —
P-38 Foggia, Italy. 25.8.43 P.38
Der Adler

George T. Fitzgibbon 1 Lt.
Staten Island
— N.Y. —
Castelvetrano Sicily 10-7-43
Sicily Invasion

Paul K. VanOorn
Ferrysburg
— Michigan
P-38 Naples Italy. 20-8-43.
Two of us Mothey

Bruce L. Campbell 2 Lt.
Belgrade
— Nebraska
P-38 Trapani Sicily 18-6-44
Arold Pal

75

HENRY H. FARMER 2ND LT.
1557 Monroe Avenue, Memphis, Tenn.
B-17 Schweinfurt, Ger. Oct 14, 1943
"FLAK HAPPY"

Mathew Harren
441 E. 15 Street
New York, N.Y.
P-38 Aug 28, 1943 Naples

Leo L. Ghadin 2nd Lt
3937 La Grange St. Toledo, Ohio
B-17 Hamburg, Germany
Black Magic navigator
1519 cherry St.
apt 22R.
Toledo

Richard Perle 2nd Lt. 0-683512
72-36, 112 St. Forest Hills, N.Y
B-17 Munich March 18, 4
Navigator
"Bongo" — round the bend
in a parachute!

William R. Griffith
7617 Canoga Ave, Canoga Pk, Calif
B-17 Hamburg 6-25-43
Lohananki C.P.
"Willie the Wabbit"

Weldon F. Holmes 1st Lt
34 Searles Place, Brockton, Mass
B-17 Hamburg, Germany June 25, 1943
Lohananki Pilot
"Suck'em"

STANLEY M SANDS 1ST LT
McGILL, NEVADA
B-17 - AUGSBURG, GER. 3-16-44
NAVIGATOR - 24 RAIDS -
(TRUCE?)

WALDO M PAGE DWF
67 No. MAIN ST
PITTSFIELD, MAINE
NAVIGATOR - 3 RAIDS - B-24
ANCONA, ITALY JUNE 13 44

DANIEL J. READING 1st Lt.
2018 Eagle Ave
Alameda, Cal.F
B-24 Berlin, Germany June
NAVIGATOR 21, 1944
28 Raids

MELVIN H. WILLIAMS 1st Lt.
COPE, COLORADO.
B-24 BERLIN, GERMANY
JUNE 21, 1944
PILOT 28 RAIDS.

76

Arthur C. Twitchell
Westhampton Beach, L.I., N.Y.
Munster   Oct 10, 1943
B-17 – Bombardier

J. Oliver Morton   2nd Lt.
23 West 28th Street
Covington, Kentucky
B-17 Navigator
August 12th, 1943 Gilsen-Kirchen, Ger.
"Happy Valley"

W. P. Morris – F/O A.C.
122 East 16th St.
Cheyenne, Wyoming
Sept 27, 1943 Emden, Germany
Copilot – B-17 "Thunderbird"
Raids-not many-but enough.

H.F. Corson   2nd Lt.
617 Wilfred Ave.
Dayton, Ohio.
B-26 – Bombardier
Capua, Italy. 5/21/44
"Remember Bolzano"   (27 Raids)

Frank M. Bigelow – 2nd Lt.
208 CLINTON ST.
FAYETTEVILLE - NEW YORK
Bombardier – B-17 – Aug. 1, 1943,
"I went to Naples, one time too many"

John H. Arlitt   2nd Lt.
242 DENTON AVE.
LYNBROOK, L.I., NEW YORK
B-17 BOMBARDIER
SEPT 27, 1943 AT EMDEN GER.

E. Wendell Roberts   %
5504 LUPTON AVE
SAN JOSE, CALIFORNIA.
PILOT – B-24 – "CHARROUGHE McGOON"
WIENER-NEUSTADT, AUS. OCT 1, -43

Charles A. Jacobson 2nd Lt.
1120 Second Ave No.
Great Falls, Mont.
B-17 Bomb.
Foggia, Italy. Aug. 19, 1943
                    19 Raids

Jos. V. Lilly   2nd Lt. O
13407 SUSSEX
DETROIT, MICHIGAN
NAVIGATOR B-17 "THUNDERBIRD"
EMDEN, GERMANY SEPT 27, 1943
12TH. MISSION INCOMPLETE

ROBERT BERGHOLZ   1st Lt.
2216 S.E. 38th Ave
PORTLAND, OREGON
NAVIGATOR B-17 "DEVIL'S DAUGHTER"
BREMEN, GERMANY, Oct 8, 43

Allan B. Lemley %
324 S. Morgan St.
Waynesburg, Penn.
B-17 Co-Pilot
Sept 6-43 Stuttgart Ger.   10 Raids

Millard B. Kesler
448 Elm Street
Hillsboro, Ohio
Navigator B-24
July 16, 1943   Bari, Italy
27th missions

Donald G Smith
19 No 33rd St
Billings, Mont.
B-17   Co-Pilot
Sept. 13, 1943   Paris   5 Raids

J. Paul R. Boswell
783 Ashby St, S.W.
Atlanta, Ga.
Pilot B-17
Oct. 8, 1943   Bremen Ger.

Burt L Talcott -
2020 4th Ave North
Great Falls, Montana
B-24 Co-pilot   8 Raids
March 19, 1944 Styr, Austria

CHARLES H. MIDGLEY
633 TURRENTINE AVE.
GADSDEN, ALABAMA
BOMBARDIER B-24 D
JULY 16, 1944 BARI, ITALY

GORDON D. SEIBERT -
2815 BRYANT AVE N.
MINNEAPOLIS, MINN.
B-24 - NAVIGATOR - 33 RAIDS
WEINER-NEUSTADT, AUS. 10-1-43

James H. Goff
Minatare, Nebraska,
P-38
Middle of the Ned.
May 16- 43

Richard F Hull
847 E. Colfax Ave.
Denver, Colorado
B-17 - Bombardier - 6 raids
Emden, Germany Sept 27-43

Samuel D. Rose
R 2 - Box 864
Visalia - California
Pilot B-24-D - 28 missions
Bari Italy - July -16-43

81

Albert J Chudoba - 2nd Lt
1012 Brown St.
Akron, Ohio
Schweinfurt, Germ - Oct 14, 1943
Navigator - "Picaddilly Jim"
"Saddang"

JAMES BARDAKJIAN
1153 PRESIDENT ST
BROOKLYN, N.Y.
VIENNA, AUSTRIA June 24, 1944
CO-PILOT "RAGGED BUT RIGHT"
(B-24 H)

Alvah Allen - 2nd Lt.
149 Howard Street
Keene, New Hampshire
Bombardier - "Stormy Weather"

Ruklam, Germany. Oct. 9th '43

Clair M. Dietrich
5816 N. Dietrich ave.
Portland, Oregon
Ruhr Valley aug. 12, 1943
Co - Pilot B-17
"Cindy"

Ernst A. Galloway
129 - 5th St
Henderson, Ky.
Bombardier - "Cindy"

Rhur Valley - aug 12, 1943

Norman J. Sansom
6329 N Wayne ave
Chicago, Ill.
Bombardier -

Bremen Oct 8, 1923.

THURMAN W. COMER 2nd Lt.
1104 North Dixon St.
GAINESVILLE, TEXAS
NAVIGATOR

GYOR, HUNGRY 13th April 1944

ALVIN F MULLER
48 FRANKLIN ST.
EAST ROCKAWAY
LONG ISLAND N.Y.
BOMBARDIER (RAGGED BUT RIGHT)

VIENNA AUSTRIA 6/26/44

John S. Acker
Jan 27, 115 St.
Richmond Hill, L.I., N.Y.
Co Pilot B-17F
"Beer House Bess"

Bremen, Germany Oct 8, 1943

John O. Hall
Scarborough-on-Hudson
New York
Pilot - B-17

St. Nazaire, May 29, 1943

82

Winford A. Gaines 1st Lt.
Route 3.
Elberton, Ga.
Pilot. A-36

Mt. Etna "Sicily"

Edward T. Connelly Jr
26 Emroff Terrace
New Rochelle, NY
C.P. B-17

Munster Oct 10, 1943

J. Owen Burgess 1st Lt
601 W. Main St.
Brownsville, Tennessee
Nav. B-17 "Miss Fortune"

BREMEN - Oct. 8, 1943

Robert L. Miller
1096 Everett Ave.
Louisville, Kentucky
Bombardier - B-17
"War Eagle"
Bremen, Oct. 8, 1943

William Daniel Daly
509 West 189 St
New York City
Bombardier B-17

Munster Oct 10 43

Emmette Gordon Wells Jr 1st Lt
308 Caledonia Road
Laurinburg NC
Co Pilot B-17   (RCAF)
"What goes up must come down"
"Happy Valley" Aug 12, 1943

Eugene M. Wiley, 1st Lt.
5815 Forest Ave
Kansas City, Mo.
Pilot - B-17
Ruhr Valley.
Aug 12, 43, 16 raids

Wm. D. Hand 2nd Lt
Brookfield
Georgia
Nav. B-17 "Scarlett O'Hara"

Ruhr Valley Ger. Aug 12, 1943

Robert E. Branch
1440 South Boston Ave
Tulsa, Oklahoma
Nav. B-17
Ruhr Valley
August 12, 1943

Herman Beckerman
204 Grand Ave
New York City
Bomb - Nav B-17

Oaklam Oct 9 1944

84

Edward G. Stork 2nd Lt
114-20-138 Street, Jamaica
Long Island. N.Y.
Pilot B17

Munster - October 10, 1943

George Shorty Hausted
125 Macamley St.
Buffalo, New York
Nav- B-17 - "Delta Rebel"
Class of Aug 12 - Ruhr Valley

Luther H. Baker (TheGoat)
R.R. # 5   WOOSTER, OHIO
NAV. B-17
HAPPY VALLEY   AUG. 12, 1943
This is the roughest war I've ever
been in.

George A. Dickerson
245 E. High St.
Jackson, Michigan
Bomb. B-17 "Fightin Pappy"
Oct 9-43. Anklam Ger.

Leslie E. Jones
#C39 Wiley Portland Rd
Warren, Ohio, Co-Pilot B-17
Happy Valley Aug. 12, 43

George W. Davis Jr
329 Shelton Ave.
Brownsville Pa.   (Ruhr)
RH- B-17 Sylvia II Aug12,43
"this too shall pass away"

Daniel G. Gillhouse, 95Lt
295 Rhodes Ave
San Jose, Calif.
Plt 9-20 Sicily Aug43

Michael Covazi
807 So. 9th St,
Hamilton, Ohio
(B) "Delta Rebel" 8/12/43

Sergie Klimkow   "Delta Rebel"
1430 S. Millard Ave.
Chicago, Illinois
Co-Pilot B-17   Aug 12, 1943
Ruhr Valley.

H.C. Holden
710 W. Wabash
Enid, Oklahoma
Co-Pilot B-17 July 30, 1943
Kassel, Germany
"Yankee Doody"

Norman Niemczyk Rural Route 2 Dorr, Mich. Co-Pilot B-17 Eagles Wrath Schweinfurt - Aug 17 '43	William L. Booth 1526 Addington Rd. Toledo, Ohio Co-Pilot - B-24 Zagreb, Yugoslavia June 26, 1944
Joseph C. Jernigan 65 W. ___ Ave. Chicago, Ill. Co-Pilot - B-17 Bremen Oct 8, '43	Vaience P Walker Menomonee Falls, Wis Co-Pilot - 24-B Bremen Germ Oct - 2 - 43
Lloyd H. Thompson 1819 10th Ave. Huntington, W. Va. Pilot - P-40 Forli, Italy June 29, 1944	Eugene W. Zepeck North Irwin, Pa. Co-Pilot - B-17G Anklam, Germany Oct. 9 -43
Del Porter, 1st Lt. 111 North Palm Drive Beverly Hills, Calif. Pilot B-17 Sept. 9 1943 - Paris "Wee Bonnie II"	George ___ 897 Porter St. Meadville, Penna Pilot B-17 Jul 28, 43 Kassel "LITTLE CHUM"
James L. Loftin 2nd Lt. Box 142 Lone Lake, Texas Pilot B-17 Oct. 9, 1943 ANKLAM GER. "Saboteur"	___ A Peterson 3427 W. Jackson Blvd. Chicago, Ill. June 21, 1944 Big "B" NAVIGATOR "BABOON McGOOLI"

88

Arthur H. Backtoff 2nd Lt.
W. Arlington
Vermont
Pilot B-17

Bremen Oct. 8, 1943

Paul A. LaChance 2nd Lt.
2nd Armored Div. 7th Army
2302 5th Ave.
Phenix City Ala.
Captured at Gela Sicily
P.G. 66 - PG 21 - Stalag. 7A.

Edward A. Wick
Le Center, Minn.
1st Lt. Pilot B-17
Wolfpack

Stuttgart Sept. 6, 1943

HARLAN F. HIGHFIELD
PILOT - P-40   2nd Lt.
606 W. 23rd ST.
WILMINGTON, DELAWARE

SFAX, AFRICA MAR. 29, '43

Avery L. Blount
Gulfport Miss
1st Lt. Bomb. B-17

BRUSSELLS JUNE 23, 1944

W. CLAYTON CATES
Bomb B-24 2nd Lt
224 No 19th st
BILLINGS, MONT.

STYRE, AUSTRIA Feb. 22, '44

John F. Pettenger
Ella Street
Bloomingdale, New Jersey
1st Lt. Pilot B-17 March. 6, 1943

Richard W. Bell
624 New ct
Oklahoma City, Oklahoma
Bomb. B-17

Regensburg, Ge. Aug 17, 1943
"SATAN'S MATE"

Bill Smoke
Devils Lake
North Dakota

John A. Brickley 1st Lt.
Deephaven Park
Wayzata, Minn
Schweinfurt Aug 17 1943
Now Air

Frank J. Ghiselli 2nd Lt. San Francisco 1454 24th Avenue Bombardier B-24 June 30, 1944 Lake Balaton Hungary	Milton M. Feldman 2nd Lt. New York, nav. B-24 555 Ft. Washington Ave., "Wolves Lair" 29 June, 1944 Aschersleben, Germany
Roger G. Menges Pilot B-24 1st Lt 12 Gardner Terrace Delmar, N.Y. Budapest, Hungary July 2, '44	RANDELL S. MAYER JR. NAV. B-24 F/O 3346 BARONNE ST. NEW ORLEANS, LA. MAGDEBURG, GERMANY JULY 7 1944
Victor O. Lysso 2nd Lt. Co-pilot B-24 478 So. 11 St. Newark, New Jersey. Budapest, Hungary, July 2, '44.	LEO RUVOLIS JR PILOT B-24 - 1ST LT. 29 NORTH STREET PLYMOUTH, PENNA "Rap 'Em Pappy" - shot down July 7, 1944, Magdeburg GERMANY
Benjamin W. Grant, Jr. 2nd Lt. Navigator (B-24) 1133 New Scotland Rd., Slingerlands, N.Y. Budapest, Hungary - July 2, '44	August J. Fleischbein Bombardier - 17's 2nd Lt 468 43rd Ave Chula Vista, California Down Feb 10, 1944 - Holland
Bob L. Abakarith 2nd Lt. Pilot "Lightning" Joliet, Illinois "Baight" /Yitlilltebonne France	ROY J. MAGGARD CO-PILOT B-17 F/O 6015 MISSION ROAD MISSION KANSAS DOWN MARCH 23 1944

90

Meredith DeMerit J 123 Ridgeside Road Chattanooga, Tenn. Pilot P 47 Feb. 10, 1944	A W. Williams Paris, N.C. Nov B-24 Steyr 3-19-44
James D. Moos 2617 James St. Shreveport, La. Bombardier B-24 July 7, 1944	James S Purtle 412 W. 7th Corona, Calif. B-24 Jun 44 Bomb
Walter L. Stilwell Spattspring, New York B.pilot B6-24 Steyr 3-19-44	Robert A. Schoch 409 Willow Ave. Altoona, Penna. Pilot B-17 Emden Dec 11, 43
John P. Kernochan 9 Marwood Rd. Port Washington, L.I., N.Y. Co-Pilot B-17 Emden - Dec 11, 1943	W R S Stewart 1615 So. 5th Ave Sioux Falls, S.D. B24 - NOV Bologna, June 22, 44
Arthur R. Tilley 300 Mt Hope Ave. Bangor, Maine Bombardier B24 Vienna June 26, 1944	Thomas B Casey Jr. (General Delivery) Boston, Mass. Bomb B-17 Munster Oct 9, 1943

92

Juan S Rodriguez, 2nd Lt. 7432 W. Wildwood Dr. Fort Wayne, Indiana. Bombardier - B-24.	Peter Val Preda. capt. East Wallingford. Vermont. Pilot - B-24J
Politz, Germany June 20, 1943	Politz Germany June 20, 1944
Lazaro Brusola 2nd Lt. 713 Bartholdi Street Bronx, New York. Navigator B-17	Richard T Walker 2nd Lt. 407 Pasadena Albany Georgia Bomb. B-17
Regensburg Aug 17, 1943	Munster Germany 10/10/43
Myron Soiden 2nd Lt. Webster, Iowa Nav. B-17 Bremen Oct. 8, 1943	Arlin Rennels Jr. 1st Lt. R. H. D. 1 Charleston, Ill. Pilot. B-17 Bremen Germany Oct. 8, '43
Avon Burgess 1st Lt. Brownsville, Tennessee Nav. B-17 "New Factors" Bremen Oct 8, 1943	Erwin Mc Craw 1st Lt. Berkeley, New Hampshire Washington Station Mc Craw Berlin June 21, 1944
Thomas J. Fitzgerald 2nd Lt. 361 Mt. Washington Rd. Los Angeles, California Co-pilot B-17 Berlin 5/21/44	Frank C Ward 2nd Lt. Rt 5 Box 208 Compton Washington Pilot B-17 Munster Gd 11-43

114

RICHARD C. LUNT 2ND LT
CO-PILOT B-17 "G" COMBINE
146 No. 1ST EAST
CEDAR CITY UTAH
LATE OF CALIFORNIA

LEIPZIG - JULY 20, 1944

JAMES T. FITZ GERALD, JR 1ST LT
PILOT P47 AIX-J "G" COMBINE
So. PITTSBURG, TENNESSEE
Sw LILLE, FRANCE AUG 2, '44
40 MM FLAK WHILE
STRAFING TRAIN LOADED W/ V-1'S

Charles J. Zubovik
1728 S. 69 St.
West Allis, Wis.
P 38

Sardinia   May '43

Harry S. Golden
1865 Hillywood Rd.
Grosse Pte (Woods), Mich.
B - B-17 Miss-Fortune

BREMEN - Oct 8, 43

Walter K. Boyd
702 S. Ross Ave.
Mexia, Texas
N-B-17 Heavenly Body

Leipzig July 20, 44

ROBERT W. Willen
1045 OVERLOOK AVE.
CINCINNATI, OHIO
PILOT B-24

MUNICH June 13, 1944

Bruce Yarwood
2646 East 71st Street
Cleveland, Ohio
Bombardier B-17

Kassel - July 30, 1943

Robert R. Ladig
1709 Boyer Ave
Ft Wayne Ind
Nav-Bomb B-24

Vienna June 26 1944

William E. Becker
Ogallala, Nebraska
Nav- Bomb B-24

Vienna June 26 '44

David L. Williams
Bangor, Pennsylvania
Hamburg July 30th 1943
Bomb. B-17

116

1ST LT. JAMES H. HEABERG
898 POPLAR CORNER ROAD
JACKSON, TENNESSEE
B-17 SQUADRON BOMBARDIER

JUNE 21, 1943, NAPLES, ITALY.

2d LT. SAMUEL BIER.
2404 HOLT AVE.
INDIANAPOLIS, INDIANA.
B-24 BOMB.

13 SEPT 1944. OSWECIUM, POLAND.

2ND LT. MERLE M. KURTZ
NYSSA, OREGON
P-51 SQUADRON
JUNE 29, 1944

Joseph Lojewski
RFD# 3
East Syracuse, NY
Flying Fortress

August 12th 44

2nd Lt. James R. Brown
1206-16th St.
Wichita Falls, Texas
B-17 Bomb

Oct. 9, 1943 Ankam, Germany

T/o Bernard D. Dooley
19 Norton Avenue
Poultney, Vermont
Bomb -- B-17

June 21, 1944 - Berlin

1st Lt. THOMAS W. LOCKE
MT. HOREB, WISCONSIN
B-24 PILOT

JUNE 26, 1944 VIENNA

2nd Lt. John S. Minerich
Keewatin, Minn.
B-17   C.P.
Oct. 10, 1943   Münster

2nd LT. W. M. Aldridge
213 EAST 3rd ST.
CLAREMORE, OKLA.
P-38

July 16, 1944 VIENNA

M/o H. Harland Leggate
Superior, Wis.
B-24   P
SEPT 10, 44 Vienna

117

1st LT. VERNON L. PRICKETT 1098 Blue Ridge AVE N.E. ATLANTA, GA P-51 Pilot ENGLAND. OCT. 17th 1944 Dusseldorf Ger.	1st LT. ROBERT F. CORENTHAL 2 HINCKLEY PLACE BROOKLYN 18, N.Y. B-17 PILOT ITALY AUG. 28, 1944 KARLSTADT, CROATIA
P² LT. JAMES O. JUNTILLA 128 CEDAR LAKE RD. No. MINNEAPOLIS, MINNESOTA P-51 PILOT OCT 5, 1944 Holland	CAPT. Clarence H. Corning SQ. S.2 Salem Mass. I met 'Pop' at camp L.S. Noir St. Valery F.7. Shot down as observer on B-25 Mission.
1st LT. THEODORE B. SCARLETT 1849 BUFFALO ROAD ERIE, PENNSYLVANIA B-24 PILOT OCT 1, 1943 WIENER NEUSTADT	Maj. Wallace Reyerson SQ. S.2 Officer Hutchinson Pilot in 1st World War. MINN. Later Gp. Executive Off. *Told me NOT to stick my neck out!*
2nd Lt. B. H. Hinckley R.G.D. #1 Rigby Idaho Bg C.P Oct. 10, 1943 Münster	1st Lt. Charles W Melvin 812 Niobrara St. Alliance, Nebraska B-17 ~ Bomb. Italy ~ 1-Nov-44 Hungary ~ ~ Best of Luck Always ~
1st Lt. Keith Conley Box 55 Portage Utah B-17 P July 22, 1943 Kiel	2nd Lt. Mark B. Calnon Rte. #1 Meridian, Idaho B-17 Pilot Anklam Oct. 9, 1943

120 _____

A W Wanaman Brig. Gen. USA
Millville N J Amiens Fr 6/27/44 B-17

Emma C Weytenbach 1st Lt
Worden, Mont.   P-47

James W Dalzell   Captain A.C.
441 Cheney St. Reno, Nevada   B-17

Elbert S Hammond 2nd Lt
Route #3 Rupert, Idaho — B-17

130

MEMBERS IN CAMP

Homer P. Anderson   Logan 1ST Ward
   R.F.D. #1   Logan Stake
     Logan   Seventy.
      UTAH

Richard F. Carter   Stratford Wd.
   2528 Chadwick   Highland STk.
    Salt Lake   Elder

   T   Byington   Kelly Wd
   Lava Hot Springs   Idaho STk
     Idaho   Elder

Appendix G

Kriegie Members of the Church of Jesus Christ of Latter-day Saints in Stalag Luft III and Stalag VIIA

L.D.S. Groups in Stalag Luft III

West Compound

Charles W. Arnett and three other L.D.S. men somehow found each other in West Compound after his arrival in the early summer of 1944. Blair Hale, Grant Ash and Julius Herrick constituted with Arnett the L.D.S. group there, although it appears there were one or two other church members in that compound.

Arnett wrote to his home stake president about their situation. Spencer W. Kimball, who by then was an apostle, replied in a letter authorizing him to hold group meetings and bless the sacrament.[1]

Center Compound

The (South Compound) Branch minutes refer to Leland Hawkley as the "guiding hand" of L.D.S. men in Center Compound. Richard knew of "Keith Conley and the other boys" in South but mentions only Richard Lunt and Harold Schauer as other L.D.S. men in Center. We can presume that the group held at least periodic meetings, however, since the *Kalender* records on Sunday 9 April 1944 "Air Raid just before church" and "Church this A.M." a few months later on Sunday 17 September.

South Compound
(Stalag Luft III Branch[2])

When Bill McKell reached Stalag Luft III in the early summer of 1943, he wrote to President Zimmer of the Swiss Mission asking for church materials to be sent.[3] By Sunday 7 November he had contacted other LDS men so that thirteen of them held an organizational meeting of the Stalag Luft III Branch of the Church of

---

1. I am indebted to Arnett's son Wayne for this information.
2. David Farrell's Stalag Luft III Branch records were donated to the Church History Library by his daughter Susan Bankhead, by whose kind permission they are used here.
3. William Hale Kehr, "Stalag Luft III Branch," *Ensign* July 1982: 35.

Jesus Christ of Latter-day Saints and elected a Presiding Elder, two counselors and a secretary.[4]

The minutes penned by David Farrell state, "There are thirteen of us here, all prisoners of war, all members of the Air Corps. We are searching for more of the truth of the Gospel which we all sincerely believe. Most of us have been out of contact with the Church for over a year. All are eager to live a better life here in camp. We are all vividly aware of the part that the Lord has taken in allowing us life. With His help and our labors' here, perhaps we can bring to this camp the truth as shown by our Prophet Joseph Smith. We feel deeply this obligation and duty. May God bless this group and help it to prosper and grow." (*Branch Minutes* 2) The official history of South Compound notes this meeting and mentions that officers were elected with W.E. McKell as Presiding Elder. (*South History* 1032)

One Kriegie memoir mentions "the Mormon combine," so we can assume that a good many of the LDS men had contrived to live together. Moreover, they were known as entrepreneurs; the same Kriegie recalls that, one night in March 1945 (after the move to Stalag VIIA), they "had come around with their well-displayed cabinets of goods for sale. Chocolate (D-bars), cigarettes, and clothing were the common currency of the camp, but they would take just about anything on consignment. Being non-smokers, they had a particular advantage in this trade." (Petersen "Stalag VII-A")

Although Branch members met weekly, due to the attendance of nonmembers and members uncomfortable with formal meetings, the sacrament was administered only on first Sundays; for the same reasons, lessons with discussion were emphasized over formal "talks." On occasion the group met in the compound's theater and at least once (per Tolman's account) in the cookhouse; otherwise, the venue is not recorded, and we may suppose that they might sometimes have met in the Mormon combine's room. Branch members held a range of Priesthood offices from Deacon to Seventy.

On 9 April 1944 the minutes note that it was "conference time throughout the church," and a sustaining vote of current officers (including Marion F. Barnhill as choirmaster) was taken. On 5 November 1944 the "presidency" was released and new leadership elected. David Farrell remained as secretary, and on the 12th he presented a statistical Report of the Year 7 November 1943 to 4 November 1944, noting that the Branch membership had grown to 24 and average attendance had been 72%; the new "presidency" members spoke and announced a revised meeting format.

---

4. Eldon Tolman heard about the group on Sunday 14 November during Appell announcement of religious services: "'There will be an L.D.S. discussion group meeting at 6:00 p.m. today in the cook house.' To this time I was not aware that there were other Mormon kriegies in the compound. It turned out that there were sixteen of us." (Tolman unpaged 23)

Late on Saturday 27 January 1945 South was the first compound to take the road on the winter evacuation march; the Branch was unable to meet together again until 25 February in Stalag VIIA. Though David Farrell was temporarily separated from the others, the four men from West Compound were able to join the Branch; by the next Sunday Farrell could attend. On 9 April South Compound was transferred across the street to move in with Center Compound in doubly-cramped quarters, so Richard and the other LDS men of Center were able to enjoy their fellowship and meet with the Branch for the two remaining Sundays before liberation.

Stalag Luft III Branch Leadership

7 November 1943–5 November 1944
William E. McKell, Presiding Elder
Bud H. Hinckley, First Counselor
Homer P. Andersen, Second Counselor
David Farrell, Secretary
Marion F. Barnhill, Choir-master[5]

5 November 1944–9 May 1945
Marion F. Barnhill, Presiding Elder
Parley Madsen, First Counselor
Frank D. Bailey, Second Counselor
David Farrell, Secretary
William E. McKell, Choir-master

---

5. Andersen and Barnhill are not mentioned in the 7 November 1943 minutes but did function in their positions and were sustained in the confirming conference-time vote.

Richard's Stalag VIIA attendance list (Richard M. Butler papers MSS 8849, L. Tom Perry Special Collections, Harold B. Lee Library, Brigham Young University)

LDS Kriegies[6]

Name	Compound	Hometown

*~   **ANDERSEN, Homer P.**   **South**   **Logan UT**
1Lt , Co-Pilot, B-17; 16 April 1943, Lorient (France)
  • Second Counselor in the original "presidency" of Stalag Luft III Branch
  • Richard's Kriegie Registry, *Wartime Log* p. 130
  • Minutes: Prayers, Lessons, Talks

+   **ARNETT, Charles W.**   **West**   **Duncan AZ**
2Lt, Pilot, B-24; 19 May 1944, Bad Langensalza (Germany)
  • Presiding Elder of West Compound (*Branch Minutes* 35)
  • Minutes in Stalag VIIA: Talk

+   **ASH, Cecil Grant**   **West**   **Lehi UT**
Flight Officer, Bombardier, B-24; May 1944, Vienna (Austria)
  • Minutes in Stalag VIIA: Prayers, Talk

*   **BAILEY, Frank Donald**   **South**   **Salt Lake City UT**
2Lt, Bombardier/Navigator, B-17; 15 October 1944, Cologne (Germany)
  • Second Counselor in Stalag Luft III Branch's second "presidency"
  • Minutes: Prayers, Talks, Sacrament, Lesson

*^ **BARNHILL, Marion Francis**   **South**   **Hampstead NC**
1Lt, Pilot, B-17; 14 October 1943, Bad Aibling (Germany)
  • Second Presiding Elder of Stalag Luft III Branch
  • Minutes: Prayers, Lessons, "choir-master," Sacrament, Talks

^   **BRIMHALL, Delbert Creed**   **Belaria**   **Provo UT**
2Lt, Co-Pilot, B-24; 20 November 1944, Munich (Germany)

*^ **BUTLER, Dee Jack**   **South**   **Ogden UT**
2Lt, Pilot, B-24; 18 June 1944, Süderbrarup (Schleswig-Holstein, Germany)
  • Minutes: Prayers, Lessons, Talks

---

6. Source Notations
*Stalag Luft III Branch (South Compound) member list
+Stalag Luft III Branch (South Compound) minutes only
^Richard's Stalag VIIA list
~Richard's *Log* registry and/or *Journal*
q Richard's *Quaderno* notebook
b Delbert C. Brimhall in *My Mission to Fulfill*
s *Behind the Wire: South Compound*
? We see the name only after the move to Stalag VIIA and have no other information.
  Additional sources of information: Stalag Luft III Compound Rosters and the following notable websites: http://www.americanairmuseum.com/person, familysearch.org, https://valor.military times.com, http://aad.archives.gov.

BUTLER, Richard Marsh   Center   Garland UT

Flight Officer, Pilot, P-38; 20 August 1943, Bay of Naples (Italy)

*~   **BYINGTON, Telford Smith**   South   Lava Hot Springs ID

2Lt, Pilot, F-5A[7]; 16 May 1943, sea off Dieppe (France)
   • Richard's Kriegie Registry, *Wartime Log* p. 130
   • Minutes: Prayers, Lessons, Talk

*   **CAHILL, Paul R.**[8]   South   Medford City MA

2Lt, Bombardier, B-17; 29 July 1943, sea off Heligoland Island (Germany)
   • Minutes: Prayer

*~   **CARTER, Richard Fielding**   South   Salt Lake City UT

2Lt, Co-Pilot, B-24; 22 August 1944, Lake Balaton (Hungary)
   • Richard's Kriegie Registry, *Wartime Log* p. 130

*^~ **CONLEY, Keith**   South   Portage UT

1Lt, Pilot, B-17; 29 July 1943, Kiel (Germany)
   • Conley's home was near Garland, and Richard knew that he was in South
camp but, of course, was not able to see him. Conley tells his shoot-down story
in "Turnabout" (Consolmagno *Needle* 135).
   • Richard's Kriegie Registry, *Wartime Log* p. 117
   • Minutes: Prayers, Lessons, Sacrament, Talks

b   **DOWNS, John W.**   (SL III)   Provo UT

1Lt, Navigator, B-17; 8 October 1943, Bremen (Germany)
   • Brimhall mentions meeting him in Stalag VIIA.

*^   **FARRELL, David**   South   Long Beach CA

1Lt, Pilot, B-17; 17 April 1943, Oldenburg (Germany)
   • Farrell served as Stalag Luft III Branch Secretary from its creation in South
Compound of Stalag Luft III through Liberation Day in Stalag VIIA.
   • Farrell was baptized into the Church shortly before Pearl Harbor and his
enlistment. His shoot-down account as well as his conversion story and testi-
mony can be found at his Family Search file.
   • Minutes: Prayers, Lessons, Sacrament, Hymn Conductor, Talks

b   **FOOTE, Warren**   Center   Idaho Falls ID

2Lt, Co-Pilot, B-17; 6 September 1943, Stuttgart (Germany)
   • Brimhall mentions meeting him in Stalag VIIA.

*^   **FRAZIER, Leo Odean**   South   Oakley UT

1Lt, Navigator, B-24; 8 March 1943, Rouen (France)

---

7. P-38G photo reconnaissance model
8. Cahill was "a non-member who has been interested and attending for some time."
(*Branch Minutes* 14)

• Frazier was initially in "the predominantly British compound" (presumably North, which was located adjacent to South and with which there would have been rudimentary communication). A transfer was arranged and by 13 February 1944 Frazier had joined the LDS group in South.

• Minutes: Lessons, Prayers

*   **GUNN, Harold Woodrow**   **South**   **Salt Lake City UT**
2Lt, Co-Pilot, B-17; 22 June 1943, Hüls (Germany)

• A 7 February 2000 *Deseret News.com* account of Gunn's shoot-down and his time as a POW can be found at his Family Search file. A number of his drawings of camp life can be seen at www.303rdbg.com/pow-halgunn.html as well as in "Stalag Luft III Branch," an article in the July 1982 *Ensign*. Gunn's account of the liberation of Stalag VIIA can also be found at the 303rd website.

• Minutes: Prayers, Lessons, Sacrament, Talks

*^   **HALE, Blair Allred**   **South/West**   **Afton WY**
2Lt, Bombardier, B-17; 13 June 1943, sea off Kiel (Germany)

• Details of his shoot-down and captivity can be found at his Family Search file.

• On 23 April 1944 it was announced that he would be transferring to West Compound; he rejoined the Branch after the move to Stalag VIIA.

• Minutes: Prayers, Lessons

^   **HAWKLEY, Leland George**   **Center**   **American Falls ID**
2Lt, Co-Pilot, B-24; 7 July 1944, Westeregelm (Germany)

• Richard does not mention him in the *Log*, but the (South Compound) Branch minutes refer to him as "the guiding hand" of the LDS group in Center Compound. (*Branch Minutes* 35)

• Minutes in Stalag VIIA: Talk

+   **HERRICK, Julius Finley**   **West**   **Craig CO**
2Lt; Co-Pilot, B-17; 28 May 1944, Hentern (Trier, Germany))

• Herrick had only been baptized three months before he went down.

• Minutes in Stalag VIIA: Prayer, Talk

s   **HERRINGTON, Glen Marshall**   **South**   **Ogden UT**
2Lt, Navigator, B-17; 3 January 1943, sea off St. Nazaire (France)

• His right leg was amputated below the knee due to injury sustained in his downing; he was repatriated 26 October 1943.

*~   **HINCKLEY, Bud Henry**   **South**   **Rigby ID**
2Lt, Co-Pilot, B17; 10 October 1943, Münster (Germany)

• First Counselor in the original "presidency" of Stalag Luft III Branch.

• Richard mentions a long talk with him after South Compound moved in with Center Compound at Stalag VIIA.

- Richard's Kriegie Registry, *Wartime Log* p. 117
- Minutes: Prayers, Lessons, Sacrament, Talks

b   HUNT, Dave   **Cedar City UT**

Among others from Utah, on 6 March 1945 Brimhall mentions that he "Recently met Dave Hunt from Cedar City, Utah." (Williams 69)

*   KEELER, Hyrum G.   **South**   **Culver City CA**

1Lt, Pilot, B-17; 2 November 1944, Detmold (Germany)

*   LISH, Gilbert Robinson   **South**   **Pocatello ID**

S/Sgt, Gunner, B-24; 9 June 1944, Innsbruck (Austria)

~   LUNT, Richard Corry   **Center**   **Cedar City UT**

2Lt, Co-Pilot, B-17; 20 Jul 44, Leipzig ("late of California")

- From 21 August 1944 to 6 January 1945 Lunt was a resident with Richard of Combine G in Center Compound's Block 56.

*b   MADSEN, Parley William Jr.   **South**   **Provo UT**

1Lt, Navigator, ; 29 May 1943, Plumieux (France)

- First Counselor in second "presidency" of Stalag Luft III Branch
- Brimhall mentions him as someone he knew from Provo.
- Minutes: Lessons, Prayers, Sacrament, Talks

*^   MALIN, Robert O.   **South**   **Salt Lake City UT**

2Lt, Navigator, B-17; 17 April 1943, Bremen (Germany)

- Minutes: Sacrament, Prayers, Lessons

*^   McKELL, William Ellsworth   **South**   **Payson UT**

1Lt, Pilot, B-17; 13 June 1943, sea off Pellworm Island (Germany)

- Original Presiding Elder of Stalag Luft III Branch and its second choir-master
- Minutes: Prayers, Talks, Lessons, Sacrament

~b   MELVIN, Charles W.   **Alliance NB**

1Lt, Bombardier, B-17; 1 November 1944, Italy/Hungary

- Melvin appears in Richard's Kriegie Registry contiguous to Bud Hinckley, Keith Conley and Mark Calnon, *Wartime Log* p. 117.
- On 6 March Brimhall says "Lt. Melvin and I are still together. . . ." They celebrated Melvin's 30th birthday on 11 April 1945, and on 22 April Brimhall "attended L.D.S. meeting with 19 other fellows including Charles Melvin." (Williams 70, 71, 72)

b   METZER, Charles

Lt, Co-Pilot, B-17

- At the 22 April L.D.S. meeting Brimhall "Also met Lt. Charles Metzer, a co-pilot of Capt. Richardson. He was shot down very early in the [465th Bombardment Group 783rd] squadron." (Williams 72)

*   **MINER, George Calvin**   **South**   **Salt Lake City UT**
2Lt, Navigator, B-17; 17 October 1944, Koblenz (Germany)

*^   **NIELSON, Thorman Rudea**   **South**   **Los Angeles CA**
2Lt, Pilot, P-38; 24 June 1943, sea off Spassari (Sardinia, Italy)
Minutes: Prayer

+^   **PORTER, Harold Wesley**[9]   **South**   **Wellsville MO**
2Lt, Pilot, B-17; 28 July 1943, Giessenlanden (Netherlands)
  • Porter's Family Search file has a number of war-related photos and documents.
  • Minutes: Lessons, Prayers, Talks

b   **RODGERS, Harvey B.**   **Center**   **Clarsdale MS**
Capt, Pilot, B-17; 28 September 1943
  • Brimhall mentions meeting "Captain Rodgers a past co-pilot of Bob Hodson" with other L.D.S. men in Stalag VIIA. (Williams 69)

*^   **SANSOM, Donald Clyde**   **South**   **Salt Lake City UT**
2Lt, Bombardier, B-17; 14 June 1944, Garcin (Yugoslavia)

~b   **SCHAUER, Harold Craig**   **Center**   **Berkeley CA**
2Lt, Pilot, B-24; 26 July 1944, present-day Poland (likely southwestern)
  • Richard mentions him in the *Log* as a relative of the Taylors of Garland.
  • Brimhall mentions a Lt. Schauer in VIIA as someone he knew from the "Columbia Steel car pool."

*^   **SMITH, Clyde Dale**   **South**   **Centerville UT**
Flight Officer, Pilot, P-47; 10 August 1943, Deventer (Netherlands)

*^   **SMITH, Roland Miller Jr.**   **South**   **Salt Lake City UT**
2Lt, Navigator, B-17; 25 June 1943, Bremen (Germany)
  • Minutes: Prayers, Lessons

*   **SMITH, Stanley George**   **South**   **Salt Lake City UT**
2Lt, Pilot, B-17; 15 October 1944, Baden (Germany)
  • Minutes: Sacrament, Talks, Prayers

*^   **STEELE, Kay Brunt**   **South**   **Idaho Falls, ID**
2Lt, Pilot, B-24; 3 April 1944, Szeged (Hungary)
  • Steele's life story at his Family Search file includes a gripping shoot-down account and brief description of his time at Stalag Luft III and Stalag VIIA.
  • Minutes: Sacrament

---

9. "Lt. Harold W. Porter, a non-member from Wellsville, Missouri . . . is sincerely interested in the Gospel. He first encountered the beliefs of our Church in California, then again in Idaho. . . . He has attended every meeting and has proven himself intelligent and humble in his searching after the truth." (*Branch Minutes* 9) Porter was baptized 19 June 1945.

+^ **THOMPSEN, Charles Richard**   **Center**   **Spring City UT**
2Lt, Pilot, B17; 17 August 1943, Ober-Massfeld (Germany)
• Several stories on his Family Search file recount aspects of his downing and POW experiences.
• Minutes in Stalag VIIA: Prayer

b   **TIPTON, Vernon John**   **West**   **Springville UT**
2Lt, Bombardier, B-24; c. 26 April 1944, Toulon (France)
• Brimhall mentions meeting him in Stalag VIIA.

*^ **TOLMAN, Eldon M.**   **South**   **Lovell, WY**
2Lt, Bombardier, B-17; 25 July 1943, Neumünster (Germany)
• Tolman's Family Search file includes a long, detailed and well written history of his time in the US military.
• Minutes: Sacrament, Prayers, Lessons, Talk

*^ **WATSON, Frank M.**   **South**   **Reno NV**
1Lt, Pilot, B-17; 17 April 1943, Bremen (Germany)
• Minutes: Prayers, Sacrament, Lessons, Talks

?+ **WILSON**
• Minutes in Stalag VIIA: Talk

Guests noted on Richard's attendance list Stalag VIIA, 15 and/or 22 April 1945

BROWN, John F.   **South**   **Oakland CA**
1Lt, Navigator, B-17; 25 June 1943, sea off Wangerooge Island (Germany)
• RLDS

CAHILL, Paul R.
(See above.)

McCRIGHT, Ewell R.   **South**   **Benton AR**
2 Lt, Bombardier, B-17; 23 January 1943, Pontivy (Nantes, France)
• Renowned designated compiler of secret South Compound individual POW histories (best known from Arnold Wright's publication of them in *Behind the Wire: South Compound*).

PINSON, William H. Jr.   **Center**   **Atlanta GA**
1Lt, Pilot, B-17; 11 June 1943, sea off Wilhelmshafen (Germany)

Other Kriegies possibly also in attendance

~   **CALNON, Mark Brooks**   **Center**   **Meridian ID**
2Lt, Pilot, B-17; 9 October 1943, Anklam (Germany)

• The University of Idaho Library holds Calnon's wartime and POW materials in the Mark Brooks Calnon Collection.[10]

• Richard's Kriegie Registry, *Wartime Log* p. 117.

~ **DALZELL, James W.**   **Center**   **Reno NV**
Captain, Co-Pilot, B-17; 18 April 1944, Blutehn (Wittenberge, Germany)
• Richard's Kriegie Registry, *Wartime Log* p. 120.

~ **HAMMOND, Elbert Lee**   **Center**   **Rupert ID**
2Lt, Pilot, B-17; 7 July 1944, Burkhorst (Germany)
• Richard's Kriegie Registry, *Wartime Log* p. 120.

~ **WYTTENBACH, Emmett C.**   **(Stalag VIIA)**   **Worden MT**
1Lt, Pilot, P-47; 13 September 1944
• Richard's Kriegie Registry, *Wartime Log* p. 120.

---

10. See also his lengthy 2013 oral history interview at https://www.youtube.com/watch?v=KWb9aJvuYBM&feature=youtu.be. and his written account "Some Lived, Some Died: It Was Understood" at http://384thbombgroup.com/_content/Stories/CALNON -Some%20Lived,%20Some%20Died,%20It%20Was%20Understood.compressed.pdf

Appendix H

Tribute to
General Delmar T. Spivey

At the time of Pearl Harbor "there was not a single gunnery school, nor was there even much thought on the subject." (Spivey 2) Then-Colonel Spivey worked in Training Command, where he and his colleagues had to try to make up for the lack of pre-war preparation. "The theory as well as the art of flexible gunnery had to be developed from scratch." (Spivey 1) Training outcomes in the ETO early in 1943 were bad enough to suggest the need "for several of us in the Training Command . . . to take a trip to the war theatre to see our graduate gunners in action. . . ." (Spivey 2)

Once there, they impatiently underwent "training and briefing in order to get into battle," not just as observers but as operational members of flight crews; Spivey was nose gunner on his first mission, a supposed "milk run." "The takeoff, assembly, and run to the target on August 12, 1943, were routine and uneventful. The weather was excellent." (Spivey 3) So, unfortunately, were the enemy flak and fighters; Spivey's B-17 instructional platform crash-landed near the German-Dutch border and he found himself a prisoner of war.[1]

Soon he would be Senior American Officer of Stalag Luft III's Center Compound with responsibility for a contingent of young American fliers whch would grow to some 2,000. On arrival in Center he saw a collection of twelve shabby, ill-constructed barracks intended to shelter men from the rigors of northern Europe's climate. More significantly, Spivey also found an entrenched culture of undisciplined, lackadaisical and disrespectful prisoners.

He not only recognized the immediate problems this presented but could see effects beyond the present. Those issues, if allowed to continue, would worsen a set of dangers he foresaw evolving for Kriegies in the final months of the conflict as the Nazis' military prospects and German life in general became ever more precarious. Helped by the massive influx of American airmen over the following year, Spivey worked to change Center's culture, imposing discipline and instilling esprit de corps by developing elements of military tradition such as a dress code and parade marching to appell.

These accrued to Kriegies' benefit not only in daily camp life but subsequently in moments of ultimate extremity during the evacuation march and their time

---

1. See Lt. Jay R. Overman's entry in *Appendix F* at page 436.

Colonel Delmar T. Spivey by Lt. Leslie Breidenthal (Arthur A. Durand Collection SMS 792, Clark Special Collections Branch, McDermott Library, US Air Force Academy)

in Stalag VIIA when they encountered frostbite, starvation, degradation, threat of execution. I credit my father's survival in large measure to Colonel Delmar Spivey's foresight and thoughtful planning and to his work late in the war with senior Nazis to ensure that Kriegies received desparately-needed food and were spared execution.

An image from the first day of the winter march exemplifies Spivey's leadership and his concern for the men of Center: As the Kriegies trudged over icy cobbles in desolating cold and stinging snow, the Colonel walked backward and forward along the column, urging and encouraging his men.

My heartfelt thanks.

AUTHOR'S NOTE

There is much more to be learned about Richard's odyssey and about other men who lived similar experiences. I hope to post additional material in an online Appendix, and there is also the distant specter of a second edition.

I am eager to hear from descendants of men who trained with Richard, of 82nd Fighter Group pilots and/or of Richard's fellow Kriegies. Relevant reminiscences, journal entries, photos or other artifacts would be most welcome.

I would very much like to hear from anyone who can identify men in the Stalag VIIA post-Liberation photos. Descendants of Combine G internees are especially encouraged to help me identify their family members.

I would also like to hear from descendants of LDS men interned in Stalag Luft III and Stalag VIIA—especially those not included in the material I have compiled, but certainly as well from anyone who can contribute additional information for existing entries.

Please contact me at 38odyssey@gmail.com.

SOURCES CONSULTED

Arbon, Lee. *They Also Flew: The Enlisted Pilot Legacy 1912–1942*. Washington: Smithsonian Institution Press, 1992.

Bender, Edward M. *Lest They Forget Freedom's Price: Memoirs of a WWII Bomber Pilot*. Bloomington: Author House, 2008.

Blake, Steve. *P-38 Lightning Aces of the 82nd Fighter Group*. Long Island City: Osprey Publishing, 2012.

Blake, Steve with John Stanaway. *Adorimini ("Up and at 'Em!"): A History of the 82nd Fighter Group in World War II*. Marceline MO: Walsworth Publishing: 1992.

Bodie, Warren M. *The Lockheed P-38 Lightning: The Definitive Story of Lockheed's P-38 Fighter*. Hiawassee GA: Widewing Publications, 1991.

Brew, Alec and Barry Abraham. *Shropshire Airfields*. Stroud UK: History Press, 2011.

Brooks, Robin J. *Shropshire Airfields in the Second World War*. Newbury UK: Countryside Books, 2014.

Buckham, Robert. *Forced March to Freedom*. Toronto: McGraw-Hill Ryerson, 1990.

Burbank, Lyman B. *A History of the American Air Force Prisoners of War in Center Compound, Stalag Luft III, Germany*. Chicago: University of Chicago, 1946. [Master's thesis. PDF in author's possession.]

Burda, Vernon L. "I Saw Ten Thousand Men Cry." Typed memoir enclosed in POW tour prospectus, Wilsonville Travel, 1994. Unpaged. [Copy in author's possession.]

Burgess, Alan. *The Longest Tunnel: The True Story of World War II's Great Escape*. New York: Grove Weidenfeld, 1990.

Burwell, Roger W. *My War.* Sandpoint ID: Selkirk Press, 1990.

Butler, Heber Marsh. *I Remember When . . . : Faith-Promoting Experiences from the Life of Heber Marsh Butler.* Garland UT: privately published, c 2005.

Caine, Philip D. *Aircraft Down! Evading Capture in WWII Europe.* Washington DC: Brassey's, 1997.

Cedergren, Hugo. Cablegram of 8 January 1945 reporting Soderberg's Christmas visit to Stalag Luft III. [Referenced in the text as *Soderberg Cable.* PDF in author's possession courtesy of Albert P. Clark Collection, SMS 329, Clark Special Collections Branch, McDermott Library, United States Air Force Academy.]

Charles, Roland W. *Troopships of World War II.* Washington, D.C.: The Army Transportation Association, 1947.

Chorlton, Martyn. *Staffordshire Airfields in the Second World War.* Newbury UK: Countryside Books, 2007.

Clark, Albert P. *33 Months as a POW in Stalag Luft III: A World War II Airman Tells His Story.* Golden CO: Fulcrum Publishing, 2004.

_____. *World War II Prisoner of War Scrapbook—Stalag Luft III—Maj Gen A.P. Clark.* [Referenced in the text as *Clark Scrapbook.* PDF in author's possession courtesy of Albert P. Clark Collection, SMS 329, Clark Special Collections Branch, McDermott Library, United States Air Force Academy.]

Consolmagno, Joe. "The March," *Kriegie Klarion: Newsletter of Stalag Luft III Former Prisoners of War,* Jan. 1995. [Copy in author's possession.]

_____, ed. *Through the Eye of the Needle: 68 First-Person Accounts of Combat, Evasion and Capture by World War II Airmen.* Baltimore: Gateway Press/Stalag Luft III Former Prisoners of War, 1992. [Referenced in the text as Consolmagno *Needle.*]

Cook, Milton. *That's the Way the Ball Bounces: A Nonplused* [sic] *Soldier's Mundane Exploits During WW II.* Xlibris.com, 2008.

Cook, Ruth Beaumont. *Guests Behind the Barbed Wire. German POWs in America: A True Story of Hope and Friendship.* Birmingham: Crane Hill Publishers, 2006.

Corson, Herb. Letter of 5 December 1991. [Referenced in the text as *Corson Letter.* Copy in author's possession.]

_____. Personal account published in Thobaben. [Referenced in the text as *Corson/Thobaben.*]

Cullen, Jim. "Young Man With a Horn," *Kriegie Klarion: Newsletter of Stalag Luft III Former Prisoners of War,* Jan. 1995. [Copy in author's possession.]

Daniel, Eugene L. *In the Presence of Mine Enemies: An American Chaplain in World War II German Prison Camps.* Attleboro MA: Colonial Lithograph, 1985.

Davisson, Budd. "Analyzing the Ryan Recruit." *Air Progress,* Sept. 1983.

Diggs, J. Frank. *The Welcome Swede.* New York: Vantage Press, 1988.

Directorate of Military Intelligence, at the National Archives, Kew. *Stalag Luft III: An Official History of the 'Great Escape' PoW Camp.* Barnsley UK: Frontline Books, 2016. [Referenced in the text as *Official History*.]

Durand, Arthur A. *Stalag Luft III: The Secret Story.* Baton Rouge: Louisiana State University Press, 1988.

Ethell, Jeffrey L. and Rikyu Watanabe. *P-38 Lightning.* New York: Crown, 1983.

Goodrich, Charles G., et al. *History of the USAAF Prisoners of War of the South Compound, Stalag Luft III.* 1945. Bound paper, unpaged. [Referenced in the text as South History; page references are to frames on the scanned microfilm roll from which it was copied. PDF in author's possession courtesy of US Air Force Historical Research Agency, Maxwell Air Force Base.]

_____. "Annexes" to *History of the USAAF Prisoners of War of the South Compound, Stalag Luft III.* 1945. Bound paper, unpaged. [Referenced in the text as South Annexes. Page references are to frames on the scanned microfilm roll from which it was copied. PDF in author's possession courtesy of US Air Force Historical Research Agency, Maxwell Air Force Base.]

Greening, C. Ross, and Angelo M. Spinelli in collaboration with John R. Burkhart. *The Yankee Kriegies.* New York: National Council of Young Men's Christian Associations, 1946. Unpaged. [Copy in author's possession.]

Griffiths, Arthur, *Secrets of the Prison-House or Gaol Studies and Sketches.* Vol. 1. (Reprint.) London: Forgotten Books, 2017.

Gurney, Gene. *The P-38 Lightning.* New York: Arco, 1969.

Halvorsen, David. Reprint of series of seven articles published 7–13 February 1965, *Chicago Tribune.* Delmar Spivey Collection, SMS 699, Clark Special Collections Branch, McDermott Library, United States Air Force Academy. [Referenced in the text as *Spivey/Halvorsen.* PDF in author's possession,]

Holmstrom, Carl. *Kriegie Life: Sketches by a Prisoner of War in Germany.* Privately published, 1946. Unpaged.

Hoover, R.A. "Bob." *Forever Flying: Fifty Years of High-Flying Adventures, from Barnstorming in Prop Planes to Dogfighting Germans to Testing Supersonic Jets.* New York: Atria paperback, 2014.

Hopewell, Clifford. *Combine 13.* Dallas TX: Merrimore Press, 1990.

Keeffe, James H. III. *Two Gold Coins and a Prayer: The Epic Journey of a World War II Bomber Pilot, Evader, and POW.* Fall City WA: Appell Publishing, 2010.

Kimball, R.W. and O.M. Chiesl. *Clipped Wings.* Privately published, 1948.

Kingsbury, Bud. *Wartime Log.* [Selected page JPGs in author's possession courtesy of the Kingsbury family.]

Koppenhöfer, Gertrude. *My Experiences as a Wartime Censor in Stalag Luft III 1942 to 1945.* Printed brochure/typed manuscript, c. 1946. [PDF in author's possession courtesy of Albert P. Clark Collection, SMS 329, Clark Special Collections Branch, McDermott Library, United States Air Force Academy.]

Korson, George. *At His Side; The Story of the American Red Cross Overseas in World War II.* New York City: Coward McCann, 1945.

Lett, Brian. *An Extraordinary Italian Imprisonment: The Brutal Truth of Campo 21, 1942–1943.* Barnsley UK: Pen & Sword Military, 2014.

Makos, Adam with Larry Alexander. *A Higher Call.* New York: Berkley, 2012.

Maloney, Edward T. *Lockheed P-38 "Lightning."* Fallbrook CA: Aero Publishers, 1968.

Mamaux, Maj. Harry O. III. *The Enlisted Pilot Program in the USAAF 1941–42: Was It Successful?* (Student Report 84-1655). Maxwell Air Force Base AL: Air Command and Staff College, Air University, 1984. [PDF in author's possession.]

McKee, Daniel C. *A Kriegie Recall 50 Years Later: Stalag Luft III Diary.* N. Richland Hills TX: Smithfield Press, 1999.

Millar, George Reid. *Horned Pigeon.* London: William Heinemann, 1946.

Mulligan, Thomas E, Lyman B. Burbank and Robert R. Brunn. *History of Center Compound—Stalag Luft III, Sagan, Germany.* Bound paper, hand paged. Delmar Spivey Collection, SMS 699, Clark Special Collections Branch, McDermott Library, United States Air Force Academy. [PDF in author's possession. Pages cited are per hand lettering on original manuscript.]

Murphy, Frank D. Letter of 3 April 1995. [Copy in author's possession.]

Murray, Claude. *Camp History of Stalag Luft III (Sagan), Air Force Personnel, April 1942–January 1945.* Typed manuscript c. 1990. [PDF in author's possession courtesy of Albert P. Clark Collection, SMS 329, Clark Special Collections Branch, McDermott Library, United States Air Force Academy.]

Neal, Toby. *Shropshire Airfields.* Telford UK: Langrish Caiger Publications, 2008.

Neary, Bob. *Stalag Luft III: A Collection of German Prison Camp Sketches with Descriptive Text Based on Personal Experiences.* North Wales PA: privately published, 1946.

Neave, Airey, *Saturday at M.I.9: The Inside Story of the Underground Escape Lines in Europe in World War II.* London: Hodder and Stoughton, 1969.

Nichol, John and Tony Rennell. *The Last Escape: The Untold Story of Allied Prisoners of War in Germany 1944–45.* New York: Penguin Putnam, 2002.

Orsini, Eric A. "Speech Before Former POWs of Stalag Luft III, 23 May 1987." *Kriegie Klarion, Newsletter of Stalag Luft III Former Prisoners of War*, Summer 1987. [Copy in author's possession.]

Paris, Pete. "67 Sad Sacks," *Yank: The Army Weekly* 1, no. 51 (1943): 18. [PDF in author's possession.]

Petersen, Quentin Richard. Undated. "Stalag Luft III, " "The March" and "Stalag VIIA." *Recollections chosen from a Fortunate Life: The War Years*, 3rd Edition. Retrieved from www.seniornet.org/ww2/gallery/memories/quentin/title.shtml.

Roessler, Gus. "Memoir based on wartime notebook." Typescript, 1990. [PDFs in author's possession courtesy of Maurice M. Bloom Collection, SMS 802,

Clark Special Collections Branch, McDermott Library, United States Air Force Academy.]

Rowan, Jack. "Christmas at Stalag Luft 3." *Kriegie Klarion, Newsletter of Stalag Luft III Former Prisoners of War*, Spring 1997. [Copy in author's possession.]

Salter, James. *Burning the Days: Recollection.* New York: Random House, 1997.

Simoleit, Gustav. "Prisoner of War Camps of the Air Force in World War II." Typed manuscript, c. 1970. [PDF in author's possession courtesy of Delmar Spivey Collection, SMS 699, Clark Special Collections Branch, McDermott Library, United States Air Force Academy.]

Soderberg, Henry. "An Outsider's View: Stalag Luft III As I Saw it." Unpaged, typed manuscript, c. 1993. [PDF in author's possession courtesy of Henry Soderberg Collection, SMS 25, Clark Special Collections Branch, McDermott Library, United States Air Force Academy.]

Spivey, Delmar. Interview with War Department General Staff G-2, Military Intelligence Service, 17 May 1945. [Referenced in the text as *Spivey G-2.* Copy in author's possession courtesy of National Archives and Records Administration.]

_____. Letter of 10 December 1945 (to Kriegies of Center Compound). [Referenced in the text as *Spivey Letter.* Copy in author's possession.]

_____. *POW Odyssey: Recollections of Center Compound, Stalag Luft III and the Secret German Peace Mission in World War II.* Attleboro MA: Colonial Lithograph, 1984.

Stalag Luft III Branch general minutes, Church History Library, Church of Jesus Christ of Latter-day Saints. Typescript on microfilm. Used by permission of Susan Bankhead. [Referenced in the text as Branch Minutes.]

Stanaway, John. *P-38 Lightning Aces of the ETO/MTO (Osprey Aircraft of the Aces 19).* Long Island City: Osprey Publishing, 1998.

Thobaben, Robert G., ed. *For Comrade and Country: Oral Histories of World War II Veterans.* Jefferson NC: McFarland & Co., 2003. [Referenced in the text as *Corson/Thobaben.*]

Tolman, Eldon M. *Eldon M. Tolman's Military History.* Digital document appended to Tolman's file on familysearch.org. [PDF in author's possession.]

Vrilakas, Robert "Smoky." *Look, Mom—I Can Fly: Memoirs of a World War II P-38 Fighter Pilot.* Tucson: Amethyst Moon Publishing, 2011.

Walton, Marilyn Jeffers and Michael C. Eberhardt. *From Commandant to Captive: The Memoirs of Stalag Luft III Commandant Col. Friedrich Wilhelm von Lindeiner genannt von Wildau. With postwar Interviews, Letters, and Testimony.* San Bernardino: Lulu Publishing Services, 2015. [Referenced in the text as *Walton & Eberhardt/Lindeiner.*]

_____. *From Interrogation to Liberation: A Photographic Journey. Stalag Luft III— The Road to Freedom.* Bloomington: AuthorHouse, 2014.

Wick, Edward A. "Distinguished Visitors," *Moosburger Zeitung*, 29 April 1995: 12. [This was a commemorative anniversary edition honoring ex-Kriegies.]

Williams, Angela Brimhall. *My Mission to Fulfill: The Military History of Delbert Creed Brimhall During World War II*. Privately published, 2006.

Wordell, Lt. M.T. and Lt. E.N. Seiler, as told to Keith Ayling. *"Wildcats" Over Casablanca: U.S. Navy Fighters in Operation Torch*. Washington, D.C.: Potomac Books, 2006.

Wright, Arnold A. *From Out of the Blue: Acts of Heroism by U.S. Airmen during World War II*. Privately published, 1963. [PDF in Arnold Wright Collection, SMS 936, Clark Special Collections Branch, McDermott Library, United States Air Force Academy.]

Young, Robert H. "North African Memoirs," *Lightning Strikes* 6, no. 1 (January 1993).

ACKNOWLEDGEMENTS

Marek Lazarz, Director of the Muzeum Obozów Jenieckich/P.O.W. Camps Museum, Zagan, Poland. For his warm welcome and generosity with his time. In the course of our daylong conversation and tour, Marek shared many details of local setting and background as well as nuggets of Stalag Luft III daily life and history. With special thanks for period maps and local photographs.

    Steve Blake, P-38 historian and author. Besides making his photo archive available and digging out of it shots I had asked to use, he spent personal time foraging in his notes to help in my search for the Sad Sacks and their personal stories. His boundless personal enthusiasm for the P-38 and the 82nd Fighter Group has been inspiring.

    Marilyn Jeffers Walton, Kriegie daughter, researcher and author. Marilyn has been endlessly knowledgeable and generous with her time, her photo collection and, not least, her massive virtual rolodex!

    Dr. Mary-Elizabeth Ruwell, Academy Archivist and Chief of Special Collections at the US Air Force Academy's McDermott Library, and **Ruth Kindreich**, Assistant Archivist. For their warm welcome and kind help with my research and for rescanning some of the photographs I have used.

    Shaun Farrelly, a knowledgeable, indefatigable and generous local historian and resident of Yarnfield, Staffordshire, England. For my copy of *The Yarnfield Yank* along with much information and helpful suggestions.

    Toby Neal, historian and author. For providing background, suggestions and photographs related to the US Army Air Corps in Great Britain.

    Sir Michael Leighton for his kind permission to use period Atcham Field photos from his family's collection.

John Murphy, Curator, 20th & 21st Century Western and Mormon Americana Manuscripts, L. Tom Perry Special Collections, Harold B. Lee Library, Brigham Young University. For making available scans of material from the Richard M. Butler Papers (MSS 8849).

Susan Bankhead, another Kriegie daughter. For her permission to use the David Farrell Stalag Luft III Branch minutes.

Jennifer Kingsbury and all the Kingsbury family for pages from Grandpa Bud's *Wartime Log* and for permission to use them. The documentary *Bud's Odyssey*, seen at festivals across the country and internationally, is now available on DVD.

Rose Butler Hensley, my cousin and daughter of Heber Marsh Butler, who shared the early years of Richard's odyssey. For her generous help with family photos, in particular and above all the shot of Richard flying his brother's ship.

Floyd & Elaine Jensen, my family historian cousins. For discovering and sending me the *Missing Air Crew Report* of Richard's last combat mission.

Anna Butler, my sister-in-law, for discovery of the signed Sad Sack $1 bill; nephew **Michael Butler** for drawing attention to the Sad Sack article in *Yank* magazine; niece **Danielle Butler Wright** for her photo of my uncle Lester Butler's model of Richard's P-38 "Geneil."

Marny K. Parkin, editor and formatter. For her bottomless well of patience with my broken promises, missed deadlines and endless corrections, additions and changes. Not to mention her beautiful work.

Manuscript readers **Maren Toone**, **Jessica Anderson** and **Trix Dahl** and early proofers **Cosette Dover** and **Jeremy Wang**.

Special thanks to my sister **Christine Anderson** for constant thoughtful consultations and suggestions; to my daughter **Emily** for scanning, proofing and frequent editorial conferences; and to my wife **Gigi** for her unfailing patience and encouragement along with whatever else the moment required, from proofing to close reading and editing of key passages.

INDEX

Bold type indicates illustrations. Numbers are alphabetized as if spelled out.

ABOUT THE AUTHOR

Dick Butler walking part of Winter March route (Butler family collection)

As an Air Force brat, Dick Butler acquired the yen for travel. He's a retired bookseller (Phileas Fogg's Books and Maps for the Traveler, Palo Alto CA and Marco Polo & I, Tucson AZ) and teacher of writing and literature.

Dick is addicted to the printed page, particularly in the genres of history, historical fiction and historical mystery. He pursues the archaeology of three empires: Mayan, Incan and ancient Roman; is an amateur musician passionate for Bach and Chopin; and finds artistic expression in the garden and in watercolors. He has a double major in French and English and an MA in Twentieth Century French Literature.

He enjoys a circle of delightful and accomplished family and friends. His proudest associations are those with his wife, an engineer, and their daughter, a medievalist.

Made in the USA
Las Vegas, NV
27 November 2023